Research, Measurement, and Evaluation of Human Resources

Research, Measurement, and Evaluation of Human Resources

Alan M. Saks

York University

Neal W. Schmitt

Michigan State University

Richard J. Klimoski

George Mason University

Monica Belcourt, Series Editor

Australia • Canada • Denmark • Japan • Mexico • New Zealand • Philippines
Puerto Rico • Singapore • South Africa • Spain • United Kingdom • United States

NELSON E D U C A T I O N

ISBN-13: 978-0-17-646249-9
ISBN-10: 0-17-646249-X

Consists of:

*Research, Management, and
Evaluation of Human Resources*
Alan M. Saks
ISBN-10: 0-17-616736-6

Brief Contents

Detailed Contents

About the Series

More than ever, HRM professionals need the knowledge and skills to design HRM practices that not only meet legal requirements but also are effective in supporting organizational strategy. The books in the *Nelson Series in Human Resources Management* are the best source in Canada for reliable, valid, and current knowledge about practices in HRM.

The texts in this series include:

- *Managing Human Resources through Training and Development*
- *Occupational Health and Safety*
- *Human Resources Management Systems*
- *Recruitment and Selection in Canada*
- *Compensation in Canada: Strategy, Practice, and Issues*
- *Strategic Human Resources Planning*

The *Nelson Series in Human Resources Management* represents a significant development in the field of HRM for many reasons. Each book in the series (except for *Compensation in Canada*) is the first Canadian text in its area of specialization. HR professionals in Canada must work with Canadian laws, statistics, policies, and values. This series serves their needs. It also represents the first time that students and practitioners have access to a complete set of HRM books, standardized in presentation, that enables them to access information quickly across many HRM disciplines. This one-stop resource will prove useful to anyone looking for solutions for the effective management of people.

The publication of this series signals that the field of human resources management has advanced to the stage at which theory and applied research guide practice. The books in the series present the best and most current research in the functional areas of HRM. Research is supplemented with examples of the best practices used by Canadian companies who are leaders in HRM. Each text begins with a general model of the discipline, then describes the implementation of effective strategies. Thus, the books serve as an introduction to the functional area for the new student of HR, and as a validation source for the more experienced HRM practitioner. Cases, exercises, and references provide opportunities for further discussion and analysis.

As you read and consult the books in this series, I hope you share my excitement in being involved in the development of a profession that has such a significant impact on the workforce and on our professional lives.

Monica Belcourt
SERIES EDITOR
AUGUST 1999

About the Author

Alan M. Saks

Alan Saks is currently an Associate Professor of Human Resources Management in the Department of Administrative Studies, Atkinson College, York University. He earned a B.A. in Psychology at the University of Western Ontario, an M.A.Sc. in Industrial-Organizational Psychology from the University of Waterloo, and a Ph.D. in Organizational Behaviour and Human Resources from the University of Toronto. Prior to joining York University, Professor Saks was a member of the Department of Management in the Faculty of Commerce and Administration at Concordia University in Montreal. He has conducted research in a number of areas in human resources, including recruitment, job search, training, and the socialization and work adjustment of new employees. His research has been published in journals such as the *Journal of Applied Psychology, Personnel Psychology, Academy of Management Journal, Journal of Organizational Behavior*, and the *Journal of Vocational Behavior.* Professor Saks is currently on the editorial board of the *Academy of Management Journal, Journal of Organizational Behavior, Journal of Vocational Behavior*, and the *International Journal of Selection and Assessment.* He is the editor of the *HRM Research Quarterly*, and is the chair of the Applied Research Stream of the Human Resources Professional Association of Ontario. In addition to this text, Professor Saks is a co-author of *Managing Performance Through Training & Development*, which is also part of the Nelson Series in Human Resources Management.

Acknowledgments

This book is the result of a number of individuals who made important contributions during its development. Monica Belcourt, series editor, was particularly instrumental in helping to make this book possible. I am grateful for her support and encouragement throughout the development and writing of this text. I am also grateful to Neal Schmitt and Richard Klimoski, who agreed to allow me to adapt their text, *Research Methods in Human Resources Management*.

The manuscript of this work was reviewed at various stages of its development by a number of reviewers. I wish to thank those who shared their insights and their constructive criticism which helped to improve this text. They include: Carolin Rekar, Durham College; Timothy DeGroot, McMaster University; Arla L. Day, Saint Mary's University; Nelson Lacroix, Niagara College; Nina Cole, Brock University; and Willi H. Wiesner, McMaster University.

I also thank my research assistants, Dara Potton and Cindy Hutchinson.

I am also grateful to the team at Nelson who helped in the development of this text. Frank Burns and Tim Sellers were responsible for the early stages of development, and Dolores Pritchard provided me with electronic copies of the original text. I am especially thankful for the dedication and commitment of the Project Editor, Mike Thompson, and Production Editor, Natalia Denesiuk.

Finally, I am grateful to my family. To my parents, Renee and Simon, for their continued support and encouragement, and to my wife, Kelly, for her patience and understanding.

Preface

During the last decade, the field of human resource management has undergone a tremendous amount of change. No longer just the record keepers and administrators whose budgets were often slashed during difficult times, human resource professionals are now widely recognized as playing a critical role in an organization's effectiveness. The growth in human resources can be seen in the academic arena, where increasing numbers of students are majoring in human resources, and more courses and programs are being offered by colleges and universities at the undergraduate and graduate level; in the growing number of practical and research journals that publish articles on human resources; in the increased visibility of the human resource profession and the certification of human resource professionals; and in the greater number of job opportunities available.

One of the most important prerequisites for effective human resource management is research. Whether one is required to determine training needs, develop a valid employment interview, investigate the reasons for absenteeism, or just interpret research reports or consultant proposals, the effective management of human resources requires sound, rigorous, and continuous research. This is likely to become more important, given the increasing role played by the human resource function in today's organizations and the greater demands for accountability and value-added human resource practices and systems. Thus, students who are majoring in human resources, professionals currently working in human resources, and those seeking employment in human resources must have a good understanding of the research process and its role in the effective management of human resources.

When I began to develop an honours-level undergraduate research methods course in human resources several years ago, I searched for a textbook that was written for students who were majoring in human resources, rather than a general business research methods text. There are many issues that are unique to human resources, and I wanted my students to have a textbook that presented those issues with examples relevant to human resources. The good news was that such a book existed. Neal Schmitt and Richard Klimoski had written exactly what I was looking for in *Research Methods in Human Resources Management*. The bad news, however, was that it was no longer in print.

For me, this was a serious problem. While there are many textbooks on business research methods, they rarely deal with issues of concern that are specific to human resources. The only option for me was to write the kind of textbook I was searching for. At the same time, I felt that Schmitt and Klimoski had already written an exceptional book that was extremely thorough in its coverage of human resource research methods and in its examples from the human resource research literature. It made no sense for me to start from scratch. Fortunately, both authors agreed to allow me to adapt their textbook, and for this I am grateful to them.

Much of the content of this textbook comes from Schmitt and Klimoski's original text. My contribution was to restructure and reorganize the text; to update the text with recent examples of human resource research (most visibly in the "HR Research Today" boxes appearing throughout the book); and to add new material and exercises to accompany each chapter. Among these exercises is a Running Case, "The VP of Human Resources," which appears intermittently in the chapter closing exercises (see chapters 1, 3, 4, 5, 6, 10, 13, and 14). This case asks students to imagine themselves in a senior HR management role, and present them with problems that tie into the material covered in the chapter.

While my primary intent was to write a textbook to teach college and university students majoring in human resources how to do research in their field of choice, this text can also serve as a useful resource for individuals who are already working in the field. The book is written in three major sections to emphasize the three major elements of doing research in human resources: the major research designs for conducting human resource research (chapters 2 through 6); the development and measurement of individual-, group-, and organization-level variables (chapters 7 through 10); and the approaches for evaluating human resource research (chapters 11 through 13). The Introduction provides a brief history of human resource research and a discussion of the main aspects and issues of the research process. Chapter 14 concludes the book with an examination of the changes and innovations taking place in the field of human resources, as well as an overview of how to write a research report.

Each step in the design and implementation of successful human resource practices and systems requires research. One cannot know what programs are needed, how to design and implement them, or how effective they are without sound and continuous research.

In addition to becoming more aware and knowledgeable of the research process in human resources, it is my hope that readers of this textbook will also be stimulated by the ability to understand, interpret, and conduct research, as well as to practise human resource management.

Alan M. Saks
MAY 1999

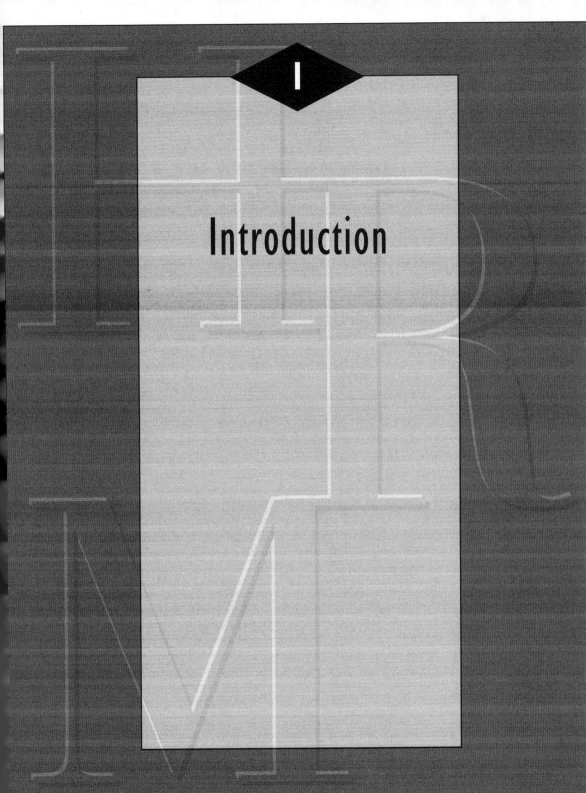

Introduction

◆ ◆ ◆
INTRODUCTION

This book describes the methods for designing and conducting research as well as for measuring and evaluating human resource practices. Knowledge of how to design and conduct research and the ability to draw correct inferences from the data collected are important for human resource professionals and researchers. This belief is based on the premise that research-based human resource management is superior to intuition-based management.

In the last decade, the human resource profession has grown dramatically, and is expected to transform itself in the next decade (Ulrich, 1997). Human resource professionals in many organizations are now involved in the strategic planning process and are considered to play a vital role in the success and long-term survival of their organizations (Phillips, 1996). As a result, it is becoming increasingly important that sound research be used to evaluate and solve human resource problems, and to develop knowledge and theory in human resource management.

Consequently, individuals involved in the management and practice of human resources in all types of organizations need to be well informed about research issues and capable of understanding research methods. Today more than ever, human resource professionals must have the skills and ability to evaluate research proposals, reports, and studies that will be of importance to human resources in a wide variety of contexts.

After reading this chapter, you should be able to:

- Understand the differences between research-based versus intuition-based human resource management.

- Discuss the origins of human resource research.

- Discuss the reasons why human resource research is becoming more important in organizations today.

- Discuss and understand the model of human resource research and practice and how these two functions are related.

- Understand the steps in the research process and the development of hypotheses.

- Discuss and understand the meaning of independent and dependent variables, and mediating and moderating effects.

2

■ Be able to review the literature on human resource topics and develop testable hypotheses.

■ Discuss and understand the human resource measurement and evaluation matrix.

◆ ◆ ◆

RESEARCH-BASED VERSUS INTUITION-BASED HUMAN RESOURCE MANAGEMENT

Although research in human resources is important in the development of a successful organization, there are still many cases in which human resource management practices are driven more by intuition than research. This is clearly an unfortunate practice because there is considerable evidence that the use of intuition rather than research in the management of human resources is a risky endeavour that is likely to result in poor human resource practices and policies.

Perhaps some examples will clarify the distinction between research-based and intuition-based human resource management. One of the most common examples of intuition-based human resources is the continued use of unstructured interviews in the selection of new employees. Dozens of studies have demonstrated that unstructured interviews, in which the decision maker relies on his or her intuition to judge the interviewee, have relatively little predictive validity. In other words, unstructured job interviews do not predict future performance on the job. On the other hand, structured interviews that are carefully and systematically developed, that are based on job analysis information, and in which job-related questions are presented to each job candidate, have been found to provide useful and valid data on which to make selection decisions (Campion, Palmer, & Campion, 1997; McDaniel, Whetzel, Schmidt, & Maurer, 1994; Wiesner & Cronshaw, 1988). The research methods discussed in this text will contribute to (1) the development of better selection interviews, (2) increased ability to assess the claims of consultants who help to develop selection interviews, and (3) greater ability to evaluate the contribution of new selection programs.

Another good example of intuition- versus research-based human resource management is the use of traditional versus realistic job previews during the recruitment process (Wanous, 1992). Many recruiters and managers like to present a glowing picture of their organization to job applicants. Their intuition is based on the belief that by presenting a job and an organization in a positive light the company will attract more job applicants and increase the rate of job acceptance.

Extensive research on job previews, however, has found that an intuitive approach to recruiting can be short-sighted. In fact, a recent review of 40 studies on job previews found that realistic job previews, which present both the positive and negative features of a job and organization to job applicants, are related to lower attrition from the recruitment process, lower turnover, and higher job performance. Thus, the use of intuition-based human resource management in this case not only can result in negative consequences (e.g., lower job performance and higher turnover), but also prevents an organization from adopting a relatively inexpensive and effective recruitment technique (i.e., a realistic job preview) that can lower the costs of selection and turnover (Philips, 1998).

Another common example of intuition-based human resource management is the use of compliments regarding a training program as indices of the training program's effectiveness. Compliments or complaints about a training program may have a significant impact on the trainer but may not be related to what the trainee learns or to improvements in job performance. Furthermore, unless an appropriate sample of trainees is interviewed or surveyed, we know nothing of the opinions of the group of persons who chose not to comment. As a result, it is not known to what extent a training program is effective. Decisions to continue to invest in a training program because some trainees said they enjoyed it could result in the use of programs that do not improve trainees' skills or job performance (Alliger, Tannenbaum, Bennett, Traver, & Shotland, 1997; see also the HR Research Today box).

In each of these examples, the point is not that the decision made is always wrong, but rather that the manager is acting only on a hunch, or intuition, about human behaviour. Such decisions could have been much better informed had an effort been made to collect data and specify how one's observations led to particular conclusions. Those who continue to use unstructured interviews and their "gut" instincts as the basis for employment decisions, traditional job previews during the recruitment process, and affective reactions to evaluate training programs would realize the limitations of these techniques if they took a moment to read the research literature in these areas, or if they made an attempt to check interview validity and the effects of traditional job previews in their own organization, or if they incorporated measures of learning and behaviour in their evaluation of training. Not surprisingly, in his research on the practices that characterize effective companies that have achieved competitive success through their management of human resources, Jeffrey Pfeffer (1994) found that one of the sixteen best practices is "Measurement of the Practices." As Pfeffer (1994) notes, "organizations seriously committed to achieving competitive advantage through people make measurement of their efforts a critical component of the overall process" (p. 56). Over the years, the evolution of research in human resources has demonstrated the important contribution that research-based human resource management can make for organizations.

HR RESEARCH TODAY

Many Companies Waste Money Because They Don't Evaluate Training

Every day, people are being trained to do their jobs better. Staff training is a way of work life in capitalist economies because, as everyone knows, training people to work better results in a better bottom line, right?

Then again, what if the sales guru you brought in to teach your sales people to sell better hasn't quite got the message across? What if your staff really didn't understand the information in the training kit that you bought to teach them how to run new software? What if they haven't learned the soft skills the management consultant was hired to teach? Would you know? And would you be able to see it in the company's performance three months from now?

The problem is that many companies waste their training dollars because they don't measure whether the training has been effective and that staff has actually learned something. Companies often assume they've measured the effectiveness of a training program by giving their employees a so-called "smile-sheet," a questionnaire they complete shortly after the completion of training.

This only provides an emotional reaction to the training. It does not measure what was learned or any change in employees' skills or abilities. Most importantly, it does not measure whether the training is being applied in the workplace. Unfortunately, this is how most companies evaluate their training programs.

There are several ways to assess the effectiveness of training programs. Surveys, questionnaires, interviews, and observations can be used. Company records can also be used by providing information on financial statistics, turnover, and absenteeism. The combination of various methods and measures can provide useful information to evaluate the effectiveness of a training program.

Source: Adapted from Whittaker, S. (1999, January 23). Training sometimes flops. *The Montreal Gazette.*

◆ ◆ ◆

THE HISTORY OF HUMAN RESOURCE RESEARCH

The origins of research on human resource issues can be traced to the work of psychologists in the early part of the 20th century as well as to individuals in other fields, such as industrial engineering, management, marketing, and sociology.

THE EARLY YEARS

During the early 1900s industrialists showed little interest in what psychologists could do for them. They were confident that they could solve whatever problems faced their companies because they had the requisite abilities and experience. But several factors were operating to change this initial disinterest. First, it was a time of industrial growth and of labour unrest. Workers were making demands. Baritz (1960) also notes that in the 1890s there appeared to be a greater acceptance by industry of the role of government in the affairs of business. Government commissions were often staffed with experts from universities. Perhaps it was felt that academics could, after all, bring some new and effective ideas to bear on their problems.

Psychology, too, was changing. Wilhelm Wundt's promotion of psychology as an experimental (empirical) science had a tremendous effect on the field. As an offshoot of philosophy, the emphasis in psychology to that point had been the search for universal laws (or truths), especially those that could explain our mental processes. But these endeavours had been frustrated by a reliance on traditional methods of investigation, such as introspection. Wundt and others promoted empiricism, measurement, and operational definitions as opposed to speculation. New researchers also began to study physical and psychological differences between people. For example, James McKeen Cattell (who took his doctorate at Leipzig, where he worked for Wundt) developed mental measurement techniques for assessing mental characteristics and traits, and became impressed with the work of Galton on the nature and measurement of individual differences. Moving to the University of Pennsylvania, he became the first professor of psychology in the United States. Cattell was not interested only in recording and listing human variabilities (in physical and mental abilities) or investigating their implications. The issue for him and many others of the day quickly shifted to uncovering the *causes* of these measured differences.

Increasingly, the work of academic researchers seemed to many industrial managers to have some relevance. If individual differences (for example, in numerical or mathematical aptitude) could be shaped by experience, management might feel that it was appropriate to stress worker training. But if this variability came about largely as a result of genetic (hereditary) factors, such an emphasis on training would be wasted. Instead, the key to good performance might lie in personnel selection.

The implications of research on human behaviour also were noticed because of the work of another psychologist, William McDougall. A Harvard professor, McDougall published his book *Introduction to Social Psychology* in 1908. In it he described and promoted a theory of human behaviour that stressed the role of instincts. Instincts were felt to be relatively enduring properties of individuals, perhaps genetically determined, that shaped perceptions and actions. For over twenty years, his book appealed to the public, and several editions sold out immediately. His theory of instincts became a popular way to think about what motivates people. Thus, it was especially valued by those who made a living trying to affect human motivation on a regular basis—advertisers.

The first application of psychological theory and research to the world of business and industry was probably in advertising (Baritz, 1960). Experiments in the psychology of advertising are reported to have begun as early as 1896 (Benjamin, 1997). In response to requests from business leaders, Walter Dill Scott began a series of well-received lectures to advertising executives in Chicago in 1901 (Benjamin, 1997; Landy, 1997). Interest in applications of psychology to advertising was further promoted by the publication of two books by Scott. His first book, *The Theory of Advertising* (1903), is considered to be the first book that applied psychological principles to the world of business (Landy, 1997). This was followed by a second book, *The Psychology of Advertising* (1908). In his books Scott emphasized the possibility that ads might be used to appeal to people's instincts, such as hoarding and hunting.

By 1910, Scott was well known in business circles and established a successful relationship with industry that was to last for many years. In addition to advertising, Scott also began to write about leadership, industrial efficiency, selection, and motivation (Landy, 1997). In 1910, he wrote one of the original textbooks in the field of industrial psychology, *Increasing Human Efficiency in Business*, in which he discussed the application of psychological principles to industry (Landy, 1997). By 1915 Scott was working on selection programs for the American Tobacco Company, Western Electric, and National Lead Co. He also studied the psychological characteristics of piece-rate pay systems, as well as organizational culture, worker attitudes, and motivation (Landy, 1997).

As industrialists saw the value of behavioural science for the areas of marketing and staffing, and as more opportunities became available to them, the field itself began to take form. One individual who was to accelerate this process was Hugo Munsterberg, who began work in business psychology in 1909 (Benjamin, 1997). Munsterberg was also trained in Germany. He received an MD in 1885 and a Ph.D. under Wundt in 1887. While at the University of Berlin he developed a series of lectures that were first published in German (1910) and later translated into a classic book that is considered to be the first modern book on industrial psychology (Landy, 1997), *Psychology of Industrial Efficiency* (1913). According to Landy (1997), the "book was the bible for the application of differential psychology in industry and established the concepts of validity and utility" (p. 470). Munsterberg felt that this new science lay somewhere between basic psychology and economics. In his book he took care to detail its application and potential in areas as diverse as vocational guidance, training, personnel selection, and marketing. He also acknowledged an intellectual debt to scientific management theories of the time but felt that it was up to psychologists to study the human element in organizations.

Munsterberg emphasized the importance of vocational guidance and personnel selection. The goal was to help organizations select workers who would perform better and experience greater job satisfaction (Moskowitz, 1977). He also believed that industrial psychologists, as staff or as consultants, should stay out of policy decisions, even those that affected workers. He felt that psychologists should remain detached scientists who had no right to proclaim what effect (result) was good or bad. It was management who should decide when and where to apply the "psychological levers" that were uncovered by research. And, certainly, the profitability of the firm should always be kept foremost in mind.

It was not only Munsterberg's writings but also his work in industry that had a great impact. He developed tests for the selection of personnel in such diverse fields as sales (for the American Tobacco Company), bus driving (for the Boston Street Railway), and even ship captaincy. In response to a request from the director of the San Francisco and Portland Steamship Company, which wanted to prevent accidents by testing the decision-making ability of captains before hiring them, Munsterberg designed a time sorting task to measure decision-making ability (Van De Water, 1997). He was eclectic in his interests. Moreover, he was well read, building on the work of others such as Gilbreth, F.W. Taylor, and Woodworth (Moskowitz, 1977), and was in great demand as both a consultant and entrepreneur (Landy, 1997).

By the middle of the decade, the reputation of academic research in human behaviour was growing, both within universities and in work organizations. In 1915, the Applied Psychology Division at the Carnegie Institute of Technology (now Carnegie-Mellon University) in Pittsburgh was founded by Walter VanDyke Bingham (who received his Ph.D. from the University of Chicago in 1908), the first program that offered a consulting service to industry (Benjamin, 1997). Shortly after his arrival, Bingham was asked by a group of local business leaders to develop a program for training sales representatives (Landy, 1997). The modest program grew steadily. Bingham set up the Bureau of Salesmanship Research (focusing on the selection of sales personnel) and later created a Research Bureau for Retail Training. It is note-worthy that he persuaded several major retail companies in the area to contribute to the bureau as a consortium of sponsors. In return, he and his staff did work relevant to their concerns in the areas of employment tests, training manuals, and programs of work adjustment and better supervision. Also significant is the fact that Bingham was able to persuade Walter Dill Scott to come to Carnegie (from Northwestern) in 1916 as America's first professor of applied psychology (Baritz, 1960).

These early efforts on the part of behavioural scientists were clearly interdisci-plinary, involving sales, marketing, management, training, and so on.

THE WAR YEARS

The period of the First World War was important in the development of human resource research. In 1916, the National Research Council was organized in the United States. A year later the Committee for Psychology was formed and given the responsibility for finding ways of using this new group of specialists. The unit was led by Robert Yerkes (on leave from Harvard) and others with applied psychology interests.

As well, a Committee on Classification of Personnel in the Adjutant General's office was formed in which Walter Dill Scott was the director and Walter VanDyke Bingham the secretary (Van De Water, 1997). Both Scott and Bingham applied their techniques for selection, training, and performance assessment (Landy, 1997). By the end of the war the committee had created 112 tests that were give to nearly 3.5 million soldiers in order to place them in 83 different jobs (Van De Water, 1997). All of these people were to leave the military with some awareness (for better or for worse) of testing, and by the end of the war in 1919, mental testing was well established (Landy, 1997).

Theories and procedures of performance appraisal were also developed during those years. As early as 1912, the Larkin Company had used management ratings of its supervisors to make annual bonus awards. During this period, the Committee on Classification did a great deal of work on performance appraisal for purposes of promotion and future military assignments.

All this created a supportive climate for the use of the behavioural and social sciences immediately after the war. The growth of the civilian economy and the rapid demobilization caused managers to seek out and employ psychologists. In a survey of the period, many members of the American Psychological Association claimed to be doing work in industry in such areas as selection testing, job analysis, and the measurement of worker attitudes and worker morale. Progress was being made in areas such as criterion definition, test construction, test validation, and statistical analyses, and testing became more common in education and industry (Van De Water, 1997).

About this time, the *Journal of Applied Psychology* was founded (1917) and still exists today as a key research and professional journal that publishes research articles on human resource issues. In 1919, Scott formed his own consulting company in Philadelphia and Cattell started the Psychological Corporation. The growth and acceptance of human resource specialists and research in industry was also occurring in other countries at this time, especially in Europe. For example, in Germany in 1922, 22 firms had personnel research laboratories.

As well, more and more companies were developing personnel departments and employing industrial psychologists to design and conduct attitude or morale surveys. In 1932, Rensis Likert developed a valuable attitude measurement technique that was to become a standard in the field of survey work (Seashore & Katz, 1982). He also wrote an influential book (with Gardner Murphy) titled *Public Opinion and the Individual* (1938). Kornhauser and Sharp, at the University of Chicago, did survey work for Kimberly-Clark. Other companies active in the area of employee surveys included Armstrong, Sears Roebuck & Co., and Procter and Gamble.

The 1930s also witnessed the widespread use of formal training programs in organizations. Casual (on-the-job) training had traditionally been used, but until then only a few companies (U.S. Steel, Eastman Kodak, Chrysler) had established classroom-like training programs. Much of this new formal training was aimed at managers and supervisors and, in the spirit of the human relations movement, emphasized leadership skills.

The employment of psychologists and human resource specialists in government and the military during the Second World War increased rapidly. Over 1700 were involved in the armed forces. They did research, development, and implementation work in a wide variety of areas. Some worked in personnel selection, training (especially management training), and on problems of absenteeism, turnover, and morale. Others were involved in unusual assignments (e.g., selecting and training bomber pilots, espionage agents, submariners), analyzed propaganda, developed campaigns to sell war bonds, trained personnel to deal with foreign cultures, and designed military hardware and technology. With the advent of new, expensive, and more complex and sophisticated weapons (especially aircraft), many psychologists became more interested not only in the selection of people to operate these weapon systems but also in the optimal design of the hardware itself. They did research and development work on such things as gun sighting mechanisms, cockpit design, and tank controls. As a result, human factors research received a great deal of prominence during this period. Performance appraisal programs also enjoyed a great deal of popularity at this time. The military had found them useful for making promotion decisions with regard to officer ranks.

The new technology of worker attitude measurement derived in the 1930s was also put to use in the war effort. For example, Likert worked for the Department of Agriculture to conduct surveys of farmers regarding crop planting habits and intentions. He also designed studies to determine civilian plans for war bonds redemption (Seashore & Katz, 1982). In a large-scale effort, Ford Motor Company sent surveys to over 124,700 production and salaried employees to assess their concerns (Baritz, 1960). Although "only" 22,000 replied, some major problem areas were uncovered in this way.

THE POSTWAR YEARS

A historical review of the development of human resources research reveals the origins of interest in various human resource content areas and research issues, many of which continue to be important today. For example, the measurement of employees' abilities and attitudes, as well as the use of survey techniques, interviews, and experimental research, had all been introduced and applied to human resource problems by the end of the Second World War and continue to be fundamental issues in human resource research. As well, in 1947, *Personnel Psychology* was founded and, along with the *Journal of Applied Psychology*, still exists today as a key research and professional journal on human resources.

In the years since the Second World War, a number of developments have had a substantial impact on the evolution and importance of human resources research. Of particular importance has been the effect of federal and provincial government legislation, particularly in the areas of employment equity, which has had substantial implications for human resource research in areas such as recruitment, selection, performance appraisals, and training and development. Pay equity issues have stimulated research on compensation and the methods that organizations use to establish their compensation plans. Interest in quality of work life programs in the 1970s stimulated renewed interest in worker attitudes and perceptions and how these perceptions might relate to productivity and perceived quality of life and job satisfaction. During the 1980s, an increasing concern and interest in productivity led to the development and evaluation of human resource programs that were designed to improve worker motivation and productivity.

In recent years, the importance of human resource research has become more evident than ever. As discussed in the next section, human resources have become recognized as fundamental for the effectiveness, competitiveness, and survival of organizations. As indicated at the beginning of this chapter, the key to successful human resource management systems and programs is a research-based approach.

◆ ◆ ◆
HUMAN RESOURCE RESEARCH TODAY

As the field of human resources continues to grow and develop, so does the importance of research. Today more than ever, research is becoming a vital, if not critical, part of the human resource function. While the usefulness of research in human resources for developing and testing theory and solving organizational problems is now well understood, a number of compelling changes are driving the need for human resources research. These include:

1. Human resource practices and organizational effectiveness.
2. Accountability of human resource departments.
3. Strategic human resource management.
4. The value-added of human resource programs.
5. The new human resources.

HUMAN RESOURCE PRACTICES AND ORGANIZATIONAL EFFECTIVENESS

Although the history of human resource management and research is comprehensive in terms of topics and studies, only in the last decade has research begun to demonstrate empirically that human resource practices are related to an organization's success and effectiveness. Previously, it was known that particular human resource practices (e.g., incentives) are related to individual-level outcomes (e.g., individual performance). We now know that human resource systems also have an effect on organization-level outcomes. Numerous studies have been conducted that demonstrate a strong relation between human resource practices and bottom-line outcomes, including productivity, turnover, and financial and accounting performance indicators (Phillips, 1996).

In one of the first studies in this area, Arthur (1994) studied the human resource systems of steel mini-mills in the United States. He found that the human resource policies and practices used by the mini-mills could be categorized as being either commitment or control systems, and that the mills with commitment systems had higher productivity and lower scrap rates and employee turnover than those with control systems.

In 1995, Mark Huselid conducted one of the most comprehensive studies of the linkages between human resource systems and firm performance. In his study, questionnaires were completed by almost 1000 senior human resource professionals who answered questions about the human resource work practices in their firms. Huselid (1995) determined that high-performance human resource practices had two major dimensions. The first dimension he called employee skills and organizational structures, which includes various practices to enhance employees' knowledge, skills, and abilities (e.g., job design programs, formal training, incentive plans). The second dimension he called employee motivation, which includes practices that recognize and reinforce desirable employee behaviours (e.g., formal performance appraisals, linking appraisals to compensation). He also measured several outcomes, including the annual rate of employee turnover, productivity, and corporate financial performance.

Huselid found strong support for the impact of human resource practices on organizational outcomes. In particular, human resource practices were significantly related to lower employee turnover and higher productivity and corporate financial performance. Furthermore, the impact of human resource practices on corporate financial performance was due in part to lower employee turnover and higher productivity.

Since Huselid's research, an increasing number of studies have investigated the relation between human resource practices and organizational performance. In fact, in 1996, the *Academy of Management Journal* published a special issue devoted to human resource management and organizational performance. Several of the studies published in this issue provide additional evidence of the relation between human resource management and organizational outcomes. For example, Delery and Doty (1996) found that profit sharing, results-oriented appraisals, and employment security were strongly related to accounting measures of performance. Delaney and Huselid (1996) found that selectivity in staffing, training, and incentive compensation were positively related to perceptual measures of organizational performance.

As evidence linking human resource practices and systems to organizational outcomes continues to grow, so does the need for human resource research. That is, there will be growing interest in identifying, developing, implementing, and evaluating the effectiveness of human resource practices, given the important role they have in organizational effectiveness. Human resource research will therefore be key to the ability to determine which practices an organization should develop and implement, and the effect they have on employees and the organization. Thus, human resource research and practice are likely to become intricately interrelated.

Figure 1.1 presents a model of the relations between human resource research and practice. This model demonstrates the critical role of research in the development, implementation, and evaluation of effective human resource practices. Central to the model is the notion that human resource research is required in order to identify problem areas, determine the best solutions for a problem, design programs as part of the solution, and implement human resource practices and systems to help organizations achieve their goals and objectives. As well, human resource research is required to monitor and evaluate the effectiveness of these programs in order to ensure their contribution and value-added to the organization.

While human resource practices can have a positive effect on organizational outcomes, it is not possible to have effective human resource programs without conducting the research required to identify those programs that will in fact be effective in meeting an organization's needs and objectives in the first place. As well, failure to conduct the research necessary to evaluate human resource programs makes it impossible to determine the effectiveness of programs and to make decisions regarding the need for adjustments or changes. For example, many organizations adopt training programs without first conducting research to determine training needs. As a result, organizations run the risk of investing in and implementing training programs that do not result in positive outcomes or, even worse, have a negative effect on employee attitudes and behaviour. As reported earlier, many organizations also fail to evaluate the effectiveness of training programs. Thus, they are unable to determine the effect, if any, of their training programs on employee learning, behaviour, and organization results (Sarri, Johnson, McLaughlin, & Zimmerle, 1988).

Thus, human resource research is required throughout the process of developing, implementing, and evaluating human resource programs and systems. The feedback loop in the model indicates that this is an ongoing and cyclical process, since the evaluation process can result in changes and modifications in the design and implementation of human resource interventions. While there is increasing research evidence, as well as a realization among managers and organizations, that the man-

FIGURE 1.1 Human Resource Research and Practice Model

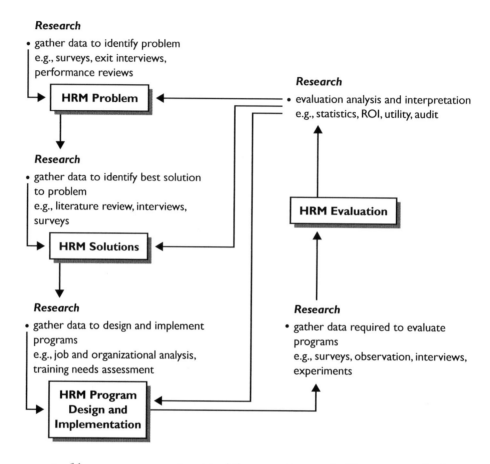

agement of human resources is critical for organizational effectiveness, the key to effective human resource practices is ongoing human resource research.

ACCOUNTABILITY OF HUMAN RESOURCE DEPARTMENTS

The growth in the stature and role of human resources in organizations over the last decade has been a long-awaited goal of human resource practitioners and professionals. Once considered a relatively unimportant part of an organization, the human resource department in many organizations today is considered a partner equal to all other divisions and functions within an organization.

However, with such equality comes expectations. Like all functions in an organization, human resource departments must now be accountable for what they do and how they do it. They must be able to explain why they invested in a particular training program, for example, or why they developed a new and expensive selection system. There will continue to be increasing demands on human resource professionals to justify their use of company resources and their decisions to invest in particular human resource practices and policies.

Research, therefore, must become an essential part of the human resource function in order to address the increasing need and demand for accountability. Failure to provide data based on sound research to the same extent as other departments in an organization will only weaken the role and status of the human resource function. Being equal also means being accountable and comparable to other organizational functions.

STRATEGIC HUMAN RESOURCE MANAGEMENT

During the last decade, organizations have become more aware of the competitive advantages that can be achieved through human resources (Pfeffer, 1994). In fact, human resource practices are most likely to lead to sustained competitive advantage when they are aligned with an organization's competitive strategy (Huselid, 1995). In other words, human resource management and practices are important factors in the successful implementation of an organization's strategies. As a result, the role of the human resource function in organizations has become increasingly more strategic. Today, human resource professionals in many organizations are involved in the strategic planning process. This involves the development and implementation of human resource practices and policies that will help the organization achieve its goals and objectives by supporting and reinforcing its business strategy. Strategic human resources also requires that human resource practices be consistent with one another and carefully aligned with the organization's corporate goals.

Strategic human resources, therefore, requires a considerable degree of data gathering in order to identify inconsistencies between human resource practices and organizational goals, as well as within the human resource system. In addition, human resource professionals will be required to design, implement, monitor, and evaluate human resource practices to ensure that they are consistent with and supportive of business strategies. Human resource practices and systems that fail to support an organization's strategies can seriously undermine organizational competitiveness.

VALUE-ADDED

In recent years, the human resource field has been accused of not adding value to organizations. For example, several years ago an article in *Fortune* magazine (Stewart, 1996) argued that human resource departments should be eliminated because they do not add value. In the article, human resource leaders were accused of not being able to describe the value-added of their department in meaningful and quantifiable terms, and the writer recommended that many traditional HR functions be outsourced. These observations and the recommendations to outsource many HR functions are based on the belief that human resource departments do not provide organizations with a competitive advantage.

As indicated previously, this is simply not the case. Human resource practices can and do make a difference. The issue is whether human resource professionals are capable of demonstrating their contribution and value-added to management and others in their organizations in a meaningful and quantifiable way. Failure to do so is not only likely to result in ridicule and disdain toward the human resource function and HR professionals, but it is also likely to affect human resource budgets, decision making, and influence in the organization. The only way for human resource departments and professionals to demonstrate their contribution to organizations is to provide meaningful data and information that clearly indicate the outcomes of human resource practices, policies, procedures, and programs in a meaningful manner comparable with other organizational departments. This, of course, requires that sound, ongoing research be carried out, and the results reported and communicated throughout the organization.

THE NEW HUMAN RESOURCES

Over the last several decades the field of human resources has evolved and developed from being a "personnel" department, which was primarily an administrative and record-keeping function, to becoming a policy-maker and regulator, and more recently a strategic partner in organizational planning. The change and evolution of human resource management, however, is about to undergo a revolution. In his book *Human Resource Champions*, David Ulrich (1997) outlines the changing role of human resources.

According to Ulrich (1997), human resources needs to change from a paradigm that has existed for the last 40 years and to focus not on what HR professionals "do" but what they "deliver." In other words, Ulrich believes that the new HR must focus on outcomes, or the results of HR efforts, such as strategy execution, administrative efficiency, employee contribution, and the capacity for change.

In making this transition, Ulrich argues that HR professionals need to assume four distinct roles: strategic partner, administrative expert, employee champion, and change agent. The HR function is undergoing a major transformation, so much so that Ulrich predicts that the next ten years will be the HR decade. Making this transition and assuming the roles of the new HR will require sound research that can result in innovative approaches to helping organizations meet the challenges of an increasing pace of change and competition. The new HR will be value-driven, results-oriented, and, inevitably, research-based. Therefore, the successful transition to this new paradigm of human resources will require that human resource professionals increasingly conduct and use research in the management of human resources.

In summary, the need for research in the management of human resources is being driven by a number of important developments in the human resource field. With increasing evidence of the impact of human resources on organizational outcomes, the need for greater accountability and evidence of value-added, combined with the increasingly strategic role played by human resources and the impending paradigm shift, the practice and management of human resources will require an approach that is guided and driven by research. This means that understanding the research process will need to become one of the competencies required by human resource professionals.

◆ ◆ ◆
THE RESEARCH PROCESS

Human resource research is a means of learning about aspects of behaviour or phenomena in organizations. Through such research we become more informed and capable of making more valid human resource management decisions. In this respect, human resource research can be used for description, prediction, and/or understanding. It can also be used to develop and test theories and to solve human resource problems in organizations. However, regardless of its purpose, the actual research process is the same, and understanding it is fundamental to conducting good research. Therefore, this section presents an overview of the human resource research process.

As indicated in Figure 1.2, the human resource research process consists of a number of steps or stages. Each step is an important and necessary stage in the research process and is discussed in more detail below.

SELECT RESEARCH ISSUE

The starting point in the research process is an issue or concern that requires the gathering of data and information. The need for research in human resources is based on a number of factors. Some of these will reflect the investigators' interests or motives; others will reflect institutional needs and organizational problems. For the academically based investigator, research might be conducted to develop a new theory; test or refine an existing theory; resolve contradictory predictions derived from two or more theories in a particular area; reconcile discrepant findings reported in the published literature; test the effects of a human resource intervention; or bridge

FIGURE 1.2 The Human Resource Research Process

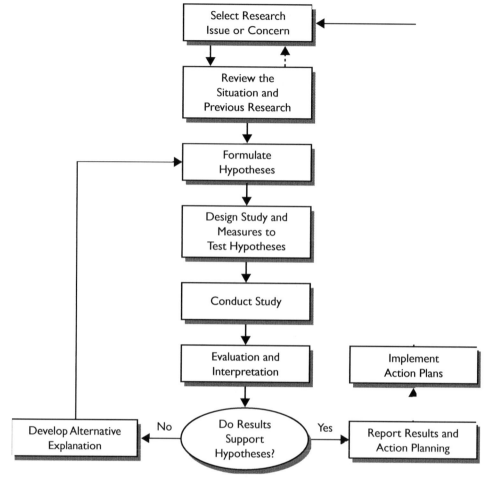

Source: Adapted from Boehm, V.R. (1980). Research in the "real world"—a conceptual model. *Personnel Psychology*, 33, 495–504.

and build linkages between two or more streams of research. In a more fully developed form the researcher's ideas might be offered as a **framework, model,** or **theory**.

On the other hand, human resource practitioners, as staff professionals or as consultants, will have other reasons for conducting research. They are likely to be interested in assessing organizational needs for human resource programs or interventions (e.g., training needs); resolving conflicts or competing preferences by members of management with regard to practices or policies (e.g., whether a flexible or a traditional work schedule should be followed); creating components of human resource systems (e.g., establishing pay grades); evaluating current programs, policies, or practices (e.g., the impact of a benefits package); meeting government agency reporting requirements (e.g., compiling employment equity data); providing data for arguments in litigation (e.g., product liability); or diagnosing the causes for organizational problems (e.g., high rates of voluntary turnover).

Thus, research can be self-motivated, generated by pragmatic concerns, or legally mandated. However, regardless of the impetus for the research or the particular form it takes, the "rules" for quality research will be the same. A person who masters these rules (and the skills associated with their implementation) will be more likely to produce higher-quality decisions and recommendations. Thus, good research, like good thinking, is required in all domains of human resource management.

REVIEW THE SITUATION

Once a research issue or problem has been recognized, the researcher will want to review the situation to gather some background information about the topic. This can involve a review of the existing research and literature on a topic, as well as informal discussions with members of the organization. Before conducting an expensive new study on some issue, it is important that we know the existing database and whether an additional study with a potentially small sample size could significantly alter the conclusions drawn from that database. For example, many academics and HR managers are concerned with turnover. Therefore, before conducting a study on the causes of turnover, one would want to find out what is currently known about the causes of employee turnover. As well, an HR manager might want to review the situation in his or her organization to get an idea about why turnover is a problem before beginning a large-scale study.

An important way to review a research topic is to learn about the existing frameworks or theories. In its simple form, a framework or model consists of a number of variables and the relationships thought to exist among them (e.g., variable x causes variable y, which in turn affects variable z). Usually a framework will include a number of such variables thought to be necessary and sufficient to understand or explain the human resource phenomenon of interest. In such a framework, it is common to think and speak in terms of the independent or causal variable and the dependent or resultant (criterion) variable.

A theory is more sophisticated than a framework in that it goes beyond merely identifying the variables of interest and their approximate relationships. Rather, it describes the functional or precise nature of how the factors interact. A theory would include a statement of the boundaries or conditions within which such relationships would be valid. It also would provide or imply propositions or conclusions which can be reasonably expected to follow from the theory, based on logical deductions. Similarly, a theory is a creation of the researcher who attempts to model some aspect of the "real world" in order to simplify and understand it. A theory or theoretical model is scientific only if it is possible to subject the theory to an empirical test (Dubin, 1976). A great deal of research in human resources involves testing or modifying some framework or theory. For example, Figure 1.3 depicts a simplified model of employee turnover.

FIGURE 1.3 Simplified Model of Employee Turnover

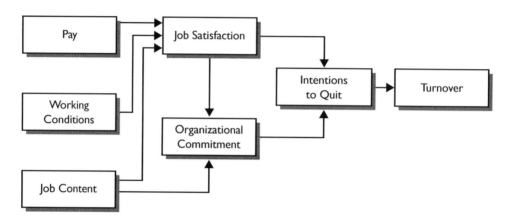

As we shall see at various points in this text, theories serve as a source of propositions and hypotheses. They provide understanding of the phenomenon we study, they direct or stimulate research, and they can be used to organize and interpret research results. We turn next to a consideration of the more explicit purpose for which we conduct research—that is, to test hypotheses derived from our frameworks, models, or theories.

FORMULATE HYPOTHESES

Based on a review of the situation as well as the existing research and theory, the investigator must begin the process of developing testable hypotheses. In effect, propositions or conclusions implied by a theory are made into **hypotheses**. These are formalized statements specifying key variables and their supposed relationships. What is special about hypotheses is that they are worded to include appropriate empirical indicators needed for testing (Dubin, 1976). Moreover, good hypotheses are stated in such a way as to be complete enough that the reader knows the conditions that would allow them to be tested (Runkel & McGrath, 1972). Thus, one of the hallmarks of a good hypothesis is that it is stated in such a way that it can be disproved.

Consider, for example, the following hypotheses that were tested by Gary Johns (1994) in an interesting study of employees' estimates of their own absenteeism and that of their co-workers:

Hypothesis 1: Employees will estimate that their work group exhibits less absenteeism than their occupation in general.

Hypothesis 2: Employees will estimate that they exhibit less absenteeism than the average member of their work group.

Hypothesis 3: Employees' actual absenteeism will be greater than their own self-report estimates.

These are clear, testable hypotheses that can be easily disproved. In research, then, investigators would use a framework or theory to position or justify the statement of the problem they are addressing. The research hypotheses narrow this down to the specific relationships of interest. It also turns out that hypotheses usually imply (or shape) the measures to be used, the research design to be followed, and even the methods involved. Thus, hypotheses constitute an important bridge between concepts (theory) and the operations that will be used (practice).

One of the most important aspects of hypotheses is that they indicate the key variables of interest. In this respect, there are two types of variables usually included in a hypothesis and that are the focus of research: an **independent variable** and a **dependent variable**. In most cases, the hypotheses will state the expected relation between these variables or the effect of the independent variable (e.g., selection test) on the dependent variable (e.g., job performance). In this respect, it is sometimes said that the dependent variable is "dependent" on the independent variable. Thus, we are interested in understanding or predicting the reasons for any variability in the dependent variable (e.g., job performance) as a result of the independent variable (e.g., selection test).

The goal of much research is to establish cause-and-effect relations among variables such that an independent variable is hypothesized to be the cause of some dependent variable. In the case of human resource interventions this usually means that we are interested in knowing if a planned intervention (e.g., a training program) has had a desired and predicted effect on some aspect of individual or organizational functioning (e.g., job or organizational performance).

While a hypothesis, in its simplest form, predicts a relation between an independent and dependent variable, it is important to realize that other relationships are possible and are often the focus of research in human resources. For example, two important types of relationships that are often of interest in human resources are known as **mediation** and **moderation** effects.

As indicated earlier, the goal of research is not only to predict a relationship, but also to understand and explain it. In many cases, then, we are interested in understanding why a human resource practice has an effect on some outcome. It could be that a relationship exists between an independent and dependent variable because some other variable serves as an intervening or mediating variable. For example, research on the effects of training on job performance has found that trainees' self-efficacy, their confidence that they can successfully perform the trained task, is an important mediating variable (Saks, 1997). In other words, training improves job performance in part because it increases trainees' self-efficacy. Therefore, self-efficacy is considered to be a mediating variable in the relationship between training and job performance.

In still other situations, it is possible that an independent variable such as training has an effect on a dependent variable such as job performance only under certain circumstances. In this case such an effect will occur only when some third variable takes on certain values. Thus, the third variable is referred to as a **moderating variable** because it *moderates* the effect of the independent variable on the dependent variable. Such a relationship is sometimes referred to as an **interaction** because the relationship between two independent variables and a dependent variable is a function of the levels of the two independent variables and how they interact. For example, if pay is more strongly related to job performance for workers who are paid according to piece rate compared with workers who are paid by the hour, we would conclude that there is an interaction between pay and pay system because the relationship between pay and job performance depends on the pay system.

In general, a moderating variable affects the nature of the relationship between two other variables. Research on training has found that the effectiveness of some training programs depends on trainees' levels of self-efficacy. In particular, some training programs have been found to be more effective for trainees who have low levels of self-efficacy (Saks, 1997). In these situations, self-efficacy is considered to be a moderating variable because the effect of training on training outcomes depends on the level (e.g., low or high) of trainees' self-efficacy, or the interaction between training and self-efficacy.

In summary, a critical step in the research process involves the development of testable hypotheses that are derived from existing research and theory as well as from one's knowledge of the situation in a particular organization. The hypotheses state the expected relationships between variables that will be the focus of the research and also help to guide and direct the subsequent steps in the research process. The remaining steps in the research process involve designing, conducting, and evaluating the study.

RESEARCH DESIGN AND METHODS

Once the problem or issue has been identified and reviewed, and testable hypotheses have been stated, the researcher needs to decide on the most appropriate research design and methods to test the hypotheses. This is a difficult and complex process because there are many factors that need to be determined. The most fundamental aspect of conducting research is the actual method or plan for conducting or carrying out a research project. Therefore, chapters 2 through 6 of this book are devoted to the different research methods that can be used to conduct research in human resources.

Chapter 2 presents an overview of the major issues involved in the research design stage of the research process. At this stage the researcher needs to decide on a number of important methodological issues such as the research sample, how and when to measure the variables of interest, and how the data will be analyzed. One of the most important decisions the researcher needs to make at this stage is which of several possible research designs to employ. Chapter 2 presents a brief overview of the various research designs and notes some of the important factors to consider in choosing the most appropriate design. Chapters 3 through 6 are devoted to each of the major research designs.

Chapter 3 describes the use of survey research in human resources. Chapter 4 discusses the different types of nonexperimental, experimental, and quasi-experimental designs. Chapter 5 presents an overview of the use of qualitative research designs in human resources, including interviews, observation, and archival sources of data. Chapter 6 describes how to use the existing literature for research and explains how a process called meta-analysis can be used to combine the results of many studies in a particular area of human resources (e.g., employment interviews) as a way to learn about the effects of a human resource intervention or the strength of a relationship between variables.

MEASUREMENT

All research methods require the measurement of some set of variables. As will become apparent throughout this text, failure to properly and adequately measure the relevant variables in a research project can be a fatal flaw in a study and severely limit the interpretations and conclusions that can be made. The most rigorous and sophisticated research design will not prove very useful if the key variables have not been adequately measured.

Chapters 7 through 10 of this book deal with measurement issues in human resources research. Chapter 7 focuses on the issues involved in developing measures for human resources, and Chapter 8 outlines methods for ensuring the quality of the measures. Chapters 9 and 10 describe different techniques for the measurement of variables in human resources. Chapter 9 describes individual measurement techniques, and Chapter 10 describes group and organization level techniques.

EVALUATION AND INTERPRETATION

Once the data have been collected, the researcher must begin the task of preparing the data for evaluation. While research in human resources can be conducted for purely descriptive reasons—for example, to gauge levels of employee attitudes and morale—very often the goal of human resource research is to evaluate a human resource practice or intervention (e.g., a new selection test or training program), a human resource function (e.g., selection procedures or system), or the entire human resource system.

Figure 1.4 presents a human resource measurement and evaluation matrix. The matrix indicates the various possibilities for evaluating human resources by combining three different levels of measurement (e.g., individual, group, and organization) with three levels of evaluation (practice, function, and system). For example, the effects of a new selection test (practice) can be evaluated in terms of its effect on individual performance, group performance, and/or organizational performance. Similarly, the effect of the entire selection function can be evaluated on the same outcomes, as well as the entire human resource system. The matrix can be used to identify the focus of evaluation and the level of measurement.

FIGURE 1.4 Human Resource Measurement and Evaluation Matrix

LEVEL OF MEASUREMENT

HRM LEVEL OF EVALUATION	Individual	Group	Organization
1. HR Programs	- attitudes	- interactions	- profit
	- perceptions	- dynamics	- productivity
2. HR Functions	- reactions	- processes	- quality
	- behaviours	- performance	- absenteeism
3. HR System	- performance	- quality	- turnover

Chapters 11 through 13 describe the methods for evaluating human resources. Chapter 11 presents an overview of the types of statistics that can be used to evaluate human resources. Management and other consumers of human resource research, however, often require more than just statistical evaluation. Human resource programs cost a great deal of money, and, as indicated earlier, it is increasingly necessary for human resource professionals to demonstrate the value-added of human resource programs. Therefore, in Chapter 12 the focus is on how to evaluate human resources in financial terms. Chapter 13 describes methods for evaluating the human resource system, including human resource audits and benchmarking.

REPORT WRITING AND ACTION PLANNING

In the final stage of the research process, the researcher usually prepares a report in which the results of the research are presented. In organizations, this will often include recommendations for solving the organizational problem that originally instigated the research process. For example, in recent years a number of organizations have conducted attitude surveys in an attempt to deal with turnover problems. This has caused organizations to design new human resource programs, such as career management, to meet their employees' desire for career growth and development. Thus, action plans in the form of new programs are often the result of research that was designed to solve an organizational problem.

Finally, Chapter 14 presents an overview of the research process in which the different stages of the process are integrated to demonstrate the different issues involved in the design of human resource research. The book concludes with an overview of how to write a research report and innovations in human resource research.

◆ ◆ ◆
SUMMARY

This chapter has introduced you to the nature and rationale of human resources research. Learning and understanding the issues presented in this book will help human resource professionals make better data-based human resource decisions and realize the practicality of a research and data-based approach to human resource problems. The field of human resources is undergoing major changes, and the need for research to guide future practice has never been greater. You should now have a basic understanding of the research process and the types of activities and decisions that need to be made at each stage. In the following chapters you will learn more about how to design, measure, and evaluate human resource practices, functions, and systems.

Definitions

Dependent variable   The variable that is expected to vary as a function of an independent or predictor variable.

Framework or model   A depiction of the relationships thought to exist among a set of variables of interest.

Hypothesis   A formalized statement that specifies the expected relationships between variables.

Independent variable   The variable that is manipulated and is expected to cause or predict one or more dependent or outcome variables.

Interaction   The relationship between two independent variables and a dependent variable is a function of the levels of the two independent variables and how they interact.

Mediating variable   A variable that intervenes or "mediates" the relationship between an independent variable and a dependent variable.

Moderating variable   A variable that affects the nature of the relationship between two other variables. That is, the relationship between an independent and dependent variable is a function of the level of a third or "moderating" variable.

Theory   An explanation of the precise nature of how a set of variables of interest interact and are related and the boundaries or conditions within which such relationships are expected to occur.

Validity   Refers to the appropriateness of the inferences and interpretations that are made from a test score.

Variable   Refers to a measure that can take on differing values. At the very least, a variable must be either present or absent, but in most cases it can have multiple levels.

EXERCISES

1. What is the difference between research-based and intuition-based human resources management? Describe a research-based and an intuition-based approach to a human resource practice (e.g., employment interview) and the implications of each approach for how the practice is conducted and for the potential outcomes.

2. Discuss the origins of human resources research. What factors led to the development of research in human resources, and what were the main topics and issues that were the focus of the early research? Why is research in human resources necessary for operating and maintaining an effective human resource system in organizations today?

3. Discuss the five human resource issues that are driving the need for human resources research today, and explain the research implications that stem from each.

4. Choose an area in human resources that interests you (e.g., selection, training, compensation, performance appraisals). Conduct a literature review on the topic and identify any existing frameworks or theories. Based on your review, develop a set of testable hypotheses, and then make a list of all of the issues you will need to consider in the remaining stages of the research process.

5. Using the human resource measurement and evaluation matrix presented in Figure 1.4, provide an example for each level of evaluation with each level

of measurement (e.g., effects of a training program on employee job performance).

6. Review the three hypotheses proposed by Gary Johns (1994) for his research on employee self-estimates of absenteeism. Consider the following:

   a) What are the key variables of interest and what needs to be measured to test the three hypotheses?

   b) What is the expected relation between the variables stated in the hypotheses?

   c) If you were to conduct a study to test the three hypotheses, what would you do?

   d) What do you think were the results of Johns's study?

RUNNING CASE: THE VP OF HUMAN RESOURCES—PART I

You are the vice-president of human resources for a large retail organization. In recent years, your organization has faced increasing competition from new competitors. Sales and profits are down and are expected to continue to decline unless something is done about it soon. As a result, the president of the company is looking for ways to cut costs and downsize. During a meeting with all of the department VPs, the president has asked each of them to prepare a report which demonstrates the value-added of each department and its programs to the organization. The president will decide what departments and programs will be cut based on the value-added of each department. As VP of human resources, you must demonstrate the value of human resource practices and the contribution of your department and programs to the organization.

Describe some of the things you will do to demonstrate the value-added of the HRM department and its programs to the organization. For each action you propose, describe the knowledge and skills that are required to perform it effectively.

References

Alliger, G.M., Tannenbaum, S.I., Bennett, W., Jr., Traver, H., & Shotland, A. (1997). A meta-analysis of the relations among training criteria. *Personnel Psychology, 50,* 341–358.

Arthur, J.B. (1994). Effects of human resource systems on manufacturing performance and turnover. *Academy of Management Journal, 37,* 670–687.

Baritz, L. (1960). *The servants of power.* Middleton, CT: Wesleyan University Press.

Benjamin, L.T., Jr. (1997). Organized industrial psychology before division 14: The ACP and the AAAP (1930–1945). *Journal of Applied Psychology, 82,* 459–466.

Campion, M.A., Palmer, D.K., & Campion, J.E. (1997). A review of structure in the selection interview. *Personnel Psychology, 50,* 655–702.

Delaney, J.T., & Huselid, M.A. (1996). The impact of human resource management practices on perceptions of organizational performance. *Academy of Management Journal,* *39*, 949–969.

Delery, J.E., & Doty, D.H. (1996). Modes of theorizing in strategic human resource management: Tests of universalistic, contingency, and configurational performance predictions. *Academy of Management Journal, 39*, 802–835.

Dubin, R. (1976). Theory building in applied areas. In M.D. Dunnette (Ed.), *Handbook of industrial and organizational psychology.* New York: Rand McNally.

Huselid, M.A. (1995). The impact of human resource management practices on turnover, productivity, and corporate financial performance. *Academy of Management Journal, 38*, 635–672.

Johns, G. (1994). Absenteeism estimates by employees and managers: Divergent perspectives and self-serving perceptions. *Journal of Applied Psychology, 79*, 229–239.

Landy, F.J. (1997). Early influences on the development of industrial and organizational psychology. *Journal of Applied Psychology, 82*, 467–477.

McDaniel, M.A., Whetzel, D.L., Schmidt, F.L., & Maurer, S.D. (1994). The validity of employment interviews: A comprehensive review and meta-analysis. *Journal of Applied Psychology, 79*, 599–616.

McDougall, W. (1908). *An introduction to social psychology.* London: Methuen.

Moskowitz, M.J. (1977). Hugo Munsterberg: A study in the history of applied psychology. *American Psychologist, 10*, 824–42.

Munsterberg, H. (1913). *Psychology and industrial efficiency.* Boston: Houghton Mifflin.

Pfeffer, J. (1994). *Competitive advantage through people: Unleashing the power of the work force.* Boston, MA: Harvard Business School Press.

Phillips, J.J. (1996). *Accountability in human resource management.* Houston, TX: Gulf Publishing Company.

Phillips, J.M. (1998). Effects of realistic job previews on multiple organizational outcomes: A meta-analysis. *Academy of Management Journal, 41*, 673–690.

Runkel, P.J., & McGrath, J.E. (1972). *Research on human behavior: A systematic guide to method.* New York: Holt, Rinehart and Winston.

Saks, A.M. (1997). Transfer of training and self-efficacy: What is the dilemma? *Applied Psychology: An International Review, 46*, 365–370.

Sarri, L.M., Johnson, T.R., McLaughlin, S.D., & Zimmerle, D.M. (1988). A survey of management training and education practices in U.S. companies. *Personnel Psychology, 41*, 731–743.

Scott, W.D. (1910). *Increasing human efficiency in business.* New York: Macmillan.

Seashore, S.E., & Katz, D. (1982). Rensis Likert (1903–1981). *American Psychologist, 37*, 851–53.

Stewart, T.A. (1996, January 15). Taking on the last bureaucracy. *Fortune,* 105–108.

Ulrich, D. (1997). *Human resource champions: The next agenda for adding value and delivering results.* Boston, MA: Harvard Business School Press.

Van De Water, T.J. (1997). Psychology's entrepreneurs and the marketing of industrial psychology. *Journal of Applied Psychology, 82*, 486–499.

Wanous, J.P. (1992). *Organizational entry: Recruitment, selection, and socialization of newcomers.* Reading, MA: Addison-Wesley.

Wiesner, W.H., & Cronshaw, S.F. (1988). A meta-analytic investigation of the impact of interview format and degree of structure on the validity of the employment interview. *Journal of Occupational Psychology, 61*, 275–290.

2

Research Methods and Designs

◆ ◆ ◆
INTRODUCTION

Once a research issue has been identified and hypotheses have been stated, the researcher must make some important decisions regarding the research design and methods. The purpose of this chapter is to identify the main research designs that are used in human resource research, and the issues that need to be considered when choosing a research design.

After reading this chapter, you should be able to:

- Describe the four major research designs used in human resource research.

- Be aware of the major questions that need to be answered when formulating a plan for a research design and method.

- Understand and discuss the five criteria involved in choosing a research design.

- Understand the three research design issues and how they influence the quality of research information and data.

- Explain the meaning of Type I and Type II errors and their implications for research interpretations and conclusions.

- Understand the problems of self-report data and how to deal with them.

◆ ◆ ◆
THE RESEARCH DESIGN

As discussed in Chapter 1, when designing a research study we try to establish two or more types/levels of one variable (the independent variable) in order to observe its effects on other variables (the dependent variable). In order to do this, the researcher must make choices about how to deal with the most important variables and how to study them. The outcome of thinking through these choices is an overall research method and design.

According to Sackett and Larson (1990), "*Research methodology* concerns the procedures and activities used to collect and analyze a set of empirical data bearing on some question of interest" (p. 428). A research design is the master plan or blueprint for conducting a study whose results can be interpreted with minimal ambiguity. In all research, the goal is to remove the most likely alternative explanations of hypothesized relationships in order to conclude that whatever happens to the dependent or outcome variable is due to the independent or predictor variable.

In experimental research, this means that we want to make statements about the causal effect of the independent variable on a dependent variable(s). To put it another way, in a well-designed study we want to be able to conclude that the variability of the dependent variable is a function of variability in the independent variable and is not due to other factors. In survey research we try to make statements that there is a relation or association between the independent and dependent variable and that the existence of a relationship is not due to some other extraneous factor(s).

In establishing a research design, we need to consider the following questions (Runkel & McGrath, 1972; Rosenthal & Rosnow, 1984):

1. Who or what will be the focus of the study?

2. What attributes of individuals, groups, or organizations will be observed?

3. In what contexts will observations be made?

4. What methods will be used to analyze the data produced?

5. How are we going to deal with relevant and nuisance variables?

It should be kept in mind that there are numerous alternatives available. Moreover, there is no one best design. The final choice for a study will depend on a number of factors. Certainly, the design will be a function of the specific hypotheses to be tested. But it will also depend on patterns established by previous research; the constraints and resources available; the needs or preferences of the sponsors or the ultimate consumers of the research; and the personal strengths, capacities, and expertise of the researcher. These factors determine the research strategy, whether it be survey research, experimental research, qualitative research, or some combination.

◆ ◆ ◆

HUMAN RESOURCE RESEARCH DESIGNS

Research in human resources usually takes the form of one of the following four research designs:

1. Survey.

2. Experimental.

3. Qualitative.

4. Existing research and meta-analysis.

Each of these designs will be described in detail in separate chapters of this book. Below is a brief summary of each design.

SURVEY RESEARCH

Survey research is popular for a wide variety of applications. Moreover, the careful and appropriate use of survey data can provide a reasonable basis for human resource decision making. In its most basic form, survey research can be used to gauge people's opinions or attitudes about a certain topic. For example, Figure 2.1 shows the results of a survey conducted by *Workforce* magazine on what HR professionals think about the term "human resources" to describe their profession. In this survey, respondents simply responded "Yes" or "No" to a number of questions.

More often, however, survey research is used to examine the relations between variables. Survey research is most appropriate when the researcher wants to learn about the relation between variables and to be able to predict the level of one variable with knowledge of another. In human resources, survey research is most often used to test the relations between individual perceptions, ability, personality, and work outcomes. For example, in selection research we often are interested in the correlation between a test score and job performance. This usually involves gathering data on job applicants' test scores and correlating them with later job performance for those who are hired. Survey research is often used to conduct attitude surveys and to study the relations between job attitudes such as job satisfaction and employee behaviours like absenteeism and turnover.

But the survey approach has limitations. Survey data can provide only the most indirect evidence for cause-and-effect relations. Because we often require cause-and-effect knowledge to make valid choices or decisions, this is an important limitation. We often use survey data and the relationships they reveal to rule out certain factors as likely causes. Some might use survey information as tentative support for a theory or policy assumption. Given the nature of survey study designs, asserting knowledge of causality is inappropriate. There are usually too many alternative explanations for the results.

EXPERIMENTAL RESEARCH

Experimental research designs provide the strongest evidence regarding cause-and-effect relationships and are important to human resources for building and testing theories. Experimental research also has an important role to play in the development and assessment of organizational policies and practices.

While all of the research designs discussed in this book provide insights into the nature of human resources, experimental design can produce research findings that allow us to form conclusions with the least ambiguity (Rosenthal & Rosnow, 1984). Experimental designs are most appropriate when the researcher wants to learn about the effect of an intervention or program on some outcome. In human resources this often takes the form of testing the effects of a human resource

FIGURE 2.1 "Human Resources": What's In A Name?

HR professionals were asked what they think about using the term "human resources" for their profession. In all, a whopping 94 people responded. Following is what HR professionals said about "HR." See if you agree.

1. Do you still refer to your department as "human resources"?

4. Do you think the term "human resources" is outdated for the 21st century challenges?

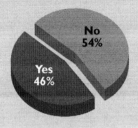

2. Did you previously refer to your department as the "personnel department"?

5. Would you like to see a new term or phrase created for your profession?

3. Does "human resources" connote a more strategic role for HR professionals?

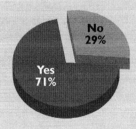

6. Have you and your colleagues exchanged ideas about new titles for your profession?

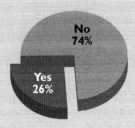

Source: Adapted from " 'Human Resources': What's In a Name?" by Jennifer J. Laabs. Copyright March 1998, p. 17. Used with permission of ACC Communications/Workforce, Costa Mesa, CA. All rights reserved.

intervention such as a training program or an incentive plan on employee attitudes and behaviours.

However, as powerful as the experimental method can be, it has theoretical and practical limitations. Even the best planned and most carefully executed experiments can have weaknesses. Given the realities of organizational life, this is likely to be the case when we try to investigate any phenomenon in an actual organizational setting. One must become skilled to recognize and distinguish between minor and major (or "fatal") flaws in any research design or method. Rather than reject the result of a study outright, we need to let our knowledge of good experimental research guide us when assessing a particular set of findings. Only under these circumstances will clear-cut conclusions regarding the value of a study be possible or warranted (Runkel & McGrath, 1972).

QUALITATIVE RESEARCH

Qualitative research refers to the gathering and sorting of information through informal methods. In its most typical form, managers or researchers may rely on the personal experiences and comments of colleagues. In its most sophisticated versions, the researcher may use a variety of qualitative techniques including interviews, observations, and the use of archival data in organizational files, records, or reports.

Qualitative research is most useful when the researcher wants to obtain a rich, in-depth description of some event or activity. In human resources, qualitative methods are often used in combination with other research methods. For example, job analysis interviews are often used along with survey data to determine the tasks and responsibilities required to perform a job. Similarly, exit interviews can be used along with survey data to study employee turnover. Observation methods are often used to measure employee behaviour and job performance.

EXISTING RESEARCH AND META-ANALYSIS

Given the large amount of research on human resources, it is often not necessary to conduct new research. Instead, useful information can be obtained by reviewing and summarizing existing research.

In recent years, a new technique called *meta-analysis* has been used to study human resource issues. This technique allows the researcher to combine the results of existing research in a particular area and to calculate the overall effect of an intervention or the correlation between a predictor and outcome(s). For example, meta-analyses on selection tests provide information on the utility of various tests for predicting job performance as well as the generalizability of test validity to other organizations (Hunter & Hunter, 1984).

The use of existing data and research is helpful for developing theory, identifying research needs in a particular area, and determining the relative effectiveness of an intervention or the strength of a relation between variables. The results of meta-analysis can be particularly useful to small organizations that do not have the ability to conduct the large-scale research studies that are often required to test the validity of a selection test or the effect of a human resource program. As well, conducting a meta-analysis study can be useful for human resource professionals who want to determine the effectiveness of a human resource program before deciding to implement it in their organization.

In summary, research in human resources can take several forms. In many cases, a topic or research question can be studied using any of the designs discussed above. The challenge facing the researcher is choosing the right research design to study a particular research issue.

◆ ◆ ◆
CHOOSING A RESEARCH DESIGN

With so many research designs to choose from, it is not always easy to choose a research method. However, the importance of this choice should not be underestimated. Failure to choose an appropriate research design can prevent the researcher from answering important research questions, and can restrict the interpretation of research findings. Therefore, it is important to carefully consider how to choose the most appropriate research design given the particular research question and the situational constraints facing the researcher.

A research design must meet several criteria. First, it must allow the researcher to adequately test the hypotheses and answer the questions he or she is asking. If a research design will not allow the researcher to properly test the hypotheses then it should not be considered. Second, **nuisance** or **extraneous factors** that could influence the results of a study must be identified and controlled. Failure to do so can severely limit the researcher's ability to make sound conclusions about the relation between an independent and dependent variable. Third, the results must tell us how other people would react in different contexts. In other words, the results must generalize to situations and people beyond the study. Fourth, the research design should enable the researcher to determine statistically whether the research hypotheses are to be accepted or rejected. Failure to do this could result in inaccurate conclusions. Finally, the research design should be efficient—we want to get the information we need with the available resources. The design must also be feasible within the context of the research site. That is to say, the investigator must recognize legitimate constraints and plan accordingly.

Each of the criteria for choosing a research design is discussed in more detail below.

TEST STUDY HYPOTHESES

Above all else, the research design should be derived from the nature of the research question and the conceptual or theoretical issues involved. Thus, the study hypotheses should be a major factor in choosing a research design. As indicated earlier, the study hypotheses should dictate who the participants should be (nurses, managers, students, etc.), what variables should be measured (ability, personality, job attitudes, etc.), and what methods should be used to analyze the data. For example, if we were interested in the effect of a program on some outcome variable(s), we would be more likely to choose an experimental design than a survey design. A survey design would not allow the researcher to make sound conclusions about the effect of an intervention on some outcome(s) of interest.

CONTROL NUISANCE AND EXTRANEOUS FACTORS

Nuisance or extraneous factors are variables that the researcher is not usually interested in studying per se but that might interfere with or influence the relation between an independent variable and a dependent variable. For example, in a study of the relationship between age and job performance, a researcher might find that age is positively related to job performance. However, if older workers have more work experience and tenure in the organization, then it is possible that these "extraneous" variables (i.e., work experience and organization tenure) are related to job performance and not age. If the researcher did not consider these other variables, then his or her conclusions could be misleading.

Therefore, when choosing a research design, it is important to identify all possible nuisance factors and then to choose a design that allows you to control them. Failure to control for nuisance factors can result in several plausible and rival hypotheses or explanations for the results of a study, therefore limiting the researcher's ability to make conclusions about the effect or relation between independent and dependent variables. In fact, the failure to adequately control for nuisance variables in a study (especially in an experiment) is often considered to be a fatal flaw and is likely to result in the rejection of any inferences, conclusions, or assertions that may be based on the findings. This would be unfortunate insofar as they could have been effectively dealt with by using an appropriate research design.

In most instances, nuisance and extraneous factors are controlled by simply measuring them and including them in the data analysis as statistical controls (hence the term "control variable") or through the use of an experimental design that has high internal validity. Thus, quite often a researcher will measure a variable because it may be useful in helping to better understand the forces operating in a study. If we are worried that a particular factor might confound or obscure the results, we might be able to put our fears to rest by measuring its magnitude, distribution across experimental conditions, or relationships with key variables. For example, if a researcher were concerned that he or she had inadvertently obtained highly motivated research participants, then it would be appropriate to measure levels of motivation to see if this was indeed the case. The researcher could then attempt to rule out or statistically control for the effects of this variable.

In the example described above, concerning the relation between age and job performance, the astute researcher would measure work experience and organization tenure to determine if they were extraneous variables and then control them. Ultimately, the researcher would want to determine if age is related to job performance even when potentially extraneous factors such as work experience and organization tenure have been controlled.

EXTERNAL VALIDITY

It is often desirable to randomly select individuals to participate in a study. In the case of an experiment, we randomly assign participants to experimental conditions. In survey research, it is often impossible to collect data from all participants about whom we hope to make inferences and statements. However, if we sample randomly from some defined population, we can use the data from this sample to make statements about the whole population with specified levels of confidence. The ability to do this is called **external validity**.

External validity is also referred to as generalizability. It reflects the extent to which the results of a study will hold up or generalize to other samples of participants and to other contexts (e.g., departments or organizations). The external validity of a study could be limited because of the nature of the sample used and the setting, both of which could influence the results and therefore limit the generalizability of the results to other samples and settings.

In experimental research the issue of external validity is often associated with generalizing the results of laboratory studies that take place in an artificial setting and often involve student participants to organizational settings. In survey research the results of a study using participants who are not randomly sampled may not generalize to other groups of participants. Unfortunately, this is more often the case than not. While this might not be a problem in organizations that are only concerned with studying their own employees, very often it is important that the results of human resource research be generalizable and applicable to other settings. Thus, the ability to generalize the results of a study to a larger population and to other organizations is often an important consideration when choosing a research design.

STATISTICAL CONCLUSION VALIDITY

Most research in human resources is conducted to determine the effects of a human resource intervention or the relationship between variables. But the outcomes of a study may be influenced (unintentionally) by forces promoting instability or unreliability. To the extent that these forces are numerous or their impact great, we would question the statistical conclusions made (Cook & Campbell, 1976).

Statistical conclusion validity is less concerned with bias (effects in a systematic direction) than with sources of error variance. Anything that might contribute to randomness in the data would be seen as a threat. Relevant factors include the reliability of measures and sample size. For example, if a variable has low reliability or a study involves a small number of participants, there is an increased likelihood that the researcher will not detect real differences between experimental groups or real relationships between variables even when they do exist. As a result, it is possible to reject the hypothesis although it is actually correct.

In other instances, one might accept a hypothesis for an effect or relation between variables and reject the **null hypothesis** when in fact there is no effect or relation. When a researcher rejects the null hypothesis and concludes that there is an effect or relation between variables although there is none, he or she is making a **Type I error.** A Type I error is the probability that we will conclude that there is a significant effect or relationship even when none exists. When a researcher accepts the null hypothesis and concludes that there is no effect or relation between the variables when in fact there is one, he or she is making a **Type II error.** A Type II error refers to the probability that we will conclude that there is no effect or relationship even when one actually exists.

Therefore, it is important that the research design allow the researcher to make valid statistical conclusions and avoid making Type I and Type II errors. This issue has much to do with **statistical power** decisions and the cost associated with making a decision error. Certain designs might be adequate under circumstances of minimal consequences but would not be so when a lot is at stake. Arvey, Cole, Hazucha, and Hartamo (1985) have stressed that the sample size must be large enough to detect true effects and to avoid making Type I and Type II errors. Previous research on a topic, the level of confidence desired by the researcher, and statistical power (calculations of the probability that you can conclude a real effect or relationship exists given the sample size) computations can be used to help determine the appropriate sample size.

RESEARCH DESIGN EFFICIENCY

In addition to the above factors, one must also consider issues related to design efficiency. Most research requires a considerable investment in time and resources, and some designs require much greater investments. Resources include the time available for research, the number of participants (cases) that can be studied, and the funds that exist for staff time, instruments, inducements, and so on. More rigorous designs usually consume more resources. As well, the level of expertise that the researcher has in using the various designs must also be considered in terms of efficiency. Ultimately, the choice of a design requires a careful balance between the need for an appropriate design given the goals of the research and the available time, resources, and expertise of the researcher.

◆ ◆ ◆
RESEARCH DESIGN ISSUES

In addition to choosing a research design, conducting research involves considering a number of other important issues. Generally, the combination of choices made by the researcher will determine the quality of the data obtained and the kinds of inferences that can be made from the data. The results of all these choices will, in effect, also determine the kind of design involved. These issues constitute themes that cut across all research methods for conducting human resource research and include the research context, the nature and size of the sample, and the sources of data.

THE RESEARCH CONTEXT

Human resource research can be conducted in a number of research contexts. Most often it is desirable to conduct the research in an actual organization. This might involve one organization, such as an experiment to test the effects of a new training program. In other cases, the research might involve several organizations to allow the researcher to study differences in particular human resource programs or policies. For example, Huselid's (1995) study of the impact of human resource practices included data from close to 1000 organizations. This is often necessary when the objective of the research is to study the relations between different human resource practices and outcomes. Research on organizational socialization practices often includes newcomers from many organizations. This ensures that there will be differences in the types of practices used to socialize new hires. However, if you were interested in the socialization of newly hired police officers, then you might focus on a particular police department, as did John Van Maanen in his classic study on police socialization (Van Maanen, 1975).

The above examples involve research in an organizational setting. However, human resource research can also take place in laboratory settings and involve individuals who are not currently employed. For example, research on realistic job previews, which involves presenting job applicants with both the positive and negative features of a job and organization, has been conducted with samples of actual job applicants and employees in an organizational setting, as well as with students who participated in a contrived laboratory setting. Research in an organizational context has been particularly useful for demonstrating the effects of realistic job previews on job survival. However, research involving students in a laboratory setting has been useful for studying the processes or psychology involved in understanding the effects of job previews. When the goal of research is to examine such processes, the setting or context is often irrelevant to the research question.

The investigator has to decide how important it is for the purposes of the research to conduct it in one or more organizational settings. In many areas of human resources, there are any number of questions that can be studied in laboratory or contrived settings. This is because for many investigators the goal is to establish the existence (or the nature) of certain dynamics or processes that are presumed to be operative in most contexts. To put it another way, the investigator's model or theory places little emphasis on the importance of the specific setting in which the phenomenon occurs. In contrast, the researcher's interest, his or her theory, or the purpose for the research may place a premium on specific features of a setting as they directly affect or modify events.

THE NATURE AND SIZE OF THE SAMPLE

There will be occasions in which the investigator may wish to study all of the people in a particular organizational context (e.g., all the employees of a small company). However, in most cases, research is done with a sample of individuals. Two features of the sample that are particularly important are the sample characteristics and sample size.

The phrase *sample characteristics* is used to convey the nature of the sample relative to the population of interest. The sample may be constructed to be representative of the population or to have some known relationship to the latter. Thus, we may use random or stratified sampling strategies, or our sample may be one of opportunity or convenience. More to the point, our actual sample plan will determine whether or not we can legitimately generalize to the population from the data we obtain from research participants.

Sample size will also affect representativeness. That is to say, it is harder for a small sample (relative to the population) to be representative. Thus, larger samples drawn with a known sample plan allow for the greatest confidence in generalizing results. But sample size also affects the statistical power of a study to detect the true effects of an intervention or a variable (if there are any). Recall the discussion of power and Type I and Type II errors.

DATA SOURCES

A research design usually implies just who (or what) is going to be measured, assessed, tested, or monitored. As emphasized throughout this text, an investigator has any number of options at his or her disposal. However, in human resource research, it is quite common to make use of **self-reports**, in which the individuals who are the focus of the study (e.g., employees) also provide the data (e.g., individual characteristics, job attitudes, job performance, etc.). This is an important factor to consider, as there is always the potential for self-report data to be biased.

Podsakoff and Organ (1986) found that self-report data represent a common form of data collection in human resource research. According to their analysis, self-reports are used in human resource research in the following ways:

1. Obtaining demographic or otherwise factual data (e.g., years of work experience).
2. Assessing the effectiveness of instructions or experimental manipulations.
3. Gathering personality data.
4. Obtaining descriptions of a respondent's past or characteristic behaviour, or how they would behave under hypothetical conditions.
5. Measuring internal or psychological states of respondents (e.g., work attitudes).
6. Assessing respondents' perceptions of context or organizational variables.

Despite its popularity, Podsakoff and Organ (1986) argue that investigators often do not appreciate important weaknesses of self-reports. In particular, they point out potential problems when measures of two or more variables are collected from the same respondents and attempts are made to interpret any correlations among them. This relates to the potential problem of **common method variance**. Because both measures come from the same source (and usually at the same time), variables may be spuriously related. This could be due to the fact that the measures make use of the same response format, are not perfectly reliable, or induce a desire on the part of respondents to be consistent across sections of a survey.

Also, self-reports have the potential to induce **socially desirable responses**—responses that are intended to make the respondent look good in the eyes of the investigator or society at large. Thus, to ask a person in a survey or an interview if he or she "learned anything" as a result of a training program or workshop is likely to produce an affirmative answer. Most people will reason that, irrespective of the truth of the matter, they would look foolish if they did not answer "Yes" to this question. The investigator can check on the possibility of distortion in self-reports and otherwise try to deal with it, and Podsakoff and Organ (1986) suggest a number of ways of doing this.

The best advice for dealing with some of the problems of self-report data, however, is to use a research method that involves separation of measures. This might require obtaining self-report data at slightly different times or using different designs (e.g., questionnaire and face-to-face interview). One of the best solutions, however, is to ensure that some variables or some of the data are obtained from more than one source (e.g., the employee and his or her peers or supervisor). For example, in assessing the effect of a training program on learning, the investigator could develop and use a paper-and-pencil achievement test, ask for self-evaluations of what was learned, or obtain assessments of the use of new knowledge as perceived by co-workers and supervisors. He or she might then have more confidence that the actual impact of the program has been estimated accurately.

The extent of bias or distortion in self-reports cannot always be established beforehand. It may not be a problem under certain conditions. For example, Spector (1987) examined the issue of method variance in published studies involving measures of job satisfaction and perceived job characteristics. The former is often treated as a criterion or dependent variable and the latter as an independent (causal) variable. That is to say, investigators have been interested in the (causal) impact of job characteristics on job satisfaction. In fact, many studies apparently have found a positive correlation between the two.

However, as Spector (1987) points out, data on both variables usually are obtained from self-reports on a single questionnaire. Thus, he reasons, instead of a true relationship between the two, the results are due to common method bias. Using published research, he found six studies that had assessed social desirability along with these measures. His conclusions were somewhat reassuring. In very few instances did he find evidence of method bias at either the item or the scale level. Consequently, the positive relationship between key job characteristics and worker-reported job satisfaction that has been found is likely to be a true one. He also points out that these results may have occurred because of the quality of the particular measures involved. Both the Job Descriptive Index (the preferred measure of job satisfaction) and the Job Characteristics Inventory (the common measure of job attributes) have been carefully developed. Thus, he warns that the results may not be similar when scales with less demonstrated construct validity are used.

One other aspect of self-reports deserves to be highlighted because, very often in human resource research, data are gathered from respondents at several points in time. Hence self-reports are obtained on more than one occasion. For example, in training evaluation studies it is common to take measures before and after a training program. But Sprangers and Hoogstraten (1989) point out that any comparison of pretest and post-test scores from self-report measures may be misleading because of what is termed a **response shift bias**. This refers to a change in the internal standards used by a respondent in making a judgment about his or her level of knowledge or functioning. Simply stated, after a person has gone through training, he or she is likely to reconsider any self-reports or self-assessments (as given on a pre-measure) in light of what was taught. Thus, participants may feel that they have *less* skill than they originally thought, given the competency of the instructor, the rigorous nature of the course content, or the behaviour of their classmates. This shift in standards becomes a bias when, paradoxically, people come to feel and report less competency after training. This also would lead to the uncomfortable conclusion on the part of an investigator that the training might actually have hurt rather than helped participants.

The researcher must also remain alert when several measures are taken over time in order to assess a change in employees' perceptions, attitudes, or behaviours. While any change found is often assumed to be an "actual" change in the variable of interest, this might not always be the case. In fact, there are three possibilities, known as alpha, beta, and gamma changes (Golembiewski, Billingsley, & Yeager, 1976). These refer to the reasons for changes in an individual's responses to a given survey item or variable over time. Such changes can be the result of at least three things.

First, they may reflect actual changes in the level of the item or variable. This is known as **alpha change**. For example, a moderate rating of job satisfaction at Time 1 (a rating of "3" on a 5-point scale) becomes stronger at Time 2 ("4"). This could be the result of a change in job design. However, a second possibility is **beta change**, which is a recalibration of the levels. For example, the "3" at Time 1 is interpreted as a "4" at Time 2. The third possibility is called **gamma change** and refers to a redefinition of the construct or variable itself. For example, the very meaning of "job satisfaction" is transformed, and this is why the rating changed from a "3" to a "4."

Using a sample of newcomers to a bank, Vandenberg and Self (1993) demonstrated the presence of gamma change over a six-month period in measures of affective and continuance commitment. They concluded that researchers should test for the presence of beta and gamma changes when assessing changes in attitudes following entry, and that some measures might not be appropriate for use at entry. Thus, researchers need to be aware of the possibility that changes in individuals' responses over time might not reflect alpha changes but could, rather, be the result of beta or gamma changes. The HR Research Today box discusses how to deal with this problem when conducting attitude surveys.

While self-reports are and will continue to be important in human resource research, they must be used with skill and caution. As well, whenever possible, other sources of data such as co-workers and supervisors should also be used. For example, it is quite common to obtain supervisor ratings of job performance when one is interested in the effect of a human resource intervention on employees' job performance.

HR RESEARCH TODAY

Is a Change in Attitude a Change in Conditions or Perspective?

Very often in human resource research, employees are asked to complete a survey over a period of time. The purpose of this is to assess any change in employees' perceptions and attitudes. For example, after implementing a new performance appraisal system, an organization might want to track employees' perceptions of fairness to see if they have changed as a result of the new system. However, if there is a positive change over time, does it represent an actual change in employees' perceptions of fairness or does it represent something else?

As it turns out, the change may actually represent a change in employees' *perspective*. That is, an employee may apply different perspectives on different occasions. This is because time, experience, and events can change people's perception and interpretation of what they are rating. This type of change is called a *beta change* and represents a recalibration of the levels that one uses when making ratings. For example, a fairness rating of "3" (on a 5-point scale) at Time 1 might be interpreted as a "4" at Time 2. Thus, the difference between these two values appears to indicate an improvement in fairness perceptions. However, it might also mean that at the time of the second survey the rater perceives a rating of "3" to actually be a "4." In this case, the rater has not changed his or her perception of fairness but, rather, has changed his or her perspective and now feels that the condition at both time periods is actually a "4." Thus, what has changed is the rater's perspective or frame of reference and not his or her perception of fairness.

So how does one know if a change in ratings represents an actual change or just a change in perspective? In most cases, you can't tell, and this can lead to confusion and incorrect interpretations of survey results. Fortunately, there is a rather simple solution to this problem.

The solution is to include a section on the follow-up or Time 2 survey that asks the rater to make *hindsight ratings*. This means that in addition to asking employees to rate the present condition, they also re-rate or re-evaluate past conditions. The idea is to apply the rater's present perspective to past conditions. In effect, they are being asked, "If you knew then (i.e., Time 1) what you know now (i.e., Time 2), how would you have rated things then?" With hindsight ratings it is possible to disentangle real change from a change in perspective by comparing the three ratings: Time 1 past ratings, Time 2 present ratings, and Time 2 hindsight ratings.

For example, if the hindsight rating in our example is a "4," we can compare this with the past rating of "3" and the present rating of "4." To measure a change in condition, we compare the present and hindsight ratings. This comparison indicates no change in fairness perceptions. To measure a change in perspective, we compare the past rating with the hindsight rating. When people rate Time 1 fairness differently in hindsight, they are

◆ ◆ ◆
SUMMARY

A research design is the master plan or blueprint for conducting research. In human resources, research is most often conducted using survey, experimental, or qualitative methods as well as summarizing existing data. The decision to use a particular research design must involve consideration of a number of factors including the ability to test hypotheses, the amount of control over extraneous factors, external and statistical conclusion validity, and research design efficiency. Finally, when choosing a research design it is also necessary to determine the most appropriate context and sample for conducting the research, and the sources that will be used to gather research data.

Definitions

Alpha change   Occurs when changes in respondents' scores over time reflect actual changes in the level of the item or variable.

Beta change   Occurs when changes in respondents' scores over time are due to a recalibration of the levels rather than an actual change.

Common method variance   Occurs when variables are highly related to one another due to the fact that they were measured using the same method of measurement; for example, self-report.

External validity   The extent to which the results of a study will hold up or generalize to other samples of participants and to other contexts.

Gamma change   Occurs when changes in respondents' scores over time reflect a redefinition of the construct or variable itself rather than an actual change.

Nuisance/Extraneous factors   Variables that might interfere with or influence the relation between an independent variable and a dependent variable and the results of a study.

Null hypothesis   Statement of the absence of a relationship between variables or the absence of an effect of an experimental manipulation.

Response shift bias   A change in the internal standards used by a respondent in answering the same questions over time.

Self-reports   Research in which individuals who are the focus of a study provide the data for the study.

Socially desirable responses   Occur when research participants respond to questions in a manner they believe will make them look good.

Statistical conclusion validity   The extent to which one can be confident about the validity of the statistical conclusions that are derived from a study.

Statistical power   The ability to detect the existence of a real effect or relationship and avoid a Type I and Type II error.

Type I error   The probability of concluding that there is a significant effect or relationship when in fact there is none.

Type II error   The probability of concluding that there is no effect or relationship when in fact one does exist.

E X E R C I S E S

1. a) Using the turnover model presented in Chapter 1 (Figure 1.3), state several testable research hypotheses.

   b) Briefly discuss how you would test your hypotheses using each of the four research designs.

   c) Evaluate the effectiveness of each design using the five criteria that need to be considered when choosing a research design.

   d) Discuss the research context, the nature and size of the sample, and the sources of data for testing your hypotheses.

2. Soon after starting her new job as a human resource assistant, Marika was contacted by several consulting companies who wanted to implement an intervention to reduce absenteeism. Since absenteeism was a costly problem in the organization, she thought that such an intervention might be worthwhile. However, before making a decision, Marika asked each consultant firm to provide her with research data on the effectiveness of the intervention. What research design issues should Marika address when evaluating the research material provided to her by the consulting firms? How should she use this information to help her determine the potential effectiveness of the intervention for reducing absenteeism and in making a decision about purchasing such an intervention?

3. Review the Human Resource Research and Practice Model in Chapter 1 (Figure 1.1). Choose a human resource topic that interests you (e.g., selection, recruitment, turnover, absenteeism, job attitudes) and work it through the model by identifying the research required at each stage and the effect it will have on human resource practice.

References

Arvey, R.D., Cole, D.A., Hazucha, J.F., & Hartamo, F.M. (1985). Statistical power of training evaluation designs. *Personnel Psychology, 38,* 493–507.

Cook, T.D., & Campbell, D.T. (1976). The design and conduct of quasi-experiments and true experiments in field settings. In M.D. Dunnette (Ed.), *Handbook of industrial and organizational psychology*. New York: Rand McNally.

Fishel, B. (1998). A new perspective: How to get the real story from attitude surveys. *Training, 35* (2), 91–94.

Golembiewski, R.T., Billingsley, K., & Yeager, S. (1976). Measuring change and persistence in human affairs: Types of change generated by

OD designs. *Journal of Applied Behavioral Science, 12,* 133–157.

Hunter. J.E., & Hunter, R.F. (1984). Validity and utility of alternative predictors of job performance. *Psychological Bulletin, 96,* 72–98.

Huselid, M.A. (1995). The impact of human resource management practices on turnover, productivity, and corporate financial performance. *Academy of Management Journal, 38,* 635–672.

Podsakoff, P.M., & Organ, D.W. (1986). Self-reports in organization research: Problems and prospects. *Journal of Management, 12,* 531–44.

Rosenthal, R., & Rosnow, R. (1984). *Essentials of behavioral research.* New York: McGraw-Hill.

Runkel, P.J., & McGrath, J.E. (1972). *Research on human behavior: A systematic guide to method.* New York: Holt, Rinehart and Winston.

Sackett, P.R., T.D., & Larson, J.R., Jr. (1990). Research strategies and tactics in industrial and organizational psychology. In M.D. Dunnette & L.M. Hough (Eds.), *Handbook of industrial and organizational psychology,* vol. 1 (2nd ed., pp. 419–489). Palo Alto, CA: Consulting Psychologists Press, Inc.

Spector, P.E. (1987). Method variance as an artifact in self-reported affect and perceptions at work: Myth or significant problem? *Journal of Applied Psychology, 92,* 438–43.

Sprangers, M., & Hoogstraten, J. (1989). Pretesting effects in retrospective pretest–posttest designs. *Journal of Applied Psychology, 74,* 265–72.

Van Maanen, J. (1975). Police socialization: A longitudinal examination of job attitudes in an urban police department. *Administrative Science Quarterly, 20,* 207–228.

Vandenberg, R.J., & Self, R.M. (1993). Assessing newcomers' changing commitments to the organization during the first 6 months of work. *Journal of Applied Psychology, 78,* 557–568.

3

Survey Research Designs

INTRODUCTION

One of the most popular methods of human resource research is the survey. Surveys are often used to measure employees' attitudes, beliefs, and intentions, or to collect demographic and background data. A survey usually consists of a series of questions requiring a written response on some topic of concern in either a structured or open-ended format. The objective of survey research is to discover how events or variables compare or relate to one another. In practice, however, most investigators also seek an explanation of why such patterns of data come about (Rosenthal & Rosnow, 1984).

Questionnaires, interviews, and observations are commonly used as part of survey research. But whatever the method, the key is to include measures of the relevant variables. This implies both those variables of primary interest (analogous to independent and dependent variables) and those that are included as control or nuisance variables. The pattern of the correlations between these variables is used by the investigator to make inferences and test hypotheses and to offer potential explanations.

After reading this chapter, you should be able to:

- Understand the purposes and content of survey research in human resources research.

- Know the differences and implications of cross-sectional and longitudinal survey research.

- Understand and explain the main questions and issues that need to be addressed when planning survey research.

- Describe the process of random sampling and what is involved in obtaining a representative sample.

- Be familiar with the guidelines for writing survey items and questions.

- Understand how to make comparisons when analyzing and interpreting survey data.

- Explain the special issues that are of concern when conducting survey research and how they should be dealt with.

- Understand the ethical issues involved when conducting survey research.

♦ ♦ ♦
SURVEY RESEARCH IN HUMAN RESOURCES

Surveys have a long history in human resource research. In fact, "by the 1930s employee attitude surveys were being frequently used in business to assess and document employee morale" (Schneider, Ashworth, Higgs, & Carr, 1996). Today more than half of the companies in the United States conduct surveys of employees (Kraut, 1996a). According to Kraut (1996a), "the term **organizational survey** describes a number of methods of systematically gathering data from the members of an organization." Further, "they are a methodical way of gathering data from people in an organization for specific purposes" (p. 2).

In human resources, survey research designs are generally used for assessment or change purposes (Kraut, 1996a). Kraut (1996a) has identified the following eight specific purposes of organizational surveys that fall within the two general categories of assessment and change:

1. *To Pinpoint Areas of Concern.* Surveys are often used in organizations to keep abreast of how employees feel about different aspects of the work environment. Sometimes the focus might be on particular issues and how employees feel about them. In effect, it is useful to know if employees are satisfied or dissatisfied and the reasons for their attitudes.

2. *To Observe Long-Term Trends.* Organizations are sometimes interested in particular issues over a period of time. Survey data might be collected as a means of generating a database regarding employee opinions on various matters. This allows an organization to monitor how changes in the organization impact employees over time and therefore to respond to any potential problems.

3. *To Monitor Program Impact.* Employee surveys are often used to monitor the impact of organization changes or human resource programs. For example, a survey might be used to evaluate a new incentive plan or performance appraisal system. This is important in order to determine if a program has been effective.

4. *To Provide Input for Future Decisions.* Organizational surveys can be used to provide important information to make policy or program decisions. For example, decisions about the types of benefits or training programs to implement can be aided by the systematic collection of survey data that measure employees' preferences and needs.

5. *To Add a Communication Channel.* Surveys can be an important source of communication throughout the organization. This is especially the case if the results are fed back to employees, thereby allowing two-way communication between employees and management on important issues.

6. *To Perform Organizational Behaviour Research.* A great deal of research in organizational behaviour and human resources involves survey research. For example, research on the relationship between perceptions, job attitudes, and work behaviours, as well as the effects of training programs and other human resource programs involves surveys. Surveys are often used to develop and test models and theories of organizational behaviour.

7. *To Assist Organizational Change and Improvement.* Many organizations use surveys as part of an ongoing process of assessment and change. In some respect, the survey itself serves as the basis of an intervention. For example, a survey might ask questions about worker concerns, such as supervision, work conditions and work procedures, pay and promotion policy, and so on. These responses are then summarized for various work units and discussed with members of those units in order to generate some action plan so that any important problems or dissatisfactions can be addressed. In such cases survey feedback is used as a means for organizational change and continuous improvement.

8. *To Provide Symbolic Communication.* Although organizational surveys are often conducted for some of the reasons mentioned above, they are inevitably a form of symbolic communication. In other words, the survey process, in terms of how it is conducted and its content, sends a message to those who are involved in the process. For example, survey questions about employees' satisfaction with their work, compensation, or careers sends the message that these are matters that are important to management. As well, failure to provide employees with survey feedback or to respond to survey results can send the message that the survey is not very important and that management does not care about employee perceptions and attitudes. Thus, survey content and conduct can be a form of both positive and negative symbolic communication to employees.

In summary, organizational surveys can be used for any of the purposes discussed above. Occasionally, a survey serves more than one purpose. In organizations such as IBM and Sears, data regarding employee opinions have been collected for many years. The data are used for survey feedback purposes and as a basis for evaluating various research hypotheses.

◆ ◆ ◆
SURVEY RESEARCH CONTENT

Survey research has been used in human resources to investigate many issues such as leadership, motivation, and attitude formation, as well as other basic human resource practices. Research on employee attitudes, however, is often a major part of survey research. This is, in part, because attitudes (as measured in surveys) have important implications for behaviour in organizations. Job satisfaction, organizational commitment, climate, and culture are constructs that almost always are important variables in survey research and reflect the notion that the affective reactions to organizations and beliefs about organizations measured in surveys have significant behavioural correlates that impact organizational effectiveness.

Job satisfaction research was initiated partly because of the belief that a happy worker is more productive. While subsequent research has failed to produce evidence of a substantial relationship between job satisfaction and performance (Iaffaldano & Muchinsky, 1985), job satisfaction does seem to be related to attendance at work (Steers & Rhodes, 1978), turnover (Mobley, Horner, & Hollingsworth, 1978), and unionization activity (Friedson, 1985). In fact, the relationship between survey measures of job attitudes and pro-union voting behaviour is so strong that surveys have been used by some organizations and consultants in their efforts to keep organizations union-free. Organizations and researchers usually collect survey data on the assumption that the expressions in these surveys have behavioural implications.

While organizational surveys have long focused on attitude-related issues such as satisfaction with various job facets, employee morale, and commitment, work and family as well as diversity issues have become increasingly popular (Kraut, 1996a). However, according to Kraut (1996a), the greatest increase has been in the areas of cultural change, quality, and customer satisfaction. In addition, employee attitude surveys are now being used to monitor an organization's success in achieving its strategic goals (Schneider et al., 1996; See HR Research Today box). Whatever the purpose or issue, organizational surveys are an important research method in human resources.

HR RESEARCH TODAY

Strategically Focused Employee Attitude Surveys

Researchers and practitioners have recently begun to use employee attitude surveys to focus on the strategic objectives of an organization. These surveys ask employees questions about organization practices and policies in terms of the organization's strategic goals. Strategic goals have included customer service quality, accident prevention, leadership, and the integration of two organizations following a merger. Research has found that employee reports are similar to judgments made by observers outside of the organization. Thus, employee reports of such practices appear to be valid indicators of the extent to which an organization is carrying out its strategic objectives.

An important aspect of this new use of employee attitude surveys is the development of the survey itself. Schneider, Ashworth, Higgs, and Carr (1996) recently reported on how

HR RESEARCH TODAY (continued)

they developed, implemented, and validated a strategically focused employee attitude survey that covered a broad range of issues related to quality management.

The survey was developed for an insurance company that had established a total quality environment for its customers, shareholders, and employees. The business strategy designed to accomplish these goals contained the following seven elements:

1. Customer-focused quality.
2. Customer satisfaction.
3. Customer retention.
4. Profitability.
5. Competitive position.
6. Sustainable growth.
7. Employee opportunity and development.

Together with some of the key players involved in the implementation of the strategy, the authors designed a survey to track, over time, employee views of the degree to which the elements of the initiative were being accomplished, rather than employees' personal feelings or satisfaction, and to establish the degree to which implementation of those policies and practices was related to the outcomes of customer satisfaction and customer retention.

The original survey consisted of 39 items and was designed so that respondents would be asked to report on the frequency with which practices and policies that defined their work situation were experienced. The authors also collected customer satisfaction data. After analyzing the results, the authors determined that seven items made up the final scale, which they called the Customer Orientation Index (COI) (see Table 3.1). These seven items were strongly related to customer satisfaction.

This research demonstrates the usefulness of employee attitude surveys for diagnosing the extent to which organizational strategies have been implemented. The data can be used by management to identify those practices that need attention in order to improve strategy implementation, as well as those initiatives that are most strongly related to important outcomes such as customer satisfaction and retention. Not surprisingly, the data were received with considerable enthusiasm by human resource and marketing executives.

Source: Adapted from Schneider, B., Ashworth, S.D., Higgs, A.C., & Carr, L. (1996). Design validity, and use of strategically focused employee attitude surveys. *Personnel Psychology, 49*, 695–705.

TABLE 3.1 THE ITEMS SCORED FOR THE CUSTOMER ORIENTATION INDEX (COI)

1. When customer requirements are not met, how often do people in your work group take action so the problem does not occur in the future?
   (Response scale: 1 = *All of the time*; 6 = *Never*)

2. How often do you receive feedback as to how satisfied your customers are?
   (Response scale: 1 = *Frequently*; 5 = *Never*)

3. How much does our company actively solicit input from customers?
   (Response scale: 1 = *A great deal*; 6 = *Not at all*)

4. Would you recommend the purchase of (our company's) insurance to a friend or relative? (Response scale: 1 = *Definitely would*; 5 = *Definitely would not*)

5. In the past 12 months have you had a formal performance appraisal discussion to compare your performance against your goals or Major Responsibilities and Performance Standards? (Response scale: 1 = *Yes*; 2 = *No*)

6. How much opportunity is there for you to pursue your job and career interests [in our company]? (Response scale: 1 = *A great deal*; 5 = *Not much*)

7. How often does your (immediate manager/team leader) talk to you and your co-workers about how the work of your group contributes to: a) customer-focused quality, b) customer-satisfaction, c) customer retention, d) profitability, and e) competitive position? (Response scale: 1 − *Frequently*; 5 = *Never*)

Source: Schneider et al. (1996). Design validity, and use of strategically focused employee attitude surveys. *Personnel Psychology, 49,* 695–705. Reprinted by permission.

♦ ♦ ♦
CROSS-SECTIONAL AND LONGITUDINAL SURVEY RESEARCH DESIGNS

An important part of survey research is the timing of data collection. Rosenthal and Rosnow (1984) distinguish between cross-sectional and longitudinal research designs. Quite often an investigator is concerned with examining a variable or set of variables at one point in time. This is referred to as **cross-sectional** research. Other times the investigator is interested in changes that occur over time or in successive periods of time. Survey research that is designed to measure change over time is referred to as **longitudinal** research.

Longitudinal research designs are particularly useful when studying change in some phenomenon or variables. Longitudinal data collection allows the identification of trends in employee opinions, attitudes, and behaviour. One group of large firms, called the Mayflower group, has organized their survey research efforts so as to take maximum advantage of survey results. The members of this group use a common core of questions across organizations and across time. This practice allows them to make interorganizational and longitudinal comparisons of survey results and to evaluate the possible impact of external or internal change.

Longitudinal research is also useful when the researcher wants to predict the effect of some group of independent variables on a dependent variable(s). For example, if a researcher were to test the relationship between job attitudes and job performance, he or she could measure job attitudes at one point in time (Time 1), and then measure job performance at some future time (Time 2). This would enable the researcher to test the prediction that job attitudes *cause* or lead to levels of job performance. If, however, the research design were cross-sectional, then the researcher would measure job attitudes and job performance at the same time. This, however, makes it much more difficult to draw conclusions about the causal relations between the variables. For example, if job attitudes and job performance were found to be positively correlated in a cross-sectional study, it would not be possible to know which was the cause and which the effect. Thus, if the researcher wished to test such cause–effect relations, then longitudinal research would be more suitable.

If a longitudinal survey is desired, there are many variations in designs to choose from. For example, if more than one measurement period is preferred, when should they occur? How long should the intervals between measurements be? How many "waves" of measurements should be taken? Usually these and related questions cannot be answered for the general case but must be resolved by considering the theories or models guiding the research, with reference to practicality and, not infrequently, with some amount of intuition on the part of the investigator. For example, research on organizational socialization has found that the effects of socialization processes on new employees' work adjustment occur relatively rapidly and then appear to be stable for the first six to ten months (Saks & Ashforth, 1997). Thus, longitudinal research on organizational socialization would require collecting survey data from new employees before they enter the organization and shortly thereafter, probably between two and four months.

One other issue that comes up in longitudinal research is that of participant mortality. When repeated measurements are taken over time, a percentage of research participants may drop out of a study or become otherwise unavailable for participation. This means that measures taken later in time will be based only on a subgroup of original respondents. This shrinking sample size implies lower statistical power. But, more importantly, if those who cannot be reached or who no longer want to continue with the study represent a particular class of individuals (e.g., less educated), it also creates the possibility of an inadvertent bias in the results. To review earlier terminology, such a bias would be a threat to the external validity of the study.

◆ ◆ ◆
SURVEY RESEARCH DESIGNS

Surveys can be either of an interview or questionnaire type. However, because most organizations use questionnaires in collecting survey data, and since interview methods are discussed in Chapter 5 on qualitative research, this chapter will focus on written surveys. Written surveys are popular because of the ease and low cost of their administration and response analysis. Recently, some organizations have computerized their surveys. Survey questions are presented and employee responses are obtained via the desktop computer or touch-tone telephone. Computerization has significant advantages: it eliminates the need for paper and mailing costs, and minimizes errors associated with the coding or reading of answer sheets. Perhaps of greatest advantage, however, is the fact that data collected by computer can be analyzed more quickly and made available as feedback to employees and/or organizational decision makers.

Once a researcher has clearly identified the variables of interest and has decided to collect data via a written questionnaire or survey, he or she must then design the survey. This usually begins by planning the survey and involves a consideration of the survey's goals in order to obtain valid measures of the variables of interest and methods of data analysis. This is a critical phase, since changes to questionnaires and sampling plans are impossible after the survey has been distributed. (This is less true for interview research or participant observation methods, which frequently can be modified according to the type of information uncovered during the research.) The following sections present the issues that need to be considered in designing a survey, including the practical issues in survey construction, administration, data analysis, and interpretation.

◆ ◆ ◆
PLANNING THE SURVEY

In planning a survey, it is important to consider the final needs for data and to work backwards to the beginning of the survey research process. Figure 3.1 provides an outline of the steps involved in survey research. With a clear understanding of the need for data, one can consider the type of analyses and tables that would be useful in answering those needs. This will lead to a consideration of the subgroups to be included in the survey, the items that will unambiguously identify those subgroups, and whether the potential available sample will allow separate analyses of all subgroups. Consideration of the type of respondents required will lead to issues involving sampling from various subgroups and how the reading level and perceptions of individuals in these subgroups will affect questionnaire items.

FIGURE 3.1 **Steps in Survey Research**

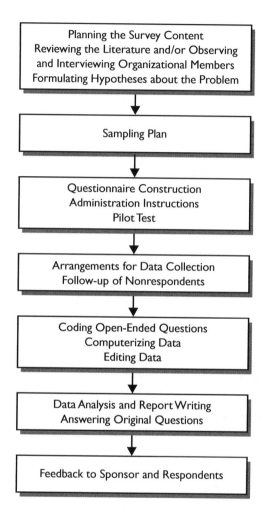

Many surveys in actual organizations are initiated with only a vague notion that something is wrong and that a survey might identify the nature of the problem (for example, turnover, absenteeism, or high accident rates). Frequently unstated at early stages of survey research projects is the desire that the survey tell organizational decision makers what to do about the problems that are identified. In order to make informed policy recommendations based on survey results, appropriate questions must be included in the survey. This demands that the authors of the survey understand the issues well enough through interviews, literature reviews, or observation that they can ask questions that will allow the evaluation and testing of the hypotheses. In planning a survey, there are a number of questions that must be asked. In the remainder of this section, some of these questions will be discussed using the example of a hypothetical company seeking to reduce turnover among its highly trained computer scientists.

WHAT ARE THE SURVEY OBJECTIVES?

The first and most important questions that require detailed answers during the planning phase are what information the survey is supposed to supply and what the organizational sponsors or researchers expect to get from the survey. A researcher typically will want to address theoretical questions, while an organizational client will usually want to know why some problem has occurred and what can be done to solve the problem. For example, the organization manager concerned about the turnover of computer science personnel undoubtedly will want to know why people are leaving and what actions can be taken to decrease the turnover rate. In planning the survey, it would be useful to find out what the current rate of turnover is and how that rate compares with other similar organizations, and, if possible, to compile information about the performance and demographic characteristics of those who recently left the organization. This information can tell us whether the organization's turnover is unusual, whether turnover is functional (that is, the least competent leave), and whether there are any subgroups that should be surveyed to clarify the problem.

Interviews with people who have recently left might lead to hypotheses about the following: role of pay, department supervision, promotion opportunities, attractiveness of alternate job opportunities, opportunities to increase work-related skills and knowledge, and so on. Questioning those individuals about what might have made them stay may lead to the development of survey questions that have direct policy implications. Perhaps this initial gathering of information will lead to hypotheses that suggest that education, marital status, gender, or ethnic status play a role in turnover rates. These hypotheses will lead to questions that will allow the breakdown of data into meaningful subgroups and will also have implications for decisions regarding the nature of the respondent sample, as well as information on the constructs relevant to the issue of turnover.

Once answers to these questions are determined, the researcher can begin to formulate some of the questions in the survey. Before proceeding, however, it is important to ask whether the survey is necessary. Because of the widespread use of surveys in human resources, they have a significant nuisance value and should be used sparingly. Will the survey design provide the information needed? For example, if a survey that is designed to examine turnover includes only current employees, it may not generate information about the actual reasons for quitting. Alternatively, a literature review, exit interviews, and a consideration of the labour market and where people go when they leave may tell human resource administrators what they need to know about the turnover problem in order to initiate actions to reduce turnover rates. They then may decide to evaluate such actions using one of the experimental or quasi-experimental research designs discussed in the next chapter.

It is also important to consider whether a survey is the best way to obtain the needed information. Frequently, information about a problem is already available in company records. For example, the organization should have information on educational background, gender, absenteeism, tardiness, performance, and marital and family status that might suggest some potential explanations of the turnover problem. The use of surveys is often criticized for providing only a superficial understanding of a problem. If one is interested in the process whereby individuals finally come to a decision to leave an organization, it might be necessary to use a series of in-depth interviews with employees or retrospective interviews with former employees. These interviews should be carried out in preparation for questionnaire construction, unless of course the problem is so simple that the interviews provide the needed answers. Most often, however, there will be a desire to gather information from a broader group of people in a less expensive and less time-consuming way than through interviews. Surveys or questionnaires, for which appropriate planning has taken place, include questions that should be responsive to the superficiality criticism.

Finally, there should be a consideration of all the likely stakeholders in a survey research project. In addition to policymakers or personnel who want specific information from the survey and may even want to use the survey results to promote a particular point of view or program, individual workers also may use the survey to "get even." The union almost always will have concerns about a survey and may want access to survey data. Questions about who has access to the data or who owns the data should be clearly spelled out prior to survey administration. The sequence of feedback to survey participants, degree of feedback, and who will give feedback should be considered so as to plan adequately for this critical aspect of survey research. The level of aggregation of the results (i.e., supervisory unit, work group level, department, etc.) must also be determined prior to survey administration to ensure appropriate safeguards regarding confidentiality and to provide appropriate expectations regarding the level of feedback possible.

WHAT IS TO BE MEASURED?

After defining the goals of the research and deciding that a survey is an appropriate means of data collection, the researcher must then decide how to translate the general concepts or terms expressed in the research objectives and hypotheses into actual questionnaire items. Some variables such as gender, age, and level of education may be quite concrete and easily translated into a questionnaire item with discrete options as possible answers. Even variables such as these, however, are occasionally difficult to place in a structured format (see the discussion below on questionnaire design with regard to item formats). Variables such as job satisfaction, social skills, and achievement motivation are abstract constructs that require careful conceptual consideration as they are translated into questionnaire items.

Some variables, such as marital status or employment status, may appear fairly concrete, but also require careful definition. For example, marital status defined as single, married, divorced, and widowed may appear fine, but individuals who are divorced or widowed also are single and some of those who are married may have been divorced. Also neglected in this classification are individuals who live with each other but who never have been formally married. These persons likely would respond "single" to the marital status question but be more like married persons in various ways that are relevant to the research. In considering employment status, we must decide how many hours a person must work to be considered fully employed. Also, are members of a family business all considered employed? How are seasonal workers treated? In many areas, standard definitions are available. Unless there is good reason to do otherwise, the adoption of accepted items is to the investigators' advantage. In the case of all items, there is no substitute for clear conceptual definitions. We must consider the realm of behaviours represented by a particular concept—for example, job satisfaction—and then include items that sample the domain in which we are interested.

In deciding which questions to ask and how to ask them, it is often quite useful to seek the opinions and input of the individuals who will use the survey results. Oftentimes, people will try to explain away survey results that indicate the need for change or an unfavourable reaction to some policy on the grounds that the question was worded in a way that they think demands a negative response. If these individuals participate in writing the questions, they feel more involved and are more likely to use the data. Of course, a researcher who wants to use existing scales to be consistent in measuring a previously researched construct could not tolerate this kind of participation. For research purposes, most often it is advisable to use existing measures to allow comparisons across research studies. As well, the quality of many existing measures is well documented and the researcher can choose measures that are known to be reliable and valid (measurement reliability and validity are discussed in Chapter 8).

WHO WILL ANSWER THE SURVEY?

Once there are clear conceptual definitions of the variables that interest the investigator, it is necessary to consider the groups of individuals to whom the survey is directed. The findings of a survey are applicable only to the population from which we draw a sample. Human resource practitioners are often interested in the results of a survey applied to a particular organization, while academic researchers are often interested in employees from a number of organizations. Survey questions should be directed to some or all of the following groups:

1. Employees working in different geographic locations.

2. Employees working in different functional units (sales, marketing, finance, production, research and development, etc.).

3. Employees working in different supervisory units.

4. Employees working at different hierarchical levels (hourly versus salary employees).

Consideration of the nature of the variables one is interested in measuring may dictate that the survey not apply to one or more of these groups. For instance, questions regarding the availability of public transportation would be inappropriate in a rural community. Or questions regarding the boring nature of work might not be relevant for a research and development division.

If one's interest is in making more general statements about working people (i.e., statements with external validity), the question of whom to survey is even more difficult. If we were interested in the degree to which people working at different occupational levels experience stress at work, we would want to make sure our sample included members in a range of occupational levels. If we wanted to investigate the degree to which physicians experience stress, we would be interested in sampling physicians who serve a variety of patients under different types of working situations (i.e., physicians working with other physicians, physicians working in a research institution, or physicians practising alone). In the latter example, stress might be affected by the degree to which responsibility and working hours are shared. Whether this hypothesis is correct or not, the point is that the type of respondent we seek to include is dictated by the variables in which we are interested.

Once we have decided that a particular group of individuals is to be the target of a survey, it is very likely that this group will be too large to allow each person to be surveyed. In this case, we will want to select a sample from the population whose responses we would like to be able to represent. In the next section, on the development of sampling plans, it will be noted that one can achieve very accurate estimates of population statistics from samples containing a relatively small proportion of the population. While accuracy of estimates can often be achieved with a small sample of a total population, it may be desirable to include all potential respondents when the survey is to be used as an intervention. Telling a group of employees that survey results come from a sample may lead to criticism that the results do not represent their views but those of someone else.

◆ ◆ ◆
THE SAMPLING PLAN

For a sample to be representative of some larger group, it must reflect the similarities or differences found in the larger group or population. Human resource researchers frequently use what is called a **convenience sample**—that is, a sample that is easy to obtain, a sample of people who will respond, or one for which we have been able to achieve organizational approval. Despite the prevalence of this practice, it is not recommended. Instead, the best way to achieve a representative sample is to randomly select the respondents from the population of interest. Without random sampling of respondents, the results may be biased in some unknown or unanticipated way.

This section discusses the basics of sampling and the confidence with which one can make inferences about a population from a sample, as well as some ways in which one can check on the representativeness of a sample when circumstances force the use of the nonrandom selection of respondents.

In discussing sampling, it is important to remember that the **population** is the total group about whom we are interested in gaining information. The **sample** is the set of respondents from this population from whom we actually collect information. From the measurements taken from this sample, we *estimate* the characteristics of the population.

RANDOM SAMPLING AND POPULATION ESTIMATES

To obtain a **random sample** of a group of individuals we first must have a complete list of all the people in the population. In most organizations, such a list would be relatively easy to compile. If one is interested in the members of a community or province or the unemployed in a particular region, such lists may be more difficult to obtain. When this list is compiled, people are selected in such a way that each person has the same chance to be selected. Names of individuals can be drawn from an urn that includes all individual names or one could use random number tables. Or, if the set of respondents is computerized, most software packages include a random sampling routine that would save a great deal of work.

Note that random sampling is not the same as taking anyone who is available on a street corner or who happens to leave a particular exit at a workplace. Random sampling means that each and every specific individual or element in the population has exactly the same probability of being included in the sample.

We rarely get responses from the first randomly selected individuals. Some of them cannot be located or some refuse to participate. In some instances, researchers try to select replacement participants who match the characteristics of the persons who cannot be located. This is not desirable, since there are usually many variables on which a match may be wanted and the process of matching rapidly becomes unmanageable. It is best to randomly select additional persons until the desired sample size is achieved.

After collecting data from this sample, the investigator can compute averages, standard deviations, frequencies, correlations between items or variables, and other descriptive statistics. At this point, one is interested in making statements about the degree to which these summary statistics apply to the population as a whole. For example, we may have sampled 200 people from the marketing division of a large organization and are now interested in saying that their responses represent the opinions of the marketing division. Thus, even though the survey included only 200 respondents, because they were randomly selected it is now possible to draw conclusions about employees in the marketing division as a whole. Unfortunately, there are many circumstances in which random sampling is not possible, and in such cases modifications are required.

MODIFICATIONS OF RANDOM SAMPLING

Sometimes the requirements of random sampling cannot be met because some unit(s) will not cooperate with a research project or there is no complete or up-to-date listing of all the persons in a given community, occupation, or area. In other instances random sampling might not be possible for practical reasons, and some modification of random sampling must be used.

One modification of random sampling involves the use of stratification. **Stratification** involves dividing the population into subgroups and then selecting randomly from these groups. Use of stratification is usually undertaken to ensure the representativeness of the sample on some critical variable(s). For example, an organization might want to sample equal proportions of people from different supervisory or functional units. Or they might want representative proportions of different gender, ethnic, or tenure subgroups. Simple random sampling might not give exactly representative samples, particularly if the total sample size is relatively small and the number of different critical subgroups is large. Occasionally one subgroup of particular interest may be oversampled or different selection procedures may be applied because of data collection problems with a particular group.

A second modification of simple random sampling is **cluster sampling**, in which participants are chosen as members of a group rather than as individuals. Let's imagine we are interested in the adoption of safety procedures among workers who handle asbestos. If we randomly sampled all such workers, the project would be tremendously costly and might involve negotiating permission to survey workers in a very large number of organizations. If we had a list of work sites or facilities at which asbestos poses a safety hazard, a possible solution would be to randomly select organizations as opposed to individuals. This approach to sampling might be a convenient, cost-effective way to conduct research on human resource issues. Only these randomly selected organizations would be asked to cooperate; if one refused, another organization or a similar organization (in type of product manufactured, demographics of the work force, size, etc.) could be selected.

The major disadvantage of using cluster sampling is the effect it has on the sampling error of the statistics computed. In the extreme case, if all the individuals in a particular cluster, or organization, were identical on a key variable and totally different from members of other organizations, then the sample size would be equal to the number of organizations rather than to the number of people in those organizations. At the opposite extreme, all of the organizations would show the same variability on key variables as a simple random sample. In practice, Warwick and Lininger (1975) indicate sampling errors 1.5 times as large for cluster samples as for simple random samples.

Another approach to selecting a sample is to order the people in the group to be sampled, to decide on the portion of the sample needed to achieve a desired sample size, then to randomly select a start point, and then to select every 5th, 10th, or 20th person after that point. For example, in an organization of 2000 employees, we might decide to survey 200; hence, every 10th person in an alphabetized listing would provide N equal to 200. If random selection of numbers between 1 and 10 produces 7, we would select the 7th, 17th, 27th, and so on. This systematic selection is essentially equal to random selection if the potential respondents are *not* ordered on any characteristic that is related to the variables of interest. It is unlikely that an alphabetical list would be ordered in such a fashion.

Occasionally, it might be desirable to sample unequally from certain subgroups. For example, if one's analysis objectives include the capability to describe a very small group, then a large portion of that group will need to be included in the respondent sample in order to get reliable data on that subgroup. However, when the research objective is to describe the total population, the responses of this one subgroup would be overweighted. In this latter instance, some type of compensating weights must be applied to the underrepresented individuals. For example, if an organization were particularly interested in the responses of a small minority group, it might sample from that group at three times the rate of the remaining members of the organization. In computing organizational-level descriptive statistics such as the mean, median, and percentages, the responses of the majority should be weighted three times the responses of the small minority.

Assuming we have developed a satisfactory sampling plan, one additional complication arises when not all of the sampled persons respond to the survey or we replace our original randomly selected respondents with others either themselves randomly selected or matched to the nonrespondent in some way. The question of the representativeness of the final sample then arises. There is, perhaps, no way of ascertaining that the sample is completely representative, although in many cases we are likely to have data regarding the characteristics of the population as a whole. These data can be compared with similar data collected on the sample to check the possibility of nonrepresentativeness.

In comparing the respondent sample and the population sample, it is of interest to include comparison variables that might potentially influence the variables in which one has a substantive interest. As stated above, without random sampling and a high response rate (perhaps above 80 percent), we can never be sure of the representativeness of our sample, but with some obvious comparisons of sample and available population data, we can assess in some degree the relative representativeness of the sample. When these comparisons reveal a nonrepresentative sample on key variables, then appropriate reservations should be made when the data are interpreted. Finally, it is often a good idea to include in the survey itself questions that allow these comparisons with known population characteristics. When surveying individuals, these questions are often demographic (e.g., gender or age of respondent) and background (e.g., education, work experience) in nature.

There also are times when, because of the homogeneity of a sample, nonrandom sampling makes no difference. For example, unless one believes or has evidence that role conflict is experienced differently by men and women, it might not be disturbing that a study on role conflict and stress has a sample that contains more men than women. Such assumptions, however, should be made only with a thorough knowledge of the construct one is measuring and how it might be influenced by the characteristics of the individuals in the population.

◆ ◆ ◆
QUESTIONNAIRE DESIGN

Once a decision has been made about the variables and sample to be included in the survey, it is necessary to begin to write questions and design the survey itself. Frequently, researchers and practitioners are interested in constructs that have been widely researched elsewhere and for which existing measures are available. Particularly when one of the objectives is to contribute to the scientific literature, existing measures should be used unless there is a compelling measurement (lack of reliability, too many items, etc.) or conceptual reason to develop a new measure.

Use of previously existing measures, even when the primary objective is a local, practical, or policy one, will allow comparability of survey results across organizations and situations. The spectrum of previous literature is an aid to the interpretation of findings. As well, by using existing measures for common variables in human resource research such as personality, ability, job satisfaction, organizational commitment, intentions to quit, and so on, one can be sure that reliability and validity are satisfactory. As discussed in Chapter 8, measures of high quality are those that have high levels of reliability and validity. The process of designing new measures and establishing their reliability and validity is extremely expensive and time-consuming, but failure to do so can result in measures that are not very good.

Thus, one way to ensure that survey measures are good is to use existing measures with known and acceptable levels of reliability and validity. Fortunately, many such measures in human resources have been developed and can be readily obtained. Table 3.2 contains several such measures, including job satisfaction, organizational commitment, and intentions to quit.

TABLE 3.2 SURVEY MEASURES IN HUMAN RESOURCE RESEARCH

Job Satisfaction (Cammann, Fichman, Jenkins, & Klesh, 1983)

1. All in all, I am satisfied with my job.
2. In general, I don't like my job. (Reverse scored)
3. In general, I like working here.

Organizational Commitment (Allen & Meyer, 1990)

1. I would be very happy to spend the rest of my career with this organization.
2. I enjoy discussing my organization with people outside it.
3. I really feel as if this organization's problems are my own.
4. I think that I could easily become as attached to another organization as I am to this one. (Reverse scored)
5. I do not feel like "part of the family" at my organization. (Reverse scored)
6. I do not feel "emotionally attached" to this organization. (Reverse scored)
7. This organization has a great deal of personal meaning for me.
8. I do not feel a strong sense of belonging to my organization. (Reverse scored)

Intentions to Quit (Colarelli, 1984)

1. I frequently think of quitting my job.
2. I am planning to search for a new job during the next twelve months.
3. If I have my own way, I will be working for this organization one year from now. (Reverse scored)

Response scale: 1 = *Strongly disagree,* 2 = *Disagree,* 3 = *Slightly disagree,* 4 = *Neither agree nor disagree,* 5 = *Slightly agree,* 6 = *Agree,* 7 = *Strongly agree.*

STRUCTURED VERSUS OPEN-ENDED ITEMS

An important decision in questionnaire design is whether to use structured or open-ended questions. Examples of these two item types are contained in Figure 3.2. In making this decision, the primary considerations include the type of respondent, the purpose of the research, and the type of question. If the respondents are not likely to be very involved or if they are not likely to be accustomed to writing, open-ended questions will yield low response rates and incomplete surveys. In this instance it would be better to use structured questions. If the purpose of the research is primarily exploratory and you want the respondents to give their opinions on issues without a great deal of "prompting" or "leading" by the question itself, then it might be better to use open-ended questions.

Frequently the responses to open-ended questions are obtained from a small pilot sample whose responses are used as a basis for developing structured items. If the question is such that obvious options exist (gender, ethnic identity, province or country of residence), there is little reason for an open-ended format. Sometimes not all options can be specified or anticipated. In these instances, it may be best to use an item similar to that in Figure 3.2 (Question C6), in which one of the options allows for an unanticipated response.

Finally, a major consideration in questionnaire design is the number of respondents one expects and the time and money available to code and analyze their open-ended responses. In the case of mail surveys, while all possible options should be included, an open-ended format should be used sparingly. Responses to open-ended formats require a great deal of time for developing codes to categorize the responses, and low agreement among raters in the use of those codes usually means that the responses to these items are not analyzed even when respondents have answered them. Their primary advantage is the freedom they give respondents to express the depth of their feelings about an issue or some unconventional response. For example, in research on the job searches of university graduates, the author of this book asked participants to comment on their job search experiences with open-ended questions at the end of a survey. This resulted in many bits of insightful information about the job search experience that could not have been gained from the structured questions.

WRITING ITEMS

The primary aim in writing items or questions for survey research is to obtain complete and accurate information about the object of interest. At the same time, item writers must be sensitive to the need to maintain the potential respondents' cooperation and goodwill and to recognize their privacy and dignity.

While item writing is as much an art as a science, there are various guidelines that are useful for evaluating questionnaire items. The reader should be aware, how-

---

FIGURE 3.2 Example of Structured and Open-Ended Survey Questions

A. Open-Ended Questions
1. What are the most dissatisfying features of your job?
2. What aspects of your job are most likely to make you happy?
3. If you had a choice, how would you change your job?

B. Structured Questions
Indicate in the space to the left of each item how happy you are with each of the following aspects of your job using the response scale below:

     5 = Very happy
     4 = Happy
     3 = Neutral, neither happy nor unhappy
     2 = Unhappy
     1 = Very unhappy

_____ 1. The work you do
_____ 2. Your supervisor
_____ 3. Your co-workers
_____ 4. The conditions in which you work
_____ 5. The employee cafeteria
_____ 6. Your work hours

C. Structured Questions with an Open Response Option
Circle the number that best represents the reason you arrive at work late.
1. I never come late
2. Problems with car
3. Problems with bus or train
4. Family problems at home
5. Illness
6. Other (please specify) _____

---

ever, that little research has been conducted to evaluate these guidelines. Remember that the primary objective in writing items is to represent faithfully the constructs in which you are interested in measuring. The list of guidelines that follows is adapted from Warwick and Lininger (1975).

1. *Make sure all words are simple, direct, and familiar to potential respondents.* Sometimes researchers unintentionally include technical jargon in items. For

example, instead of using the word "feedback," it might be better to ask how often a supervisor or co-worker tells you "how well you are doing your job." Or a question regarding the degree of "personal initiative" one can exercise in one's job might be rephrased to ascertain whether or how often the worker "can decide how to do a task" or "which task will get done."

2. *Make the question as clear and specific as possible.* In most instances, a lack of clarity results when the respondent is given an inadequate frame of reference for an answer. If we ask a worker how many people work with her or him, we may get answers that indicate how many workers are in the company, a supervisory work unit, a work group, and so on. If we ask how many times someone comes in late for work, the item should specify whether we mean in a year, a month, a week, and so forth. "How long did you look for a job?" is a question that might generate respondent questions such as: "When? My first job? My current job?"

3. *Avoid double-barrelled items.* Double-barrelled items are questions that actually address two issues. They usually elicit an answer to only one of the two issues addressed, even when the question is open-ended. When structured response options are given, it is, of course, impossible to address both issues at once. Consider the following items:

Do you plan to leave your job and look for another one during the coming year? Do you plan to retire and travel? Are you unemployed because of a lack of training?

4. *Avoid leading or loaded questions.* Questions can be leading when one or more option is listed with the question as in the following item: "How often do you complain about some aspect of your work, such as the pay you receive?" If all options are listed, as should be the case for an item with a structured format, then the item would not be subject to this bias.

Another leading item might read: "How often do you drink to excess?" This item makes the presumption that the respondent has indeed drunk too much on occasion. Again, a structured format with a "Never" response option would correct this item.

Leading questions are frequently used by political candidates in surveys of constituents' opinions. Consider the following:

- Do you agree with my opponent's support of legislation, which would infringe on your rights, such as gun control legislation?
- Do you agree with my opponent's support of tax breaks for big business?

Leading questions are phrased so as to make it difficult for the respondent to disagree with the stated position, whatever the respondent's real positions. For example, the tax breaks referred to may have positive implications for individuals as well as business, and while no one likes to lose their rights, gun control legislation may not affect individual rights.

It is tempting to ask leading questions on attitude surveys in such a way that the survey indicates support for human resource policies espoused by management.

5. *Be sure the question applies to all respondents.* Very often surveys contain questions that are not applicable to all respondents. For example, questions to single respondents asking how long they have been married or to unemployed persons about how long they have worked on their current jobs are typical examples. Sometimes the question is applicable to all respondents but the options in a structured item are not. People might then respond to one of the options simply to oblige the researcher or to avoid embarrassment. This often occurs when they are asked their opinion on some topic they have not previously considered and for which they have no opinion.

The most convenient way to handle the problem of questions and their applicability to some subset of the potential respondents is to use a branching or skip format in which respondents are directed to additional detailed questions based on an affirmative response to a previous question. Individuals who do not respond in the affirmative to a particular question, and would therefore find the more detailed questions meaningless, would be instructed to skip such questions and be directed to the next set of questions. Computer-administered surveys can be used in a manner such that branching is done automatically and the respondents see only those questions that are relevant to them based on their previous answers.

6. *The likelihood of response styles should be considered and appropriate steps should be taken to minimize their effects.* A response style is the tendency of a respondent to choose a certain response category regardless of the item's content. For example, sometimes survey responses form a series of straight lines, indicating that the respondent probably only read one item (if any) from each set of items, decided on a response, and then responded the same way to all items.

Two such response sets have been extensively studied by researchers using surveys to measure attitudes. **Acquiescence response styles** are characterized by persons who indicate a positive response to all statements in a scale. (Sometimes these yea-sayers are distinguished from naysayers, who indicate negative responses to all questions.) The most frequently recommended way to minimize this response set is to word some items positively and others negatively (e.g., to measure job satisfaction: "In general, I really like my job" [positive], and "I do not like my job very much" [negative]). This forces the respondent to read all items to discern their negative–positive nature and hopefully their content. However, the most effective way of avoiding or minimizing this type of response bias is to maintain respondents' motivation to respond carefully by keeping the survey short. People are more apt to read items rapidly and cursorily when a survey is long and boring due to the repetitive nature of some response formats (e.g., "strongly disagree" to "strongly agree").

A second major response style is called **social desirability**. People who respond in a way that they think will present them in a favourable light are answering in a socially desirable way. For example, it is socially desirable for some people to say that they like challenging work, that they like opportunities to learn at work, or that they like to be able to exercise their own initiative at work.

One way of dealing with the social desirability response style is to use a forced-choice format, in which the respondent is forced to make a choice from a group of potential responses. Another way to minimize social-desirability responses is the use of *content-specific anchors* as opposed to *agree–disagree* or *high–low continua*. This practice is used in performance ratings that use *behaviourally anchored rating scales*. Another attempt to minimize both social-desirability responses and acquiescence is to intermingle the items measuring a given construct throughout a survey to force respondents to read and think carefully about each item before responding. The best way to deal with these problems, however, is to first conduct a pilot test of the survey with a sample of the people to whom the survey will be directed and see how they respond to the survey. As well, respondents are more likely to answer honestly if they know that the survey results will be confidential and that they are not required to reveal their identify on the survey.

In summary, writing items is a time-consuming and difficult task. However, failure to write good questions can result in incomplete and inaccurate data. Kraut (1996b) provides the following guidelines for writing good items:

- Use simple words.
- Make items short.
- Use unambiguous terms.
- Use familiar language.

As well, Kraut (1996b) recommends avoiding:

- Double-barrelled items.
- Double-negative items.
- Strange or exotic terms.
- Imprecise words.

- Asking about issues outside of the respondent's experience.

- Asking "loaded" questions.

- Asking overly demanding questions.

- Using overlapping alternatives.

RESPONSE OPTIONS IN LIKERT-TYPE SCALES

When structured response options are used, it is necessary to have a number of response options. For example, questions about job attitudes usually have five or seven options that range from "strongly disagree" (low response option) to "strongly agree" (high response option). An important consideration is whether respondents use all of the options presented or only a portion of the total options, either all at one end of the scale, in the middle, or at both ends. This lack of variability, or *bimodal responding*, has important measurement consequences. In human resources research, we often make judgments about the amount and frequency of some activity or behaviour. In some performance evaluation instruments, the rater judges amount—how much or how often the behavioural statements apply to an employee. The respondent to an attitude survey judges frequency—how much or how frequently the statements reflect her or his opinion.

Bass, Cascio, and O'Connor (1974) have collected information about a large number of frequency and amount descriptors. Their objective was to provide descriptors that were equally spaced along a continuum. The results of their research are presented in Figure 3.3, which indicates optimal verbal anchors when using scales of frequency and amount for scales with four to nine response categories.

In some cases the accuracy of responses can be increased by using a frequency response scale. For example, a frequency response scale might include anchors such as "once a week," "twice a week," "once a day," "twice a day," or "many times a day." Such a scale has been developed by Blau (1994) to measure the frequency of job seekers' job search behaviour. Respondents are asked to indicate the frequency with which they have performed different job search activities (e.g., "Sent out copies of your résumé to potential employers") by responding to a 5-point scale where 1 = Never (0 times); 2 = Rarely (1 or 2 times); 3 = Occasionally (3 to 5 times); 4 = Frequently (6 to 9 times); and 5 = Very frequently (at least 10 times). Providing these types of anchors ensures that verbal anchors such as "Occasionally" and "Frequently" mean the same thing to all respondents. Furthermore, when using these types of scales it is also important to indicate the relevant time frame within which participants are to respond. For example, in the case of the job search behaviour scale, respondents might be asked how often they have performed each job search activity during the past three months.

FIGURE 3.3 Numerical Equivalents for Expressions of Frequency and Amount

A. Statistically Optimal Scales of Frequency
(with Percentage of Overlap Between Scale Points)
No. points in scale

9	8	7	6	5	4
8 Always 24%	7 Always 24%	6 Always 24%	5 Always 5%	4 Always 2%	3 Always <1%
7 Continually 21%	6 Continually 21%	5 Constantly 4%	4 Frequently, if not always 8%	3 Very often 12%	2 Often <1%
6 Very often 24%	5 Very often 13%	4 Often 25%	3 Quiet often 1%	2 Fairly many times <1%	1 Sometimes <1%
5 Quite often 42%	4 Rather frequently 2.5%	3 Fairly many times 6%	2 Sometimes 10%	1 Occasionally <1%	0 Never
4 Fairly many times 6%	3 Sometimes 45%	2 Sometimes 10%	1 Once in a while 2%	0 Never	
3 Sometimes 45%	2 Now and then 16%	1 Once in a while 2%	0 Never		
2 Occasionally 16%	1 Not often 7%	0 Never			
1 Not very often 7%	0 Never				
0 Never					

FIGURE 3.3 **Numerical Equivalents for Expressions of Frequency and Amount (continued)**

B. Statistically Optimal Scales of Amount

(with Percentage of Overlap Between Scale Points)

No. points in scale

9	8	7	6	5	4
8 All 44%	7 All 39%	6 All 18%	5 All 10%	4 All 2%	3 All <1%
7 An exhaustive amount of 18%	6 Almost entirely 31%	5 An extraordinary amount of 7%	4 Almost completely 16%	3 An extreme amount of 3%	2 A great amount of <1%
6 An extreme amount of 29%	5 An extreme amount of 8%	4 A great amount of 17%	3 Very much 2%	2 Quite a bit of <1%	1 A moderate amount of <1%
5 A great deal of 20%	4 A lot of 7%	3 Quite a bit of 5%	2 Fairly much <1%	1 Some <1%	0 None
4 Quite a bit of 5%	3 Fairly much 9%	2 A moderate amount of 12%	1 To some degree <1%	0 None	
3 An adequate amount of 32%	2 Some 9%	1 Somewhat 2%	0 None		
2 Some 5%	1 A limited amount of 4%	0 None			
1 A little 6%	0 None				
0 None					

Note: Each percentage shown represents the overlap in distribution between the accompanying entry's scale point and the scale point directly below that entry. For example, there is 44% overlap in response distribution between response at Point 7 and response at Point 8 for the 9-point scale.

Source: Reprinted with permission from Bass, B.M., Cascio, W.F., & O'Connor, E.J. (1974). Magnitude estimations of expressions of frequency and amount. *Journal of Applied Psychology*, 59, 313–320.

Another important issue to consider is the optimal number of scale points on structured survey questions of this type. Research on this issue (Lissitz & Green, 1975) indicates that reliability will increase up to five points but that it levels off beyond that point, so that adding additional scale points gains little or nothing.

A final issue regarding questionnaire design has to do with layout, instructions, and the ordering of items in the survey. If structured items are used and respondents are asked to indicate their answers on computerized answer sheets or directly into a computer terminal, detailed instructions with examples should be provided. These instructions should be pilot tested as many older or less educated respondents may have had no previous exposure to computerized answer sheets and may be confused about the requirements of these forms.

The physical layout of the survey should be attractive, easy to use, and easy to code and process (if it is not read by computer). There must also be some means to identify each survey and each page of the survey, in the case of multiple pages, and the possibility that the survey parts will become disconnected. To reduce paper and mailing costs, it is tempting to reduce the physical size of the survey by reducing print size or by cramming many items onto a single page, but this should never be done at the expense of readability. Numbering of items should be consecutive throughout the questionnaire rather than restarted in different sections. Numbering sections separately increases the possibility of respondent confusion and errors in coding the data. Different typefaces, boxes, asterisks, and underlining can be useful in alerting respondents to branches in the surveys, special instructions, negative wording, important exceptions, and so forth.

PRETESTING THE SURVEY

The importance of pilot testing a survey has been noted. This involves pretesting the survey before actually distributing it to the sample population. As part of the development of survey items, it is useful to include members of the respondent population in discussions regarding readability and even item content when the survey is to addresses policy issues. In addition, the final version of the survey should be given to a small number (perhaps twenty) of potential respondents. These people are asked to answer the survey and also to note any problems, confusions, or ambiguities. Pretests of components of the survey should be conducted face-to-face by someone who is working on the preparation of the survey. The pilot respondents who are answering the preliminary completed drafts of the survey should be encouraged to mention any issues that arise and to ask for clarification as they proceed through the survey.

As a next-best alternative to personal interviews, pilot respondents could be asked to tape-record their comments as they are responding. No matter how thoroughly the development phase has been conducted, a pilot test will reveal additional problems. It is an indispensable part of survey development and research and should always be conducted before distributing the survey to the sample population.

OPTIMIZING THE RETURN RATE

Survey research costs less than individual or group interviews or telephone surveys, and it is the most frequently used approach. The major disadvantage of survey research, however, is that people can and do simply ignore it, and this often results in a low return rate. The effects of a low return rate on a carefully selected sample are difficult to assess. This is another reason why it is important to compare the characteristics of the respondents with the population and the sample to which the survey was mailed, when such information is available. If the respondents are different from the population in some meaningful way, then one must be extremely cautious in generalizing the findings to the overall population. Therefore, a number of actions should be taken to maximize the return rate of a survey.

In human resources research, surveys are frequently distributed at the workplace. In these instances, return rates can be enhanced by support from top-level executives and/or union officials. Such support can come in the form of an accompanying letter or previous announcements in newsletters or at worker meetings. Returns can also be increased if time is allocated at work for the completion of the survey, although this may result in feelings of coercion. The respondent should have the option to refuse without any real or perceived penalty. The most important determinant of survey return rates, however, is the degree to which a workforce believes in the value of the research. When it comes to problem-solving survey research, this feeling is enhanced when respondents believe that real and timely feedback regarding the results of this survey will be provided, and that action on problems identified by the survey will be taken.

Mailed surveys, however, are often the only alternative, especially when the goal is to obtain the responses of persons working in different organizations. In general, the best returns come from surveys that look professional. As well, inclusion of a stamped, pre-addressed return envelope, personally typed cover letter, and a well-prepared and structured questionnaire all contribute to this professional appearance. The use of first-class mail has also been found to result in a 9 percent higher return (Armstrong & Lusk, 1987).

Letters and postcards to inform and remind respondents about a survey can also improve the response rate. This involves mailing a postcard informing respondents that they will be receiving a survey and in some cases asking for an indication of the respondents' willingness to respond. Postcard follow-ups can be sent in the weeks following the distribution of the survey as a reminder to complete the survey for those who have not responded. While these techniques can improve the response rate, they require additional time and costs. Further, it is possible that, by the time the postcard arrives, the individual has lost or discarded the survey, and unless a new copy is provided, he or she cannot respond. Most responses to survey research come within the first two to four weeks after the surveys are mailed.

Return rates are also increased when the respondents are personally involved or have an interest in the subject matter addressed in the survey. This can be enhanced by including with the survey a cover letter that provides a convincing but realistic statement of how the survey is relevant to the respondent and what purposes it is intended to serve. For example, a cover letter sent to university students by the author of this book for research on job search indicated that the results would provide important information to help graduates find employment. Needless to say, the response rate for this research was very good, and all respondents received a summary of the major findings of the study.

Paying respondents and providing incentives for completing a survey can also improve return rates. For example, the author of this text conducted research in which respondents received $5.00, a lottery or movie ticket, and had their names entered into a cash lottery for completing and returning the survey. While it is not known to what extent these incentives improved the return rate, the number of surveys returned in these studies was above the average for survey research. Higher response rates have been reported when a cheque was included with the mailed survey (Berry & Kanouse, 1987).

Finally, the best way to ensure an optimal return rate is to keep the survey short. Long surveys are less likely to be completed, and when they are returned they are often incomplete. Besides resulting in lower rates of return, the quality of the information obtained from lengthy surveys may also suffer.

ELECTRONIC MAIL AND THE INTERNET

With the increased availability of personal computers, conducting survey research via electronic mail is likely to increase (Sproull, 1986). Electronic mail uses computer text-editing and communications tools to provide a high-speed message service. Anyone with a computer account can use a terminal to compose a message and send it to anyone who has a setup to receive messages by computer.

The primary advantage of electronic mail is its speed and low cost. In addition, as noted earlier, an electronic survey can include branching and prompts that may be difficult or impossible to incorporate in a mailed survey. Furthermore, there is no need to transcribe or score data, thereby eliminating the time and errors associated with these tasks in a typical written survey.

Sproull (1986), however, identifies three issues relevant to the use of electronic mail as a research tool. Obviously, respondents must have access to a computer, and large segments of the working population still do not. Respondents must be willing to use this mode of data collection, and their responses should not be different than responses gathered using more traditional methods of data collection.

In a study conducted with divisions of a large firm, Sproull (1986) found that electronic mail produced a 73 percent response rate, certainly higher than what is typical of mailed questionnaires (Heberlain & Baumgartner, 1978), but lower than participation rates among a similar group whose cooperation was requested by telephone and who were then interviewed. The time of response was less than a week (about half that of the conventional method); incomplete data occurred on about 1 percent of the items; participants were fairly neutral toward this method of data collection, but did indicate a willingness to participate in a similar study in the future; and, perhaps most importantly, there were no substantive differences in mean responses to questions when compared with the interview-administered questionnaire method.

The questions in the Sproull (1986) study were relatively factual in content. In another study (Kiesler & Sproull, 1986), in which items were more subjective or attitudinal in nature, the authors reported that responses were more extreme and less socially desirable (Kiesler, Siegel, & McGuire, 1984). The potential for facilitating the collection of survey data and perhaps enhancing the quality of the data is apparent, but data comparability as well as ethical issues discussed later in this chapter must be considered when developing the capacity to use electronic mail for survey research.

Like e-mail, the Internet or World Wide Web (WWW) can also have great potential for survey research and data collection. Besides the lower costs associated with using the Internet, there exists the potential to reach large numbers of employees with different backgrounds and in many organizations (Stanton, 1998). However, would the data obtained through an Internet survey be comparable and of the same quality as data obtained from a more traditional paper-and-pencil survey?

In a recent study, Stanton (1998) set out to answer this important question. Stanton designed two identical surveys and gathered data from two samples of professional employees. One sample responded to a survey that was implemented on the Internet, and another sample completed a traditional paper version of the survey. The survey was designed to measure the determinants of individuals' perceptions of fairness in their interactions with their supervisors. The on-line version of the survey was published on a university Web server. Participants were contacted by e-mail and requested to complete the survey.

The results indicated that the data obtained through the Internet were comparable to the traditional paper-and-pencil survey in terms of quality, usefulness, and structural and relational patterns. Nonetheless, Stanton (1998) points out that a number of concerns need to be considered when using the Internet for survey data collection. For example, there are likely to be sampling problems to the extent that, unless the sample is targeted, anyone can respond to a survey placed on a Web server. Because the majority of individuals who have access to the Web tend to be male, professionals or managers, and university- or college-educated, their responses are not likely to be representative of the larger population. In addition, respondents who complete a survey on the Internet control the time and setting in which they complete the survey. As a result, the psychological state of the respondent is likely to vary considerably (e.g., sleepy, angry, bored, etc.) and this too can influence and bias the results. Therefore, considerable caution has to be used when implementing an electronic survey.

In summary, the computer as well as other new technologies have provided the researcher with new alternatives for survey research in addition to the traditional paper-and-pencil survey. Choosing an appropriate survey method is no longer a straightforward decision, and the researcher needs to consider a number of important factors, including confidentiality, flexibility, time and logistics, ease of use, and facilities and cost (Kuhnert & McCauley, 1996). Table 3.3 compares four nontraditional survey methods on these dimensions.

◆ ◆ ◆
DATA ANALYSIS

After the surveys have been returned, the investigator can begin the process of data analysis. However, it is important to realize that data analysis should actually be planned before the survey research is conducted. If such planning takes place, then most of the work described in this section is a relatively mechanical execution of these plans. Prior to the planned analyses, a number of steps should be taken to ensure the quality of the data being analyzed.

PRELIMINARY DATA CLEANING

The data analysis begins with a check of the surveys for any inconsistencies and obvious errors. If data are collected by computer-scored answer sheets, this checking should include a scan of answer sheets to make sure important identification information (ID numbers, department, organization, city, etc.) has been included. At this stage, such information may be obtained from the envelope or from other sources from which the data have been sent. If physically damaged, answer sheets may be copied to another sheet, thereby making computer scoring possible and saving the respondent's answers. Also, answer sheets that were filled out in a careless manner should be discarded. This might include answer sheets in which the same response option was always used (i.e., response bias), in which the same pattern (1, 2, 3, 4, 3,

2, 1, 2, 3, 4 etc.) was used throughout, or on which a picture or figure was drawn. A count of these discarded sheets should be kept and reported. Another common problem involves the respondent's use of pen as opposed to pencil, which makes the form unreadable. These answer sheets can be saved by copying responses to another sheet in pencil.

Answers that require an open-ended response entail much more work, assuming these answers will be translated into some quantifiable form. Coding categories must first be established and will most likely be developed by reading all or a large number of the responses and establishing a tentative list of mutually exclusive and exhaustive categories. These then must be described fully, and rules for assigning a response to one category or another must be written. The appropriateness of the categories is then tested by the degree to which independent coders can use the categories and can agree on the type of response given. When there is a low degree of interrater agreement or the coders are unable to assign a large portion of the responses to any response category, the system of categorizing is inadequate.

As stated above, the amount of work involved in processing open-ended questions dictates that they be used sparingly. They can, however, be useful in explaining responses to structured responses (Dunham & Smith, 1979). For example, low scores on a job satisfaction scale may be explained by a large number of comments about a new work procedure.

Once data are computerized, a listing of the file should be obtained and scanned. Data are usually input in a fixed format; that is, the answers to a particular item are always in the same place on a record and there are always the same number of responses on each record. This means that responses that are out of the input field can be readily recognized, often indicating a problem with the computerized scoring of the sheets, coder or data entry inaccuracy, or a respondent who failed to place answers in the correct position on the answer sheet. These problems occasionally indicate that an entire record (or major portion thereof) has been incorrectly read or coded. A scan of the data listing may also reveal out-of-range responses; for example, 7s and 8s appearing in a field in which there should only be responses from 1 to 5 should be checked and corrected.

The next step is to compute basic descriptive data on all survey items. Inspection of item means can direct you to a coding or formatting problem. For example, a mean of 6.6 to an item with response options of 1 to 5 is impossible and would alert you to some type of problem. Likewise, a standard deviation that is unreasonably large or small may represent some problem with data coding. If the range of possible responses is 6, then the standard deviation is likely to be about 1.5 (6 divided by 4, because two standard deviations on either side of the mean include most cases).

TABLE 3.3   COMPARISON OF SURVEY METHODS

	Automated Telephone	Fax	PC	E-mail
Confidentiality	Perceptions of confidentiality are enhanced when individual initiates call.	There may be concerns related to linking of identification / phone number stamp.	Perceptions of confidentiality are enhanced when a central PC or set of PCs is used for administration.	Concerns centre around linking of responses to e-mail addresses.
Flexibility	There is a lower level of tolerance for length, complex questions/responses, and open-ended questions. Item-branching capabilities are available.	Once faxed, flexibility is similar to paper-and-pencil survey.	There is greater flexibility for longer surveys, multiple question-and-response formats, open-ended items, and graphics. Complex item-branching capabilities are available.	Initial applications contain limited flexibility.
Time and logistics	Using external vendor technology, system can be running within a few weeks.	A short survey can be developed, distributed to limited population, and analyzed in a few days.	Requires more extensive development time. Central administration sites help control complexity.	Survey can be programmed within a week. Constructing extensive mail lists and integrating multiple e-mail systems can increase time requirements.
Ease of use	Responding becomes more difficult and frustrating with complex questions and long surveys. Providing a hard copy of survey for reference reduces frustration.	Completing survey is similar to completing paper-and-pencil survey.	Because survey may be administered to employees not familiar with PCs, detailed instructions may be necessary.	Because survey may be administered to employees not familiar with PCs and e-mail, instructions may be necessary.
Facilities and cost	Costs include specialized vendor technology and phone charges.	Costs include a PC equipped with fax board and phone charges.	Costs include software and additional hardware, if necessary.	Main cost is software.

Source: Kuhnert, K., and McCauley, D.P. (1996). Applying alternative survey methods. Table 9.1, p. 239. In A.I. Kraut (ed.), *Organizational Surveys*, Copyright 1996. (pp. 233–254). San Francisco, CA: Jossey-Bass Inc., Publishers.

One also may detect potential problems by comparing the responses to items with one's knowledge of the respondent sample. If the survey indicates 80 percent of the respondents are male and you know the sample included an approximately equal proportion of males and females, some checking should take place. The problem could be a mistake in coding or scoring the data, differential male–female response rates, or inadequate sampling. When all of these potential problems or inconsistencies are checked and corrected, one is ready to begin the analyses related to the original objectives of the survey.

ANALYZING AND INTERPRETING DATA

Analyzing and interpreting the results of survey data usually begins with an examination of descriptive statistics such as means, standard deviations, and frequencies. This can also involve comparisons of basic descriptive data that are usually conducted and are necessary to make the results meaningful and useful for initiating appropriate policy changes. At least four types of comparative data are possible:

1. Comparisons of different departments, locations, occupational groups, and so on, within an organization.
2. Comparisons with similar groups in other organizations.
3. Comparisons of the responses of similar groups across time.
4. Comparisons of the same group to different aspects of some content area, such as a training program or a work situation.

Without such comparative data, the survey is of little or no use. Examples of these types of comparisons are presented in Chapter 11 on statistical evaluation.

In addition to analyzing the descriptive data and making group comparisons, survey data are often used to test relationships between variables. Relational or correlational research attempts to identify how variables are connected. Investigators search for patterns and systematic linkages that might inform theory or guide practice. In certain conditions, survey data allow us to establish plausible arguments (but not really test) for causation, especially when the survey research is longitudinal. For example, research on employee turnover typically tests the relations between various predictor variables such as job satisfaction, organizational commitment, and intentions to quit and actual turnover. Thus, survey data can be used to establish relations among variables of interest and to predict outcome or dependent variables such as turnover using a set of predictors or independent variables such as demographic variables and job attitudes. More will be said about this type of analysis in Chapter 11.

◆ ◆ ◆
SPECIAL CONCERNS IN SURVEY RESEARCH

This chapter has emphasized the usefulness of survey research for providing answers to practical and theoretical questions or as a guide to organizational policy decisions. In this section, several issues that are particularly important in survey research are discussed. Some of these issues have been mentioned previously at various points in this chapter, but require special attention because of their importance.

SCALE REDUCTION

First, it has been noted that it is important to keep research surveys short. Too often, however, this requirement means that researchers use only certain items from existing measures. For example, a fifteen-item measure of organizational commitment might be shortened to five items, or a 50-item climate scale might be reduced to ten items. While the measures from which these items are derived may have desirable psychometric characteristics, subsets of items may or may not be appropriate representations of the same construct. It is not correct to cite earlier studies on the full scale as support for the reliability and validity of shortened scales. If the survey instrument is too long in these instances, it might be better to reduce the number of variables (or scales) included in the survey or to find alternate methods of measuring some variables rather than to randomly shorten an existing scale.

PERCEPT–PERCEPT PROBLEM

A second problem that occurs in survey research has been labelled the percept–percept problem. Researchers are often interested in determining the relationships among the variables they measure. For example, a researcher interested in organizational commitment might think job satisfaction, organizational climate, and job perceptions all contribute to people's commitment to an organization. However, if all these variables are measured in a single instrument, any mood or general response tendency possessed by the respondents will affect their responses to all measures and serve to inflate the observed correlations between variables. The fact that correlations between questionnaire measures tend to be positive and relatively high may be due at least in part to this percept–percept problem. This problem is, of course, important when the researcher hypothesizes a functional relationship between variables; that is, one or more of the variables measured is a dependent variable and the others are conceptualized as causes or independent variables.

Studies in which all variables are collected via survey are called **percept–percept studies**. That is to say, both the independent or presumed causal variables and the dependent variables are gathered at the same time in the form of employee perceptions. These studies are especially susceptible to *response bias*—that is, measures of all variables are influenced to some degree by the fact that they are collected via questionnaire. Consequently, inferences that correlations between these measures reflect a real relationship between underlying constructs are likely to be flawed.

Some measures can be taken to minimize or eliminate the percept–percept problem. The best solution, of course, is to consider whether all variables should be measured by a survey. The best guide here is to consider whether you are theoretically interested in the research participants' perceptions or in some other "objective" reality. If the latter, then an alternate form of measurement should be considered. In job design research, we might be interested in perceptions of job or task design, but at some point in a program of research one would almost certainly want to take some objective measurements of how the work is arranged.

If one does decide to measure all or some of the variables in a survey, then it might be best to separate those items measuring independent variables from those measuring dependent variables. Or it may be wise to collect the two sets of variables at different points in time. In this way, any temporary mood or reaction on the part of participants will not serve to inflate correlations between measures, although there still might be some inflation in observed relationships due to stable personal dispositions that are not relevant to the measured constructs.

As indicated earlier, longitudinal research involves the separation in time of measurement of the variables and can help reduce the problem of percept–percept measurement as well as help the researcher establish some causal sequence in the observed relationships between variables. This is another advantage of longitudinal survey research compared with a cross-sectional survey. For example, if job satisfaction at Time 1 is correlated with turnover intentions at Time 2 (e.g., several months later), we are somewhat more comfortable with the assertion that job satisfaction "causes" subsequent turnover intentions than we would be if both measures were taken at the same point in time. Of course, the timing of these two data collection efforts would also affect the appropriateness of causal attributions. At the very least, it would not be likely that turnover intentions caused job satisfaction.

SURVEY MATCHING

If data are collected at two different times, then the researcher must also take care to identify the respondents in order to match their answers in the two instruments. This, of course, raises issues regarding the confidentiality of answers. In almost all cases, it is imperative that respondents' surveys be anonymous and confidential. Unfortunately, this makes it difficult to match respondent surveys in longitudinal research. One way of dealing with this problem is to ask respondents to use an identification number such as their mother's birth date to allow matching across time while retaining respondents' anonymity. If this type of solution is impossible or unsatisfactory, then respondents must be informed how their identity is being established and what confidentiality safeguards are being employed.

CONTROL OF NUISANCE VARIABLES

In survey research, as in other types of research, it is important to consider what other "nuisance" or contaminating variables might affect the measures and variables in which you are primarily interested. Age, gender, experience, education, socioeconomic status, and/or organizational policies are examples of variables that may be related to various measures of interest to human resource researchers. These variables may affect the range of scores on other measures or interrelationships between variables of interest. Careful review of the literature, a clear conceptual understanding of the variables of interest, and knowledge of the respondent sample will suggest what these nuisance variables might be. Measures of these variables must then be included in the survey to enable an assessment of their effect, or some alternate means must be taken to eliminate or minimize their effect.

RESPONSE VARIABILITY

Finally, theoretical research also necessitates a careful consideration of the scale anchors used with each item or set of items to ensure that respondents will exhibit some response variability. In applied research, it may be appropriate to have survey respondents indicate "Yes" or "No" to items indicating whether they have experienced certain stress symptoms. A finding that none or all of the respondents have experienced a stress symptom would be useful knowledge. Theoretically, however, this variable would be of no use since it has very little variability (i.e., "yes" or "no"). Only prior knowledge of the variable being measured or a pilot effort will tell a researcher whether there is likely to be any response variability on items with a certain response scale. Therefore, it is important in survey research to ensure that the measures being used have enough variability to obtain meaningful results.

◆ ◆ ◆
ETHICAL ISSUES IN SURVEY RESEARCH

The proper conduct of survey research must include an awareness and concern for the ethical issues involved. The conduct of survey research usually involves at least three significant concerns. First, the participants must be informed adequately as to the objectives of the research and the intended use of the data generated by the survey. Second, adequate safeguards must be taken to preserve the anonymity of the respondents. If it is necessary to identify the respondents who gave certain answers (as it might be when data are gathered from other sources as well, or data collection is part of a longitudinal study), then precautions to safeguard the identity of particular individuals must be taken. Sometimes it is possible to let the respondents supply an identification code (last four digits of a social security number, birth date, mother's birth date, etc.) when the research involves tracking respondents across time. Third, the ethics of survey research demand some type of feedback be given or made accessible to the respondents.

Regarding the first issue, there is usually no reason to hide the objectives of survey research; if there is, it is quite likely that respondents will guess or form their own hypotheses regarding the purpose of the survey. If it is anticipated that results are to be broken down in various ways, it might be useful to indicate this information in a cover letter. By the same token, it is probably advisable to tell the respondents what concepts you are interested in measuring with a set of items. If the survey is concerned with organizational or product loyalty, job involvement, or satisfaction with promotion opportunities, then tell the respondents that these are issues of concern. Aside from ethical concerns, it likely that a respondent who is informed about the purpose and nature of the questions asked will be better able and more motivated to provide accurate responses.

Respondents are often concerned that management or the people responsible for conducting a survey have some method of identifying them. Obviously, this becomes more likely under conditions of organizational stress and/or as we increase the number of demographics we ask of the respondents and the size of the group in which they are located is relatively small. In a group of twenty, there probably are not many female workers aged 35 with three children and a master's degree. Ultimately, the belief that responses will indeed be treated confidentially is a function of many organization–employee interactions, and no assurance of confidentiality will suffice in an atmosphere of low trust. It is usually true that data become less valuable and interpretable as we aggregate over larger and larger groups. The need for confidentiality and the desire for specificity are often in conflict. However, because of ethical concerns and for reasons of collecting quality data on other occasions, it is mandatory that confidentiality of responses be scrupulously protected.

A special case of a threat to anonymity occurs when survey data results are to be broken down by work unit or department in such a way that the effectiveness of particular managers is implied. Because many survey items convey an evaluative tone (e.g., "How well does your group work together?"), this is very easy to do. Thus, average scores on items like this may be computed for each work group, published, and compared. The end result is that specific managers may appear to look better than others.

There is no easy solution to this dilemma. However, the investigator should be certain that there indeed is some legitimate business or scientific need for such an analysis. If there is not, perhaps some other way of aggregating the same data should be considered. If there is such a need, participants/respondents all must be told at the outset that such clustering and reporting is intended. It may also be possible to code work groups so that, while differences may be seen, only the members of a work team will know of their specific identity. As stated above, people have the right to know what will be done with the survey information they provide.

The issue of anonymity is particularly problematic in the case of electronic surveys, because the respondents' e-mail addresses are typically returned to the researcher along with their surveys (Stanton, 1998). Although there are ways to overcome this, respondents may not feel comfortable enough to respond honestly. In fact, respondents' beliefs about anonymity have been shown to influence responses to computer-based attitude surveys (Kantor, 1991). Therefore, it is particularly important to implement controls to ensure respondent anonymity when using electronic surveys (Stanton, 1998).

Finally, the researcher has an obligation to provide feedback to respondents or to provide access to such feedback. If the only interest in conducting survey research is to examine research hypotheses, it might be expedient to provide only a short overall summary of the research findings to respondents. However, even in this instance, such a strategy would seem shortsighted. Surveys are widely used, and if we are to expect serious responses and high rates of return, we must be prepared to provide feedback at the level of detail desired by respondents. A three- to five-page feedback report with an overall summary of the findings, their implications, and any planned action and the option of obtaining additional data upon request is usually sufficient. In those instances in which no feedback is possible or intended, the respondent should be informed before completing the survey. The desired degree of specificity of the feedback will vary with the level of respondent interest in the survey and perhaps his or her ability to understand the research data. The importance of this should not be underestimated. In fact, it has been reported that the major reason for the ineffective use of survey research is the failure to provide feedback and a lack of action planning and follow-up (Kraut, 1996a).

◆ ◆ ◆
SUMMARY

This chapter began with a discussion of why human resource researchers do survey research. Research areas in human resources in which surveys are commonly used were discussed, followed by a description of the steps involved in conducting survey research. It was indicated that a clear formulation of survey objectives and the theoretical constructs of interest is required in order to guide what questions will be asked of what group of people and how their responses will be analyzed. The chapter also described how to sample from a population (so as to realize an adequate representation of the population without depleting the resources to conduct the study) and how to write questionnaire items and construct a professional survey with clear directions. Finally, the chapter concluded with a consideration of the special issues involved in conducting survey research and the ethical issues involved. While survey research is extremely important and popular in human resources research, conducting effective survey research requires a sound theoretical or conceptual rationale for conducting the survey. Thus, survey research should always be preceded by consideration of the underlying theoretical and practical issues involved.

Definitions

Acquiescence response styles   Occur when survey respondents indicate a positive response to all questions in the survey.

Cluster sampling   A form of sampling in which participants are chosen as members of a group rather than as individuals.

Convenience sample   Refers to a sample that is either easy to obtain or likely to respond to the survey.

Cross-sectional survey   A survey in which a variable or set of variables is measured at one point in time.

Longitudinal survey   A survey in which a variable or set of variables is measured over time or in successive periods of time.

Organizational survey   A method of systematically gathering data from people in an organization for specific purposes.

Percept–percept survey   A survey in which both the independent or presumed causal variables and dependent variables are gathered at the same time in the form of respondent perceptions.

Population   Refers to the total group from which one is interested in gaining information.

Random sampling   A process in which one selects randomly the respondents to complete a survey from the population of interest.

Sample   Refers to the set of respondents from the population from whom one actually collects information.

Social desirability   Occurs when survey respondents respond in a way they think will present them in a favourable light and in a socially desirable way.

Stratification   Involves dividing the population into subgroups and then selecting randomly from these groups.

E X E R C I S E S

1. In groups of two or three, design a survey using the measures in Table 3.2 (job satisfaction, organizational commitment, intentions to quit). Also include demographic and background variables that you feel are important for your survey as either comparison variables or control variables. Then make up several hypotheses about the relations between the variables in your survey. Before the next class, each group member is to ask five people to complete the survey. Bring your completed surveys to the next class and be prepared to discuss how to analyze the data and test your hypotheses.

2. Many news programs today include phone-in surveys in order to gauge viewers' opinions and attitudes about important news events. These surveys usually pose a question to viewers and ask them to indicate if they agree or disagree with a statement such as "Do you think that Canadians are spending too much time at work and not enough time with their families?"

   a) Discuss the sampling plan used to conduct these surveys and the effects this has on the results of such surveys.

   b) What factors need to be considered when interpreting the results of these surveys?

   c) What advice would you give about how to improve these surveys?

3. Select an HRM topic of interest to you and pose a series of questions to which you would be interested in knowing the answers (e.g., Is self-esteem related to job performance?). Then state several testable hypotheses based on your questions and explain how you could test your hypotheses by conducting survey research. Refer to each stage of the survey design research process to describe how you would conduct your study. Do you think that this would be a good research design to test your hypotheses? What are the advantages and disadvantages?

4. The following are just some of the questions a researcher interested in studying the research that is conducted by human resource departments might want to ask: Do human resource departments conduct research? What kind of research do they conduct, and what methods do they use? What major topics or issues are the focus of the research? Do they conduct survey research, and if so what is its purpose? How do they design surveys, and what kinds of variables do they measure? What do they do with the results of the research?

   For this exercise, you are required to design a survey to try to answer some of these and related questions. In small groups, design a survey on the topic "Research in Human Resource Departments." Before the next class, ask several human resource professionals to complete your survey, and bring the results to class the following week.

RUNNING CASE: THE VP OF HUMAN RESOURCES—PART 2

Describe how you can conduct survey research to demonstrate the value-added of the HRM department and its programs to the organization. Be sure to discuss how you will proceed in terms of each stage of the survey design process. Based on your answer to the above, would you conduct survey research in order to demonstrate the value-added of HRM to your organization? What are the advantages and disadvantages of doing so?

References

Allen, N.J., & Meyer, J.P. (1990). The measurement and antecedents of affective, continuance and normative commitment to the organization. *Journal of Occupational Psychology, 63*, 1–18.

Armstrong, J.S., & Lusk, E.J. (1987). Return postage in mail surveys. *Public Opinion Quarterly, 51*, 233–248.

Bass, B.M., Cascio, W.F., & O'Connor, E.J. (1974). Magnitude estimations of expressions of frequency and amount. *Journal of Applied Psychology, 59*, 313–320.

Berry, S.H., & Kanouse, D.E. (1987). Physician response to a mailed survey. *Public Opinion Quarterly, 51*, 102–114.

Blau, G. (1994). Testing a two-dimensional measure of job search behavior. *Organizational Behavior and Human Decision Processes, 59*, 288–312.

Cammann, C., Fichman, M., Jenkins, G.D., Jr., & Klesh, J.R. (1983). Assessing the attitudes and perceptions of organizational members. In S.E. Seashore, E.E. Lawler, III, P.H. Mirvis, & C. Cammann (Eds.), *Assessing organizational change: A guide to methods, measures, and practices*. New York: Wiley.

Colarelli, S.M. (1984). Methods of communication and mediating processes in realistic job previews. *Journal of Applied Psychology, 69*, 633–642.

Dunham, R.B., & Smith, F.J. (1979). *Organizational surveys*. Glenview, IL: Scott-Foresman.

Friedson, A.S. (1985). The legality of employee attitude surveys in union environments. *Employee Relations Law Journal, 8*, 648–669.

Heberlein, T., & Baumgartner, R. (1978). Factors affecting response rates to mailed questionnaires. *American Sociological Review, 43*, 447–462.

Iaffaldano, M.T., & Muchinsky, P.M. (1985). Job satisfaction and job performance: A meta-analysis. *Psychological Bulletin, 97*, 251–273.

Kantor, J. (1991). The effects of computer administration and identification on the Job Descriptive Index (JDI). *Journal of Business & Psychology, 5*, 309–323.

Kiesler, S., Siegel, J., & McGuire, T. (1984). Social psychological aspects of computer-mediated communications. *American Psychologist, 39*, 1123–34.

Kiesler, S., & Sproull, S.E. (1986). Response effects in the electronic survey. *Public Opinion Quarterly, 50*, 402–414.

Kraut, A.I. (1996a). An overview of organizational surveys. In A.I. Kraut (Ed.), *Organizational surveys* (pp. 1–17). San Francisco: Jossey-Bass.

Kraut, A.I. (1996b). Planning and conducting the survey. In A.I. Kraut (Ed.), *Organizational surveys* (pp. 149–176). San Francisco: Jossey-Bass.

Kuhnert, K., & McCauley, D.P. (1996). Applying alternative survey methods. In A.I. Kraut (Ed.), *Organizational surveys* (pp. 233–254). San Francisco: Jossey-Bass.

Lissitz, R.W., & Green, S.B. (1975). Effect of the number of scale points on reliability: A Monte Carlo approach. *Journal of Applied Psychology, 60,* 10–13.

Mobley, W.H., Horner, S.O., & Hollingsworth, A.T. (1978). An evaluation of precursors of hospital employee turnover. *Journal of Applied Psychology, 63,* 408–414.

Rosenthal, R., & Rosnow, R. (1984). *Essentials of behavioral research.* New York: McGraw-Hill.

Saks, A.M., & Ashforth, B.E. (1997). Organizational socialization: Making sense of the past and present as a prologue for the future. *Journal of Vocational Behavior, 51,* 234–279.

Schneider, B., Ashworth, S.D., Higgs, A.C., & Carr, L. (1996). Design validity, and use of strategically focused employee attitude surveys. *Personnel Psychology, 49,* 695–705.

Sproull, L.S. (1986). Using electronic mail for data collection in organizational research. *Academy of Management Journal, 29,* 159–169.

Stanton, J.M. (1998). An empirical assessment of data collection using the Internet. *Personnel Psychology, 51,* 709–725.

Steers, R.M., & Rhodes, S.R. (1978). Major influences on employee attendance: A process model. *Journal of Applied Psychology, 63,* 391–407.

Warwick, D.P., & Lininger, C.A. (1975). *The sample survey: Theory and practice.* New York: McGraw-Hill.

4

Experimental
Research Designs

◆◆◆
INTRODUCTION

An important goal of human resource research is the ability to make conclusions about the *effect* of human resource programs or interventions on individual, group, and organizational outcomes. Accomplishing this goal requires experimental research designs. The purpose of this chapter is to review experimental and nonexperimental research designs, with an emphasis on making strong inferences about cause–effect relations. Concepts, strategies, and different designs are discussed in order to conduct research to assess the impact of human resource interventions.

After reading this chapter, you should be able to:

■ Understand the importance of construct and internal validity in experimental research.

■ Be aware of the threats to internal validity and how to deal with them.

■ Know the differences between, as well as the advantages and disadvantages of laboratory and field experiments.

■ Be able to discuss the various types of nonexperimental, experimental, and quasi-experimental research designs for conducting human resource research.

■ Be able to discuss the ethical issues involved in experimental research.

To evaluate the impact of human resource interventions such as training and development, incentive programs, job redesign, and so on, requires more than survey research. As stated earlier, survey research usually results in data about the relations between variables rather than causality. Therefore, in many cases a different research design is required. A research design is the plan for conducting a study in such a way as to answer certain questions, and many research questions in human resources focus on the effects of a particular program or intervention on some outcome. In this chapter we assume that for many researchers and human resource professionals, the question of primary interest has to do with assessing the degree of (causal) impact of some theoretically interesting variable or some intervention. Thus, the emphasis will be on designs that allow us to interpret the results of research with a minimum amount of equivocality. This requires experimental research designs that allow causal inferences to be made.

◆ ◆ ◆
CAUSAL INFERENCE AND EXPERIMENTAL VALIDITY

The goal of conducting experimental research is causal inference. In other words, the researcher usually wishes to be able to understand why, how, when, or where some form of intervention (e.g., training) will have a predictable effect. In general, when the goal is causal inference, the preferred approach is an experimental one. Whether conducted in a laboratory or a field setting under the right conditions, experiments will provide the kind of evidence on which to base strong inference. In this section, these conditions will be reviewed.

In Chapter 2, external and statistical conclusion validity were discussed because they are relevant to all research methods and designs. In this chapter, two other types of validity—construct and internal validity—are discussed because they are particularly relevant to experimental research methods.

CONSTRUCT VALIDITY

The **construct validity** of an experiment refers to the degree to which the investigator has been successful in creating or arranging for the conditions of conceptual or theoretical interest. For example, if a researcher wished to study the effects of stress on job performance, the notion of construct validity would be raised in order to question the degree to which he or she defined operationally or created the essence of and the levels of stress correctly.

Cook and Campbell (1976) have highlighted several factors that affect the potential construct validity of experiments. These include the following:

1. *Method bias.* This refers to the possibility that the method used to create or produce variability (in the independent variable) is incorrect or flawed. The manipulation may not capture the richness or complexity of the construct of interest, or it could be contaminated (it creates forces that are not part of the construct). A special form of this bias is **monomethod bias**, in which a set of findings (even a theory) is incorrect because everything gets built upon a single method for operationalizing a construct. We would have far greater confidence in the construct validity of an investigation if we found convergence of the results of studies involving multiple approaches to the manipulation and measurement of the variables of interest.

2. *Hypothesis guessing on the part of subjects.* The results of a study may be affected by the ease with which research participants can correctly guess the purpose of the experiment and the observed tendency on their part to "give the researcher what he/she wants" (Rosenthal, 1967). In this case, the construct validity of the

study would be in question because the observed behaviour would not be a function of the independent variable.

3. *Confounding levels of constructs.* The investigator may create the wrong (e.g., weak) level of the construct. For example, in a study on the effects of stress on job performance, the level of stress created in the experiment might be much lower than what employees actually experience. When no effects are found, it might not reveal the true nature of the variable, but reflect the fact that an inappropriate level had been created. This is a major problem for laboratory studies, in which the magnitude of the conditions created may be much less than the same phenomenon in an actual work setting.

The construct validity of an experiment can only be estimated and involves making inferences about the appropriateness of the methods involved. At times the pattern of data obtained can be used to judge the construct validity of a study. Any time that the investigator makes a claim for the construct validity of a study, he or she has an obligation to demonstrate the basis for this claim. Such a demonstration is a necessary (although not a sufficient) indication of a quality study.

INTERNAL VALIDITY

Internal validity refers to the degree to which the results of a study can be explained unambiguously by an experimental intervention (e.g., incentive program), and cannot be explained by alternative factors related to the design and/or conduct of a study (Blackburn, 1987; Cook & Campbell, 1976). The concept of internal validity focuses on a specific set of plausible rival (alternative) hypotheses for a particular pattern of results obtained from a study. A study with strong internal validity increases our confidence that a particular manipulation, change, or human resource intervention actually caused observed outcomes.

We usually increase the level of internal validity by expending greater effort at careful design and control of factors in the research setting. However, as will become clear, the specific factors we choose to be concerned with should depend on such matters as the nature of the phenomenon itself and the setting in which the study is to take place.

Cook and Campbell (1976) and, more recently, Cook, Campbell, and Peracchio (1990) have identified a number of potential threats to internal validity. These are, in effect, things that can turn out to be rival or alternative explanations for the results of an experiment. For example, if an experiment on the effects of an accident prevention training program found that, after the training program, the rate and seriousness of accidents declined, the researcher would want to demonstrate that the decline was due to the training program and not to something else. However, to the extent that any threats to internal validity are in evidence, they might explain the reduction in accidents and not the training program. Therefore, it is important to improve the internal validity of an experiment by controlling for the following threats to internal validity:

1. *Selection of participants.* Internal validity depends in part on how people (groups, organizations) become subjects or participants in a study or how they are assigned to various treatments or conditions in experimental research. To the extent that individuals are not *randomly* selected or assigned to conditions, it is possible that the results are due to pre-existing differences in knowledge, skill, ability, attitudes, and so forth. For example, if participants are not randomly assigned to a training program, it is possible that any differences in job performance between those who participated in the training program and those who did not are due to pre-existing differences and not to the training program. Thus, if the most promising employees were sent to a training program, they would probably differ from other employees in terms of their abilities and job performance.

2. *Testing.* In human resource research it is not uncommon to measure or observe participants prior to the actual conduct of the study or the onset of an intervention. For example, prior to a training program it is often desirable to obtain a baseline of trainees' pretraining knowledge, behaviour, and/or job performance. However, the process of doing this itself may sensitize or change people, especially if they are not used to being assessed in this manner. Similarly, many studies involve taking repeated measures over a period of time. This, too, may change respondents in some unintended manner. Under certain circumstances this may produce fatigue or resentment, which may cause poorer scores. Or it may induce participants to produce later answers that are consistent with previous ones. In any event, the data would be suspect, seriously affecting the results and internal validity of the study.

3. *Instrumentation.* The nature of the procedures or instruments used to take measures may also have an effect on internal validity, especially if different techniques are involved during different parts of the study. For example, two different measures of job satisfaction may not be entirely equivalent. In a similar vein, self-reported or observer-generated data on stress may not show the same results. To conclude that true changes have occurred as a result of an intervention when, in fact, they are a consequence of using different instrumentation would be inaccurate, the result of an instrumentation effect rather than the independent variable.

4. *Statistical regression.* Statistical regression is a special type of selection problem. In many contexts, an investigator may identify and select individuals (groups, organizations) for study or receipt of particular treatments because they scored

extremely high (or low) on some measure such as ability or skill level. For example, employees who receive low scores on a test of social skills might be sent to a training program to improve interpersonal and social skills. If the same individuals were assessed again after the training, the researcher likely would obtain different scores. Statistical regression reflects a tendency for scores, upon remeasurement, to change in the direction of the mean. It would be incorrect to conclude that such shifts in patterns of data were a result of an intervention. Regression to the mean could be a plausible alternative explanation.

5. *History.* Very often during the course of a study events or factors occur that are not part of the study but may result in changes in the dependent variable. For example, if during the course of a training program there is a change in the organization's compensation plan, then an improvement in job performance following training might be due to the change in compensation and not to the training program. Thus, any event or happening that occurs at the time of an experimental intervention might be an alternative explanation for changes in a dependent variable rather than the independent variable.

6. *Maturation.* Changes in scores on a dependent variable may sometimes be due simply to the normal evolution of psychological or biological changes in individuals that occur over time. For example, an improvement in the work adjustment of newly hired employees after several months might be the result of an orientation program, increased job experience, or greater familiarity with the organization that occurs with the passage of time.

7. *Mortality.* Some participants usually drop out of a study before it is completed. To the extent that certain types of individuals (groups, organizations) choose not to come to sessions, complete surveys, or provide data, the pattern of results over time may be more a function of mortality effects than of any real change or impact of an intervention. For example, if participants who remain in a study are more motivated than those who drop out, then the results might be due to the fact that only the most motivated and perhaps best employees remained to the end of the study. This might explain an improvement in job attitudes or job performance rather than any human resource intervention.

8. *Diffusion/imitation of treatments.* In experimental research, investigators provide treatments or interventions to some potential participants (experimental condition), and withhold or postpone the intervention to others (**control condition**). They would then look for differences between these groups in terms of their scores on the dependent or outcome variable. However, if those in the control condition were to inadvertently learn about or otherwise be affected by the intervention and change their own behaviour as a result, such comparisons would be misleading. A finding of no difference between conditions could reflect

the impact of this threat to internal validity rather than a lack of effect of the intervention.

9. *Compensatory effects.* Similar to the scenario just described, individuals in a control condition may learn about the fact that they will not be receiving the presumed benefits of an intervention such as a training program. As a result, they might resolve to make up for having been left out with an increased effort or similar strategy aimed at making them look just as good on the dependent variable. Alternatively, such knowledge may produce a feeling of having been left out and of demoralization. Either dynamic can obscure the true effects of the intervention and lead to false conclusions.

10. *Interactions among the threats.* Finally, it is possible for more than one of the above threats to internal validity to be operating at one time and to affect the results of a study. For example, selection procedures may either exaggerate or mitigate the consequences of maturation, history, or instrumentation effects. Individuals chosen for a study may be more or less able to read, comprehend, and complete a complex survey than a different sample (selection × instrumentation effects).

Estimating the internal validity of a study is essentially a deductive process. Cook and Campbell (1976) characterize the investigator who does this as a critic, who assesses the extent to which the study embodies one or more flaws. Threats to internal validity must be assessed for their plausibility and severity as early as possible in the design and development stages of research so that certain changes or precautions can be taken beforehand. It is also important to understand the setting in which the research is to be carried out. Ultimately these considerations become the "lenses" through which we scrutinize the study and its design for any potentially serious weaknesses and threats to internal validity. Threats to internal validity, however, can be reduced by conducting a true laboratory or field experiment.

◆◆◆
LABORATORY AND FIELD EXPERIMENTS

Experimental designs in human resources research can take one of two forms: laboratory experiments or field experiments. A laboratory "is defined as any setting specifically created for the purpose of conducting research" (Sackett & Larson, 1990). Thus, the main difference between these two settings is the amount of realism and control involved. **Laboratory experiments** typically involve a contrived situation in which the task, setting, and/or the participants are in some way artificial. **Field experiments**, however, take place in organizational settings. As a result, they tend to involve actual employees and organizational phenomena. On the other hand, a laboratory experiment might involve individuals who are not employees (e.g., student participants) and/or who are asked to work on an artificial task or some sort of role-play or simulation.

The major trade-off in conducting laboratory versus field experiments involves the degree of internal and external validity. Typically, laboratory experiments have a high degree of internal validity because the researcher is able to control many if not most of the threats to internal validity. However, because of the lack of realism and the contrived nature of laboratory experiments, they are often limited in terms of external validity, especially when the study involves students who are participating in an experimental task as part of a course requirement. Field experiments, however, have a high degree of external validity, but due to the constraints of conducting research in an actual organization, have lower internal validity.

The priority we give to a particular type of validity often depends on the purpose or the goal of the research. When the concern or objective is mostly of an applied nature, such as to study the effectiveness of a human resource intervention in the workplace, then a field experiment with its high degree of external validity is often more appropriate. However, for theory building or studies on the psychological processes involved in some known phenomena, a laboratory experiment in which one can ensure a high degree of internal validity would be more appropriate. For example, research on the effects of realistic job previews on employee turnover is best conducted in an organization. However, if the purpose of the research is to study the psychological processes of job previews or how they work, then laboratory research can be very effective (Olian, 1986). Sackett and Larson (1990) provide a more in-depth discussion of the strengths and weaknesses of laboratory and field research for the interested reader.

Regardless of whether an experiment is to be conducted in the laboratory or the field, the main principles and issues of conducting a true experiment remain the same. In the sections that follow, the main types of nonexperimental, experimental, and quasi-experimental research designs are discussed.

◆ ◆ ◆
NONEXPERIMENTAL RESEARCH DESIGNS

Before the various designs of so-called true experiments are described, it is important also to understand what are known as **nonexperimental research designs**. Nonexperimental research designs are weak in terms of providing a basis for making a strong argument that a human resource intervention has had an effect on some outcome. Because they often are perceived as easy to conduct and less costly and disruptive (to the routine of the organization), they probably are the most prevalent kind of designs used. Key examples of nonexperimental research designs include the post-test-only design and the pretest/post-test design.

POST-TEST-ONLY DESIGN

In this design, participants are assessed only after they have been exposed to an intervention. For example, trainees' job performance might be measured after they have attended a training program or some other HR intervention. Schematically, this design is portrayed as follows:

HR Intervention ⟶ Post-measure

Any conclusions about the effects of the training program would have to be tentative at best. For example, with this design we don't know what the trainees were like before training, so post-measures may reflect levels of prior knowledge rather than program effectiveness. Thus, a serious limitation with this design is that a baseline measure is not obtained, so it is not possible to determine if a change has occurred following the intervention. In addition, there are many threats to internal validity. In other words, it is very difficult to know if the intervention or something else led to the results.

However, it is worth noting that in some cases it might not be necessary to know if the effect of an intervention is the cause of the post-measures. In some cases it might only be necessary that trainees achieve a certain level of knowledge or job performance following a training intervention. If this is the goal of the research and intervention, then this design would be adequate. This is a good example of how the goals or purpose of research should drive the research design.

In other instances, an investigator might use a post-test-only design because he or she is interested in the nature of the intervention itself and only incidentally about its causal effect. In this regard, measures of a training intervention might be taken and data reported for such things as the number of class hours taught, the number of students enrolled, trainee reactions to the training, and so on.

THE PRETEST/POST-TEST DESIGN

The pretest/post-test design adds a pre-measure to the post-test-only design. Therefore, it includes a baseline measure of things such as initial levels of individual knowledge, skill, or behaviour. The pretest/post-test is diagrammed as follows:

Pre-measure ⟶ HR Intervention ⟶ Post-measure

The logic of this design is that the effectiveness of a human resource intervention can be inferred from any change in scores observed between the pre-measures and post-measures. Thus, it enables one to determine if there is a change in some outcome following the intervention. However, despite this advantage, one can have only limited confidence in the ability to interpret the meaning of any differences found. This is because there are many possible threats to internal validity. For example, it is possible that something else occurred contemporaneously with the intervention, and it, not the intervention, was responsible for the change in scores. This would be the case if an organization instituted a new incentive pay plan (history effect) at the same time as a training program was implemented as an experimental intervention. In such an instance it would be difficult to determine what caused an improvement in a dependent variable such as job performance, and it might be concluded that the training program was a success when in fact the improvement in job performance was due to the new incentive plan. Other threats to internal validity such as selection, maturation, testing, and instrumentation are also possible explanations for any changes that are found in a pretest/post-test design.

In an attempt to deal with some of the limitations of the pretest/post-test design in training research, Haccoun and Hamtiaux (1994) developed an innovative approach called *internal referencing*. Using this approach, the researcher collects data that are relevant to the training content as well as data that are not relevant. Pretest and post-test comparisons are then made on the content areas covered during training as well as those areas not covered during training. Training effectiveness is demonstrated when pre/post changes on the items relevant to training are greater than pre/post changes on the nonrelevant items. The logic behind this approach is that changes should only occur for the data that are relevant to the training content. If similar pre/post changes are found for the data that are not content-related, it suggests that something else besides or in addition to training is responsible. If the training program is the cause of a pre/post change, then a change should only be found when comparing the data that are content relevant.

While the internal referencing strategy is very helpful when using the pretest/post-measure design, nonexperimental designs have only limited potential for concluding that a human resource intervention caused some change in a dependent variable. A preferred strategy is to use a **true experimental design** that allows the researcher to more confidently establish cause–effect relations.

◆◆◆
EXPERIMENTAL DESIGNS

True experimental research is designed to control many of the threats to internal validity by incorporating two important features into the study design. First, true experimental designs have a *control group*, which consists of individuals who are part of the research study but do not actually receive the experimental treatment or HR intervention. This allows the researcher to rule out threats to internal validity such as history, maturation, and testing effects, since any differences between the experimental and control groups can be interpreted as being due to the experimental treatment or intervention. Since the experimental intervention is the only thing that distinguishes the experimental and control groups, any differences between them following an intervention can only be due to the intervention.

The second important feature of a true experiment is the use of *random assignment* of participants to experimental and control conditions. This ensures that the participants in all groups are equal on factors such as age, gender, education, work experience, and so on. These are factors that could influence the results due to a selection effect. However, to the extent that participants are randomly assigned, such differences should not exist and the groups can be considered to be equivalent. Thus, one can be more confident that any differences between the experimental and control groups are due to the experimental intervention rather than pre-existing differences (Cook & Campbell, 1976).

There are numerous examples of "true" experimental research designs in human resources. These include the pretest/post-test control group design, the pretest/post-test control group with multiple post-measures design, the after-only control group design, and the Solomon four-group design. As discussed in the box below, some of the earliest experimental designs in human resources research were conducted in the 1920s at the Western Electric Company and became famous for a phenomenon known as the **Hawthorne effect**.

THE HAWTHORNE STUDIES AND THE HAWTHORNE EFFECT

An important series of research studies in the history of human resource research was carried out over a span of fifteen years at the Western Electric Company. These are known collectively as the Hawthorne Studies because they were conducted at the Hawthorne plant of the company in the Chicago area. Numerous descriptions of these studies exist (e.g., Bramel & Friend, 1981; Parsons, 1974), and their significance is still being debated. These studies provide some important insights into the forces that shaped human resource research for years afterward.

In 1924, the National Research Council decided to support studies on worker productivity. In particular, it called for an examination of physical working conditions and the role of lighting in the workplace. After considering a number of offers from companies who wanted to co-sponsor the project, Western Electric Company was selected. At the time Western Electric provided the telephones and switching equipment needed by AT&T. The company had over 20 000 employees and was considered a progressive (even a worker-oriented) company. Management was pleased to have been chosen as the site for such important and nationally visible research.

One of the Hawthorne Studies involved actual experiments on illumination. It was organized by engineers in cooperation with an industry-supported group called the Committee on Industrial Lighting (Bramel & Friend, 1981). Following reasonable experimental design and procedures, workers were assigned to a control or experimental

THE HAWTHORNE STUDIES AND THE HAWTHORNE EFFECT (continued)

condition. Levels of illumination were varied (manipulated) for the latter groups in a systematic manner, and records of worker productivity were kept.

These studies turned out to be somewhat frustrating to those conducting them. It was found that worker productivity actually did improve. But output was unrelated to the levels of illumination experienced. Moreover, during the same periods, those in the control group also raised their productivity. Clearly, something other than physical working conditions was operating to affect productivity. But the researchers were unable to pinpoint what it was.

A second set of experiments was conducted from 1927 to 1930 on groups of workers in the relay assembly and mica-splitting areas. The former were responsible for making electromechanical switching devices called relays; the latter prepared materials (mica) for use. Two things were noteworthy about this series of studies. One was that workers were selected for participation and relocated in special areas of the plant. This meant they could be isolated from other workers not in the studies and could be more closely observed. It was thought that this would lead to "cleaner" (less ambiguous) results. Another feature of this second series was that they marked the earliest participation of social scientists, primarily Elton Mayo, in the Hawthorne Studies. The first study in this series was one of the most publicized.

Five women workers were exposed to varying combinations of starting and stopping times and work breaks. But once again the results were complex and confusing. It did not seem to make a great deal of difference what combination of starting times, pauses, and so on, was in effect. Worker productivity seemed to increase beyond levels typically found on the factory floor.

After some deliberation, the conclusion drawn by Mayo (and others) was that productivity increased largely as a result of the unique social conditions surrounding the workers in the experiment. It was felt that the special attention paid to them by the researchers, and their friendly style, was reciprocated by the workers in the study in the form of greater effort and productivity. Over the years, this effect, in which the phenomenon under study is inadvertently influenced by the process of studying it, is frequently referred to as the Hawthorne effect. In this case, the social scientists actually caused productivity to increase through their intrusive research methods. The participants (workers) apparently were not affected so much by the formal manipulations (e.g., work break schedule) as they were by the questions being asked of them about their feelings toward the work breaks.

It should be noted that other interpretations of the reasons for the results of this well-publicized study have been offered. For example, Parsons (1974) argues that the more explicit measurement of worker performance used by the psychologists provided new and valuable feedback to the workers and that it was this that spurred effort and productivity. Others, such as Bramel and Friend (1981), emphasize that the workers were responding to implied threats and pressures by management. In fact, they point out that some workers resisted the notion of higher productivity and were ultimately dismissed during the course of the experiment.

THE PRETEST/POST-TEST CONTROL GROUP DESIGN

The pretest/post-test control group design attempts to deal with potential threats to internal validity by having a separate group of participants who are in a control group and do not receive the experimental intervention but do provide the same measures as participants in the experimental group. This design is represented as follows:

Experimental group: Pre-measure ⟶ HR intervention ⟶ Post-measure
Control group: Pre-measure ⟶ Post-measure

The control group is not exposed to the HR intervention, but the investigator does obtain the same pre- and post-measures as those obtained from the experimental group. By comparing and contrasting the scores on these measures, one is in a better position to conclude that extraneous factors and threats to internal validity were not responsible for pretest/post-test changes. The expectation is that there will be an increase or improvement in scores (pretest to post-test) for those in the experimental group who receive the HR intervention but not for participants in the control group.

The pretest/post-test control group design allows the researcher to make a number of important comparisons in order to determine the effects of an HR intervention on the dependent measures. In particular, the following comparisons can be made:

1. *Between-group comparisons on pre-measures scores:* Comparison between the experimental and control groups' pre-measure scores to determine if the groups are equivalent. There should be no difference between the groups on pre-measure scores (e.g., job performance should be the same).

2. *Between-group comparisons on post-measures scores:* Comparison between the experimental and control groups post-measure scores to determine if the groups are different. The post-measure score for the experimental group should be better than the control group's (e.g., job performance should be higher).

3. *Within-group comparisons:* Comparisons between the pre- and post-measure scores for the control and experimental groups. The post-measure score for the experimental group should show some improvement compared with the pre-measure score. There should be no difference between the pre- and post-measure score for the control group (e.g., post-measure job performance is higher than pre-measure job performance for the experimental group but remains relatively the same for the control group).

Given the above pattern of results, we would be able to conclude that the HR intervention had the desired impact and is an effective intervention in terms of its effect on the dependent or outcomes variable(s) of interest.

An important component of experimental designs is that the employees in the experimental and control groups are from the same population. That is, they do not differ from each other in some important way that might affect the outcome in an unintended fashion (e.g., the experimental group might have a higher aptitude as a whole). As indicated above, the best way to ensure this is through random assignment. Operationally, this means that we might take the pool of eligible employees and divide them into the two groups according to some unbiased procedure. Those assigned to the control group would be presumed to be similar in most ways to those in the experimental group.

However, it is not always possible to randomly assign participants to experimental and control groups. This is especially the case when conducting field research in organizational settings, since the investigator must contend with numerous constraints that exist in organizations. In such circumstances it is important to use a matching strategy to create equivalent groups. Using such a strategy, the researcher identifies factors that might affect the variables being investigated (e.g., work experience might affect job performance), and then assign participants on the basis of such factors to ensure that the groups are matched on those variables deemed to be most relevant and important for a particular study. For example, if it is believed that work experience is related to an outcome variable such as job performance, then the investigator would want to match the groups to ensure that they are equivalent in terms of work experience.

One of the advantages of the pretest/post-test design is that it allows the investigator to check the assumption of unbiased or equal assignment to conditions. This can be done by comparing the experimental and control groups on the pre-measures. If assignments were done properly and if the groups are equally matched, they should be equivalent. When they are not equivalent it is important to control for these variables when analyzing the data.

THE PRETEST/POST-TEST CONTROL GROUP WITH MULTIPLE POST-MEASURES DESIGN

When evaluating the effects of HR interventions, it often takes time for a program to take effect. As well, the researcher may be interested in how long the effect of the intervention will persist. For example, a researcher is usually more interested in the effects of a training program after six months than after one week. In such situations, the investigator will want to obtain post-training measures over a period of time. Thus, it is important to know the effects of a training program in the short term (e.g., after one month) and the long term (e.g., after one year).

Latham and Frayne (1989) studied the long-term effects of self-management training to improve job attendance. They measured job attendance for experimental and control groups prior to training and three, six, and nine months after training had been completed. Thus, they were able to report on the persistence of the training effects, and found that trained employees had significantly better attendance records and reported fewer family and transportation problems that interfered with coming to work months after the program.

The pretest–post-test control group design with multiple post-measures is represented as follows:

Experimental group: Pre-measure ⟶ HR intervention ⟶ Post-measure 1, 2, 3 ...
Control group: Pre-measure ⟶ Post-measure 1, 2, 3 ...

The only difference between this design and the pretest–post-test control group design is that the post-measure data collection takes place at several times after an intervention.

One variation on this design is worth describing because it has practical as well as scientific implications for organizations. In general, it is usually a challenge to get organizations to support the extra effort that a control group design requires. Specifically, they have to agree to withhold an intervention such as training from some employees and yet authorize the time needed to obtain pre-measures and post-measures from them. From the workers' perspective, there is the imposition and inconvenience of participating in the measurement process as well as the question, "What's in it for me?"

An approach used by some investigators to deal with this problem is to design the intervention and the study in such a way that members of the control group ultimately receive the intervention. In the ideal format, all potential participants are identified and invited to the program with the understanding that, for some of them, the actual intervention will take place at a later time. Employees are then randomly assigned to the experimental or control group and the necessary pre- and post-measures are taken. After this, however, the employees in the control group receive the intervention and another set of measures is taken. Thus, all employees eventually receive the intervention. When diagrammed, this design has the following features:

Initial experimental group:
Pre-measure → HR intervention → Post-measure → Control → Second post-measure

Initial control group:
Pre-measure → Control → Pre-measure → HR intervention → Post-measure

This design was used by Basadur, Graen, and Scandura (1986) in a field experiment to test the effects of training on the attitudes of a group of engineers toward divergent thinking in problem solving. A second group served as the control group in the first part of the experiment and vice versa for the second part. A positive effect for training was detected by comparing the scores of the two groups after the training. The performance of the experimental group was higher after they received the training, and both groups were about the same after the control group also received the training. A version of this design also was used by Latham and Frayne (1989) in the study described above. The control group received the training in self-management subsequent to the nine-month measurement period.

THE AFTER-ONLY CONTROL GROUP DESIGN

The after-only control group design is an experiment in which measures are only taken after the intervention. This approach relies on an assumption that participants are, in fact, randomly assigned to experimental and control groups or that they have been carefully matched on relevant factors. This design can be represented as follows:

Experimental group: HR intervention $\longrightarrow$ Post-measure
Control group: $\longrightarrow$ Post-measure

This design is sometimes used when there is not enough time to obtain measures prior to the intervention. It might also be used if there is reason to believe that the completion of pre-measures would constitute a *treatment*, that is, would have its own effects (i.e., "testing" effects). For instance, asking managers questions about their management style might cause them to become sensitized to this aspect of their behaviour and, inadvertently, cause even those in a control group to change their style in some systematic way (e.g., to become more open or participative with their subordinates). As a result, the post-measure scores of the experimental and control group might be similar and lead to the conclusion that the intervention is not effective.

Thus, in such cases it is desirable not to include a pretest measure. However, the downside is that the researcher does not have a baseline measure and is therefore unable to determine if there has been a pre/post change. However, differences between the post-test measures are usually sufficient evidence of a significant experimental effect to the extent that the participants in the experimental and control groups have been randomly assigned and are equivalent.

THE SOLOMON FOUR-GROUP DESIGN

The Solomon four-group design is a complex design that is meant to reduce equiv-ocality as much as possible. Several experimental and control groups are created in order to measure and control for many of the threats to internal validity. This design can be outlined as follows:

Experimental group:	Pre-measure →	HR intervention →	Post-measure
Control group:	Pre-measure	→	Post-measure
Experimental group:		→ HR intervention →	Post-measure
Control group:		→	Post-measure

In effect, the Solomon four-group design is a combination of the pretest–post-test control group design and the after-only control group design. The logic of com-parisons as developed earlier would then be followed to infer the degree to which an intervention had an impact. The design allows the investigator to assess the extent to which pretesting has an effect for both the experimental and control group. For example, if there is a difference in the post-measure scores between the two control groups, there is the possibility that pretesting is having an effect.

In practice, however, the complexity of the Solomon four-group design makes it difficult to implement. The degree of management support needed is considerable, and large numbers of employees are also required. The patience of those not involved in the intervention (i.e., control group) must be great to tolerate all of the measurements taken. In addition, the results can be difficult to interpret if they do not turn out as expected.

◆ ◆ ◆
QUASI-EXPERIMENTAL DESIGNS

Very often in organizations there is a need to evaluate the effectiveness of a human resource program or intervention, but the conditions required for a true experimen-tal design are lacking (e.g., there may be too few participants involved, the investi-gator may not be able to create or manipulate the intervention, or random assignment to experimental conditions may not be feasible). In these circumstances, **quasi-experimental designs** are a reasonable alternative (Cook & Campbell, 1979; Cook et al., 1990).

The logic of quasi-experimental designs is to use whatever opportunities are available to rule out the most likely threats to internal validity. Quasi-experimental designs include the nonequivalent control group design, simple time-series designs, and multiple time-series designs.

NONEQUIVALENT CONTROL GROUP DESIGN

A hallmark of a true experimental design is the capacity to rule out plausible rival hypotheses, especially with regard to the internal validity of the study. As we have seen, a practical approach to dealing with possible biases due to individual differences (e.g., in ability, experience, motivation), group differences (norms, leadership), or organizational differences (structure, resources) is to randomly assign participants to research conditions. However, there are many instances in which this is not feasible. For example, there may be only certain groups available at a point in time to participate in a program or intervention. Thus, when data are gathered and analyzed, the investigator must be cautious because the results may be an artifact of the particular (nonrandomly selected) groups involved.

From a design point of view, the nonequivalent control group looks like some of the experimental designs already discussed. However, the difference is in the special care that the investigator must exert to address possible biases stemming from the use of intact or ad hoc groups.

For example, when conducting training research it is not always practical or possible to randomly assign individuals to experimental and control conditions. This could be due to shift work, work locations, group work, or other factors. In these circumstances it might only be possible to assign groups of individuals to conditions. The day shift might be assigned to a training intervention and the night shift to the control group. The potential problem in this type of study is that the groups might be different to begin with, and this might influence the results of the study.

In such circumstances, it is extremely important to gather data on variables that might influence the results of the study (such as gender, age, education, and work experience) before the study begins. The groups can then be compared on these variables to determine if there are any differences between them. If there are no such differences on these pre-measures, then the investigator can be more confident that any differences found on post-measures are due to the interventions and not to pre-existing differences between the experimental and control groups. Furthermore, the pre-measures can be statistically controlled for when analyzing the data to determine the effect of an intervention.

Careful analyses of the data generated from quasi-experimental designs are required to cope with what is essentially a lack of experimental control. Measurement and statistical analysis become important ways to deal with rival hypotheses and to ensure internal validity. For a good example of a quasi-experimental design, see the HR Research Today box on page 111.

SIMPLE TIME-SERIES DESIGN

A time-series design involves taking repeated measures of a dependent variable (e.g., job performance) before and after participants have received an intervention. The

HR RESEARCH TODAY

Effects of a Performance Appraisal System on Trust

Trust in organizations has become an important area of concern in recent years, especially in light of the evidence that employee trust in management has been on the decline. Because trust is related to important outcomes such as productivity and turnover, an important research issue is how to build trust in organizations.

In an interesting quasi-experimental study, Roger Mayer and James Davis investigated the effects of a new performance appraisal system on trust toward top management. Employees perceived the current appraisal system as unacceptable because it did not accurately measure their performance and there was no relationship between performance and rewards. The authors hypothesized that replacing the old system with a new system that is perceived as more acceptable would increase the level of trust toward management.

The study was conducted in a small, nonunion manufacturing firm. Before the new system was implemented, several measures of trust were collected from employees. Management then implemented the new performance appraisal system, which included a self-appraisal form for employees and required supervisors and employees to meet and discuss the ratings prior to the supervisor's final evaluation.

Some of the employees were assigned to receive the new system and others continued to receive the old system. Assignment to conditions was not random, but was based on the month of the year an employee was hired. This approximates random assignment to conditions because there is no reason to believe that the month of hire should have a systematic effect on the results. To verify this, the researchers conducted analyses of demographic variables that indicated that the two groups did not differ in terms of age, tenure, gender, or propensity to trust.

After nine months, another survey was administered. This allowed the researchers to test for changes over time and between the two groups. As noted by the researchers, this analysis helped to rule out a number of threats to internal validity.

The results indicated that employees who received the new system perceived it to be more accurate. As well, they showed a significant increase in trust toward top management over time compared with the control group. Comparisons between the two groups indicated that the experimental group had a higher level of trust after receiving the new appraisal system than the control, providing evidence that the increase in trust over time was due to the appraisal system.

Source: Based on Mayer, R.C., & Davis, J.H. (1999). The effect of the performance appraisal system on trust for management: A field quasi-experiment. *Journal of Applied Psychology, 84*, 123–136.

measures are obtained over a period of time that brackets their participation in a program. The actual interval between measures can be daily, weekly, or monthly. The time-series design works best where measurement occurs naturally or as part of operational reporting requirements (e.g., sales performance data gathered weekly). Otherwise, the measurement burden becomes oppressive and may produce testing effects. A simple time-series design can be represented as follows:

Pre-measure 1, 2, 3, 4, 5 $\longrightarrow$ HR intervention $\longrightarrow$ Post-measure 1, 2, 3, 4, 5

In this example, pre-measures are taken numerous times before and after the intervention. In using the data generated by this plan, we are looking for several things. First, we are looking for some relative stability or consistency in scores within the pre- and post-event measurement sets. This provides some insight into the extent to which extraneous forces are affecting scores. Assuming that we believe in the value of the intervention, we would expect to see some sort of discontinuity or noticeable shift in scores just after the intervention. The pattern of data revealed in Figure 4.1 would appear to support the contention that a training program does have an impact. This can be gleaned from the fact that there is relative stability of performance within the pre-measurement period and then a noticeable upward shift in scores that coincides with the training intervention. Thus, a strong case can be made that the sudden upward shift that occurred only at the time of the training intervention is in fact due to the training program and not some extraneous factor(s).

A good example of this type of study was conducted by Banker, Field, Schroeder, and Sinha (1996) to examine the impact of work teams on manufacturing performance over a 21-month period during which time a plant assembly line was converted to high-performance work teams. Measures of labour productivity (i.e., the ratio of the number of units produced to total production) were taken on a monthly basis and measures of quality (i.e., percentage of total units produced that were defective) were collected on a weekly basis before and after the formation of teams. The results indicated that there was no trend in the manufacturing defect rate prior to the formation of teams; however, in the weeks following team formation there was a significant reduction in the defect rate. As well, there was no change in labour productivity prior to team formation, and a significant improvement in the weeks following the formation of teams. These results are consistent with the pattern of data shown in Figure 4.1. (See Chapter 14 for a more detailed discussion of this study.)

MULTIPLE TIME-SERIES DESIGN

The multiple time-series design provides an extra margin of confidence over the simple time-series design by including data from individuals not involved in an intervention and are control participants. Thus, we would hope that the scores of the

FIGURE 4.1 Idealized Pattern of Data of a Time-Series Design

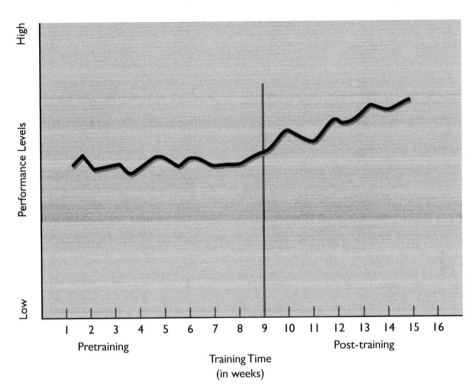

control group demonstrate some consistency across both the pre-measurement and post-measurement periods. The multiple time-series design can be represented as follows:

Group 1: Pre-measure 1, 2, 3, 4, 5 ⟶ HR intervention ⟶ Post-measure 1, 2, 3, 4, 5
Group 2: Pre-measure 1, 2, 3, 4, 5 ⟶ Post-measure 1, 2, 3, 4, 5

In general, time-series designs are effective in dealing with history as a threat to internal validity. Because of their temporal nature, they also help us get at the direction of the "causal arrow" as well. However, the emphasis on measurement also presents some liabilities. As mentioned, repeated measurements may create unintended testing effects. Similarly, if data are gathered through direct observations or self-reports and are taken over long intervals, this increases the likelihood of instrumentation problems (Blackburn, 1987). Even archival measures may be affected when the period of time involved is long. Newer scales or methods for record keeping may come into being, calling into question the comparability of data sets.

◆◆◆
ETHICAL ISSUES IN EXPERIMENTAL RESEARCH

While true experimental research designs provide the best means to test the causal effects of human resource interventions, there are many ethical concerns facing the researcher who conducts experimental research. Moreover, as one might imagine, the issues facing a researcher will vary depending on whether the research is to be carried out in a laboratory or in an actual organizational setting. Good studies are much harder to conduct in organizations, requiring at times extraordinary arrangements. Some of these imply difficult ethical choices (Cook & Campbell, 1976).

Investigators in university settings usually subscribe to professional norms regarding the treatment of participants in research. Moreover, they usually have institutional requirements for protecting the welfare of human subjects (Gardner, 1978).

It is not that such review procedures are nonexistent in business organizations, but that they are less inclusive and salient. Usually, organization-conducted research that is likely to put individuals in physical danger will be the object of close scrutiny. But most often research in human resources is not likely to be of this type. This places a greater burden on the investigator to attend to and resolve any ethical dilemmas associated with experimentation involving employees. Whether the investigator is a manager, consultant, or staff researcher, personal or professional values must be invoked and brought to bear on choices among design and procedure options (some of which may imply trade-offs regarding risk, costs, and the quality of the data that will be obtained). Many of these decisions will have to be made privately and without the benefit of external support.

These comments will serve as a backdrop for the set of issues selected for treatment in this section. The potential range of ethical concerns as they relate to experimental research that could be addressed is enormous. Four of the most important include participants' freedom of choice to participate, the right to receive beneficial interventions, the deception of participants, and the pressure to produce desirable research findings.

FREEDOM TO CHOOSE

It is unethical to force individuals to participate in research. They must have the opportunity to decline participation in a research project. A variation on this issue involves the right to reject assignment to a particular treatment or experimental condition. Professional ethics dictate that these options be open to people. Moreover, most social scientists place high value on the process of *informed consent*, whereby individuals not only know that they are to be in a study but also are aware of the nature of the research and what risks (if any) might be involved. Yet for an investigator to do these things might compromise the validity of the study or violate norms of the organization.

It should be recalled that random selection and random assignment are powerful strategies for dealing with or mitigating the effects of many biases or threats to internal validity. As pointed out, however, if potential participants can choose to get involved there is the very real possibility of an unknown bias entering into the study. This puts many researchers in a dilemma.

Nonetheless, it is imperative that people be given adequate information in order to have informed consent. However, other things should be done to assess and minimize any potential bias. First, as part of the informed consent procedures, potential participants should be told that, as a result of their involvement, they may or may not be in what we would call the experimental condition. That is, by volunteering they realize that investigator control over assignment to treatments will be retained. Thus, threats to internal validity may be minimized. It is also important that careful measurements be taken in order to detect what, if any, bias occurred as a result of the general tendency to volunteer or not to volunteer under these circumstances (Rosenthal & Rosnow, 1984). To the extent possible, relevant attributes of nonparticipants and participants (e.g., age, experience, job tenure) must be obtained, indexed, and compared. While post-study discovery of a sample bias cannot change the results, at a minimum it should condition the researcher's claims of generalizability. At most, it may call for additional data gathering.

INTERVENTIONS AS AMELIORATIVE TREATMENTS

There are circumstances in which the proposed research involves some intervention or treatment that is hypothesized to have beneficial effects for those who receive it. Moreover, this is widely believed by potential participants to be the case. For example, participation in a new training and development program, job redesign, attending an assessment centre, and so forth, are examples of human resource interventions that many employees would find desirable. Thus, the researcher may be under tremendous pressure to allow all who wish to be involved the same treatment. And yet the researcher, in order to make strong inference, usually will require that some individuals be held out as a control group. Wortman, Hendricks, and Hillis (1976) point out how such pressures become exaggerated when both the beneficial nature of the intervention and the awareness of being in a control group are discovered by accident.

Cook and Campbell (1976) suggest that assignment to attractive treatments or interventions may be carried out more easily under certain circumstances:

1. When demand outstrips supply, there is usually a credible justification for some fair allocation mechanism (e.g., lottery).

2. When interventions cannot be delivered to all units at once, one might argue for a staged introduction.

3. When experimental units can be spatially and administratively separated, it may be feasible to justify withholding treatments.

While many of these alternatives may work, the investigator must still be sensitive to the possibility that delayed treatment may be one that is, in effect, denied. For example, an employee development intervention that takes some time to introduce and evaluate effectively forecloses on the opportunities of a whole group of cohort members who will not have the benefit of the experience at that particular (and possibly crucial) time in their careers.

DECEPTION

It has been pointed out that it is an apparent paradox that experimental realism can be achieved through falsehood (Aronson, Brewer, & Carlsmith, 1985). In fact, it is not uncommon to see deception used in research, especially on topics of a social-psychological nature conducted in a laboratory. This has raised numerous ethical and methodological concerns (Kelman, 1967; Miller, 1972). For example, a researcher might wish to investigate the effects of failure on attitudes and behaviour. Instead of creating conditions that will actually produce failure on a task, he or she uses a procedure that will lead the participants to *believe* that they have failed (regardless of actual levels of performance). There are times when the investigator believes that deception is the most effective way to deal with the need for experimental control.

Deception (especially misleading or misinforming the subject, not just withholding information) should only be considered as a last resort. The investigator has an obligation to establish that alternatives (e.g., simulations [Klimoski, 1978] or role-playing [Cooper, 1976; Miller, 1972]) are not feasible or appropriate. If deception is used, it is imperative that, once the experimental session is over, the participants be carefully debriefed. This involves a description of what actually occurred in the study and why deception was involved. A number of writers have stressed how important this phase of experimental research is to both the participant and to the investigator (Fromkin & Streufert, 1976; Holmes, 1976; Tesch, 1977).

PRESSURE TO PRODUCE FINDINGS

Although we would like to think otherwise, deliberate bias or fraud in scientific endeavours does occur. There are many personal and institutional pressures operating on researchers to produce results that support a particular point of view. While this is unfortunate, the nature of research on human resource interventions has its own special pitfalls. In particular, the way that HR interventions come about may set up additional pressures to report a preferred outcome of research.

Boehm (1980) implies that the investigator doing research in organizations often is the one responsible for developing, promoting, and implementing the intervention in question in the first place. In order to get top management to accept and underwrite the expenses of a program (e.g., a large-scale training effort), the researcher often has to argue that the intervention will indeed have a desirable impact, even in the face of limited evidence. Moreover, when the research is done, the "real world" investigator then must be concerned with selling the results to decision makers. These realities hardly make for a disinterested position. Thus, it is no wonder that the systematic evaluation of the most common form of HR intervention—training— is rarely carried out (Sarri, Johnson, McLaughlin, & Zimmerle, 1988). Unfortunately, such forces create the potential for setting up weak or biased evaluation designs.

Quite clearly, it will take a strong sense of professional integrity, personal credibility, and skill to promote the notion of careful and systematic evaluation of human resource interventions in organizational settings. This usually means working with top management to create an appreciation for differences in the quality of the data (and, hence, of decisions) associated with weak versus strong designs. It also places an obligation on the organizational investigator to be flexible and resourceful in coming up with approaches to evaluation that will generate data of reasonable quality given very real constraints on resources or time. In particular, he or she should pay considerable attention to the potential of some of the quasi-experimental designs outlined in this chapter. They represent reasonable alternatives. Remember, there is no one best design. Each circumstance calls for informed judgment. The technology exists, but the investigator needs to be motivated to search for a workable solution.

◆ ◆ ◆
SUMMARY

This chapter has reviewed many of the research methods used to study the causal effects of human resource interventions. There are numerous approaches that may be used, depending on the resources available and the level of certainty regarding causal inferences required. The main difference between true experiments and other study designs has to do with internal validity. True experiments allow for strong inference because the investigator can control most (but not all) threats to internal validity through the direct creation or manipulation of the independent variable(s) and the random assignment of participants to conditions. Thus, the researcher has many choices to make. It is hoped that the material presented in this chapter will allow the reader to make these choices in a more informed manner. Similarly, those who are responsible for supporting or evaluating research also should find this chapter helpful. The ideas presented can be used as checkpoints or benchmarks with which to critically review proposed or completed studies.

Definitions

Construct validity of an experiment   The degree to which the manipulated variable adequately captures or represents the conditions of interest.

Control condition   Research participants who do not receive the experimental manipulation or treatment.

Experimental research   When a variable is changed or manipulated in a controlled situation in order to test its effect on other variables.

Field experiment   An experiment that takes place in an actual setting such as an organizational setting.

Hawthorne effect   When there is some effect on participants of an experiment that is due to some factor other than the independent or manipulated variable.

Internal validity   Refers to the extent to which the results of an experiment can unambiguously be explained by an experimental manipulation or intervention rather than by alternative factors.

Laboratory experiment   An experiment that takes place in a setting that has been created for the purpose of conducting research.

Monomethod bias   Occurs when a single method or approach has been used to study the variables of interest, as opposed to multiple approaches and methods.

Nonexperimental research designs   Research designs that are considered to be weak in terms of providing a basis for making strong causal arguments because they lack a control group and random assignment.

Quasi-experimental designs   Research designs that are lacking a control group or random assignment to conditions.

True experimental designs   True experiments are considered to be the strongest for making causal inferences because they include a control group and random assignment to conditions.

EXERCISES

1. Select an HRM topic of interest to you, and pose a series of questions that you would be interested in knowing the answers to (e.g., Is self-esteem related to job performance?). Then state several testable hypotheses based on your questions, and explain how you could test your hypotheses by conducting experimental research. Do you think that this would be a good research design to test your hypotheses? What are the advantages and disadvantages?

2. Henry Kaper had completed a course on training evaluation just in time to prepare for an evaluation study on a new training program about to be implemented in his organization. The

training program was very expensive to develop and the director of human resources wanted to make sure that the program was properly evaluated. This appeared to be a relatively straightforward task for Henry now that he was well informed about experimental research designs. He would simply gather data from a training group and a control group before and after training and then compare the mean differ-ences between the groups. Unfortunately, top management insisted on training all employees as soon as possible and would not allow a control group that did not receive the training.

Now Henry wasn't so sure about what to do. What advice would you give him about how to evaluate the training program without a control group?

RUNNING CASE: THE VP OF HUMAN RESOURCES—PART 3

Describe how you can conduct experimental research to demonstrate the value-added of the HRM department and its programs to the organization. Be sure to discuss how you will design your study and how you will collect your data. Based on your answer to the above, would you use an experimental design in order to demonstrate the value-added of HRM to your organization? What are the advantages and disadvantages of doing so?

References

Aronson, E., Brewer, M., & Carlsmith, J.M. (1985). Experimentation in social psychology. In G. Lindsey & E. Aronson (Eds.), *The handbook of social psychology* (3rd ed.). New York: Random House.

Banker, R.D., Field, J.M., Schroeder, R.G., & Sinha, K.K. (1996). Impact of work teams on manufacturing performance: A longitudinal field study. *Academy of Management Journal, 39*, 867–890.

Basadur, M., Graen, G.B., & Scandura, T.A. (1986). Training effects on attitudes toward divergent thinking among manufacturing engineers. *Journal of Applied Psychology, 71*, 612–617.

Blackburn, R.S. (1987). Experimental design in organizational settings. In J.W. Lorsch (Ed.), *Handbook of organizational behavior*. Englewood Cliffs, NJ: Prentice-Hall.

Boehm, V.R. (1980). Research in the "real-world"—A conceptual model. *Personnel Psychology, 33*, 495–504.

Bramel, D., & Friend, R. (1981). Hawthorne, the myth of the docile worker and class bias in psychology. *American Psychologist, 36*, 867–878.

Cook, T.D., & Campbell, D.T. (1976). The design and conduct of quasi-experiments and true experiments in field settings. In M.D. Dunnette (Ed.), *Handbook of industrial and organizational psychology*. New York: Rand McNally.

Cook, T.D., & Campbell, D.T. (1979). *Quasi experimentations: Design and analysis for field settings*. Chicago, IL: Rand McNally.

Cook, T.D., Campbell, D.T., & Peracchio, L. (1990). Quasi experimentation. In M.D. Dunnette & L.M. Hough (Eds.), *Handbook of industrial and organizational psychology*, vol. 1 (2nd ed., pp. 491–576). Palo Alto, CA: Consulting Psychologists Press, Inc.

Cooper, J. (1976). Deception and role playing: On telling the good guys from the bad guys. *American Psychology, 31*, 605–610.

Fromkin, H.L., & Streufert, S. (1976). Laboratory experimentation. In M.D. Dunnette (Ed.), *Handbook of industrial and organizational psychology*. Chicago, IL: Rand McNally.

Gardner, G.T. (1978). Effects of federal human subjects regulations on data obtained in environmental stress research. *Journal of Personality and Social Psychology, 36*, 628–634.

Haccoun, R.R., & Hamtiaux, T. (1994). Optimizing knowledge tests for inferring learning acquisition levels in single group training evaluation designs: The internal referencing strategy. *Personnel Psychology, 47*, 593–604.

Holmes, D.S. (1976). Debriefing after psychological experiments: Effectiveness of post-deception dehoaxing. *American Psychologist, 31*, 858–867.

Kelman, H.C. (1967). Human use of human subjects: The problem of deception in social psychological experiments. *Psychological Bulletin, 22*, 1–11.

Klimoski, R.J. (1978). Simulation methodologies in experimental research on negotiation by representatives. *Journal of Conflict Resolution, 22*, 61–77.

Latham, G.P., & Frayne, C.A. (1989). Self-management training for increasing job attendance:

A followup and replication. *Journal of Applied Psychology, 74*, 411–416.

Mayer, R.C., & Davis, J.H. (1999). The effect of the performance appraisal system on trust for management: A field quasi-experiment. *Journal of Applied Psychology, 84*, 123–136.

Miller, A.G. (1972). Role playing: An alternative to deception? *American Psychologist, 27*, 623–636.

Olian, J. D. (1986). Staffing. In E.A. Locke (Ed.), *Generalizing from laboratory to field settings* (pp. 13–42). Lexington, MA: Heath.

Parsons, H.M. (1974). What happened at Hawthorne? *Science, 183*, 922–932.

Rosenthal, R. (1967). *Experimenter effects in behavioral research*. New York: Appleton-Century-Crofts.

Rosenthal, R., & Rosnow, R. (1984). *Essentials of behavioral research*. New York: McGraw-Hill.

Sackett, P.R., T.D., & Larson, J.R., Jr. (1990). Research strategies and tactics in industrial and organizational psychology. In M.D. Dunnette & L.M. Hough (Ed.), *Handbook of industrial and organizational psychology*, vol. 1 (2nd ed., pp. 419–489). Palo Alto, CA: Consulting Psychologists Press, Inc.

Sarri, L.M., Johnson, T.R., McLaughlin, S.D., & Zimmerle, D.M. (1988). A survey of management training and education practices in U.S. companies. *Personnel Psychology, 41*, 731–743.

Tesch, F.E. (1977). Debriefing research participants: Though this be method there is madness to it. *Journal of Personality and Social Psychology, 35*, 217–224.

Wortman, C.B., Hendricks, M., & Hillis, J.W. (1976). Factors affecting participant reactions to random assignment in ameliorative social programs. *Journal of Personality and Social Psychology, 33*, 256–266.

5

Qualitative
Research Designs

◆ ◆ ◆
INTRODUCTION

In addition to survey and experimental research designs, we can also learn to better understand the nature and functioning of organizations and human resource policy and practices through careful descriptive and analytic work. To this end, this chapter reviews qualitative research designs such as observation, interviews, and archival techniques and methods. These methods have a special place in descriptive research.

After reading this chapter, you should be able to:

■ Understand the uses of qualitative research designs, and how this approach to research differs from others.

■ Understand the assumptions and philosophy that underlie qualitative research.

■ Discuss the general purposes of qualitative research.

■ Understand how to use observation, interviews, and archival data.

■ Describe the advantages and disadvantages of qualitative research.

■ Understand the ethical issues involved in conducting qualitative research, and what actions can be taken to maintain ethical standards.

Individuals who seek to understand the nature of organizations or to learn about the effects of human resource policies and practices may do so through the use of any number of techniques. They might also follow a wide variety of plans or designs for gathering the desired information. This chapter emphasizes the goal of careful and complete description of key organizational phenomena by following a relatively uncomplicated research plan with the emphasis on three powerful and useful data gathering techniques: observation, interviews, and archival analysis. Taken together, these constitute the essential tools of what has been called **qualitative research**.

It should be made clear that qualitative research is more of an approach than a particular design or set of techniques, although these are admittedly difficult to separate in practice. It is an "umbrella" phrase that covers "an array of interpretive techniques which seek to describe, decode, translate, and otherwise come to terms with the meaning of naturally occurring phenomena in the social world" (Van Maanen, 1979, p. 520). "Doing description" is therefore the fundamental act of qualitative research.

Qualitative research also implies a set of assumptions regarding the essential nature of scientific inquiry itself and its potential for discovering truths about organizational life. While the notion that research methods and assumptions are closely linked has been examined in previous chapters, it turns out to be particularly salient in the domain of qualitative research. And indeed, some of these assumptions are at the heart of disagreements as to how and when to make use of the approach. Thus it seems reasonable to start this chapter by discussing the underlying philosophy of qualitative research, before describing the major techniques and applications.

◆ ◆ ◆
ASSUMPTIONS UNDERLYING QUALITATIVE RESEARCH

Both proponents and critics tend to contrast qualitative and quantitative research to make their points. But as Morgan and Smircich (1980) point out, it is inappropriate to argue in the abstract for one or the other. Rather, the choice and appropriateness of method really depend on what phenomena you are trying to understand and on beliefs about how new knowledge can best be acquired. It turns out that choice of method is also related to assumptions about human nature as well.

Evered and Louis (1981) describe qualitative research as conducting organizational research from the "inside." In contrast to the usual natural science paradigm, this involves taking an active or participative role in the behaviour to be investigated. Usually, this means getting involved with the organization or the people you want to study. Thus, we come to know our subject by being there or being involved experientially. We gain a personal knowledge this way. It also implies that we approach a situation or research question with an open mind and with few a priori assumptions. In practice, proponents of this view argue that our hypotheses and the ways we categorize information should arise from our experience rather than be proposed in detail ahead of time.

As qualitative researchers, our goals might be different as well. Traditional inquiry from the outside stresses the discovery of generalized statements that are universally applicable. In contrast, inquiry from the inside is directed toward creating a complete description of the specific case. The researcher is seeking a rich appreciation for the context and the conditions operating at that point in time. As Mintzberg (1979) puts it, "we should ask ourselves whether we are better off to have each study 100 organizations, giving us superficial data on ten thousand, or each study one, giving us in-depth data on one hundred" (pp. 583–584). For the qualitative researcher, the answer is clear. Thus, as a rule, qualitative studies typically involve small samples of individuals, groups, or organizations.

The focus on small samples has several implications. As noted, the result may be greater insight into the particular case. On the other hand, small samples also imply a reduced capacity to detect valid but subtle phenomena. One other implication of using small numbers is limited generalizability. Even when the investigator has taken great pains to select individuals, groups, or organizations that are felt to be representative of the population of interest (e.g., managers or schools), there is a low probability that this really will be the case. This is another way of saying that the small sample study will have low external validity.

One other feature of inquiry from the inside is the willingness of the investigator to acknowledge the role of personal values in the research product. With the typical data-gathering methods used in qualitative research, it is difficult to separate the person from the process. In a sense, like the clinician, the investigator becomes the research tool. Frequently, then, it is not unusual to see levels of skill, personal assumptions, expectations, and biases acknowledged openly at the outset by the qualitative researcher, in order to allow the reader of the research to make an informed decision regarding the likely quality of the data.

To summarize, the person employing a qualitative approach seeks an in-depth and rich description of specific cases based on the belief that this is the best way to know about some aspect of organizational life. He or she approaches the task with the realization that the data of interest must be generated from the participants' point of view because it is the subjective interpretation of reality that accounts for much of the variation in the phenomenon of interest.

◆ ◆ ◆
GENERAL PURPOSES OF QUALITATIVE RESEARCH

It has been noted that one might want to conduct qualitative research in order to develop a deeper and more descriptive understanding of some phenomenon. However, it seems useful to be somewhat more explicit and systematic about the general purposes of conducting qualitative research in human resources. An investigator might wish to use a qualitative approach for any of the following purposes:

1. *To gain familiarity or insights.* The researcher may seek to gain a better understanding of a phenomenon. This may be in an entirely new area of interest, or it could reflect a desire to increase the level of specificity or precision of existing knowledge. The latter conditions might exist for the individual who is attempting to formulate a research problem or specific hypotheses.

2. *Description.* The goal might be to accurately portray the characteristics of a particular individual, situation, or group. The investigator initially may have no idea, hypothesis, or theory about the nature of these characteristics. He or she enters into the activity with few preconceived notions about the phenomenon of interest. However, in practice, most of the time the investigator is already knowl-

edgeable regarding the general issues involved and can specify certain domains or variables of interest at the outset.

3. *Frequency.* The investigator may be interested in the frequency with which something does or does not occur. This also may involve the detection of patterns of co-variation among factors or variables. When these studies are done with no real preconceived notions, the work is considered exploratory and/or purely descriptive. With hypotheses in mind, the investigator shifts the activity into the domain of theory or hypothesis testing. For example, a current theory may assert that something does not or cannot occur (with or without the presence of other variables). A qualitative study may uncover one or more nonconforming cases, thus weakening the credibility of the theory.

4. *Causal relationships.* The focus of this chapter is on the use of methods in preliminary or exploratory research work. However, a given technique (e.g., observation) may be adapted to or made suitable for the generation of quantitative data. These data, in turn, provide the basis for the testing of theories or models of phenomena involving cause-and-effect relationships (Martinko & Gardner, 1985).

So far in this chapter, reference has been made to techniques used by qualitative researchers. In the following sections, a set of those techniques that are used widely will be discussed in detail. Particular applications to human resources will also be described. Keep in mind that any of the methods described can also be used, with modification, in research of more complex designs (e.g., experiments), and with alternative goals in mind (e.g., theory testing). They are being introduced here because they have been found to be particularly useful for describing organizations and organizational life.

◆ ◆ ◆

SYSTEMATIC OBSERVATION

While all of us have the occasion to observe and comment on human nature, scientific direct observation has several features that distinguish it from casual observation. Bickman (1976) states that observation is scientific when it serves a formulated research purpose, is planned systematically, is recorded systematically, and is subjected to certain checks and controls for quality. To put it another way, Weick (1968, p. 360) describes scientific observation as "involving the selection, provocation, recording and encoding that set of behaviours and settings concerning organizations 'in situ' consistent with aims."

While many fields of social science have made use of observational methods (psychology, economics, organizational studies), it has been most refined by sociologists and anthropologists. When used by the latter it is sometimes referred to as part of (along with informant interviewing) the ethnographic method (Sanday, 1979).

When applied to cultural anthropology, the goal of systematic observation has been to obtain a complete understanding of a given group or society. Usually this includes one or more of the following objectives: (1) identifying the general themes of the culture, with reference to the way that functions get fulfilled (e.g., socialization of new members); (2) developing an appreciation of the native's point of view, including standards of thought and interpretation; and (3) gathering data in preselected categories of behaviour (Sanday, 1979). The researcher is usually most interested in description, but also seeks to gain some level of understanding as well. Similar approaches have been used to study the culture of organizations (Rousseau, 1990).

To be effective in the ethnographic method, the field worker must be trained in the method and, armed with notebooks, a tape recorder, and even a camera, must be prepared for a lengthy stay in the setting of interest. In practice, the specifics of the effort will depend on the personal tastes of the researcher and the goal involved, whether it be to focus on the whole, the meaning, or the particular behaviours of culture to be studied.

When done well, systematic observation can provide insights regarding not only what occurred, but also the time and duration of phenomena. It may uncover the nature of the relationships of the various parts to the whole, and characterize interpersonal and group processes over time. As pointed out earlier, it is sufficiently flexible to allow for the discovery of the unanticipated and the development of new insights. It can also be quantified. In short, systematic observation allows the researcher to get at the "deep structure" of person and systems properties along with the consequences of their interaction (Light, 1979).

One of the most often cited efforts in organizational research—the so-called Hawthorne Studies—made heavy use of systematic observation. In particular, as noted in Chapter 4, the third series of studies conducted at the Hawthorne works of the Western Electric Company in Chicago during the period of 1931–32 produced great insights into the nature of social relationships in the workplace (Baritz, 1960; Bramel & Friend, 1981). In these studies, investigators from Harvard University spent many hours watching teams of men in the Bank Wiring Room assemble telephone switching equipment, in an effort to better understand what could account for levels of productivity.

At the time of this investigation, managers and researchers had a view of the worker and worker performance that emphasized financial incentives. In the case of the Bank Wiring Room, because the work involved five to seven men pulling together a single, large switching device, the company had instituted a group bonus plan to spur production. Under this payment plan, the greater the output (in terms of the number of switches completed), the more money would be placed into lump-sum payments to be divided equally among team members. This bonus money would be over and above the payment of any hourly wage.

Despite the potential for some fairly large bonuses, however, the output of the work groups was remarkably consistent. They typically made between one and two switching assemblies a day. Mayo, Warner, and their colleagues from Harvard chose to study these groups to see what could be learned about this phenomenon. Using the method of observation, they uncovered a great deal. Over time, the researchers discovered that a complex network of social relationships actually controlled a large amount of work group behaviour. Most startling was the way groups seemed to regulate production. Individuals were found not working as hard as they could, and performing at some level that was felt by the employees to be a "fair day's work." Group members, especially informal leaders, used a variety of techniques (from teasing to social ostracism) to prevent deviation from the group's expectations with regard to performance. It also seemed clear that this informal influence process protected the work group from management pressure for higher production. If one team (or individual) demonstrated extraordinary output during any one period of time, management would be certain to demand it of everyone.

◆◆◆
TYPES OF OBSERVATION

Bickman (1976) distinguishes between situations in which the observer interacts with the subjects of study versus situations in which the observer is hidden or concealed. The researcher can act as a full participant, a **participant observer**, or strictly as observer, or **nonparticipant observer**. Bickman also suggests that the researcher may adopt different attitudes with regard to involvement. At an extreme, he or she may attempt to affect the situation in order to better study the phenomenon of interest.

The issue of concealment relates to concerns for potential reactivity, or what Weick (1968) has termed observer interference. In many cases, the actual or presumed presence of the researcher will change a subject's behaviour. Sometimes this effect is transitory. For example, in the Hawthorne Studies, it took some time before the investigators came to be trusted, and for the work groups to reveal their normal routines. More often, unconcealed direct observation continues to produce atypical behaviour.

Johnson and Bolstad (1973) identified several factors that influence the effects of reactivity—among them, the level of conspicuousness in the observation, the personal characteristics of the individuals being studied, and specific features of the observer (e.g., status). Most important, the purposes of the observation (real or imagined on the part of the subject) will affect the levels of anxiety or apprehension felt by those under scrutiny. To the extent that the latter perceive potential harm (e.g., loss of esteem) as a consequence of being studied by someone, one may expect efforts at self-protection in the form of behaviour change. Unless the investigator is actually interested in studying the effects of being observed, the resultant changed behaviour creates problems for valid inference.

As a participant observer, the researcher is involved in organization life in some regular way. Thus, he or she has a job to do or a role to enact while being an observer. Van Maanen (1975), for example, functioned as a police officer the entire time he was researching the socialization of new recruits. In participant observation, occupying a particular role is felt to give the researcher special insights. Clearly, it places special demands on a person as well.

One of the central issues related to participative observation is the extent to which the people being studied are aware of the presence of the investigator. At one extreme, this fact may be completely hidden. A researcher, somewhat like an espionage agent under deep cover, gains entry into the organization undetected. In fact, this may be more common in novels than in social science research (although there are some exceptions). A more common model is for the researcher to make arrangements with key people in an organization (e.g., a senior manager) to carry out a study, with a general announcement being made as to the project's existence and the methods involved. But this arrangement does not ensure that particular employees under study are aware of their situation when they are actually in a conversation with the investigator. Such announcements can easily be forgotten. Thus, unless the researcher clarifies his or her role at the point of contact, the employees involved may remain ignorant of their role as subjects. Van Maanen (1979) describes how difficult it was building a trust relationship with co-workers in order to avoid being misled by presentational data, while still reminding subjects in subtle ways that they were the objects of his research. Moreover, he found it hard to keep his roles as co-worker and investigator separate.

This last point raises aspects of another dimension of the observation technique that Bickman (1976) labels as intervention. By this he means both the intentional and unintentional ways in which the investigator can affect the processes under study. As a hidden or *nonparticipant* observer, the hope is that there will be minimal effects from the act of observation. As a participative observer, this is most difficult to guarantee. Being an actor in the setting, the investigator is bound to have some effect. On the other hand, there are times when the researcher desires to stimulate or provoke the system in order to better understand certain dynamics. For example, the researcher may sit in certain proximity to others in a park or a coffee shop to observe their reactions. Or he/she may volunteer to help out the individuals who are to be studied.

Salancik (1979) describes and advocates what he calls *field stimulations*, in which the researcher "makes things happen" and then observes how the people and the system operate under these circumstances. The kinds of things he refers to include sending memos to key people in organizations, simulating a need for help, or attempting to negotiate the price of a loaf of bread at a supermarket. He argues that this is a legitimate way to gain insight into organizations without having to get their permission to do so. He implies that this technique tends to reduce a bias that has crept into organizational studies in which findings were based on data from only those companies who were willing to be scrutinized. He does acknowledge, however, that there are legal and ethical parameters to this approach.

◆ ◆ ◆
METHODS OF OBSERVATION

There are a number of specific activities associated with carrying out observations. However, it is useful to distinguish between relatively unstructured versus structured approaches. In general, the unstructured approach is a hallmark of the qualitative researcher. As indicated, the goal of many investigators is to obtain a rich, in-depth description of an organization, its people, or one or more aspects of its functioning. In **unstructured observation** a high degree of contact with the people or entities of interest is presumed. The investigator starts out with a set of tentative hypotheses and uses these to guide how, when, where, and about whom observations are conducted, while being open to new directions.

Observations of this sort are usually recorded in field notes. Whenever possible, this would be done at the time of an event of interest. When taking notes would be intrusive physically, skill in mental note-taking becomes invaluable. In any event, ad hoc material must be reviewed daily and placed into a more systematic form. Thus, unstructured observation can still be systematic.

The content of field notes will be related to the research question involved. However, Bickman (1976), Bouchard (1976), and Weick (1968) would argue that field notes should include a description of the participants involved, the setting, the apparent purpose of the event/exchange, the activities or social behaviour, and the frequency or duration of events.

The notes should be detailed and concrete. They should reflect what occurred with minimal inferences by the observer. They may, however, make reference to the observer's feelings at the time, perhaps to indicate what was surprising or unexpected, or to reveal any potential bias created by his or her mood. Good field notes often include quotations. To the extent that the notes "can communicate the rules for proper and predictable conduct as judged by the people studied," the observer has produced a successful product (Sanday, 1979, p. 529).

While the emphasis of this chapter is on description and on the theory-generation goals of qualitative research, direct observation as a method is, more often than not, highly structured and systematic. It holds an important position in almost all areas of social science investigation. In fact, structured observation is usually conducted in such a manner as to produce data suitable for quantitative analysis. Because it is so widespread, this approach to direct observation will be described in some detail.

Structured observation is based on a clearly articulated definition of the important features of the people, behaviour, or setting as seen by the investigator. These, in turn, may derive from extensive prior experience, from a particular theory, or from past empirical research. To put it another way, the researcher has a good idea going into the study of whom to talk to, when to take observations, and what should be recorded. Just as importantly, the researcher also is relatively sure of what can be ignored (Smith, 1981).

The potential designated attributes of features to be attended to are enormous. Moreover, there are no taxonomies or standardized lists of behaviours, actions, and so on, to guide the investigator. Ultimately, these will relate to the goals of the research. However, most of the time the recording activity will include rating or coding some aspect of the following (Smith, 1981):

1. *Form.* This is defined as the features of interest.
2. *Duration.* This is defined as the length of time the form lasts.
3. *Frequency.* This is defined as the number of times an event occurs (occasionally indexed in terms of rate of occurrence).
4. *Antecedent/consequent phenomena.* This is defined as what happens before or after the target event.

In addition, investigators interested in studying some aspect of organizations might tend to focus on the following: (1) task-relevant behaviours (including the sequence involved), (2) tools and technology used, (3) manifestations of affect/emotion, (4) levels of effectiveness, and (5) behaviours on which to base inferences regarding traits or qualities.

In the area of work measurement, structured observations are used to generate data for such practical purposes as work design, staffing levels, job classification, and compensation levels. Smith (1978) argues that here the focus should be on activities that have several key attributes. That is, they would be easily observable, mutually exclusive, collectively exhaustive, and reasonable in number. In light of the fact that the conduct of work measurement studies can be controversial, and the outcome of such studies relevant to so many people, Smith (1978) emphasizes that the nature and number of activities that are to be indexed should be carefully determined and ultimately defensible.

The actual recording involved in structured observation rarely takes the form of prose as written in field notes. Instead, the investigator likely will develop worksheets to facilitate the structured observation. Frequently, these are formatted as checklists. The observer indexes whether something occurred or did not occur by placing a checkmark in the space provided. Here, the record of observation is the frequency with which something was seen. This is the essence of work measurement as practised by human factors psychologists and industrial engineers (Smith, 1978). Figure 5.1 shows such a work sampling data form.

More likely, however, the observer will attempt to classify a behaviour that is observed as belonging to one category or another. In other words, the bulk of structured observation in organizational research makes use of specially constructed rating scales. Here the investigator records, according to a pre-established format, impressions or inferences with regard to the frequency, amount, or quality of something (e.g., work behaviour). Figure 5.2 illustrates a behaviour rating scale created for the purpose of indexing effectiveness in conducting performance appraisal interviews. Notice that the investigator must use judgments to use this scale (e.g., judgments as to what frequency of occurrence warrants a rating of "always," and judgments regarding lack of the behaviour domains).

One area in which those interested in behaviour in organizations have used observation is the study of the nature of jobs. For a wide variety of practical reasons, in human resources (selection requirements, training needs, job evaluation) we often want to know just what duties, tasks, tools, activities, etc., are performed, used, or exhibited by workers. This often requires the observation of workers performing their jobs. Similarly, many theories have been proposed in which job attributes or characteristics are felt to be important to worker attitudes and behaviour. These, too, require the measurement of jobs.

In an unstructured observation, the field worker must make decisions about what to record on a regular and continuous basis. In the structured approach, a similar set of decisions is involved. In the latter case they are done a priori, well before data are gathered. Some of these decisions have already been alluded to, others have not. Thus, before making direct observations, the researcher needs to resolve the following issues:

1. *Unit of observation.* What should the unit be? In particular, how minute should it be? For example, in behaviour observation, one could record each activity exhibited (opening letters), or choose to cluster these into the tasks that are fulfilled by performing the activity in context (dealing with customer complaints).

   It's clear that while any number of actions or behaviours can be observed and recorded, investigators usually focus on instances or events that are theoretically or practically meaningful. For example, in a study of the behaviours of coaches, Curtis, Smith, and Smok (1979) chose to observe behaviours reflecting

FIGURE 5.1 **Work Sampling Data Form Used to Record the Occasion of Occurrence of Work Activities**

Hr.	Min.	Drawing (Formal Drawings)	Drawing (Pipe Sketches)	Working on Blueprints	Reading	Idle	Telephone	Miscellaneous	Not Observed
8	42								
9	37								
10	28								
11	09								
Lunch									
1	09								
2	10								
3	51								
4	52								

Source: Smith, G.L. Jr. (1978). *Work measurement: A systems approach.* Columbus, OH: Grid Publishing, Inc. Reprinted with permission.

such things as reinforcement, encouragement after mistakes, or technical instruction. These were felt to be related to or to cause player behaviour. Player behaviour, in turn, would affect key outcome variables such as player attitudes toward the team and ultimately the team's win/loss record. In fact, observations of the number of "punishment" behaviours observed correlated negatively with the team's win/loss record (–.35 and –.37) for the two years of their study. The coach's behaviours did make a difference, but in this case, in a negative direction!

FIGURE 5.2 Example of Rating Scale Used to Characterize Job Behaviour

Use the following scale to index your observations of how the employee conducts performance appraisal interviews:

Always = 1
Often = 2
Occasionally = 3
Seldom = 4
Never = 5

_____ 1. Maintained control over the interview.
_____ 2. Probed deeply into sensitive areas in order to gain knowledge.
_____ 3. Asked appropriate questions.
_____ 4. Displayed insensitivity to the subordinate's problems.
_____ 5. Responded to the subordinate's outbursts in a rational manner.
_____ 6. Used appropriate compliments regarding the subordinate's technical expertise.
_____ 7. Projected sincerity during the interview.
_____ 8. Skillfully guided discussion through the problem areas.
_____ 9. Provided good advice about resolving conflict.
_____ 10. Appeared defensive in reaction to the subordinate's complaints.

Source: Adapted from Bernardin, H.J., & Beatty, R.W. (1984). *Performance appraisal: Assessing human behavior at work.* Boston, MA: Kent.

2. *Intensiveness versus extensiveness.* Just how much detail should be recorded? Are broad, general descriptions adequate?

3. *Observer knowledge.* How much information should the observer have with regard to the purposes of the study and/or the research hypotheses? On the one hand, more information might aid the observer by clarifying what to look for and allowing for serendipity. On the other hand, specific knowledge can introduce a bias into the observations made. That is, knowing what the investigation is all about, the observer might look for specific occurrences, or might be prone to make inferences from observations that favour the research goals. Thus, as a rule, it is usually better to give only as much information as is necessary for the observer to do his or her job adequately. In other words, it is often appropriate for the observer to be blind to the research hypothesis.

4. *Observer inference.* To what extent should the observer have to estimate, conclude, or infer what is to be recorded? Should he or she simply be describing what is actually seen or not seen? As noted, most structured systems do require some inference on the part of the investigator.

5. *Time unit for measurement.* The period of structured observation may last a few seconds or several hours. The stream of behaviour or events can be arbitrarily broken into shorter or longer episodes for classification or rating.

6. *Recording and coding of the behaviour/event stream.* Should the behaviour/event stream be recorded and coded in its entirety? Or, more likely, how should it be sampled? In this regard, one can use time or event sampling. Bickman (1976) argues that to do event sampling (e.g., accidents) requires a great deal of prior knowledge regarding the frequency, duration, and location of a particular phenomenon. The investigator must be there exactly when the event occurs. On the other hand, time sampling implies not only precise definitions of what an event of interest is, but what time frame is most appropriate (five minutes or one hour). The issue of time sampling has been extensively investigated in the context of work measurement (Campion & Thayer 1985; Fleishman, 1982).

In time sampling, observations are taken according to a plan. This may imply regular (every half-hour) episodes or a random sampling. In the latter instance, electronic devices programmed for the purpose may be used to alert the investigator when to record what is occurring. Observations taken on a random basis are frequently seen as part of a job analysis effort designed to obtain a complete description of what work is involved and the knowledge, skills, and abilities required to perform it.

7. *The use of electronic recording devices.* Researchers are now able to record observations on audio or videotape. These can be reviewed and coded later. However, unless such technologies are hidden, they are likely to be intrusive and may interfere with the events to be studied. Alternatively, there exist very compact and portable event recorders that can be used instead of a checklist or rating scale. These are less obtrusive and can facilitate data reduction and coding. Indeed, with one of these devices it is possible to input data, maintain a cumulative record of the information of interest, and have an immediate preliminary analysis of the results at the time the last observation is entered. Hidden recording, however, does raise ethical issues of informed consent. See the HR Research Today box below for an innovative study that used audiotaped observations to study interview interactions and outcomes.

HR RESEARCH TODAY

Audio Observations of Interview Interactions and Outcomes

The employment interview is one of the most common methods of selection and has been studied for over 80 years (Campion, Palmer, & Campion, 1997). While a great deal has been learned about interview reliability and validity, much less is known about how interviewers conduct the interview. In an innovative study on interview interactions, Cynthia Stevens (1998) audiotaped recruitment interviews and collected survey data from interviewers and interviewees before and after the interview.

Stevens (1998) first identified two important factors that might influence how interviewers conduct themselves during the interview process. The first factor involves a screening/selection orientation versus a recruiting/attraction orientation. Some interviewers use a *screening orientation* and focus on evaluating the qualifications of job applicants. Other interviewers use a *recruiting orientation* and focus on attracting applicants. The second factor involves the extent of interviewer training. Stevens (1998) hypothesized that screening-recruiting priority and interviewer training would influence interviewer conduct.

But what exactly is interviewer conduct and how do you measure it? With the approval of the interviewers and interviewees, a microphone was concealed in the interview room in order to audiotape the interviews. For each interview, the total interview time and the time spent talking by the interviewer were assessed. Interviews were transcribed verbatim and the turns-at-talk were numbered to facilitate analysis.

The transcripts were then segmented according to the following scenes: (1) the *preamble*, or interviewer comments about how the interview would be sequenced; (2) *unprompted information* about the firm, in which interviewers offered organizational information not requested by applicants; (3) *sidebars*, in which interviewers or applicants initiated discussion of non-job-related topics (e.g., hobbies); and (4) *predisengagement*, in which interviewers attempted to (but did not) close the interview.

The interview interaction was analyzed by examining the number, length, and sequence of interview scenes. For each transcript, information about the turns-at-talk numbers, sequence, and scene classifications was tabled. These data were used to calculate the total number of scenes, the numbers of unprompted organizational-information and sidebar scenes, and percentage of exchanges associated with each scene.

Stevens (1998) also coded interviewers' question attributes and discussion topics. Interviewers' questions (those asked during interviewer question scenes) were counted and coded as either primary (i.e., topic introduction questions) or secondary (i.e., follow-up probes), and as open (providing response flexibility) or closed (providing restricted response options). In addition, question content, transparency, and differentiation were coded. *Content* was classified according to the type of information sought: facts (verifiable information), opinions (e.g., preferences), and behaviours. *Transparency* referred to whether the phrasing of the question indicated the correct response (e.g., "How would you rate your communication skills?"). Differentiation concerned whether the answers to the question would differentiate strong from weak applicants.

To assess the number of topics discussed by interviewers, all topics mentioned during scenes in which interviewers provided information to applicants were coded. Topics included: (1) organizational facts (e.g., size), (2) organizational philosophy (e.g., firm culture), (3) clients or customers (e.g., their demographics), (4) organizational benefits (e.g., fringe benefits), (5) business prospects (e.g., expected growth, industry trends), (6) fit or KSA information (e.g., characteristics associated with good organizational fit), (7) interviewers' personal experiences with their firms (e.g., career progression), (8) neutral work or job descriptions (e.g., a typical day), (9) positive job information (e.g., positive features of a job, organization, or locale), (10) realistic job information (e.g., drawbacks of a job, organization, or locale), and (11) comparative information about interviewers' organizations (e.g., comparisons of overtime hours across firms). Transcript segments were tallied for the topics interviewers addressed. The final measure was the sum of different topics covered during unprompted-information scenes.

The results of the study supported Stevens's (1998) hypotheses that interviewers' orientation and training would influence how they conducted interviews. For example, recruitment-oriented interviewers spoke 50 percent more, discussed twice as many topics, and asked fewer than half as many questions compared to screening-oriented interviewers. As well, their questions were less likely to focus on behavioural content, but were more transparent in indicating the "correct" responses. They also had more scenes involving sidebars and unprompted organizational information, with the latter scenes playing a more central role.

The results for interviewer training indicated that trained interviewers used more of their allotted time for interviews, with fewer overall scenes and fewer scenes in which they digressed into sidebars (and fewer exchanges devoted to such digressions when they did occur). Training also affected the attributes but not the number of questions asked. Trained interviewers asked more secondary, open, and differentiating questions. Of the question types asked most often, trained interviewers used higher percentages of screening-oriented and lower percentages of non-screening-oriented questions.

The results of this study are important because they demonstrate how an organization's screening—recruiting priorities and interviewer training programs can influence interview processes and outcomes. The use of an innovative qualitative research method was a key factor in obtaining in-depth knowledge about interview interactions and processes.

Source: Based on Stevens, C.K. (1998). Antecedents of interview interactions, interviewers' ratings, and applicants' reactions. *Personnel Psychology, 51,* 55–85.

◆ ◆ ◆
RESEARCH INTERVIEWS

Interviews are quite common in human resources. They are a key assessment tool in selection and promotion, and one of the most common methods for employee selection (Pulakos & Schmitt, 1995; Pulakos, Schmitt, Whitney, & Smith, 1996). In this section, special applications of the research interview will be reviewed. The point to be made is that interviews are an excellent vehicle for obtaining qualitative information.

Interviews have been characterized as conversations with a purpose. As a technique for qualitative research, they are used to gain insights regarding how individuals attend to, perceive, or otherwise deal with some phenomenon of interest. Another important feature to note is that interviews are dynamic. The nature of the exchanges that take place between the interviewer and the respondent will vary over time and be affected by such factors as the needs and behaviours of both parties, their relationship, the skill of the researcher, the topics to be covered, and the context in which the interview takes place.

This dynamism of the research interview is both a strength and a liability. On the one hand, it allows for flexibility and efficiency. Unlike the questionnaire, which programs the respondent to answer a fixed set of questions in a prescribed order, the interview allows the researcher to pursue productive and appropriate lines of inquiry. In fact, unanticipated and entirely new directions of questioning can be conducted, if so desired. But this dynamism implies difficulty in imposing standardization on the process. Thus, it is hard to ensure that, across interviews, all respondents will face the same questions, in the same order, and posed in the same manner.

As a result of this dynamism, a special problem facing those who use the interview is the need to be responsive and to maintain rapport with the interviewee, while staying on track and following the research agenda. In a sense, the investigator is like a participant observer who must be a part of the process while remaining somewhat removed from it. This becomes even more complicated when a group interview is involved.

◆ ◆ ◆
ISSUES TO BE ADDRESSED IN A RESEARCH INTERVIEW

When using the research interview, the investigator must consider a number of important issues with respect to how the interviews will be conducted. In this section, the following issues will be discussed: (1) whom to interview; (2) interview methods; (3) interviewee motivation; (4) interview structure; and (5) note-taking.

WHOM TO INTERVIEW

It seems rather straightforward to assert that the researcher should be attentive to the issue of who should be interviewed. In many situations the qualitative interview is conducted because very little is known about a phenomenon or area. In fact, a study's objective may be to establish who should be targeted for a more systematic survey. It may even be appropriate to use intact groups (e.g., club members) in the form of what are called *opportunity samples* if the kind of knowledge or experience of interest is thought to be widely shared. These points notwithstanding, normally those people (units, dependents, etc.) who are representative of the population of interest would be interviewed. If the population can be clearly defined, and the goal is to generalize with regard to findings, it is correct to select a scientifically drawn sample for the purposes of interviewing.

In organizational settings and in market research, there is usually some advantage to ensuring that formal and informal (opinion) leaders are included in a sample. These people often have well-developed and articulated views and thus would constitute a rich source of data. Moreover, to involve such individuals early in an investigation conveys an importance and legitimacy to the effort (Bouchard, 1976). Key informants may be selected for their presumed specific knowledge. For example, more senior people may be interviewed because of their capacity to provide a historical perspective. Similarly, new hires, frustrated employees, or those who are outside of the mainstream of organizational life may be targeted because they are able to provide desired insights. *Exit interviews* are often conducted with employees who quit in an effort to find out why they have decided to leave the organization and to prevent future employees from quitting (see the HR Research Today box below).

HR RESEARCH TODAY

Exit Interviews

Exit interviews are one of the most common methods used by organizations to find out why employees quit their jobs and choose to leave the organization. The information obtained from exit interviews can provide valuable information about problem areas in the organization. The data obtained from exit interviews can be used to improve jobs and the work environment, and serve as a basis for the design of programs to reduce turnover. Thus, the exit interview can be an effective research tool for improving the attraction and retention of employees.

Although there is some debate regarding the best time to conduct an exit interview, it should probably be conducted sometime during the final week of employment. However, regardless of when the interview is conducted, one of the main challenges facing the interviewer is to obtain accurate and valid data. Research has found that the data obtained from exit interviews are subject to distortion. This is because departing employees may be

HR RESEARCH TODAY (continued)

reluctant to reveal controversial information, especially if they need letters of reference and don't want to "burn their bridges." One survey found that 96 percent of human resource professionals said they conducted exit interviews, but only 60 percent thought the information was accurate and truthful.

For this reason, organizations need to take a number of steps when conducting exit interviews. In particular, they should be conducted by a member of the human resources department who is a skilled interviewer rather than by the employees' supervisor. It is also important that employees be informed that the information they provide will be confidential and used in combination with the responses of other departing employees.

The exit interview itself should be structured. In other words, a set of carefully prepared questions should be designed and asked of all departing employees. The questions themselves should be open-ended and allow for deeper probing to learn as much as possible about the departing employees' true feelings and attitudes.

Research on the exit interview has identified a broad range of questions asked by organizations. Some of the most common questions include:

- Why did you decide to leave?
- What might have been done differently?
- Would it have made a difference?
- What suggestions do you have?
- What would have made you stay?
- Have you had enough growth opportunities?

Although many organizations conduct exit interviews, they are less likely to code and analyze the data and use them in a meaningful way. The information obtained from exit interviews often winds up in personnel files rather than being acted upon. Thus, although organizations realize that the information obtained from conducting exit interviews can be extremely useful, many do not use the information as a basis for making improvements or in the development of turnover reduction programs.

In sum, in order to effectively use exit interviews as a meaningful research tool that can be used to improve practice, the following steps should be followed:

1. Develop a structured exit interview.
2. Interview all employees who voluntarily leave the organization.
3. Code the data and track them over time.
4. Analyze and interpret the data.
5. Take corrective action in areas that need improvement.
6. Follow up to evaluate changes.

Sources: Pounds, M.H. (1999, May 3). Exit interviews give employers a valuable opportunity. *The National Post*, D9 (Knight Ridder); Drost, D.A., O'Brien, F.P., & Marsh, S. (1987, February). Exit interviews: Master the possibilities. *Personnel Administrator*, 104–110; Garretson, P., & Teel, K.S. (1982, July-August). The exit interview: Effective tool or meaningless gesture? *Personnel*, 70–77; Hinrichs, J.R. (1975). Measurement of reasons for resignation of professionals: Questionnaire versus company and consultant exit interviews. *Journal of Applied Psychology*, 60, 530–532; Pearl, J. (1993, June). Exit interviews: Getting the truth. *Working Woman*, 16–17.

INTERVIEW METHODS

The various methods of interviewing also present certain advantages and disadvantages. Personal interviews can be conducted face-to-face or over the telephone. The face-to-face interview method is emphasized in qualitative research because it establishes a personal relationship with the research subjects and allows direct observation of the work context of the people involved. These factors, in turn, allow for the careful adjustment of lines of questioning and such subtle but important matters as voice tone or quality and nonverbal body cues. In particular, when interviewing individuals of low verbal ability, it is useful to work with several levels of communication (e.g., both verbal and nonverbal). Finally, in some investigations it is desirable to have the interviewee respond to physical or visual stimuli (e.g., proposed ideas for products or for ads), and face-to-face interviews allow for this.

Yet, face-to-face interviews have some disadvantages. They are costly insofar as travel time is involved (either to get the interviewer to the respondent or vice versa). This also means that the collection of information will take longer, due to the number of research staff involved. Occasionally, there is the issue of safety—travelling to some locations may pose a potential threat to the researcher.

The telephone interview, on the other hand, can be administered by staff calling from various locations or from a single location. Most studies involve this method because those conducting the interview are in one place and can be better monitored or supervised. If problems occur, they can be solved quickly and consistently by a supervisor. Moreover, telephone surveys can often be administered quickly and can reach individuals anywhere in the country. Depending on the topic, interviews as long as 45 minutes to one hour are possible, making telephone interviews desirable when quick results are needed (as in the case of research designed to evaluate the impact of the introduction of a new product or service).

The telephone interview, however, has certain weaknesses. Many people today are being contacted frequently by phone for purposes of selling a product or service. This means that respondents may not be willing to participate in a real telephone study. Thus, while telephone surveys have a good response rate (the number of individuals contacted who agree to participate), it is somewhat lower than the rate for face-to-face interviews. Moreover, the interview may be "broken off" if the respondent stops the process and refuses to answer more questions. This poses the problem of how to classify the case or to use the data.

Some individuals have limited patience and capacities. Thus, telephone interviews usually have to be shorter in length than face-to-face interviews (although, as mentioned, this will vary by respondent, characteristic, and topic). The interviewer may also be limited as to the kinds of questions and answer formats used in a telephone interview. Depending on the aural and memory skills of the respondent, the investigator may have to plan on repeating questions.

Telephone surveys may use either closed-ended or open-ended response modes. The former are choices presented to the respondent, who then picks an appropriate option (e.g., "strongly agree," "agree," etc.). In the open-ended format, the investigator needs to take down what is said as accurately as possible. Clearly, the nature of the material and the complexity of response options often preclude using a telephone interview. In these cases, it is better to collect data with face-to-face interviews.

It should be noted that both face-to-face and telephone interviews require careful development and staff training, but they are not always interchangeable. The nature of the research and of the resources available has a big impact on which method is more appropriate.

INTERVIEWEE MOTIVATION

A third issue in interview research is the ability to create and maintain motivation. A large number of factors affect a respondent's willingness to be interviewed for research. The investigator should attempt to build on these as much as possible. Some of these factors include the following:

1. *Perceived value of the research.* What the potential respondents believe to be the goals of the research will make a difference. If they believe it's for a "good cause," or if they will benefit personally from its outcome, respondents are more likely to get involved. In contrast, if they see negative consequences (in general or specifically for themselves), they will respond with at best superficial cooperation.

2. *Sponsor.* The decision to let respondents know who is sponsoring the research is a complex one. There are ethical reasons for favouring informed consent. Thus, all things considered, open disclosure regarding the sponsor is preferred. More practically, if the sponsor is reputable or well liked, it is more probable that questions posed will be answered. People will be more motivated to participate. On the other hand, knowledge of the sponsor under these conditions is also likely to create some bias. Individuals may distort answers. Instead of eliciting a truthful reply, the researcher may come away with a more socially desirable response.

3. *Rapport.* Rapport refers to the quality of the relationship between the investigator and the study participants. It is especially important in the research interview. Rapport is affected not only by many of the factors already cited, but also by the personal qualities and behaviours of the investigator. Greater rapport comes about when the interviewer is perceived as trustworthy, demonstrates empathy with the respondent without taking sides on issues, minimizes status differences in dress and in the use of language, and is a good listener. As noted, it is easier to establish rapport in the face-to-face interview, but it needs to be established

more quickly in the telephone interview (because of the limited time usually available).

4. *Topic and format.* Some topics are more intrinsically interesting to respondents. However, the phrasing of questions, voice quality (tone and modulation), and sequencing can be designed to enhance interest levels.

5. *Setting.* Where interviews take place can affect the ability to establish or maintain motivation. In most cases this implies selecting a setting free from distraction or interruption. Executives might be questioned while away from their desks, and operatives while away from their machines. Setting may impact on the level of privacy and confidentiality possible. The perception that the conversation will be overheard most likely will reduce candour. This especially is an issue in group interviews.

INTERVIEW STRUCTURE

The fourth issue to be considered in planning the interview is the structure of the interview. Almost by definition, the qualitative research interview will be relatively unstructured. However, this does not mean that the investigator does not have a plan. In general, he or she will have goals for the session, a list of potentially useful questions, as well as some outline (mental or written) of the order in which questions may be posed. In this regard, the investigator is attempting to balance several factors in order to produce the desired result.

If the researcher knows little about the phenomenon, questions must be broad enough to stimulate respondent thinking. If the investigator has some strong ideas on the topic, he or she must be aware of the possibility of influencing the respondent with leading questions. Phrases like "Don't you think ..." or "Wouldn't you agree ..." should be avoided. They imply a preferred answer. Open-ended prompts such as "Tell me about ..." or "Describe how you feel ..." are more likely to elicit unbiased information.

The sequence of questions asked and their level of specificity can have an effect on respondent motivation. Sequence may also influence the way the respondent thinks about issues and opinions or conclusions. It is the task of the interviewer to elicit whatever thoughts and ideas the respondent already has—not to create them.

A number of authors recommend the *funnel technique* for eliciting valid and uncontaminated impressions from respondents in an interview (Bouchard, 1976). This technique involves first inquiring about a domain with general questions and unspecified response options. This loosely structured line of inquiry allows the investigator an opportunity to become familiar with the respondent's level of understanding. With this insight, the researcher then can move to more specific questions, modifying them so that they are appropriate in language and direction. By going from general to specific, there is less likelihood that the respondent's answers will become contaminated or unduly influenced by the questions themselves. Over the course of a lengthy interview, there might be several cycles going from general to specific questions as one covers different topics or content domains.

The funnel technique has other advantages as well. The more or less free response format of the early questions is likely to be perceived as more natural by respondents. Thus, answers are likely to be more spontaneous and free-flowing. Because the respondent feels less self-conscious, it should be somewhat easier to establish and maintain rapport.

Regardless of specific question sequence, a key feature of qualitative interviewing is the use of follow-up questions and probes. Short or incomplete answers to questions can be followed up with requests for elaboration. Apparent contradictions can be clarified. Additional facets of an issue can be covered beyond what was originally intended. When done with skill, such probes as "Please tell me more," "What do you mean by that?," and "I'm not sure that I am clear on that" may produce additional relevant information.

In a great deal of research, the goal is to obtain information or data that can be readily analyzed by computer. Thus, the interview is designed to have a great deal of structure, both in the nature and order of questions used, and in the way people answer. In its most extreme form, the highly structured interview is conducted by reading from a prepared questionnaire. As the respondent answers, the appropriate place on a form is marked or checked off by the investigator. In contrast to simply handing out a questionnaire and hoping that it comes back filled out correctly, the interviewer can help respondents by clarifying items and motivating them to answer.

Interview structure has been shown to be especially important in employment interviews. As a research tool, the employment interview allows the interviewer to collect important information about job applicants pertaining to their ability to perform a job. As well, interview evaluations are an important part of the research process which help to determine interview reliability and validity. Thus, the development of relevant interview questions is very important, as is the way the interview is conducted and evaluated.

Campion, Palmer, and Campion (1997) noted that 80 years of research on the employment interview have shown that "few conclusions have been more widely supported then the idea that structuring the interview enhances reliability and validity" (p. 655). Based on a review of the literature, Campion et al. (1997) identified the following fifteen ways that employment interviews can be structured in order to enhance the content and evaluation process of the interview:

1. Base questions on a job analysis.
2. Ask the same questions of each candidate.
3. Limit prompting, follow-up questioning, and elaboration on questions.
4. Use better types of questions (see Table 5.1 for examples of different types of structured interview questions).
5. Use a longer interview or a larger number of questions.
6. Control ancillary information.
7. Do not allow questions from candidate until after the interview.
8. Rate each answer or use multiple scales.
9. Use detailed, anchored rating scales.
10. Take detailed notes.
11. Use multiple interviewers.
12. Use the same interviewer(s) across all candidates.
13. Do not discuss candidates or answers with other interviewers.
14. Provide extensive interviewing training.
15. Use statistical rather than clinical prediction.

NOTE-TAKING

A final issue peculiar to face-to-face interviews is whether to take notes in the interview. It is one thing to elicit information, but quite another to record it with accuracy and in a way that is appropriate to the needs of the investigator. Clearly, some way of recording what gets said in the interview is imperative. But how and when to record often present a challenge.

Taking notes as the respondent is talking often interferes with the interview. It takes time and can interrupt the free flow of ideas. It distracts from the interviewer's thinking about and sequencing of questions. Moreover, continuous note-taking produces something like a transcript. It will almost always have to be organized and copied. As noted earlier, this can be extremely time-consuming. But, most important, it makes what is already an intrusive technique somewhat more so. Continuous and obvious note-taking will cause most individuals to be more self-conscious and even uncomfortable. This, in turn, is likely to reduce spontaneity and even promote self-censorship. The respondent will be careful about what he or she says in order to avoid disclosing any self-threatening information or in order to "look good" in the eyes of the interviewer or to those who will be reviewing the notes.

The particular setting may make a difference (e.g., a manager's office versus a shop floor) in note-taking. Most experienced interviewers request permission to take

TABLE 5.1 EXAMPLES OF DIFFERENT TYPES OF STRUCTURED INTERVIEW QUESTIONS

Situational Questions:

1. Suppose a co-worker was not following standard work procedures. The co-worker was more experienced than you and claimed the new procedure was better. Would you use the new procedure?

2. Suppose you were giving a sales presentation and a difficult technical question arose that you could not answer. What would you do?

Past Behaviour Questions:

3. Based on your past work experience, what is the most significant action you have ever taken to help out a co-worker?

4. Can you provide an example of a specific instance in which you developed a sales presentation that was highly effective?

Background Questions:

5. What work experiences, training, or other qualifications do you have for working in a teamwork environment?

6. What experience have you had with direct point-of-purchase sales?

Job Knowledge Questions:

7. What steps would you follow to conduct a brainstorming session with a group of employees on safety?

8. What factors should you consider when developing a television advertising campaign?

Note: So that direct comparisons can be made, an example is presented to assess both teamwork (1, 3, 5, and 7) and sales attributes (2, 4, 6, and 8) for each type of question.

Source: Campion et al. (1997). A review of structure in the selection interview. *Personnel Psychology, 50,* 655–702.

notes first but, in fact, take only the briefest notes. This is usually done to reduce the intrusiveness of note-taking and to maintain rapport. Thus, small note cards might be used instead of a pad of paper, and the noting of information might occur at convenient points of transition within the interview. It certainly would not be continuous. More to the point, it would not be done in a manner to convey to the subject that what was just said was noteworthy or unusual. It is most disconcerting to have the interviewee anticipate what is important by noticing what does or does not elicit note-taking on the part of the interviewer.

It is tempting to use recording devices during the interview. This would free the investigator from having to worry about real-time note-taking. However, in most cases (unless they are disguised or hidden), these, too, are likely to produce undesirable consequences. The awareness of being recorded usually creates a mindset that everything said is "for the record." This has inhibiting effects. On the other hand, it makes good sense to use recorders as dictation devices after the interview is completed as a way of quickly and easily capturing impressions and thoughts regarding the session. In any event, any recorded material still has to be reviewed and edited in order to be useful, and this is time-consuming.

Typically, rough and cursory notes will be reviewed in privacy by the researcher immediately after the interview. Thus the notes become the basis or outline for a more complete documentation relying on (at most, short-term) memory. Ultimately, these too will have to be organized and summarized.

In a recent study of note-taking during the employment interview, voluntary note-taking was found to result in more valid interview ratings, especially when the notes were behavioural in terms of content (Burnett, Fan, Motowidlo, & Degroot, 1998). However, in an experiment in which participants were instructed either to take general notes, to take behavioural notes, or not to take notes, the ratings of those who did not take notes were just as valid as those who took behavioural notes, and more valid than those who took general notes. The authors concluded that "note-taking is not necessary for increasing validity, but if interviewers take notes they should emphasize information about interviewees' behaviours, and minimize attending to irrelevant behaviours occurring in the interview itself... For those interviewers who prefer or need to take notes, they could be trained to organize information and summarize important points so that note-taking does not interfere with the flow of the interview, and avoid recording extraneous or irrelevant information" (Burnett et al., 1998, p. 395).

◆ ◆ ◆
ANALYZING AND REPORTING INTERVIEW DATA

Once the interview has been concluded, the data must be summarized, analyzed, and reported. The treatment of this information is very similar to the treatment of information on observation presented earlier. In general, notes are integrated around themes as they emerge from the responses to questions. Based on a thorough review of interview-produced materials, the investigator infers and interprets the essential meaning and "teases" out implications of what he or she has read and experienced. There is ample opportunity to emphasize or weight more heavily more informed or more credible respondents. It also is common to base interpretations on what the investigator may have deduced through means other than the interview. For example, personal exposure to relevant aspects of organizational life (i.e., several staff meetings) may colour the interviewer's descriptions and inferences.

The actual reporting of qualitative interviews is dependent on the larger research effort. At times, there is no real need for documentation. As a result of interviews, the investigator may profit or grow from the experience and go on to do his or her work in a different, hopefully more informed, manner. In other contexts, the interview data may be introduced into reports containing quantitative data in order to assist interpretation or add substance. In some instances, however, the information stands alone. The investigator thus integrates the new knowledge or insights gained into an essay designed to characterize the phenomenon of interest. Examples from notes, anecdotes, or even quotations may be used to support the points being made. In many respects, the final product may resemble what is created by a good investigative reporter. The strength of the document lies in its organization, the persuasive tone of its arguments, and its liberal and effective use of interview data (its appropriateness, consistency, specificity, and detail).

When the structured interview format is used, the information obtained is much like what you would get from a questionnaire. This means that the response options chosen by research participants are translated into numbers. Thus, the analysis of the output of a very structured interview presents far fewer problems than that arrived at by qualitative insights.

◆ ◆ ◆

SPECIAL APPLICATIONS OF THE QUALITATIVE RESEARCH INTERVIEW

It seems likely that, at one point or another, any project involving information gathering will make use of the interview technique. This section highlights several particular interview applications that might frequently be encountered.

TANDEM INTERVIEWS

One special adaptation of the interview, the **tandem** or **team interview**, refers to an interview conducted by two individuals. As indicated earlier, one component of employment interview structure involves the use of multiple interviewers (Campion et al., 1997). Given the dynamics of the face-to-face interview described previously, it is easy to see the functionality of having two interviewers. While one person is primarily responsible for asking questions, the other is taking notes or listening carefully to responses. The latter can be brought into a more active role from time to time to pose questions that seem to have been overlooked or are important and deserve elaboration.

Having a team of investigators work together in this manner allows for post-interview discussions in order to summarize what was learned. In this sense, points of agreement and disagreement can be part of the database being built. In many cases this may be efficient as well. The researchers need not spend time orienting one another as they would have to if each were to interview informants individually and separately.

One other potential advantage of the tandem or team interview relates to the technical knowledge that researchers may share. For example, a research project calling for interviews of senior engineering managers regarding decision making associated with the introduction of innovative production technology might well use a team made up of a production technology expert and someone who understands decision making in complex organizations.

As with any technique, the team approach also has some disadvantages. Most notably, because a given interview ties up more than one investigator, this may limit the number of informants who might be contacted. Moreover, the team members must learn to work well together in order to create a climate that is free of tension.

GROUP INTERVIEWS

Another form of the qualitative research interview is the **group interview**, in which more than one individual at a time can be questioned. Such interviews can be conducted by one or more research team members as well.

The design and execution of successful group interviews involves several important considerations. Both the size and the composition of the group will make a difference for both process and outcomes. Larger groups are harder to manage and severely restrict the amount of time that a given individual can speak. It is harder to establish rapport as well. Groups made up of people who know each other may share the same enthusiasm (or reluctance) to participate. While they may be more spontaneous in their responses, it also is likely that their behaviour and opinions will be affected by what each has been known to do and say in the past. Private (or inconsistent) thoughts may not surface. To the extent that there are status differences between participants, stylized response and deference to the senior member of the group may not be uncommon. In fact, a major task of the group interview leader is to control the tendencies of some individuals to dominate, while eliciting information and opinions from those who tend to be quiet or reserved. Regardless of past acquaintance levels, individuals may vary in their experience and knowledge of the topic of interest. This, too, will affect group dynamics. Bouchard (1976) also points out that scheduling difficulties may be encountered when attempting to get a group of busy people together.

One potentially important limitation of the group interview is that different or conflicting views and information may not be obtained. Questioning individuals separately will reveal particular points of view, perhaps in greater detail. Follow up and probing is more feasible. The same individuals in a group setting may be reluctant to go into such detail; or, just as commonly, they may be drawn into a particular way of thinking by what others say, overlooking or forgetting important points. Thus, descriptive richness, complexity, and accuracy may be sacrificed.

Group interviews may be especially useful when the investigator is interested in how attitudes, opinions, or ideas might be stimulated by group interaction. Thus, there may be some real value in having individuals share the information or thoughts they have with one another in open discussion. Under these circumstances, group dynamics may work to some advantage.

FOCUS GROUP INTERVIEWS

The **focus group interview** is a term loosely applied to interviews conducted with small groups of individuals who are known to have had some personal experience with the phenomenon being researched. The interview thus focuses on respondents' impressions, interpretations, and opinions in this domain. Focus group interviews are used in market research by manufacturers and advertising agencies to determine consumer needs or preferences and their predilections to respond favourably to new products (Calder, 1977). Although the use of focus groups in human resources has been rare, they are becoming an increasingly popular research tool, especially when in-depth feedback is required (Phillips, 1996).

Calder (1977) identifies three different applications of the focus group interview technique. First, it is often used in anticipation of quantitative research as an exploratory approach. The purpose of the technique, then, is to stimulate the thinking of the investigators. They may use focus groups to generate theoretical ideas or hypotheses that may be verified empirically at a later time. This approach concentrates on the creation of useful and important constructs that relate to those used in everyday life. For example, focus groups are helpful in planning both the content and wording of surveys. Alderfer and Brown (1972) report how qualitative interviews contributed to the appropriate wording of a questionnaire to be used to assess organizational attitudes. This is a prototype application of a qualitative technique for exploratory research.

Second, the focus group technique is used to provide generalizations from the information generated by the focus groups themselves. Calder (1977) refers to this as the *clinical approach*. The investigator thus uses the group as a way of probing deeply into a phenomenon in order to form certain conclusions. The validity of the inferences made will depend on the degree of rapport that exists within the group and the quality of the interactions that take place during the session. It is also highly dependent on the theories, knowledge, and skill of the group leader as analyst. Calder (1977) is quite critical of this method as a means of producing generalizable scientific findings. The results of such an effort are too dependent on the skill of the investigator and, in practice, they are rarely subjected to verification by other means.

Third, the most prevalent application of the focus group technique is to obtain the point of view of a sample of people from a population of interest. Calder (1977) refers to this as the *phenomenological approach*. Contact between the investigator and his or her participants is viewed as necessary in order to better empathize with them and to anticipate their reactions to choices or decisions (e.g., about consumer products). This type of focus group emphasizes involvement with a group of people as they discuss and interpret things or events. The goal is to obtain a description of how they interpret reality in their own terms. Usually, investigators conduct focus groups of this nature until they feel confident they can "just about" anticipate what is going to be said.

For the purposes of human resources, focus groups can be useful for obtaining information about the quality of human resource programs as well as changes in employees' behaviour following an intervention (Phillips, 1996). According to Phillips (1996), focus groups provide an inexpensive way to research the strengths and weaknesses of a program, especially when the information needed cannot be obtained using other methods.

DEBRIEFING INTERVIEWS

In the course of most experimental research the investigator often finds that he or she needs to better appreciate how the participants experience and interpret instructions and manipulated conditions. In each of these situations the researcher may use another special type of interview called the **debriefing interview**.

The debriefing interview is most often used in quantitative, usually experimental, research, and is helpful when the investigator needs to gain a full understanding of the nuances of perceptions, reactions, and impressions of experimental participants. In the debriefing interview, the researcher first attempts to understand how the participant's written responses relate to his or her state of mind. If the researcher is in a position to observe the participant in a session, he or she may wish to follow up on some behaviour or action that was out of the ordinary. Thus, the debriefing interview becomes a means of remaining open to serendipity. When used on an occasional basis in the actual study it can provide an additional safeguard for quality (Aronson & Carlsmith, 1968; Tesch, 1977).

All of these special applications of the qualitative research interview require a great deal of competence and skill on the part of the investigator. He or she must be aware of and make use of interpersonal and group dynamics, have a wide-ranging behaviour repertoire, and possess great sensitivity to the impact of nuances in choice of language. These are not capabilities that are easy to acquire and refine. In most cases, they only can be developed under supervision with appropriate and timely feedback. As in the case of direct observation, the assurance of quality data is closely tied to the investigator as an intrinsic part of the technique itself. The value of the technique is related to the person using it.

◆◆◆
ARCHIVAL AND TRACE MEASURES

Archival measures are based on documents and records that are generated in the course of day-to-day organizational life. These could include notes on desk calendars, schedule books, memos, speeches made by company representatives, and financial operating data (Bouchard, 1976; Webb & Weick, 1979). **Trace measures** are based on physical evidence and artifacts often presumed to reflect the attractiveness or popularity of activities or choice options. For example, the amount of floor wear in front of a museum exhibit might be used to infer the drawing power or level of interest of the exhibit. Missing pages from the Yellow Pages section of telephone directories might be assumed to reflect frequency of need/use of services or products (Webb, Campbell, Schwartz, & Sechrest, 1966). For investigators interested in human resource management, a major source of archival and trace information is the personnel file (Owens, 1976).

There is no reason why either type of measure must be used in a nonquantitative manner. One could, for example, create a coding system for analyzing executive speeches that would result in actual numbers (e.g., frequency counts) to serve as input to standard statistical analysis (Bouchard, 1976; Weick, 1968). In fact, this was done in a study that examined the personality profiles and charisma of U.S. presidents. Measures of presidents' personality motives were based on a content analysis of presidential inaugural speeches, and measures of charisma were derived from a content analysis of newspaper editorials the day after the president's inauguration and from the biographies of former members of cabinet. Both the president's personality profile and amount of charisma were related to presidential performance (House, Spangler, & Woycke, 1991).

However, for reasons covered below, it is more likely that an investigator will use archival and trace measures in a subjective and qualitative manner. They often are gathered as incidental to other data and treated as supplementary and given a subordinate role to those generated by other methods (Miles, 1979; Pettigrew, 1979).

Both techniques are often classified as unobtrusive measures because they are presumed to be uncontaminated by reactivity dynamics (Bouchard, 1976). This is based on the belief that the actor would not be aware that he or she was being studied at the time the record or trace was being produced. However, there may be reasons to be concerned by reactivity bias even here. For example, financial data in annual reports are often presented in a manner designed to make the company look good. Public speeches may tell us more about the speaker's assumptions about what the audience wants to hear than about what the speaker really believes. According to a study that analyzed the annual reports of publicly owned corporations, and despite assertions to the contrary (Salancik & Meindl, 1984), it seems reasonable to assume that the text is carefully contrived for public consumption. Thus, a major limitation of these methods is that the investigator can never be certain about the level of self-consciousness of the actor responsible for the trace or artifact.

A second and somewhat related limitation of these measures is that their psychological meaning is problematic. More so than with other techniques, the investigator must infer and make a case for, the state of mind, intent, or motivation of the subject. To illustrate, the wear on floor tile may have little to do with the popularity of an exhibit, but instead be caused by such diverse factors as a "right turn bias" known to occur as people enter public spaces, a bathroom located in that area, or the use of floor material in that area that simply wears faster (Bouchard, 1976). Similarly, memos written to the file may reflect a conscientious attitude and commitment to the organization or a deep distrust of the system by the actor. In other words, such measures may suffer from distortion. Variance may be caused by factors irrelevant to the phenomenon of interest. In sum, there are a large number of mediating factors operating between the measure and the phenomenon itself.

Nevertheless, a number of researchers have made skillful use of archival data. For example, Pfeffer and Salancik (1974) tested a theory of how departments or units in an organization gain power in a university setting. In their study, most of the data came from university records. For example, subunit power was indexed by the number of department faculty who served on important university committees and the amount of money they had in their budget (controlling for number of faculty). The authors found that, contrary to popular belief, the number of courses or students taught (also obtained from archival records) did not relate to the amount of power held or to other, more political, factors.

Similarly, Salancik and Meindl (1984) used company archives to get copies of annual financial reports. By looking over such reports for a period of eighteen years, the authors found that the words used by CEOs in the reports were related to the nature of the context in which the organization had to operate (its environment). When the environment was changing or unstable, top managers used carefully chosen words to create "strategic illusions" to describe the causes of their firm's performance over the preceding year. This was less likely for companies in which the environment was better understood and more predictable. Through the use of archival data, this study was able to contribute to the refinement of theories of organization and environment interactions.

◆◆◆
ADVANTAGES AND DISADVANTAGES OF
QUALITATIVE RESEARCH

The data created in qualitative research would seem to have many attractive features. According to Miles (1979), they are rich, full, holistic, and usually match the complexity of what is being studied. Because of this detail and specificity, they appear to have face value, and can add credibility to research reports when presented as vignettes or illustrations.

From both a scientific and practical point of view, many methods outlined in this chapter lend themselves to the uncovering of serendipitous findings and new insights. Webb and Weick (1979) stress the fact that certain classes of data (e.g., those based on unobtrusive measures) are particularly well suited to research on less articulate populations, because the latter have neither the time, the interest, nor the skill to work with traditional survey measures. Finally, many believe that qualitative data, when combined with quantitative results, can produce more valid inferences than either one separately.

On the other hand, there are some obvious limitations and liabilities associated with the use of qualitative methods. Collecting and analyzing qualitative data can be laborious and time-consuming. Mintzberg (1979) asserts that in his study of strategic decision making in organizations he and his team spent a number of months on site to gain an appreciation for the context. To learn about socialization dynamics, Van Maanen (1975) actually worked as a police officer for the better part of a year. It was only after being accepted as a participant observer that he came to understand what were the "facts" and what were the "theories of facts" that he held as an outsider. It also took time (and trust) to discover what he calls *presentational data*. This is an idealized or manufactured image presented to outsiders, designed to protect the system and the esteem of its members. As pointed out by Van Maanen (1979, p. 544), "a central postulate of the ethnographic [participant observation] method is that people lie about those things that matter most to them." "Penetrating fronts" then becomes one of the important goals of the field worker. This takes time and effort.

Miles (1979) describes the physical, emotional, and intellectual demands placed on those working with qualitative information. The researcher is almost totally responsible for the quality (validity or accuracy) of the data. The range of phenomena to be observed and documented; the volume of notes; the time required for write-up, coding, and analysis—all can become major sources of stress. To illustrate, Miles points out that in his study of innovation in public schools, an all-day contact usually resulted in 60 to 90 minutes of taped notes, which took a field worker about 2 hours to produce, a secretary 68 hours to transcribe, and the field worker another hour to review and correct. In this project, Miles felt that this level of effort could not be reduced appreciably without losing many of the direct quotes and details that make such data so attractive. Moreover, on any major project this process must be multiplied by the number of sites, field workers, and periods of observation.

A major limitation of qualitative data is that the methods of analysis are not well formulated. For quantitative data, there are clear conventions for analysis. But for the qualitative researcher, there are "very few guidelines for protection against self-delusion, let alone presentation of 'unreliable' or 'invalid' conclusions to scientific or policy making audiences" (Miles, 1979, p. 590).

However, with the increasing popularity of qualitative methods, a number of computer programs are now available for qualitative data analyses that can be used to help sort, code, and categorize qualitative data (Weitzman & Miles, 1995).

◆◆◆
ETHICAL ISSUES IN QUALITATIVE RESEARCH

A major ethical concern in the use of qualitative research is that the investigator must deal with the issue of informed consent. The position taken by most researchers is that subjects in research should have the option of not participating and should give their consent before they become the object of study.

Informed consent in participant observation implies that subjects are aware that the investigator is going to be among them, fulfilling multiple roles. When dealing with organizations or large groups this may be difficult to accomplish. It is especially true when the study takes place over a long period of time. People tend to forget about the arrangement. New people come into the system. Moreover, while the investigator contributes to the texture of daily life as a participant, it is difficult to maintain the balance between being unobtrusive and reminding co-workers that they are the object of a study.

As part of the organization, the investigator must deal with the possibility of changing the phenomenon intentionally or inadvertently. This becomes even more problematic if we adopt Salancik's attitude toward the benefits of field stimulation. As mentioned earlier, this involves deliberately "tweaking" the system to see how it responds in order to learn something about it (Salancik, 1979). The question is: "What right do we have to do this?"

Informed consent is especially relevant if the study makes use of hidden observation. Almost by definition, the subject is not to know that he or she is the object of study. Many investigators deal with this dilemma by publicly inviting participation and securing cooperation. Then they trust that, over time, memory lapses and the use of unobtrusive measurement will desensitize subjects so that they will behave naturally.

Other researchers argue that any behaviour exhibited in public is open to study without formal consent. Such behaviour, they maintain, is available to any and all to observe. Under this assumption, why should a researcher be required to go to any length to advise people that they are under scientific scrutiny? There is no simple or easy response to this. The need for informed consent in this public context will depend on the type of phenomenon of interest (e.g., prosocial versus illegal), the significance of the problem, the absolute need to use the method, the probable quality of the discoveries that might come out (based on theory and strength of the design), as well as the potential for harm to subjects as a result of the investigator's actions or work products.

Informed consent is also relevant to the use of archival or trace measures. It will be recalled that the latter's benefits derive, in part, from the fact that subjects are presumed to be unaware of the probable use of such artifacts for research. Most often, investigators assume that, if they get permission from the current custodian of the materials of interest, they are behaving in an ethical manner. However, this does not relieve the researcher of responsibility for considering ways to contact and obtain permission from the original source. Public archival records do not require such diligence.

A second area of concern is confidentiality. Interviews, in particular, are usually conducted under the assumption that what is shared with the investigator will only be known in detail to members of the research team. Great care must be exercised not to violate this trust in talking to other respondents (especially when attempting to verify the accuracy of accounts of events) or when writing up or documenting findings. Miles (1979) reports how difficult it is to "sanitize" reports in a way that keeps the desired richness of detail while still protecting sources. Confidentiality is especially difficult to maintain when the investigator, as participant observer, uncovers information shared in confidence that, for the good of the system, really should be revealed.

One last ethical dilemma relates to certain features inherent in the use of the methods described in this chapter for strictly qualitative research. As stated many times, in most qualitative research, the knowledge, skills, attitudes, and abilities of the investigator are inextricably tied up with the nature and quality of the data produced. What this means is that the data, summaries, and inferences are not often subject to verification. Consequently, errors, biases, and distortion may not be detected.

There is the remote possibility that an investigator will consciously manipulate or distort findings. One can find examples of this when pressure for publication or the need to maintain or enhance a reputation has caused outright falsification to occur. Unfortunately, there is little that a text like this can do to prevent intentional deception. Much more insidious, however, is the well-known tendency of a person's beliefs and expectations to guide attention, to colour perceptions, and to shape inferences and conclusions. Because what gets observed, recorded, and emphasized in qualitative research is largely a function of the investigator, it is quite possible that the final product reflects the investigator's biases as much as the reality of the phenomenon. And more to the point, it would be difficult, if not impossible, to detect this distortion.

The qualitative researcher must become aware of his or her biases and assumptions regarding the object of study. With such an awareness, several actions might then be taken. At a minimum, the investigator might discipline himself or herself to follow a "devil's advocate" strategy during critical phases of the research. This would involve regularly challenging personally held assumptions by trying out reasonable, alternative perspectives on the evolving database. Or, it may be possible to create and configure teams of researchers with divergent personal views. Thus, any individual biases might be detected and minimized as a result of vigorous discussions during staff meetings.

It is necessary that the investigator's biases and assumptions be clearly stated. As the author of a technical report, journal article, or book, the researcher should clearly state his or her preconceived notions held at the time of the study. While research cannot (and should not) be value-free, it is important to recognize the need for mechanisms to make it clear how and where values might have an impact on the quality (and accuracy) of the data and the conclusions derived from them (Morgan & Smircich, 1980). This is especially important in studies using the methods described in this chapter on qualitative research.

◆◆◆
SUMMARY

In this chapter, qualitative research designs were described as a set of assumptions and a particular attitude in addition to being a set of research techniques. Further, any of the methods reviewed can be used to generate quantitative as well as qualitative data. An important aspect of qualitative research is the key role of the investigator. The investigator not only chooses a particular technique, but also functions as the guardian of its ethical use and the quality of the data generated.

Qualitative designs are an important part of human resource research. Observation and interviews are frequently used to gather data required for many human resource functions, such as job analysis, job evaluation, training needs analysis, employment interviews, assessment centres, and so on. When used in combination with other research designs, the result can be a much richer and more complete understanding of the phenomenon of interest.

Definitions

Archival measures   Information that is acquired from documents and records such as personnel files that are generated in the course of day-to-day organizational life.

Debriefing interview   Interview conducted after an experiment to better understand how participants experienced and interpreted the instructions and the experiment.

Focus group interview   Interview conducted with small groups of individuals who are known to have had some personal experience with the phenomenon being researched.

Group interview   Interview in which more than one individual is questioned at a time.

Interview   A technique for qualitative research in which the researcher gains insights and gathers information about individuals or organizations by questioning selected respondents.

Nonparticipant observer   A researcher who acts only as an observer of organizational activity and not as a functioning member of the organization.

Participant observer   A researcher who becomes involved in organizational life and has a job or role in the organization while being an observer.

Qualitative research   An approach to research that involves a number of techniques that are used to understand and describe some naturally occurring phenomenon.

Structured observation   A systematic approach to observation in which the researcher has a clear idea prior to the study of what will be observed.

Tandem interview   Interview that is conducted by two interviewers.

Trace measures   Information that is derived from physical evidence and artifacts presumed to reflect the attractiveness or popularity of activities.

Unstructured observation   An approach to observation in which the researcher learns what is important and what to observe during the course of the study rather than prior to the study.

EXERCISES

1. Refer to Exercise 4 in Chapter 3. Rather than using a survey for this exercise, use a telephone interview. In small groups, design a telephone interview on the topic "Research in Human Resource Departments." Before the next class, phone several organizations and ask to speak with a member of the human resource department. Conduct your telephone interview and bring the results to class the following week.

2. An important type of interview conducted by many organizations is the exit interview, which is held with employees just before they leave an organization. One of the purposes of an exit interview is to find out why employees have decided to leave the organization. Imagine that you are a human resource professional who must conduct an exit interview with an employee who has decided to leave

the organization. Develop a list of interview questions, and, with another member of the class, take turns playing the role of the interviewer and interviewee. For a point of reference, the interviewee should consider a previous job when answering the interviewer's questions.

3. Job analysis interviews are a common method for conducting a job analysis. Find a partner in your class and take turns conducting a job analysis interview. You must first develop a series of questions in order to find out what the key tasks, duties, responsibilities, working conditions, and requirements are for the person's job.

4. As consumers, we regularly come into contact with employees who perform service functions. Whether they are serving us in a clothing store, fixing something in our homes, or taking our orders in a restaurant, such employees perform numerous duties in the course of their interactions with customers. For this exercise, you are to use the structured observation technique in order to observe the behaviour of customer service employees. Visit your local coffee shop, order yourself a drink, and then have a seat and observe the behaviour of the employees. Prior to your period of observation, you should prepare a list of the things that you will want to study and what you will rate and code. After you have completed your observations, consider the ethical implications of this research. As a hidden observer, do you think that

you should have informed the employees that you were observing their behaviour and that they were the objects of your study? Should you have obtained their informed consent prior to your observations?

5. One way to conduct research on groups is by observation. For this exercise, you are to assume the role of a participant observer or a nonparticipant observer. If you are currently in a work group for one of your classes or at work, then take some time to observe your group as a member. If you are currently not in a group, ask a friend who is if you can attend a group meeting to observe the group. State some hypotheses that you can test about group interactions and behaviour, and prepare a checklist or worksheet that outlines the things you will be observing to test your hypotheses.

6. Select an HRM topic of interest to you, and pose a series of questions for which you are interested in knowing the answers. Then state several testable hypotheses based on your questions, and explain how you could test your hypotheses by conducting qualitative research. Describe how you would conduct your study. If you use observation, indicate whom and what you will observe. If you use an interview, indicate whom you will interview and what type of questions you will ask. Do you think that this would be a good research design to test your hypotheses? What are the advantages and disadvantages?

RUNNING CASE: THE VP OF HUMAN RESOURCES—PART 4

Describe how you can conduct qualitative research to demonstrate the value-added of the HRM department and its programs to the organization. Be sure to discuss how you would proceed and how you would use observation and/or interview techniques. Based on your answer to the above, is qualitative research a useful method to demonstrate the value-added of HRM to your organization? What are the advantages and disadvantages of doing so?

References

Alderfer, C.P. & Brown, D.L. (1972). Designing an empathic questionnaire for organizational research. *Journal of Applied Psychology, 56,* 456–460.

Aronson, E., & Carlsmith, J.M. (1968). Experimentation in social psychology. In G. Lindsey & E. Aronson (Eds.), *The handbook of social psychology,* vol. 2 (2nd ed., pp. 1–79). Reading, MA: AddisonWesley.

Baritz, L. (1960). *The servants of power.* Middleton, CT: Wesleyan University Press.

Bickman, L. (1976). Observational methods. In C. Seltiz, L.S. Wrightsman, & S. Cook (Eds.), *Research methods in social relations* (3rd ed.). New York: Holt, Rinehart & Winston.

Bouchard, T. (1976). Field research methods: Interviewing questionnaires, participant observation, systematic observation, unobtrusive measures. In M.D. Dunnette (Ed.), *Handbook of industrial and organizational psychology.* Chicago: Rand McNally.

Bramel, D., & Friend, R. (1981). Hawthorne, the myth of the docile worker and class bias in psychology. *American Psychologist, 36,* 867–878.

Burnett, J.R., Fan, C., Motowidlo, S.J., & Degroot, T. (1998). Interview notes and validity. *Personnel Psychology, 51,* 375–396.

Calder, B.J. (1977). Focus groups and the nature of qualitative research. *Journal of Marketing Research, 14,* 353–364.

Campion, M.A., Palmer, D.K., & Campion, J.E. (1997). A review of structure in the selection interview. *Personnel Psychology, 50,* 655–702.

Campion, M.A., & Thayer, P.W. (1985). Development of an interdisciplinary measure of job design. *Journal of Applied Psychology, 70,* 29–43.

Curtis, B., Smith, R.E., & Smok, F.L. (1979). Scrutinizing the skipper: A study of leadership behaviors in the dugout. *Journal of Applied Psychology, 64,* 391–400.

Evered, R., & Louis, M.R. (1981). Alternative perspectives in the organizational sciences: "Inquiry from the inside" and "Inquiry from the outside." *Academy of Management Review, 6,* 385–395.

Fleishman, E.A. (1982). Systems for describing human tasks. *American Psychologist, 37,* 821–834.

House, R.J., Spangler, W.D., & Woycke, J. (1991). Personality and charisma in the U.S. presidency: A psychological theory of leader effectiveness. *Administrative Science Quarterly, 36,* 364–396.

Johnson, S.M., & Bolstad, Q.D. (1973). Methodological issues in naturalistic observation: Some problems and solutions for field research. In L.A. Hamerlynch, L.C. Handy, & E.J. Marsh (Eds.), *Behavioral change: Methodologies, concepts and practice.* Champaign, IL: Research Press.

Light, D., Jr. (1979). Surface data and deep structure: Observing the organization of professional training. *Administrative Science Quarterly, 24,* 551–559.

Martinko, M.J., & Gardner, W. (1985). Beyond structured observation: Methodological issues and new directions. *Academy of Management Review, 10,* 676–695.

Miles, M.B. (1979). Qualitative data as an attractive nuisance: The problem of analysis. *Administrative Science Quarterly, 24,* 590–601.

Mintzberg, H. (1979). An emerging strategy of "direct" research. *Administrative Science Quarterly, 24,* 582–589.

Morgan, G., & Smircich, L. (1980). The case for qualitative research. *Academy of Management Review, 5,* 491–500.

Owens, W.A. (1976). Background data. In M.D. Dunnette (Ed.), *Handbook of industrial and organizational psychology.* Chicago: Rand McNally.

Pettigrew, A.M. (1979). On studying organizational cultures. *Administrative Science Quarterly, 24,* 570–581.

Pfeffer, J., & Salancik, G.R. (1974). Organizational decision making as a political process: The case of a university budget. *Administrative Science Quarterly, 19,* 135–150.

Phillips, J.J. (1996). *Accountability in human resource management.* Houston, TX: Gulf Publishing Company.

Pulakos, E.D., & Schmitt, N. (1995). Experience-based and situational interview

questions: Studies of validity. *Personnel Psychology, 48,* 289–308.

Pulakos, E.D., Schmitt, N., Whitney, D., & Smith, M. (1996). Individual differences in interviewer ratings: The impact of standardization, consensus discussion, and sampling error on the validity of a structured interview. *Personnel Psychology, 49,* 85–102.

Rousseau, D.M. (1990). Assessing organizational culture: The case for multiple methods. In B. Schneider (Ed.), *Organizational climate and culture* (pp.153–192). San Francisco, CA: Jossey-Bass.

Salancik, G.R. (1979). Field stimulation for organizational behavior research. *Administrative Science Quarterly, 24,* 638–649.

Salancik, G.R., & Meindl, J.R. (1984). Corporate attributions as strategic illusions of management control. *Administrative Science Quarterly, 29,* 238–254.

Sanday, P.R. (1979). The ethnographic paradigms. *Administrative Science Quarterly, 24,* 527–538.

Smith, G.L., Jr. (1978). *Work measurement: A systems approach.* Columbus, OH: Grid Publishing, Inc.

Smith, H.W. (1981). *Strategies of social research.* Englewood Cliffs, NJ: Prentice Hall.

Stevens, C.K. (1998). Antecedents of interview interactions, interviewers' ratings, and applicants' reactions. *Personnel Psychology, 51,* 55–85.

Tesch, F.E. (1977). Debriefing research participants: Though this be method there is madness to it. *Journal of Personality and Social Psychology, 35,* 217–224.

Van Maanen, J. (1975). Police socialization: A longitudinal examination of job attitudes in an urban police department. *Administrative Science Quarterly, 20,* 207–228.

Van Maanen, J. (1979). Reclaiming qualitative methods for organizational research: A preface. *Administrative Science Quarterly, 24,* 520–526.

Webb, E.J., Campbell, D.T., Schwartz, R.F., & Sechrest, L. (1966). *Unobtrusive measures: Nonreactive research in the social sciences.* Chicago: Rand McNally.

Webb, E.J., & Weick, K.W. (1979). Unobtrusive measures in organizational theory: A reminder. *Administrative Science Quarterly, 24,* 650–659.

Weick, K.E. (1968). Systematic observational methods. In G. Lindzey & E. Aronson (Eds.), *The handbook of social psychology* (vol. 2, pp. 357–451). Reading, MA: Addison Wesley.

Weitzman, E.A., & Miles, M.B. (1995). *Computer programs for qualitative data analysis: A software sourcebook.* Thousand Oaks, CA: Sage Publications.

6

Existing Research and Meta-Analysis

◆ ◆ ◆
INTRODUCTION

Given the large number of studies that have been conducted on human resource issues, you might have wondered why we need more research. In fact, sometimes we don't. In addition to conducting original research, a researcher might review the large research base that already exists on various topics in human resources. He or she might actually conduct a literature review as part of a research project, or refer to a literature review as part of the research process. Questions regarding the cumulative findings of research or what further questions can or should be addressed are often the focus of literature reviews. Whatever the purpose, understanding how to conduct and make use of existing research on human resources is an important part of the research process. This chapter outlines the methods used in conducting and summarizing existing research with an emphasis on meta-analysis review techniques. These reviews serve as a basis for estimating the magnitude of a relationship or the size of an effect one can expect from a particular human resource intervention.

After reading this chapter, you should be able to:

- Know how to conduct a traditional literature review and describe the major limitations of this type of review.

- Understand the use of meta-analysis procedures and how they extend the findings of traditional literature reviews.

- Describe research areas in human resources that have been subject to meta-analysis reviews and the major findings.

- Outline each of the steps involved in conducting a meta-analysis review.

- Understand how researchers and practitioners can use the results of meta-analyses reviews and be able to review and interpret them.

◆ ◆ ◆
TRADITIONAL LITERATURE REVIEWS

Many issues in human resources have been studied by dozens of researchers. These researchers frequently have slightly different purposes and methods of measuring key variables, and employ different procedures in data collection. Further, they are often faced with slightly different situational constraints. As discussed later in this chapter, sampling error alone can be expected to produce striking differences between the results of a set of studies that are similar in all other respects. Because of differences in the conduct of studies and the findings of those studies, researchers frequently have attempted to review and integrate studies on a topic in order to come to a general conclusion or to develop a theory that might explain inconsistencies in the results.

This task frequently can prove to be quite formidable. As early as 1949, Wagner (1949) reported 106 articles on the employment interview. Locke (1976) enumerated between 2000 and 3000 papers on job satisfaction. Traditionally, these reviews involved a recording of the major variables investigated, the direction of the relationships, and the statistical significance of the relationships. The reviewers also may have recorded particular features of the study, such as whether it was conducted in the field or the laboratory, how many subjects were involved, and their basic demographic statistics. They frequently counted the instances in which a significant relationship occurred under different research circumstances and drew their conclusions.

The traditional review, then, is criticized primarily because it does not provide an index of the magnitude of observed relationships, and, more importantly, may actually distort the findings of research because it does not take into account the variability in study results due to sampling error and other artifacts.

Glass, McGaw, and Smith (1981) cite a review of the practices and methods of research reviewers by Jackson (1978) that provides the following criticisms of the traditional review:

1. Reviewers frequently fail to examine critically the evidence, methods, and conclusions of previous reviews on the same topic. They may cite those reviews, but they rarely take a second look at them.

2. Reviewers often focus on a small subset of the articles they review. It is not clear why their attention is focused in this way.

3. Reviewers are very general or misleading in their descriptions of the findings of the studies they review. For example, studies are frequently classified only as to whether or not their findings were statistically significant.

4. Reviewers fail to recognize the role of sampling error in their findings. Variability in results across studies is taken, often mistakenly, as conflicting evidence regarding some phenomenon.

5. Reviewers frequently fail to assess the relationship between study findings and the characteristics of the study. Failure to record these characteristics is important because some reviewers simply eliminate studies they consider flawed without considering the results of those studies in conjunction with the remaining papers.

6. Reviewers often report very little about their methods of reviewing. That is, they fail to report where they searched, what papers were included or excluded, and so on.

In an experiment that illustrates the inadequacies of the typical narrative review, Cooper and Rosenthal (1980) divided 40 graduate students and faculty members into two groups and asked them to evaluate seven empirical studies on gender differences in persistence. The first group was told to read the studies and generate a single conclusion using whatever criteria they normally would in preparation of a review-type manuscript. The second group was given instructions on how to quantitatively record the results of the seven studies and accumulate the results across studies. The reviewers in both groups were then asked to indicate their opinion of the likelihood that there was a relationship between gender and persistence. Nearly 75 percent of those relying on traditional review procedures concluded that gender and persistence were unrelated, while only 31 percent of the group who had been given directions as to how to quantitatively cumulate the seven studies drew a similar conclusion.

Thus, the traditional literature review can lead to inaccurate conclusions. Fortunately, significant advances have been made in the last two decades in the way literature reviews are conducted and the way in which results are cumulated across studies. In the next section, these techniques and procedures are discussed.

◆◆◆
META-ANALYSIS REVIEWS OF HUMAN RESOURCE ISSUES

The essential character of **meta-analysis** is to statistically analyze the findings of many empirical studies. Many such reviews have been conducted on human resource topics in the last fifteen years, such as recruitment, selection, training, performance appraisals, job design, and other types of intervention programs. As a result, we now have a much better understanding of the relationships and effects of many human resource practices.

Many of the meta-analyses that have been conducted examined various predictor–criterion relationships in selection. This is not surprising since the use of meta-analyses of correlational data originated with the goal of exploring the degree to which the results of hundreds of criterion-related research studies could be generalized to other situations (Schmidt & Hunter, 1977).

The use of meta-analysis techniques was an attempt to deal with the findings that **validity coefficients** vary considerably from study to study, even when jobs and tests appear to be similar or essentially identical. This variability has been taken as evidence that test validity is specific to a given situation. This means that to justify the use of a test, even a thoroughly researched test, a human resource specialist with adequate training must conduct a validation study whenever the test is to be used in a different situation, organization, or with a different group of employees. This problem has been widely cited as the most serious shortcoming in the use of psychological tests to select employees (Guion, 1978), and has been labelled the *situational specificity hypothesis*.

Frank Schmidt, John Hunter, and their colleagues have re-evaluated this situational specificity problem using meta-analysis of existing validation data (Hunter & Hunter, 1984; Schmidt & Hunter, 1977, 1978, 1980, 1981; Schmidt, Hunter, Pearlman, & Shane, 1979). Schmidt and Hunter held that true validity does generalize across situations and that observed differences among validity coefficients are statistical artifacts. The latter are due to various defects in the study, such as variability in the reliability of the job performance criterion and/or variability in the degree of range restriction that occurs when only a small portion of the job applicant population is available when data are collected to do a criterion-related validity study. The single largest source of variability among validity coefficients was attributed to small sample sizes used in most criterion-related work. In performing their meta-analytic work, Schmidt and Hunter pooled the results of validity studies for a given test type and a given job grouping, and proceeded to determine how much of the variability in validity coefficients could be accounted for by these artifactual sources. If most of the variation in validities is accounted for by these "errors," then it is difficult to see how the situational specificity hypothesis holds, and the conclusion that validity is generalizable across situations is appropriate.

Most of the **validity generalization** work has involved reviews of paper-and-pencil measures used in a wide variety of jobs. Hunter and Hunter (1984) and Schmitt, Gooding, Noe, and Kirsch (1984) have extended this work to other types of selection instruments. The major cognitive and perceptual tests always exhibit nonzero validities for virtually all jobs, and most of the variability across situations in validity coefficients can be accounted for by statistical artifacts.

Both Hunter and Hunter (1984) and Schmitt et al. (1984) have produced comprehensive meta-analyses of selection research. Schmitt et al. (1984) summarized validity coefficients for various predictor–criterion combinations. The data indicate that there are average positive correlations for all predictor–criterion combinations.

The amount of variance left unexplained after correction for sampling error was substantial in some cases and was larger than in previous reported meta-analyses, although this can be accounted for by the fact that the Schmitt et al. (1984) studies had larger sample sizes than previous meta-analyses. The number of times some predictor–criterion relationships have been studied is relatively small and this fact may prove to be a problem for meta-analyses directed toward a study of moderator effects.

The overwhelming conclusion of these studies, however, is that various selection methods are related positively to a variety of criteria, that organizations can use these procedures with confidence, and that by doing so they will increase the effectiveness of their work force. For example, paper-and-pencil cognitive ability tests are indeed valid, and there is no empirical basis for requiring separate validity studies for each job; tests can be validated at the level of general job families (Pearlman, 1980). Further, while tests can be used in many, if not all, contexts with confidence in their validity, there are substantial differences among validities for jobs that vary in complexity.

Another conclusion drawn from meta-analysis reviews is that research results should be described as fully as possible to produce maximally useful results for practitioners and scientists. Validation work should include information on (1) the type of firm or organization sponsoring the work; (2) the problem and setting in which the research is conducted; (3) the job title and code; (4) the job description; (5) sample size and sample characteristics; (6) the predictors—their reliability, intercorrelations, and content; (7) the criteria and their psychometric characteristics; and (8) a full report of the data collected and analyzed, including any subgroup analyses.

Guzzo, Jette, and Katzell (1985) conducted a meta-analysis review of different types of human resource interventions, such as selection/placement, training, goal setting, and work redesign, to name just a few. Effects of these interventions were examined for each of three types of outcomes: (1) output, including quantity and quality of production; (2) withdrawal, including turnover and absenteeism; and (3) disruption, including accidents, strikes, and other costly disturbances. Overall, workers who experienced the interventions improved their work performance by nearly one-half (.44) standard deviation, although there were large differences in effectiveness across interventions. For example, training, goal setting, decision-making strategies, and sociotechnical interventions were among the most effective interventions.

The effects of financial incentives were not as consistently positive. However, they were much different when the studies were broken down by type of criteria. For example, financial incentives had a major impact on output criteria, but not as great an effect on other measures.

Selection/placement, which included mostly studies of realistic job previews (RJPs), had little or no effect, although more recent meta-analyses of realistic job previews report more positive outcomes (McEvoy & Cascio, 1985; Premack & Wanous, 1985). In fact, the most recent meta-analyses of realistic job previews provides evidence that they have an effect on a number of outcomes (Phillips, 1998). Philips (1998) found that RJPs were related to lower attrition during recruitment, lower expectations and turnover, and higher job performance. The results also indicated that the effectiveness of job previews was moderated by the timing of the RJP (i.e., when the RJP is provided during the recruitment process) and the medium of the RJP (i.e., written, verbal, or videotaped). For example, videotaped RJPs were related to higher job performance, and written RJPs were unrelated to job performance. Thus, the results of this meta-analysis provide useful information about what effects to expect from realistic job previews as well as how to enhance their effectiveness in achieving specific outcomes.

The results of meta-analyses on human resource interventions such as training and development provide important information about the relative effectiveness of interventions. Such information enables human resource decision makers to determine which of several programs is most effective. For example, Morrow, Jarrett, and Rupinski (1997) conducted a number of quasi-experimental studies on the effectiveness of different types of training programs, and then used the results to conduct a meta-analysis. Their results indicated that the effect of sales and technical training programs was twice as great as that of managerial training.

One area of particular importance in the training literature is the relationship among the different levels of training criteria (i.e., reactions, learning, behaviour, and results). Thus, it is important to know if trainee reactions, for example, are related to and predict learning and behaviour. Fortunately, a recent meta-analysis examined these relationships and sheds light on this important issue. See the HR Research Today box for a closer look at this meta-analysis.

HR RESEARCH TODAY

A Meta-Analysis of the Relations among Training Criteria

Training evaluation is an important part of the training and development process. It is critical to know how effective a training program is and whether the training objectives have been met. The most widely accepted model of training evaluation is Kirkpatrick's four levels of evaluation criteria. According to this model, training criteria consist of the following four levels: trainee reactions, learning, behaviour, and organization results.

Unfortunately, the evaluation of most training programs consists only of reaction measures. While it is important to know how trainees feel about their training experiences, it is also important to know whether they have learned anything and whether their job performance has improved as a result of the training. If reaction measures are related to the other levels and can predict trainee learning and behaviour, than perhaps reaction measures are satisfactory and could be used as a surrogate measure of learning and behaviour. However, what if reaction measures are not related to learning and behaviour, and only reactions have been measured?

Thus, it is important to know if the four levels of training criteria are related. In order to find out, Alliger, Tannenbaum, Bennett, Traver, and Shotland (1997) conducted a meta-

HR RESEARCH TODAY (continued)

analysis of the relations among training criteria. To conduct their meta-analysis, they identified 34 studies that provided them with 115 correlations among the training criteria. They
also modified Kirkpatrick's model by dividing reaction measures into two categories.
Affective reactions have to do with how trainees felt about a training program. *Utility reactions* measure the extent to which trainees believe the training will be useful for them in
performing their job. The authors also distinguished three measures of learning. *Immediate
post-training knowledge* measures trainees' knowledge of the training material immediately
after the training. *Knowledge retention* measures knowledge at some point after the training
program. *Behaviour/skill demonstration* measures trainees' ability to demonstrate the training
material behaviourally during the training program. Behaviour was classified as *transfer* and
refers to on-the-job performance. *Results* refer to organizational results such as productivity, customer satisfaction, or cost savings. However, because so few studies have measured
results criteria, they were not included in the meta-analysis.

   The results of this meta-analysis indicated that affective reactions were not related to
learning or to on-the-job performance (i.e., transfer). However, utility reactions were
related to learning and to on-the-job performance and were more strongly related to on-
the-job performance than immediate or retained learning. Further, while behaviour/skill
demonstration was related to on-the-job performance, the size of the relationship was
similar to that for utility reactions. The authors concluded that their "results reveal that
at most, there are modest correlations between the various types of training criteria"
(p. 351).

Source: Based on Alliger, G.M., Tannenbaum, S.I., Bennett, W. Jr., Traver, H., & Shotland, A. (1997). A meta-analysis of
the relations among training criteria. *Personnel Psychology, 50*, 341–358.

◆ ◆ ◆
META-ANALYTIC TECHNIQUES

The meta-analytic review process is outlined in Figure 6.1. It is important to realize
from the outset that a great deal of care must be taken to describe and code the
empirical studies on relevant dimensions. Actually, the work of coding and analyzing
the results of studies should be preceded by extensive preparation. The review
process begins with a compilation of all the relevant empirical studies on the topic
in which one is interested. The papers then should be read and the researcher should
formulate hypotheses about potential moderators or study characteristics that may
affect the relationship between the variables being investigated.

   One of the temptations of reviewers employing meta-analytic methods is to
rush into the data coding part of the review without thoroughly reading the research
or later merely scanning the relevant papers to find the numbers one needs to code

FIGURE 6.1 A Flow Chart of the Steps in a Meta-Analysis

Compile a List of Relevant Studies
(using abstract services, bibliographies,
computerized searches, etc.)

↓

Read the Papers and Formulate Hypotheses
and Potential Moderators

↓

Develop Coding Scheme and Rules

↓

Train Coders and Check Intercoder
Consistency and Accuracy

↓

Code the Study Characteristics and Results

↓

Analyze Data

↓

Draw Appropriate Conclusions about Effect
and Potential Moderators

data on the relevant variables. Very often, relevant aspects of the study and theoretical discussion may be missed if one proceeds in this fashion. The papers should be reviewed thoroughly to fully appreciate the sources of the data and the methods used to collect the data. From the hypotheses generated by reading the relevant papers, a list of variables that need to be coded from each study is identified, along with coding rules to guide the coders. Coders are then trained, and their accuracy and consistency checked. Finally, these data are analyzed and summarized. In the next section, some examples are presented to indicate what is important in describing and coding the studies in a meta-analytic review.

DESCRIPTION AND CODING OF STUDIES

Deciding which data are relevant will vary with the substantive and methodological issues that are important to the reviewers and to the relationships being studied. For example, Gaugler, Rosenthal, Thornton, and Bentson (1987) examined assessment centre validity as a function of various study characteristics. They coded the following characteristics: source of publication (journal, unpublished, convention presentation); percentage of minorities in the sample; number of exercises used; number of days of assessor operation; the type of assessor (psychologist versus manager); whether or not peer evaluations were collected; the purpose of the assessment centre evaluation; the design of the validation study; and the type of criterion used, as well as the estimate of assessment centre validity. One or more authors previously had suggested that these variables had some effect on the magnitude of the validity coefficient and/or the quality of the centre or validation effort. Similarly, Schmitt et al. (1984) coded the type of validation design, the occupational group studied, the type of test, and the type of criterion used in assessing the validity of various selection procedures.

These studies indicate two important points about meta-analytic reviews. First, studies are not eliminated from the review on methodological bases; rather, their methodological features are coded, and the influence of the variation in methods is empirically evaluated. Perhaps this is no more clearly evident or important than in the case of unpublished studies. Rather than being excluded automatically because of the feeling that failure to appear in the published research literature indicates a serious flaw, these studies are included so that the nature of differences between published and unpublished studies can be evaluated. This requires that reviewers be especially thorough in locating the available empirical research. Various computerized search routines are now available to help locate existing research studies, but additional efforts to locate unpublished studies may include letters and phone calls. Given the amount of time and money expended in searching for relevant studies, it is a good practice to record the sources of data in the review article.

Second, all efforts should be taken in meta-analytic efforts to ensure accurate and reliable coding of study characteristics and results. Information such as the number and gender of the subjects and the **effect size** should be clear. There should be no disagreement, other than instances of recording errors, in this information. However, information such as the type of validation design in the Schmitt et al. (1984) study or the complexity of a job (Hunter & Hunter, 1984) may involve some subjective judgment on the part of the coder. In these cases, the rules for coding these variables, the extent of coder agreement, and the means by which coding inconsistencies are resolved should be stated clearly in the meta-analytic review.

Wanous, Sullivan, and Malinak (1989) have drawn attention to the various types of judgments meta-analytic researchers must make and how those judgments may affect the results and conclusions of a meta-analytic review. Wanous et al. (1989) summarize the critical points in meta-analyses in Table 6.1. They show how differences in judgments created differences in meta-analytic reviews of the job satisfaction–job performance relationship, the relationship between realistic job previews and job survival, correlates of role ambiguity and role conflict, and the relationship between job satisfaction and absenteeism. Their conclusions in comparing these reviews were that judgment calls do affect the results of meta-analysis, and that by accounting for differences in the judgments made by the researchers, the results of the different reviews converged.

Therefore, reviewers must consider their judgments at each of the steps outlined in Table 6.1. They must report the decisions they make with the greatest detail possible, and, whenever possible, they should test the effects of their decisions. Further, as mentioned above, two independent judges should make the judgments called for in Table 6.1, and the extent of their agreement (and how disagreements are resolved) should be reported. The practice of doing a good narrative review first, in order to be able to make intelligent decisions about what to code and what studies to include, should become standard practice. Finally, in some research areas, studies of a qualitative nature are common, and it is difficult (and occasionally impossible) to quantify the study characteristics or findings. When this is the case, it is probably good practice to include a narrative review of the qualitative studies along with the meta-analytic review.

GUIDELINES FOR REPORTING STUDIES

Hunter, Schmidt, and Jackson (1982) provide a discussion of the data needed to conduct an appropriate meta-analytic review using a variety of data analysis techniques.

If one is reporting on a training evaluation study, it is important to report sample sizes, means, standard deviations, and intercorrelations of variables. We also want to know (1) how subjects were assigned to control and experimental groups, (2) when dependent variables were collected, (3) who did the training, and (4) how it was delivered, and so forth. Studies evaluating changes in pay systems should include (1) the overall effect the change had on pay levels, (2) how the decision to change was made, (3) what previous pay system the employees had been on, and (4) the relative pay status of workers in the community and organization, and so on.

In short, the researcher should strive to describe the methods of research, the sample studied, and the organization in which the study was done along those dimensions that could conceivably influence the relationships observed. How much of this information is included is, of course, partly a function of the researcher's knowledge of the human resource intervention studied and his or her good judgment. Above all, the data should be reported as fully as possible, including means, standard deviations, intercorrelations of all variables and their reliabilities, and these data should be readily available to other researchers.

Once the study characteristics have been coded, the data can be analyzed. The goal is to determine the strength of a relationship or effect, which is termed the effect size. There are two primary types of effect sizes that can be calculated in meta-analyses: effect sizes expressed as a function of average correlations, and effect sizes

TABLE 6.1 ROLE OF JUDGMENT IN META-ANALYSIS

1. Define the domain of research (judgment call)
   a. By independent variable
   b. By commonly researched variable
   c. By causes and consequences of important variable
2. Establish criteria for including studies in the review (judgment call)
   a. Published versus unpublished study
   b. The time period covered in the review
   c. Operational definitions of variables
   d. The quality of a study
   e. And so forth
3. Search for relevant studies (judgment call)
   a. Computer search
   b. Manual search
4. Select the final set of studies (judgment call)
   a. Do individually
   b. Done by more than one person
5. Extract data on variables of interest, sample sizes, effect sizes, reliability of measurement, and other noteworthy characteristics of each study (judgment call)
   a. Use all the data when multiple measures are reported
   b. Use a subset of the data
6. Code each study for characteristics that might be related to the effect size reported in the study (judgment call)
   a. Research design factors
   b. Sample characteristics
   c. Organizational differences
   d. And so forth
7. When there are multiple measures of independent and/or dependent variables, decide whether to group them a priori or not (judgment call)
   a. Theoretical diversity among variables
   b. Operational measurement diversity among variables
8. Determine the mean and variance of effect sizes across studies (calculations)
   a. Mean effect size weighted by sample size
   b. Between studies variance in effect sizes
   c. Estimate of artifactual sources of between-studies variance (sampling error, attenuation due to measurement error, and range restriction)
   d. Estimate of true between-studies variance
   e. Estimate of true mean effect size corrected for measurement error and range restriction
9. Decide whether to search for moderator variables (calculations)
   a. Significance test
   b. Amount of between-studies variance that is artifactual
10. Select potential moderators (judgment call)
    a. Theoretical considerations
    b. Operational measurement considerations
11. Determine the mean and variance of effect sizes within moderator subgroup (calculations): Procedure similar to Step 8.

Source: Wanous, J.P., Sullivan, S.E., & Malinak, J. (1989). The role of judgment calls in meta-analysis. *Journal of Applied Psychology, 74*, 259–264. Reprinted with permission.

expressed as a function of mean differences. Because the calculation of effect sizes requires some understanding of statistics, it is described in Chapter 11.

◆◆◆
USING META-ANALYSIS RESULTS IN HUMAN RESOURCES

The results of meta-analyses in human resources can be very useful for researchers and practitioners in a number of important ways. Practitioners can consult meta-analytic reviews to help them decide if an intervention will be helpful for a particular human resource problem. For example, if an organization has a turnover problem and is seeking ways to lower it, should it design a realistic job preview as part of a recruitment intervention, implement a job design intervention, or perhaps develop a new selection program? The results of meta-analysis reviews can provide information on what type of intervention is most likely to lower turnover or solve other problems. In addition, as discussed earlier, the results of validity generalization meta-analysis reviews can help one determine if a particular selection test is likely to be valid in an organization and for a particular job category.

As well, effect size estimates can be used to determine the financial impact of an intervention and whether the expected financial gain will outweigh the expected costs (see Chapter 12). The practitioner can also consult meta-analytic reviews to determine whether enough data exist to support the use of an intervention without further empirical study. Moderator analyses can also provide information about the relative effectiveness of an intervention under different circumstances.

Researchers can also benefit from meta-analytic reviews in several ways. First, they can identify those relationships that are likely to be stable regardless of the situation or sample studied. Second, they can search for moderators of the relationship even though all effect sizes may be relatively large and practically important. Third, when two variables that are correlated both moderate a relationship, as in gender and occupational group, a researcher would realize that additional data need to be collected in order to fully understand the relationships involved. In both of the latter two cases, the meta-analytic review would reveal deficiencies in the available database. Research then should be directed to these issues rather than to more studies of relationships for which there is no indication of a possible moderator effect. Finally, meta-analytic reviews allow researchers to make more confident and specific theoretical statements about the variables they investigate.

SUMMARY

In this chapter the deficiencies of the traditional narrative review and the basics of meta-analytic reviews have been described. A brief summary of meta-analysis research on various human resource topics was provided, along with some of the uses of meta-analytic reviews. Knowledge of meta-analysis is crucial to understanding and performing integrative reviews. The results of meta-analyses can be an important source of research information for both practitioners and researchers in human resources.

Definitions

Effect size   Indicates the strength of a relationship between variables or the effect of an intervention.

Meta-analysis   A procedure for statistically analyzing and cumulating the findings of many empirical studies on a particular topic or area of research.

Validity coefficient   Refers to the correlation between a selection test and a criterion measure such as job performance.

Validity generalization   Refers to the extent to which the validity of a selection test or the validity coefficient generalizes across situations.

EXERCISES

1. Conduct a literature search and find a recent meta-analysis on a topic in human resources. Review the article and answer the following questions:

   a) What is the topic area, and what has been found in previous research?

   b) What is the purpose or reasoning for doing the meta-analysis?

   c) How many studies were located for the meta-analysis and how many effect sizes were included?

   d) How were the data coded? What are the predictor and criterion variables? What moderator variables were coded and included in the analyses?

   e) What are the major results of the meta-analysis? What are the effect sizes, and are there any significant moderating variables?

   f) What are the research and practical implications of the meta-analysis?

2. Refer to the HR Research Today box on page 169, which discusses the meta-analysis of the relations among training criteria. What are the practical implications of the findings of this meta-analysis? How can the results of this meta-analysis be used by a training

director for choosing and developing measures to evaluate training programs in his or her organization? Can reaction measures be used as surrogate measures for the other levels of training evaluation?

RUNNING CASE: THE VP OF HUMAN RESOURCES—PART 5

Describe how you can conduct a literature review to demonstrate the value-added of the HRM department and its programs to the organization. Be sure to discuss how you would conduct your literature review and how you would proceed if you decided to do a meta-analysis. Based on your answer to the above, would you conduct a literature review or meta-analysis to demonstrate the value-added of HRM to your organization? What are the advantages and disadvantages of doing so?

References

Alliger, G.M., Tannenbaum, S.I., Bennett, W. Jr., Traver, H., & Shotland, A. (1997). A meta-analysis of the relations among training criteria. *Personnel Psychology, 50*, 341–358.

Cooper, H.M., & Rosenthal, R. (1980). Statistical vs. traditional procedures for summarizing research findings. *Psychological Bulletin, 87*, 442–449.

Gaugler, B.B., Rosenthal, D.B., Thornton, G.C., III, & Bentson, C. (1987). Meta-analysis of assessment centre validity. *Journal of Applied Psychology, 72*, 493–511.

Glass, G.V., McGaw, B., & Smith, M.L. (1981). *Meta-analysis in social research.* Beverly Hills, CA: Sage.

Guion, R.M. (1978). Scoring of content domain samples: The problem of fairness. *Journal of Applied Psychology, 63*, 499–506.

Guzzo, R.A., Jette, R.D., & Katzell, R.A. (1985). The effects of psychologically based intervention programs on worker productivity: A meta-analysis. *Personnel Psychology, 38*, 275–291.

Hunter. J.E., & Hunter, R.F. (1984). Validity and utility of alternative predictors of job performance. *Psychological Bulletin, 96*, 72–98.

Hunter, J.E., Schmidt, F.L., & Jackson, G.B. (1982). *Meta-analysis: Cumulating research findings across studies.* Beverly Hills, CA: Sage.

Jackson, G.B. (1978, April). *Methods for reviewing and integrating research in the social sciences.* Final report to the National Science Foundation for Grant No. DIS7620309. Washington, DC: Social Research Group, George Washington University.

Locke, E.A. (1976). The nature and causes of job satisfaction. In M.D. Dunnette (Ed.), *Handbook of industrial and organizational psychology.* Chicago: Rand McNally.

McEvoy, G.M., & Cascio, W.F. (1985). Strategies for reducing employee turnover: A meta-analysis. *Journal of Applied Psychology, 70*, 342–353.

Morrow, C.C., Jarrett, M.Q., & Rupinski, M.T. (1997). An investigation of the effect and economic utility of corporate-wide training. *Personnel Psychology, 50*, 91–119.

Pearlman, K. (1980). Job families: A review and discussion of their implications for personnel selection. *Psychological Bulletin, 87*, 1–28.

Phillips, J.M. (1998). Effects of realistic job previews on multiple organizational outcomes: A meta-analysis. *Academy of Management Journal, 41*, 673–690.

Premack, S.L., & Wanous, J.L. (1985). A meta-analysis of realistic job preview experiments. *Journal of Applied Psychology, 70*, 706–720.

Schmidt, F.L., & Hunter, J.E. (1977). Development of a general solution to the problem of validity generalization. *Journal of Applied Psychology, 62*, 529–540.

Schmidt, F.L., & Hunter, J.E. (1978). Moderator research and the law of small members. *Personnel Psychology, 31*, 215–231.

Schmidt, F.L., & Hunter, J.E. (1980). The future of criterion-related validity. *Personnel Psychology, 33*, 41–60.

Schmidt, F.L., & Hunter, J.E. (1981). Employment testing: Old theories and new research findings. *American Psychologist, 36*, 1128–1137.

Schmidt, F.L., Hunter, J.E., Pearlman, K., & Shane, G.S. (1979). Further tests of the Schmidt-Hunter validity generalization procedure. *Personnel Psychology, 32*, 257–281.

Schmitt, N., Gooding, R.Z., Noe, R.A., & Kirsch, M.P. (1984). Meta-analyses of validity studies published between 1964 and 1982 and the investigation of study characteristics. *Personnel Psychology, 37*, 407–422.

Wagner, R. (1949). The employment interview: A critical summary. *Personal Psychology, 2*, 17–46.

Wanous, J.P., Sullivan, S.E., & Malinak, J. (1989). The role of judgment calls in meta-analysis. *Journal of Applied Psychology, 74*, 259–264.

7

Development of Measures in Human Resources

◆◆◆
INTRODUCTION

In previous chapters, different approaches to research design were presented. At this point it should be clear that regardless of which design is chosen for a research project, ultimately the measurement of some set of variables will be involved. The importance of measurement cannot be overemphasized. The most elaborate and rigorous research designs can be severely undermined by poor measurement of key variables. In this chapter, the focus is on the development of predictor and criterion measures, and the different levels of measurement that can be used to operationalize and measure them.

After reading this chapter, you should be able to:

- Understand and explain the meaning of a variable, concept, and construct.

- Be familiar with the process of developing predictor and criterion measures, and the role of job and organizational analysis.

- Understand the meaning and importance of the criterion concepts of relevance, deficiency, and contamination in the development and measurement of criterion measures.

- Explain the four levels of measurement and how they influence the type of analysis and statements that can be made about the relationships between variables.

The term **variable** is used to denote a symbol that takes on differing values. It must have the potential for assuming at least two states: It can be either absent or present. In most cases, however, we assume that variables will have multiple states or levels. A variable is also used to represent a concept. A **concept** is an idea or generalization formed from the observation of particular instances. It is created to label several elements or observations that appear to have something in common. Job satisfaction is an example of a concept. A **construct** is a concept that has been deliberately created or adopted for a scientific purpose and is the basic element of theories.

Most variables, concepts, and constructs measured in the social or behavioural sciences cannot be observed directly, and are therefore measured indirectly. We may have some commonsense notions about a concept or construct, but we don't know how to measure it directly. We measure some other variable that we presume is related to it. One of the functions of the observed or operationalized variable is to provide the empirical referents for concepts or constructs (Runkel & McGrath, 1972). In this case, the empirical variable serves as an indicator of a hidden, presumed, or latent variable. We use one to infer the nature of the other.

For example, psychologists have measured the galvanic skin response as an indirect measure of emotion, the number of trials it takes to learn a maze as an indication of learning ability, and the number of academic-like tasks a child can solve as intelligence. Now consider work motivation. We may judge employee or student motivation by the number of hours spent at a task, or success at the task, or by asking them questions about how hard they work. All three are indirect, imperfect measures: the person who spends hours at work may be daydreaming or avoiding another unpleasant situation; the successful performer may simply be more able; and the worker who describes how hard he or she is working may feel that this is the socially appropriate response. Part of the research process involves identifying or creating and then using these measures in a variety of situations while checking to see if the observations coincide with our initial commonsense or theoretical notion of what we are trying to measure. This, in effect, is the first requirement of strong inference noted above—namely, that we are really measuring what we intend.

We do, however, usually assume that operational variables reflect some underlying construct continuum. Thus, when we ask workers to complete a survey item regarding the number of different jobs they have had before coming to work for a company, in all likelihood we will record and index this on a continuum from "none" to "many" and go on to relate this variable to others of interest. But notice that in doing this we are not invoking any notion of just what values on this continuum mean. It is only when we choose to label this variable "experience" that we are shifting from an empirical indicator to one that is assumed to reflect some underlying construct.

In doing so, we need to be concerned about the adequacy of how we operationalize constructs. For example, studies of leadership behaviour often refer to constructs such as consideration for subordinates and initiating work structure. The items in the consideration measure have to do with supervisors giving praise, explaining their reasons for action, asking opinions, and so on, while items in the initiating structure measure include questions about goal setting and schedule maintenance. Operationalization of these two variables, like any others, needs to be preceded by a careful consideration of a conceptual or theoretical framework that specifies the meaning of the construct, distinguishes it from other constructs, and indicates how the measure of the construct should relate to other variables.

Measures of constructs attain further meaning after data are collected and analyzed. We find out how the measure actually does relate to measures of other constructs and how the measure is affected by such things as the format of the questions, the language level of the items, and the conditions under which the measure is given. Evidence about our interpretation of the measure also may come from data that indicate the degree to which the items in a measure are related to one another. If items are highly related, we have some confidence that they are measuring the same construct. Further, the measure should be related to measures of similar constructs (leader consideration should be related to leader supportiveness) and not very highly related to dissimilar constructs (satisfaction with the leader probably shouldn't be highly related to satisfaction with one's physical surroundings unless the leader was responsible for producing those surroundings). The meaning of questionnaire measures can also be increased by observation of the behaviour in question or by interviews with respondents. That is, we hope to increase our understanding of constructs by measuring or examining them in different ways.

◆◆◆

THE DEVELOPMENT OF PREDICTOR AND CRITERION MEASURES

At this point, it is worth considering exactly how the researcher develops measures to operationalize constructs in human resources. Recall from previous chapters that there are two general categories of variables that are usually measured in research: independent or predictor variables and dependent or criterion variables. But how does the researcher know which predictor and criterion variables to measure, and how are they developed?

In this area more than in any other in human resources, researchers have developed a detailed and well-defined set of steps. In general, when selecting or developing predictor and criterion measures, the researcher must identify the abilities, behaviours, or work products that are important for the job, tasks, or persons of interest. This requires the gathering of information by conducting a job analysis. Job analysis is often considered to be a cornerstone of human resources because it influences almost all human resource functions. Job analysis provides the information necessary to develop measures in areas such as selection, job performance, and training needs and outcomes.

JOB ANALYSIS

The term **job analysis** refers to the activities associated with determining the tasks, duties, and responsibilities carried out by job incumbents. The researcher conducting a job analysis wants to know what the job is all about (job description). In most cases, a job analysis also defines worker requirements. These include the knowledge, skills, abilities (KSAs), and other related qualities that a worker needs in order to perform the job adequately.

There are a large number of approaches to job analysis. However, most make use of several techniques (e.g., interviews, observations, questionnaires) and involve gathering information from multiple sources (e.g., the job market, supervisors, staff specialists) in order to develop the most comprehensive and accurate picture possible. Job analysis provides the basis for many human resources practices, such as recruitment, selection, training, promotion, job design, and compensation programs. In all these areas, valid job descriptions and/or a complete set of worker requirements are required. Similarly, as discussed in the next chapter, job analysis is an important part of the research process involved in test validation. Finally, the nature of jobs as defined by job analyses is often the focus of theoretical work. Task and job characteristics have often been defined as central in many theories of work motivation and leadership. The researcher frequently needs to be able to measure and classify (or create) jobs that have specific attributes in order to develop or test these theories (Campion, 1988; Kulik, Oldham, & Langner, 1988).

The job analysis information also will inform the researcher as to the types of job performance and other criterion constructs that are relevant and how to measure those constructs. Good criterion measures should have a number of features. First, they should be relevant. **Criterion relevance** is the term used to describe the extent to which the actual criterion measure does, in fact, get at or index the task requirements and KSAs identified in the job analysis. For example, if communication skills are an important objective of a training program, then the measure used to evaluate the training program should include communication skills.

Second, criterion measures should not be deficient. **Criterion deficiency** refers to criterion measures that do not include important KSAs that were identified in the job analysis. For example, if the criterion measure used to evaluate the above-mentioned training program did not include communication skills, it would be criterion deficient. This might happen if the criterion used were an existing measure of job performance. When criterion deficiency is a problem, it usually means that certain components are missing either entirely or in part. Under these circumstances we say that our actual criterion measures are deficient. The concept of criterion deficiency is rooted in the notion that the actual measures used may not adequately cover the conceptual or theoretical domain of interest. What we are measuring may not be bad or incorrect per se, but it may be lacking some important components.

Third, criterion measures should be free from contamination. **Criterion contamination** exists when a criterion measure consists of components that were not identified by the job analysis as being relevant. For example, if part of the criterion measure used to evaluate the training program included trainees' job attendance, then the criterion measure would be considered contaminated because job attendance was not an objective of the training program and is, in effect, irrelevant in this case. Furthermore, to the extent that the criterion used to evaluate the training program includes attendance, this will result in inaccurate conclusions about the effectiveness of the training program. At the extreme, if trainees have poor job attendance, then the use of the contaminated criterion measure could lead to the conclusion that the training program was not effective.

Contamination can occur for a number of reasons. For example, an employee's scores on an actual measure (that are in some ways appropriate) may be systematically affected by factors that are outside the control of a person. A good example of a biasing factor is the nature of a sales territory assigned to an account representative. Features of that sales area, such as size, population, affluence, and so on, are bound to affect sales volume. The key here is that they act to affect it in a systematic way. That is, given a sales territory with certain attributes, any salesperson would do better (or worse) there. The key to this effectiveness measure is the territory, not the person. Such systematic contamination is called *bias*. In this example, the actual measures of "number of sales" and "dollar value of sales" may have a built-in bias. It should be noted that it is often difficult to know whether, in fact, actual criterion measures are biased. Another source of contamination is a lack of reliability in criterion measures (reliability is discussed in detail in Chapter 8).

In addition to the criterion concepts of relevance, deficiency, and contamination, criterion measures should also be practical. In some cases, we might be able to get actual criterion measures that possess many of the above qualities, but at too great a price. It is just not cost effective. Criterion measures must also be viewed as correct or appropriate by the people affected—management and workers alike. It is interesting to note that one of the ways to accomplish this is to ensure that the measures really do get at the important aspects of a job (that they have relevance). Good criterion measures must also be able to discriminate—they must differentiate truly effective from ineffective individuals, groups, or systems. In most organizational settings, this means that there will be variability in the scores of individuals.

While job analysis has been considered to be the major source of information required for the development of predictor and criterion measures, it is becoming increasingly apparent that in addition to job analysis, organizational analysis is also required for the development of predictor and criterion measures.

ORGANIZATIONAL ANALYSIS

As we enter the new millennium, the world of work continues to undergo rapid and dramatic changes. Among the many changes occurring in the workplace is the very nature of work itself. In his book *Jobshift*, William Bridges (1994) argues that the job, in fact, has become an extinct species, a kind of dinosaur that has outlived its time and will soon disappear. In this respect, many organizations will soon become dejobbed. As a result, the notion of jobs and job fit will need to be modified.

An important goal of human resource management is to ensure a good "fit" between employees and their organization. The traditional approach to fit has been person-job fit or P-J fit. This approach to fit is based on fitting the knowledge, skills, and abilities (KSAs) of individuals to the critical requirements of specific jobs. The objective, then, is to match KSAs to jobs. Once employees are hired, socialization as well as training and development are used to ensure that they have the KSAs needed to perform their jobs effectively. They are then evaluated on their job performance, and rewarded and compensated accordingly. The foundation for all of these activities is the job analysis and the focus is employees' knowledge, skills, and abilities.

In recent years, however, a new approach to employee fit has been emerging. This new approach focuses on employees' fit with the organization known as person-organization fit, or P-O fit (Kristof, 1996). This approach recognizes that employees must have more than the right KSAs, and differs from the traditional approach or P-J fit in several ways.

First, unlike P-J fit, which considers only parts of a person (e.g., their KSAs), the P-O fit approach takes into account the "whole" person (e.g., personality, needs, interests, values). Second, the focus of P-O fit is the organization, not the job. This usually consists of the values, norms, beliefs or culture of the organization, but might also include other aspects of an organization, such as its philosophy, goals, or objectives (Kristof, 1996). Third, the foundation of P-O fit is an organizational analysis rather than a job analysis. Finally, the types of human resource practices that are used to achieve P-O fit differ from those used to achieve P-J fit (Bowen, Ledford, & Nathan, 1991; Kristof, 1996).

Research on P-O fit in the last several years has provided a considerable amount of evidence for the importance of P-O fit for employees and organizations. Person-organization fit has been reported to be related to job attitudes and behaviour (Kristof, 1996). For example, P-O fit has been found to be positively related to job satisfaction, organizational commitment, intentions to remain, job involvement, career success, health and adaptation, and organizational effectiveness, and to lower stress and turnover (Bretz & Judge, 1994; Cable & Judge, 1996; Chatman, 1991; Kristof, 1996; Saks & Ashforth, 1997). Thus, it should not be surprising that improving person-organization fit is desirable for individuals and organizations. The difficulty, however, is being able to determine the characteristics of individuals and organizations that are important for P-O fit and how to measure them.

This is where the need for an organizational analysis becomes apparent. Like the job analysis, an **organizational analysis** provides the information necessary to measure important characteristics of individuals. These characteristics, such as values and personality, must be measured for many of the same purposes as are knowledge, skills, and abilities—for example, selection, socialization, performance appraisal, and so on. As noted by Bowen et al. (1991),

The purpose of an organizational analysis is to define and assess the work environment in terms of the characteristics of the organization, rather than just in terms of the characteristics of a specific job. It identifies the behaviours and responsibilities that lead to organizational effectiveness, and implies the personal characteristics most likely to be associated with such behaviours and responsibilities. (p. 38)

Bowen et al. (1991) described how they used an organizational analysis along with a job analysis in the development of a selection model of person-organization fit. The process begins with an assessment of the overall work environment, which includes an organizational analysis in addition to the traditional job analysis. The job and organizational analyses help to identify the KSAs and characteristics of individuals required for a job and organization. Recruitment and selection procedures can then be designed to help job applicants and organizations make assessments of fit, as well as performance and reward systems to reinforce fit once applicants are hired.

The methods for conducting an organizational analysis are not as established as those for job analysis; however, some techniques have proved useful. For example, training needs assessment often includes an organizational analysis, which identifies important dimensions of the organization that can be used to determine the characteristics required of employees. Methods for analyzing and measuring an organization's culture can also be used to identify the critical values, goals, and norms of the organization (Bowen et al., 1991).

One aspect of organizational culture that has a received a great deal of attention in the last several years is values. As indicated earlier, the fit between individual and organizational values—what is referred to as values congruence—is related to individual and organizational outcomes (Kristof, 1996). However, values congruence requires a technique for measuring individual and organizational values, something that traditional job analysis does not do.

O'Reilly, Chatman, and Caldwell (1991) developed an instrument for assessing person-organization fit in terms of work values. Their instrument, called the Organizational Cultural Profile (OCP), consists of 54 values such as flexibility, risk taking, and autonomy. To develop a profile of individual and organizational values, individuals must sort the 54 values into nine categories by answering the following question: "How important is it for this characteristic to be part of the organization you work for?" At the same time, to determine the culture profile of an organization, key members of organizations are asked to sort the values into nine categories in terms of those values that are considered to be the least and most characteristic aspects of their organization's culture. A person-organization fit score based on values congruence for each individual is then calculated by correlating an individual's value profile with the profile of his or her organization.

The Organizational Culture Profile has also been used to study interviewers' assessments of fit and organizational hiring decisions (Cable & Judge, 1997). Cable and Judge (1997) conducted just such a study in which they asked job applicants and interviewers to sort the values of the OCP. Based on a pilot study with organizational recruiters, they shortened the OCP from 54 to 40 items, which are presented in Table 7.1. Cable and Judge (1997) found that interviewers can accurately assess applicant-organization values congruence, and that their subjective assessments of person-organization fit are related to their hiring recommendations.

In addition to values, another aspect of P-O fit is personality. In this respect, a set of personality dimensions known as the Big Five has been identified as the most relevant taxonomy of personality traits for work behaviour (Mount & Barrick, 1995).

TABLE 7.1 THE REDUCED SET OF ITEMS USED ON THE ORGANIZATIONAL CULTURE PROFILE

Adaptability	Decisiveness
Stability	Being competitive
Being reflective	Being highly organized
Being innovative	Achievement orientation
Quick to take advantage of opportunities	A clear guiding philosophy
Taking identification responsibility	Being results oriented
Risk taking	High performance expectations
Opportunities for professional growth	Being aggressive
Autonomy	High pay for good performance
Being rule oriented	Security of employment
Being analytical	Praise for good performance
Paying attention to detail	Being supportive
Confronting conflict directly	Being calm
Being team oriented	Developing friends at work
Sharing information freely	Being socially responsible
Being people oriented	Enthusiasm for the job
Fairness	Working long hours
Not being constrained by many rules	Having a good reputation
Tolerance	An emphasis on quality
Informality	Being distinctive

Source: Cable, D.M., & Judge, T.A. (1997). Interviewers' perceptions of person-organization fit and organizational selection decisions. *Journal of Applied Psychology, 82*, 546–561. Copyright 1997 by the American Psychological Association. Reprinted with permission.

The Big Five personality dimensions include extroversion, emotional stability, agreeableness, conscientiousness, and openness to experience.

Research on the Big Five has reported that they are related to work outcomes (Mount & Barrick, 1995). A meta-analysis of the Big Five personality dimensions and job performance reported that conscientiousness was consistently related to different job performance criteria (i.e., job proficiency, training proficiency, and personnel data) across numerous occupations. The relations for the other dimensions varied by criterion types and occupation. For example, extroversion was related to occupations that involve social interaction such as management and sales (Barrick & Mount, 1991). Judge and Cable (1997) found that the Big Five personality traits are related to job seekers' cultural preferences, and that both objective and subjective P-O fit perceptions are related to organization attraction.

While these results demonstrate that personality is related to cultural preferences and work outcomes, it is less clear how to identify which personality characteristics are most important for a particular job and organization. Once again, this is because traditional job analysis methods do not provide such information. A traditional job analysis usually only provides information about knowledge, skills, and abilities, not personality traits. This explains in part why personality measures have only recently begun to receive serious attention in the selection process (Raymark, Schmit, & Guion, 1997).

Therefore, new forms of job analyses are required to determine the personality characteristics that will best fit a particular job and organization. One group of researchers recently developed a job analysis technique for identifying relevant personality variables (Raymark et al., 1997). Their job analysis is called the *Personality-Related Position Requirements Form (PPRF)*, and was designed to supplement more traditional methods of job analysis. The PPRF consists of 107 items that are organized according to twelve subdimensions. The twelve subdimensions are structured according to the Big Five personality dimensions.

Completion of the PPRF involves indicating the extent to which each statement indicates a requirement for effective job performance. The results of the PPRF can be used to develop hypotheses about the relationship between the Big Five personality dimensions and job performance. Further research is required to determine if the hypotheses developed based on the PPRF are supported. Table 7.2 provides definitions and sample items for each of the subdimensions of the PPRF.

Thus, in addition to a job analysis for identifying KSAs, the development of predictor and criterion measures will increasingly require an organizational analysis and new job analysis techniques that can identify important values and personality characteristics. An organizational analysis can be conducted in a fashion similar to the more traditional job analysis. However, the emphasis is on identifying key dimensions for fit and success in the organization. This should include the specification of

TABLE 7.2 BRIEF DEFINITIONS AND SAMPLE ITEMS FOR THE SUBDIMENSIONS OF THE PPRF

I. SURGENCY

1. **General Leadership:** a tendency to take charge of situations or groups, to influence or motivate behaviour or thinking of other persons. Sample items: Lead group activities through exercise of power or authority; take control in group situations.

2. **Interest in Negotiation:** an interest in bringing together contesting parties through mediation or arbitration or as a contesting party, an ability and willingness to see and understand differing points of view. Sample items: Negotiate on behalf of the work unit for a fair share of organizational resources; mediate and resolve disputes at individual, group, or organizational levels.

3. **Achievement Striving:** an ambition and desire to achieve, to win, or to do better than others, a desire to exert effort to advance, to do better than one's own prior achievement. Sample items: Work beyond established or ordinary work period to perfect services or products; work to excel rather than work to perform assigned tasks.

II. AGREEABLENESS

4. **Friendly Disposition:** a tendency to be outgoing in association with other people, to seek and enjoy the company of others, to be gregarious, to interact easily and well with others. Sample items: Represent and promote the organization in social contacts away from work; attract new clients or customers through friendly interactions.

5. **Sensitivity to Interest of Others:** a tendency to be a caring person in relation to other people, to be considerate, understanding, and to have genuine concern for others. Sample items: Listen attentively to the work-related problems of others; give constructive criticism tactfully.

6. **Cooperative or Collaborative Work Tendency:** a desire or willingness to work with others to achieve a common purpose and to be part of a group, a willingness and interest in assisting clients, customers, or coworkers. Sample items: Work as part of an interacting work group; work with one or more co-workers to complete assigned tasks.

III. CONSCIENTIOUSNESS

7. **General Trustworthiness:** a pattern of behaviour that leads one to be trusted by other people with property, money, or confidential information, a demonstration of honesty, truthfulness, and fairness. Sample items: Refuse to share or release confidential information; make commitments and follow through on them.

8. **Adherence to a Work Ethic:** a tendency to work hard and to be loyal, to give a full day's work each day and to do one's best to perform well, a tendency to follow instructions and accept company goals, policies, and rules. Sample items: See things that

TABLE 7.2   BRIEF DEFINITIONS AND SAMPLE ITEMS FOR THE SUBDIMENSIONS OF THE PPRF (continued)

need to be done and do them without waiting for instructions; work until task is done rather than stopping at quitting time.

9. **Thoroughness and Attentiveness to Details:** a tendency to carry out tasks with attention to every aspect, a meticulous approach to one's own task performance. Sample items: Examine all aspects of written reports to be sure that nothing has been omitted; remain attentive to details over extended periods of time.

IV. EMOTIONAL STABILITY

10. **Emotional Stability**: a calm, relaxed approach to situations, events, or people, emotionally controlled responses to changes in the work environment situations. Sample items: Adapt easily to changes in work procedures; keep cool when confronted with conflicts.

V. INTELLECTANCE

11. **Desire to Generate Ideas:** a preference for situations in which one can develop new things, ideas, or solutions to problems through creativity or insight, or try new or innovative approaches to tasks or situations. Sample items: Help find solutions for the work problems of other employees or clients; develop innovative approaches to old or everyday problems.

12. **Tendency to Think Things Through**: a habit of mentally going through procedures or a sequence of probable events before taking action, a tendency to seek and evaluate information, and to consider consequences. Sample items: Solve complex problems one step at a time; analyze past mistakes when faced with similar problems.

Source: Raymark, P.H., Schmit, M.J., & Guion, R.M. (1997). Identifying potentially useful personality constructs for employee selection. *Personnel Psychology, 50*, 723–736.

key organization characteristics such as an organization's culture (values, beliefs, and norms) and philosophy; the attitudes and behaviours that lead to organizational effectiveness; and the characteristics of individuals who are likely to fit into the organization. The organizational analysis can then be used to construct an *organizational description*, and should form the basis for predictor and criterion measures to be used in areas such as recruitment, selection, socialization, training, performance appraisals, compensation, and so on.

In summary, the development of predictor and criterion measures will increasingly require the incorporation of information based on both organizational and job analyses. Failure to include such information in criterion measures is likely to result in problems of criterion deficiency. In the next section, the different ways to measure predictor and criterion measures are described.

◆◆◆
LEVELS OF MEASUREMENT

Virtually all behavioural research demands the measurement of the objects in which one is interested, and this usually involves assigning numbers or symbols to objects or some property of the objects. The degree to which this assignment of numbers to people or characteristics of people results in data on which we can perform various arithmetic transformations is referred to as the scale or level of measurement. Stevens (1946) identified four types of measurement: nominal, ordinal, interval, and ratio. Understanding these different types of measurement is important because the level of measurement determines the types of statements that can be made about the relationships among observations and the types of statistics that can be calculated with the numbers we collect.

NOMINAL SCALES

A **nominal measurement scale** is one that has two or more mutually exclusive classes or categories of the variable in question. For example, if one is interested in gender, there are two mutually exclusive categories: female and male. Different past job experiences are likely measured on a nominal scale. The numbers, or categories, assigned to the people (in the case of gender) in these examples imply only that they are different in some way. The numbers do not signify any ordering of job experiences or members of different gender groups. We often use nominal values to index the existence or nonexistence of a treatment or intervention.

ORDINAL SCALES

An **ordinal measurement scale** is one that allows us to rank order people or objects on some variable. The colour of hair of a group of individuals can be ordered from light to dark, so we would say that the lightness or darkness of one's hair colour is an ordinal variable. If John's hair is darker than Judy's, whose hair in turn is darker than Joan's hair, then John's hair must also be darker than Joan's if our scale of measurement is really ordinal. In the human resource area, the kind of manipulations or treatments we usually create have clear ordinal relations (no training, some training, or a great deal of training). Usually, the variables we observe can be ordered in some way as well; for example, educational background levels probably can be ordered from high school diploma to doctoral degree, although occasionally the ordering of technical degrees or community college education may be problematic.

INTERVAL SCALES

A rank order tells us nothing about how much difference there is between the ranked objects. To extend the example above, we might assign the number 10 to

John's hair, 6 to Judy's hair, and 2 to Joan's hair. If we can establish that the colour difference between John and Judy's hair, the colour difference between Judy and Joan's hair, as well as any other difference of 4 on our scale is exactly the same, then we can say that we have **interval measurement**.

Note that variables measured in this fashion also allow us to make distinctions between objects (they are the same or different) as for nominal measurement and that we can rank order persons (ordinal measurement) on these interval scales. However, interval scales do not have meaningful zero points (consider the meaning of zero intelligence), which, practically speaking, means we cannot meaningfully form ratios of objects measured on an interval scale. For example, it would not be useful to make the statement that John's hair (darkness = 10) is five times as dark as Joan's hair (darkness = 2), when darkness is measured on an interval scale. Finally, it should be noted that most of the measures (and resultant numbers) used in the measurement of human capabilities or attitudes are treated as though they meet interval assumptions without evidence that the scale limits or differences are equivalent. For example, whether a difference between 65 and 75 on an intelligence scale is the same as the difference between 100 and 110 is debatable, even though intelligence tests are probably one of the better-developed measures of human capabilities.

RATIO SCALES

As you have probably guessed, **ratio scales of measurement** are those in which the objects measured do have interval properties. In addition, zero is a meaningful measurement; hence, we can form ratios of objects measured on a ratio scale. Zero is meaningful because it is possible to have zero length or weight. By contrast, it is difficult to conceptualize what it would mean to say someone has zero intelligence or zero empathy or motivation. Ratio scales are usually encountered only in the physical sciences. The usual examples include height and weight. It is meaningful to say that a person measuring six feet tall is twice as tall as someone measuring three feet tall. Some possible examples of ratio measurement scales in human resources include absenteeism and tardiness measures or the number of units produced in some jobs, such as the number of letters typed by a secretary.

◆ ◆ ◆

PRACTICAL CONSIDERATIONS CONCERNING MEASUREMENT SCALES

The level of measurement with which we assign numbers to objects has practical consequences when we start summarizing our measurements or performing arithmetic operations on the numbers we use to represent the objects. For example, we can transform nominal data any way at all as long as we maintain the separate classification of objects in mutually exclusive categories. Numbers assigned to objects using an ordinal scale may be added, subtracted, multiplied, divided, squared, or transformed in any way that preserves their original rank order.

Transformations of interval data must maintain both order and the relative size of scale intervals; that is, multiplying, dividing, adding, or subtracting a constant number from all values is fine, but taking the square root or squaring changes the size of the intervals between objects. Finally, the ratio properties of a scale are destroyed by the addition or subtraction of a constant number because the zero point changes.

Aside from considerations concerning appropriate transformations of numbers, the scale of measurement also has implications for the ways in which we summarize data and describe the relationships among variables. These summary statistics are described in detail in Chapter 11.

◆ ◆ ◆
SUMMARY

This chapter has presented the issues associated with measurement development. The meaning of variables, concepts, and constructs was discussed, and the development of predictor and criterion measures was described. It was noted that an organizational analysis is becoming an increasingly important source of information in the development of predictor and criterion measures. As human resources begins to focus more on person-organization fit, the measurement of values and personality will be required for purposes such as selection, socialization, performance appraisal, and compensation. The chapter also described the four levels of measurement and their relevance for operationalizing variables.

Whatever the level of measurement or the means by which measures attain meaning, all measures must be of high quality. That is, they must be reliable and valid. This basic notion of reliability and validity is central to assessing the quality of measures, and, as we shall see in the next chapter, there are a variety of ways of assessing them in human resources.

Definitions

Concept   An idea or generalization formed from observation of particular instances.
Construct   A concept deliberately created or adopted for a scientific purpose.
Criterion contamination   A criterion measure that consists of components that were not identified by the job analysis as being relevant and is therefore considered to be "contaminated."

Criterion deficiency   Criterion measures that do not include important KSAs that were identified in the job analysis.

Criterion relevance   The extent to which the actual criterion measure includes the task requirements and KSAs identified in the job analysis.

Interval measurement scale   A measurement scale that assigns values to individuals or objects to indicate differences between them although there is no meaningful zero point.

Job analysis   The activities associated with the determination of the tasks, duties, and responsibilities carried out by job incumbents.

Nominal measurement scale   A measurement scale that has two or more mutually exclusive classes or categories of the variable in question.

Ordinal measurement scale   A measurement scale that involves the ranking of people or objects on some variable.

Organizational analysis   The identification of key organization characteristics such as an organization's values and culture and the characteristics of individuals that are required for organizational success.

Ratio measurement scale   A measurement scale in which the objects measured have true interval properties and zero is a meaningful measurement point.

Variable   A symbol that takes on at least two differing values.

EXERCISES

1. Describe how job performance could be measured using each of the four levels of measurement (i.e., nominal, ordinal, interval, and ratio). Which level of measurement would you recommend for measuring job performance?

2. Consider your current job or the most recent job you held. First, conduct a job analysis by listing the major tasks and responsibilities of your job. If you have a job description, you might want to refer to it. Second, make a list of the dimensions that are used to evaluate your job performance. If you have a copy of a performance appraisal form, you should refer to this. On the basis of this information, answer the following questions:

a) What level of measurement is used to evaluate your job performance? Do you feel that the level of measurement is appropriate? If not, how would you change it?

b) Compare the job analysis information with the performance appraisal dimensions. What is the extent of criterion relevance, deficiency, and contamination?

c) What are some of the reasons why your performance appraisal is relevant, deficient, or contaminated?

d) What are the implications of a performance appraisal that is deficient or contaminated?

e) If your performance appraisal suffers from criterion deficiency or contamination, what actions would you recommend for improvement?

3. Consider the following human resource functions in your organization:
   a) recruitment
   b) selection
   c) performance appraisal
   d) compensation

For each of these functions, describe the extent to which it incorporates relevant knowledge, skills, and abilities and person-job fit, as well as values and personality and person-organization fit. What personality characteristics and values are important to you, your job, and your organization? How are they measured in your organization?

References

Barrick, M.R., & Mount, M.K. (1991). The big five personality dimensions and job performance: A meta-analysis. *Personnel Psychology*, 44, 1–26.

Bowen, D.E., Ledford, G.E., Jr., & Nathan, B.R. (1991). Hiring for the organization, not the job. *Academy of Management Executive*, 5, 35–51.

Bretz, R.D., Jr., & Judge, T.A. (1994). Person-organization fit and the theory of work adjustment: Implications for satisfaction, tenure, and career success. *Journal of Vocational Behavior*, 44, 32–54.

Bridges, W. (1994). *JobShift*. Reading, MA: Addison-Wesley.

Cable, D.M., & Judge, T.A. (1996). Person-organization fit, job choice decisions, and organizational entry. *Organizational Behavior and Human Decision Processes*, 67, 294–311.

Cable, D.M., & Judge, T.A. (1997). Interviewers' perceptions of person-organization fit and organizational selection decisions. *Journal of Applied Psychology*, 82, 546–561.

Campion, M.A. (1988). Interdisciplinary approaches to job design: A constructive replication with extensions. *Journal of Applied Psychology*, 73, 467–481.

Chatman, J.A. (1991). Matching people and organizations: Selection and socialization in public accounting firms. *Administrative Science Quarterly*, 36, 459–484.

Kristof, A.L. (1996). Person-organization fit: An integrative review of its conceptualization, measurement, and implications. *Personnel Psychology*, 49, 1–49.

Kulik, C.T., Oldham, G.R., & Langner, P.H. (1988). Measurement of job characteristics: Comparison of the original and revised job diagnostic survey. *Journal of Applied Psychology*, 73, 462–465.

Mount, M.K., & Barrick, M.R. (1995). The big five personality dimensions: Implications for research and practice in human resources management. In G.R. Ferris (Ed.), *Research in personnel and human resources management* (vol.13, pp. 153–200). Greenwich, CT: JAI Press.

O'Reilly, C.A., III, Chatman, J., & Caldwell, D.F. (1991). People and organizational culture: A profile comparison approach to assessing person-organization fit. *Academy of Management Journal*, 34, 487–516.

Raymark, P.H., Schmit, M.J., & Guion, R.M. (1997). Identifying potentially useful personality constructs for employee selection. *Personnel Psychology, 50,* 723–736.

Runkel, P.J., & McGrath, J.E. (1972). *Research on human behavior: A systematic guide to method.* New York: Holt, Rinehart and Winston.

Saks, A.M., & Ashforth, B.E. (1997). A longitudinal investigation of the relationships between

job information sources, applicant perceptions of fit, and work outcomes. *Personnel Psychology, 50,* 395–426.

Stevens, S.S. (1946). On the theory of scales of measurement. *Science, 103,* 677–680.

8

The Quality of
Measures in Human
Resources

◆ ◆ ◆
INTRODUCTION

In the previous chapter, the issues associated in the development of predictor and criterion measures and different levels of measurement were described. An important outcome of the measurement development process is the quality of predictor and criterion measures. Quality issues have to do with measurement reliability and validity. **Reliability** is the degree to which a measure results in the same values when it is repeated. **Validity** refers to the appropriateness of the inferences we draw from a test score. For example, in using test scores to make selection decisions, we are making an inference from a test score about an individual's job performance. It is important to realize that no matter how well a study has been designed, if the measures have poor reliability and validity, the results of the study will at best be difficult to interpret, and, at worst, meaningless.

After reading this chapter, you should be able to:

■ Understand and describe the meaning and theory of reliability.

■ Know the meaning of and calculation of test–retest reliability, parallel-forms reliability, internal consistency, and interrater reliability.

■ Understand the meaning of and calculation of content validity, criterion-related validity, and construct validity.

■ Understand and describe the criterion-related validation model.

■ Understand and describe the multitrait–multimethod matrix.

Imagine that after beginning a new job in the human resource department in an insurance company you are required to design a new selection system to hire insurance agents. Based on your knowledge of measurement development, you conduct a job and organizational analysis and then design an employment interview that consists of a set of structured interview questions. Eager to try out the new interview, you and a regional sales manager begin to conduct interviews. After the first week of interviews you and the sales manager compare interview notes and ratings. Although you designed a rating scale to rate applicants' answers to each question, you are surprised to find many differences between your ratings and those of the sales manager. Perhaps the sales manager is not used to the new interview and just needs a little time.

At the end of the month, all applicants have been considered and you are ready to hire 100 new sales agents. You review the interview ratings and once again find that there is very little agreement between your ratings and the sales manager's. You begin to question the results. Whose ratings are more accurate? Why is there such disagreement? Whose ratings should be used to make selection decisions? Because you cannot answer these questions, you take the average ratings for each applicant based on your ratings and those of the sales manager.

Six months later, following the new hires' first performance review, you decide to evaluate your employment interview and calculate the relationship between interview ratings and job performance ratings. You are shocked to find that there is no relationship. In other words, employment interview ratings did not predict job performance. You wonder if this is because of the interview ratings problem or if there is something wrong with the performance ratings. You don't know, and you are further dismayed to learn that 20 of the 100 people you hired have decided to quit.

This scenario highlights the importance of measurement quality in human resource research. Following the development of predictor and criterion measures, it is important to evaluate the quality of the measures. By quality we mean the extent to which your measure provides you with an accurate assessment of an individual on a particular variable, what is better known as reliability. In this scenario there appears to be a problem of reliability, as evidenced by the differences in the ratings of the two raters.

Quality also involves the extent to which a measure enables the researcher to make valid inferences. For example, based on one's ratings in an employment interview, can one predict future performance on the job? In the scenario this does not appear to be the case. As a result, the employment interview is not helping the organization to hire the best job applicants.

An important part of measurement is the quality of one's measures. One way to try to solve the employment interview problem would be to calculate the reliability and validity of the interview and performance measures. Low levels of either would require some changes and improvements to the employment interview and perhaps the performance measure as well. Thus, measurement reliability and validity are critical issues in measurement and research, and are the focus of the remainder of this chapter.

◆ ◆ ◆

RELIABILITY THEORY

When measuring physical objects, we usually can take repeated measurements without concern that the object measured will change as a result of being measured. In measuring people, however, the very act of measuring may change people because they may remember the material presented, or the questions asked may stimulate them to search for answers or change their opinions about the concept being measured. This sensitivity to being measured means that their scores may be different upon re-administration of the measure.

Reliability theory is based on the assumption that a person's score on a test is made up of a true score and an error component. Since the errors are considered to be random, the true (t) and error (e) components in a test score (t_s) are independent, and a person's test score can be presented as follows:

$$t_s = t + e \tag{8.1}$$

If we use equivalent measuring instruments, or use the same instrument repeatedly to assess a person's ability (or attitude, perceptions, etc.) many times (each time erasing the effect of measurement), the scores obtained will be different if the measure has less than perfect reliability. These different scores will distribute themselves around the person's true level of ability on the construct being measured. The error component on any given administration of the test is the difference between the person's test score (t_s) and her or his true score (t). Errors have a mean of 0 (some will be positive, some negative), are uncorrelated with one another on repeated administrations of a test, and are uncorrelated with the true score component in the test as stated above. Also, note that defining errors as random excludes consideration of constant error. Constant error is treated as part of the true score in this formulation.

◆◆◆
TYPES OF RELIABILITY

There are a number of different types of reliability that are relevant to measures used in human resources. The type of reliability depends on the purposes for which data were collected. In the following sections, each of the definitions of reliability will be related to issues of interest to human resource researchers.

TEST–RETEST RELIABILITY

Very often in human resources, measures take the form of tests that are used during selection to hire employees; in such cases we are interested in their predictive value. In a predictive sense, a test must yield the same values when it is administered at two different points in time. In estimating **test–retest reliability**, we give a test twice to the same people and correlate their scores at these two different times. The two administrations of the test must be separated by a suitable time interval so that the examinees cannot remember their previous answers. We assume that the first administration of the test does not affect scores on the second administration of the test. The extent of agreement between measurements on different occasions can be assessed by calculating the correlation coefficient between sets of repeated measurements (see Chapter 11 for a detailed discussion of correlation coefficients). The correlation coefficient in this case is called a **reliability coefficient**. If a measurement instrument is not affected by random factors, the reliability coefficient will be 1.00.

Using the notions of true and error variance developed in the previous section, it is clear that any nonsystematic changes in persons across time contribute to error variance. What is perhaps not obvious is that if all individuals change at exactly the same rate, reliability will be perfect (recall that constant change or differences are treated as true score variance). Also, since the test includes the same items on both administrations, any idiosyncrasies (called item-specific variance) in the items are treated as true variance. Only changes in the relative position of the persons measured constitute error variance.

PARALLEL-FORMS RELIABILITY

It is not always safe to assume that the responses of individuals to a second administration of a test will be unaffected by the previous administration of a test, or perhaps it is impossible to get individuals together to take a test more than once. In these cases, it is possible to estimate reliability by constructing two forms of a test and correlating the scores of both measures. This type of reliability is called **parallel** or **equivalent forms**. Two forms of a test are constructed, and the correlation coefficient between the parallel forms is calculated in the same way as that between the scores of two administrations of one of these forms. Of course, we assume that we can remove traces of the first testing on the occasion of administering the second test.

When constructing parallel forms, we try to make the items in both similar with respect to content, instructions, and format. Parallel forms should also be arithmetically equivalent in their means, standard deviations, and the intercorrelations between their items. Classical reliability theory, and the various formulas presented in this chapter, are based on the definition of reliability as the correlation between parallel forms or scores on the same form given twice when administration of the first testing does not influence the second measurement.

The two parallel forms contain similar (in terms of content) but not identical items. Item difficulty (the proportion of people who get the item correct), as well as other item statistics (i.e., correlations of the item with other items), should be as similar as possible across forms. Note that these parallel forms may be given at the same time or may be separated by a suitable interval.

When administered at the same time, the correlation between parallel forms really gives us an index of the degree to which the items in the two forms are similar in content. When the two forms are separated in their administration by a time interval, the correlation between the two forms also may be lowered because of events that have occurred between the two test administrations. Consequently, parallel forms reliability with no time interval between test administrations yields what has been called a coefficient of equivalence (of the forms). When a time interval separates the administration of the two forms, the correlation between the two forms yields a coefficient of stability and equivalence. In the latter case, both time and the nonequivalence of the items in the two forms may serve to lower the reliability; these factors, then, constitute error variance.

Frequently, this may be an appropriate measure of reliability, since we would not be interested solely in a person's answers to specific items at a given point in time, but rather his or her general ability to answer all questions related to particular knowledge or ability at any point in time. Differences across time and item content, then, are appropriately treated as evidence of a lack of reliability. If the parallel forms are administered at the same point in time (or close enough so that an intervening time interval should not have an effect on scores), then only changes in item content constitute error variance.

INTERNAL CONSISTENCY RELIABILITY

Researchers are often faced with a situation in which two forms of an instrument are unavailable and there is no possibility for a second administration of a test. One solution in this case is to take the items in the test, split them randomly into two halves, and correlate the scores of the examinees on these two half-tests. This correlation would be the reliability of a test one-half as long as the original. To obtain the reliability of the full-length test, one needs to apply the *Spearman-Brown correction formula*, which reads as follows:

$$r_{full} = 2r / (1 + r) \qquad\qquad (8.2)$$

where r_{full} is the reliability of the full-length test and r is the correlation between the two half-tests. As an example, let us assume that the correlation between two half-tests is .60. Application of this formula would yield:

$$r_{full} = 2 \times .60 / (1 + .60) = .75$$

The reliability of the full-length test would be estimated at .75. Application of this formula is based on the assumption that the items in the two halves are statistically equivalent measures of the content one is interested in measuring. This means that one would expect the correlations of individual items with the sum of all possible item scores to be equal. This, of course, is most likely to happen when the content of the items in a measure is homogeneous. Internal consistency estimates are often used as an index of the unidimensionality or homogeneity of a set of items. Differences in items constitute error variance.

Another form of internal consistency is called **coefficient alpha**. If one were to split the items in a test in all possible ways, and average the split-half reliabilities (after correction with the Spearman-Brown) obtained in this manner, one would have coefficient alpha. Fortunately, there is a simpler way to calculate coefficient alpha. The formula for its calculation is as follows:

$$r_a = n^2\, \bar{r}_{ij}\, /\, C \qquad\qquad (8.3)$$

where r_a is coefficient alpha, n is the number of items in the test, $\bar{r}_{ij}$ is the average intercorrelation between different items in the test, and C is the sum of all the items in the item intercorrelation matrix, including items above and below the diagonal and the diagonal values (all 1.00 in the case of a correlation matrix).

It is not important to memorize these formulas, but the notions underlying their use is important. First, we assume that all the items in the test measure the same concept or construct when we apply measures of internal consistency. Theoretically, any one item could be an adequate measure of an individual's position on the construct being measured. However, none of our items is a perfect measure; hence we try to minimize the possibility of measurement errors by increasing the number of items. Both the formula for coefficient alpha and the Spearman-Brown formula include in their calculation the number of items. A long test is more reliable than a short test, provided the items measure the same construct. Intuitively, students would usually rather have their grades determined by an examination with many items rather than by a single-item exam, even though the lengthier exam might be more threatening.

While, as a rule, a longer test with more items is generally recommended, primarily because it will result in a more reliable measure, there are often constraints such as cost and survey length that limit the number of items that can be used to measure a particular construct. It is therefore noteworthy that a recent meta-analysis of job satisfaction measures found that single-item measures of overall job satisfaction are strongly correlated with scale measures of overall job satisfaction ($r = .67$) (Wanous, Reichers, & Hudy, 1997). This does not mean that one should use single-item measures; however, it does provide evidence that, in the case of overall job satisfaction, single-item measures are acceptable for use in those instances in which constraints limit or prevent the use of scale measures of overall job satisfaction (Wanous et al., 1997).

INTERRATER RELIABILITY

In human resource research, many constructs are measured by asking raters to make judgments of peoples' performance or behaviour in various organizational situations. Employment interviews, for example, are sometimes conducted by more than one interviewer. The degree to which the judgments of various raters yield similar information about a group of people is called **interrater reliability**. If we view the raters as items in a test, then all the forms of reliability we discussed above apply to raters' judgments. We can compute the consistency with which raters make judgments on two different occasions. If we compute the intercorrelations of the judgments of all raters, and compute coefficient alpha from this correlation matrix, we have a measure of the reliability of the sum of all raters' judgments. Sometimes we will want an estimate of the reliability of a composite of raters' judgments over time as, for example, when ratings are used as criteria in a test validation project.

Returning to our discussion of true and error variance in considering interrater reliability, we can see that these different alternatives will lead to different estimates of reliability. If we used a set of judges to evaluate the worth of jobs and were concerned that their evaluation of jobs might change as a function of time, then we would correlate their judgments of the same jobs (requiring the evaluation in a way that memory could not influence the second evaluation) across time. In this case, time differences would constitute error variance. If the number of jobs to be evaluated were so large that we would have to rely on different judges to evaluate different jobs, then interjudge reliability with an intervening time interval would be an appropriate estimate of reliability. Differences in judges and time would contribute to error variance.

◆◆◆
COMPARING THE TYPES OF RELIABILITY AND CAUSES OF UNRELIABILITY

Whenever we measure some aspect of a person, we are really attempting to ascertain that person's "true" score on the construct we are measuring, as opposed to a score that contains some element of error. In assessing reliability, we are estimating what proportion of variability in people's scores on a particular measure represents true variability on the underlying construct. But, if we have different methods of estimating reliability, then we are likely to get different estimates of the degree to which our instrument is composed of true and error variance. Which of these estimates is correct?

The answer to this question is that it depends on the purpose for which we are measuring individuals and what types of error need to be considered and minimized when we use the measures to make decisions. Consider the case in which a supervisor observes an apprentice electrician trying to locate the source of a malfunctioning electrical circuit. The supervisor rates the performance of the apprentice on a nine-point scale ranging from "Completely inadequate, does not know how to proceed" to "Appropriately and efficiently searched for the problem." We want to determine to what extent such a rating reflects the "true score" of the apprentice and to what extent it reflects "error." In trying to provide estimates of the reliability of this rating, we might take any one or more of the following steps:

1. A second supervisor simultaneously observes and independently rates the same performance.

2. A second supervisor observes the apprentice solving a different problem immediately after the first one.

3. A second supervisor observes the apprentice solving the same problem a week later.

4. A second supervisor observes the apprentice solving a different problem a week later.

In this case, then, we have at least four different reliabilities. In the fourth example, reliability will be lowest because several potential sources of error (rater idiosyncrasies, time, and content of the test) serve to lower the reliability estimate. Which of these definitions we use depends on how we will use the data we collect to make decisions. If we are always going to use the same supervisor to make ratings of apprentices, then the supervisor should not be considered a source of error. Likewise, if we are only interested in apprentices' ability to solve a specific electrical malfunction, then we would not want to evaluate the contribution to error that results from the use of different problem types.

A more complete list of the reasons why individuals differ in performance on a test or measure of job performance is presented in Table 8.1. In the various estimates of reliability presented above, we correlate two sets of measures of the same thing. True or systematic variance causes the individuals' scores to be the same on the sets of measures and increases the correlation. Changes in people on any of the factors in Table 8.1 lower the correlation between the two sets of measures and are defined as errors.

The factors in category I in Table 8.1 will probably stay the same across different testing situations and therefore contribute to our estimate of "true" variability among persons. Some of those factors (B and C) might not be relevant to the trait we are measuring, however, and would detract from the validity of a test (see the discussion of construct validity later in this chapter). Category IIA lists sources that likely would contribute to "true" score estimates when we are interested in specific aptitudes, but category IIB includes factors that would lower reliability when we use parallel forms or internal consistency estimates. All of the category III considerations likely would lower reliability when it is defined in a test–retest fashion, and category IV factors might lower reliability estimated either in test–retest or parallel-forms fashion. You will note differences in raters are not identified in Table 8.1, but everything that applies to written or oral test items also applies to raters. Raters are best conceptualized as test items when we are estimating their reliability.

TABLE 8.1 SOURCES OF INDIVIDUAL DIFFERENCES IN TEST PERFORMANCE

I. Reasons That Are More or Less Permanent and That Apply in a Variety of Testing Situations.

   A. Some traits are general in that they influence performance on many different kinds of tests. General intelligence may influence performance on tests of verbal ability, numerical fluency, or knowledge of psychology.

   B. Some people are more "test-wise" than others; that is, because of more experience or special training in taking tests, they are able to come closer to their maximum potential scores in any kind of test situation.

   C. Some people grasp the meaning of instructions more quickly and more completely than others. Some may flounder through much of a test before catching on to what is required, regardless of the nature of the task; some never fully grasp any kind of test instructions.

II. Reasons That Are More or Less Permanent but That Apply Mainly to the Specific Test Being Taken.

   A. Some of these reasons apply to the whole test or to any equivalent forms of it.

   1. Some people have more of the ability or knowledge or skill or other trait being measured by the test.

   2. Some people find certain kinds of items easy while others may be more confused by them. For example, some people are good at "outguessing" a true-false set of items.

   B. Some reasons apply only to particular items on a test. Of all the items that *could* be included, only a small number actually *are* in the test. There is an element of luck here; if the test happens to contain a few of the specific items to which the individual does not know the answer, his or her score will be lower than if he or she is luckier in the specific questions asked.

III. Reasons That Are Relatively Temporary but Would Apply to Almost Any Testing Situation.

   A. The state of the individual's health may influence his or her score.

   B. A person may not do as well when he or she is particularly tired.

   C. The testing situation is, to some people, a challenge; they want to score high so that they can enjoy a feeling of achievement. The intensity of motivation to do well may fluctuate; the individual will score higher when highly motivated than when less motivated.

   D. Individuals react differently to emotional stress; a person tested under stress is likely to have a score different from that obtained when he or she is tested under emotionally secure conditions.

> ## TABLE 8.1 SOURCES OF INDIVIDUAL DIFFERENCES IN TEST PERFORMANCE (continued)
>
> E. There seem to be some relatively temporary fluctuations in "test-wiseness."
>
> F. A person varies from time to time in the extent of his or her readiness to be tested; such differences in set produce differences in attention to and comprehension of the test situation and, therefore, differences in scores. Those with favourable sets make higher scores.
>
> G. People respond differently to physical conditions (light, heat, etc.); individuals with the same abilities may score differently because of differences in their reactions to unusual or perhaps adverse physical conditions.
>
> IV. Reasons That Are Relatively Temporary and Have Application Mainly to a Specific Test.
>
>   A. Some reasons apply to the test as a whole (or to equivalent forms).
>
>   1. People differ in their understanding of a specific set of instructions; those who understand the instructions do better than those who do not. However, a person who has only a dim comprehension of what he or she is to do at one time might understand better if tested at another time.
>
>   2. Some tests require special techniques; some individuals may "stumble" into certain insights useful in tackling a particular test sooner than would others.
>
>   3. The differences in the opportunities for practising certain skills required in test performance produce differences in scores.
>
>   4. An individual may be "up to" a test or "ripe" for it, at one time and not at another; individual differences in readiness cause differences in scores.
>
>   B. Some reasons apply only to particular test items.
>
>   1. Momentary forgetfulness or lapses of memory while taking a test make a person miss an item he or she might otherwise get right.
>
>   2. The same thing can be said of momentary changes in level of attention, carefulness, or precision in detail.
>
> Source: Reprinted with permission from Guion, R.M. (1965). *Personnel testing.* New York: McGraw-Hill.

◆ ◆ ◆

CORRECTION FOR ATTENUATION

When we develop a measurement instrument, we are rarely, if ever, interested in the scores of individuals on that instrument only. We usually are interested in the way scores on the instrument we developed relate to other test scores, job performance, work motivation, absenteeism, or other behaviours. The reliability of a test is important because it limits the size of any observed relationship with these external variables. In the extreme case, when reliability of a measure is .00, then it does not relate to any other variable. When reliability is less than 1.00, and it almost always is, then we say that relationships with external variables are *attenuated*. Thus, reliability is a necessary condition for validity, as evidenced by correlations with external variables.

Sometimes researchers are interested in the correlation between two variables when or if measurement error (lack of reliability) can be removed. They are interested in making an estimate of the degree of relationship between the underlying constructs or true scores being measured. The estimate of the true relationship (r_{xyc}) between two variables is made by dividing the observed relationship (r_{xy}) by the product of the square roots of the reliabilities (r_{xx} and r_{yy}) as follows:

$$r_{xyc} = \frac{r_{xy}}{\sqrt{r_{xx}} \ \sqrt{r_{yy}}} \tag{8.4}$$

If one were interested in the true relationship between different measures of cognitive ability, for example, corrections for unreliability in both variables would be applied.

If two different measures were correlated .60, and their reliabilities were .81 and .64 respectively, the corrected correlation between these measures would be:

$$.60 \ / \ (\sqrt{.64} \ \sqrt{.81}) = .83$$

A frequent application of this correlation in selection research involves the correction for attenuation for unreliability in the criterion (a job performance measure that we are trying to predict). Corrections to the observed correlation for lack of criterion reliability are made to estimate the true validity of a potential predictor. Similar corrections for predictor unreliability are not made because the use of the predictor in other situations will always involve a similar lack of reliability.

◆ ◆ ◆
STANDARD ERROR OF MEASUREMENT

When a person's level of skill is being evaluated for a particular job or academic assignment, then a single score is obtained for each of the skill dimensions being measured. A relevant question, given the fact that all measures are subject to some error, concerns the accuracy of that single score as an index of the true ability of the individual being measured. Use of the **standard error of measurement** allows us to make statements about the confidence with which we have estimated the true ability level of an individual. Theoretically, the standard error of measurement would be the standard deviation of scores that a person would receive if we could obtain an infinite number of independent test scores from this individual. Because of lack of reliability, these scores would scatter around the individual's true ability level. The standard error of measurement (SEM) can be computed using the following formula:

$$SEM = SD_{test} \ \sqrt{1 - r_{xx}} \tag{8.5}$$

where SD_{test} is the standard deviation of the test and r_{xx} is the test's reliability. So a test with a reliability of .84 and a standard deviation of 10 would have a standard error of measurement equal to 4.00.

Approximately 95 percent of the cases in a normal distribution of scores fall within two standard deviations of the mean. This means, in this case, that the true score of persons with obtained scores of 20 could range between approximately 12 and 28 in 95 percent of the cases. So a person whose true score is 12 is unlikely to have an obtained score as high as 20; likewise, a person whose true score is 28 is unlikely to score as low as 20.

The standard error of measurement has a number of uses in human resources. If we are trying to decide whether to hire two individuals whose scores are three points apart when the SEM is 4.00, we clearly know that the scores these two individuals received are not significantly different from one another, and that on a subsequent test of these two people, we wouldn't be surprised if the persons' relative position on the test were to change. Note, however, that the probability that the higher-scoring individual will score higher on a second administration of the test is always greater than the reverse—that is, that she or he will score lower than the other person. Similarly, if we know this test is correlated with some important outcome measure, the probability is always greater that the higher-scoring person will outperform the lower-scoring individual.

Another use to which the standard error of measurement has been applied is in determining whether a person's obtained test score is significantly above or below a minimum cutting score. In this case, let's say that a human resource department is using the test described above to select only those persons who score above 18. The question then might be whether a person's obtained score falls significantly below 18. A person with a true score of 18 would receive a score of 14 or below only about 16 percent of the time (16 percent of the cases in a normal distribution fall beyond one standard deviation of the mean).

This latter use of the standard error of measurement has been commonly addressed in legal cases involving fair employment. Both the defensibility of a particular cutting score and the significance of the difference between a cutoff and the obtained score of rejected applicants have been at issue. One alternative is to weigh other information more heavily when an applicant's score is relatively close to the cutoff—either above or below. In the absence of other information, however, it is well to remember that one would always be more likely to select an individual whose job or academic performance were superior if his or her tested ability also were higher, assuming the test scores were valid indicators of the job or academic performance one wanted to predict.

To this point, the focus has been on issues internal to a test, such as the ways of assessing whether the scores a test provides are sensitive to changes in time, whether the items in the test are internally consistent (i.e., measure the same ability or construct), and whether the test score is an accurate assessment of a person's true score on the tested construct. The purpose of giving a test, however, is usually to make predictions or inferences about individuals' behaviour or performance in other contexts. We might also be concerned with the relationship between an attitude measure and employees' behaviour. In the next section, the focus shifts to methods of assessing whether or not a test serves this purpose.

◆◆◆
VALIDITY

The accuracy of inferences based on a score that an individual receives on a test or measure is called validity. *Validity* refers to the degree to which a test measures what it is supposed to, or, more formally, the degree to which inferences made from test scores or other instruments are accurate. A common example of this in human resources is the accuracy of inferences that can be made about an individual's job performance on the basis of his or her score on a selection test. If such inferences were correct (relatively speaking) more often than could be expected by chance, we would say that the test is valid in its predictions about job performance. These statements suggest, and correctly so, that a test has validity for particular inferences or interpretations. While it might be valid for one set of inferences or interpretations (e.g., job performance), it might not be valid for other inferences or interpretations (e.g., absenteeism).

There are three ways to establish the validity of a measure in human resources: content, criterion-related, and construct validity. Each will now be discussed.

CONTENT VALIDITY

Content validity refers to the degree to which the responses required by the test items are a representative sample of the tests, behaviours, or knowledge to be exhibited in the domain about which we want to make inferences. For example, when students write exams, they expect the exam questions to be a good representation of the course content. In human resources, selection tests and performance appraisals should include items that are representative of the jobs in question.

Content validity requires the researcher to follow three basic steps:

1. Carefully specify the area of performance or behaviour about which inferences are desired.
2. Clearly formulate the intended uses of the test.
3. Consider and then carefully specify the degree to which the test items sample the behaviour or performance domain of interest.

The extent to which these objectives are met in any given test is assessed by asking a set of subject matter experts to give their opinions regarding how well these various aspects of test construction were conducted, and to evaluate the appropriateness of the end product of these operations (i.e., the test items). Frequently, a group of judges is asked to give appraisals of a test's content, and these assessments are summarized in an index called a **content validity ratio** (Lawshe, 1975).

In human resources, content validity usually begins with a job analysis to identify the major tasks, knowledge, skills, and abilities required to perform a job. This information is then used to determine the content validity of test items. Mussio and Smith (1972) provide relevancy, accuracy (of the situation presented), and fairness scales by which judges can evaluate each of the test items. Each judge is asked to indicate whether the knowledge, skill, or ability measured by the item is essential, useful but not essential, or not necessary to the performance of the job. A content validity ratio (CVR) for each item is calculated using the following formula:

$$CVR= (n_e–N/2) / (N/2) \tag{8.6}$$

where n_e is the number of judges indicating the knowledge, skill, or ability (KSA) is essential and N is the total number of judges. By averaging the CVRs for all items in a test, one can compute a content validity index for the test. The content validity index, then, is a summary of the degree to which the judges believe that the test domain and performance domain overlap. Judgment on the part of experts is obviously crucial in good test construction, but it is also central to other methods of validating the inferences we draw from test data.

While content validity is usually discussed in connection with employment tests, it is also relevant to other measures developed and used in all areas of human resources, such as determining the content of training programs, performance appraisals, and so on.

CRITERION-RELATED VALIDITY

While content validity has to do with the actual "content" of the test or measurement instrument, **criterion-related validity** has to do with the relationship between scores on a test and some criterion. To establish the criterion-related validity of a measure, a researcher collects data from a group of individuals on a test or measure (the predictor) and on some outcome or criterion variable such as job performance. In this way, the researcher can determine the appropriateness of the inferences made from test scores about the criterion (e.g., job performance). The magnitude of the correlation between these two sets of scores is taken as evidence of criterion-related validity, and is referred to as the *validity coefficient*. The validity coefficient is often squared in order to determine the *coefficient of determination*. This coefficient is the amount of variance in the job performance or criterion measure that is accounted for by the selection or predictor measure. For example, a selection test with a validity coefficient of .60 would have a coefficient of determination of .36 and be described as a measure that accounts for 36 percent of the variance of the criterion.

In human resources, criterion-related validity research is often conducted in the development of tests used in selection. This usually involves a number of steps that begin with a job analysis to identify the knowledge, skills, and abilities (KSAs), the development and administration of selection measures to job applicants, the development and collection of job performance measures, and the computation of correlations between scores on the selection test and job performance.

The approach used in the development of predictor measures in selection is outlined in Figure 8.1 and is referred to as the *criterion-related validation model*. The first step in this process is to conduct a job analysis to define the tasks or responsibilities required of the job incumbent and the KSAs necessary to adequately perform these tasks. A group of subject matter experts will then rate the task statements using a questionnaire developed for that purpose. Rating scales may include time spent per week performing a task, task difficulty, and criticality (Levine, 1983). The nature of the rating involved can be seen in Figure 8.2. Overall task importance values can then be computed by multiplying difficulty and criticality ratings and adding the value for the time spent. Tasks can then be organized by category and ranked in terms of importance. The KSAs and their relative importance as judged by job experts and job analysts then become the blueprint for test construction. The researcher may then either use an existing selection procedure or test that measures the relevant KSAs, or construct a new measure. The job analysis information will also be used to develop criterion measures of job performance.

While the general outline of criterion-related research is well developed and widely employed, there are a variety of ways in which these steps may be implemented. Usually these variations are a result of trying to do research in a functioning organization. The major design differences in criterion-related research are discussed below.

DESIGN OF CRITERION-RELATED VALIDITY RESEARCH

Criterion-related validity has probably been the most frequently employed validation strategy for human resource researchers interested in selection research. These researchers have used two different validation strategies: *predictive* and *concurrent*. The difference between these two strategies is primarily one of the timing of the collection of the predictor data (e.g., selection instrument) and the criterion data (e.g., performance data).

In a predictive criterion-related validation study, the researcher collects test or predictor data from a group of job applicants, employs those applicants without ref-

FIGURE 8.1 **Steps in Criterion-Related Validation Research**

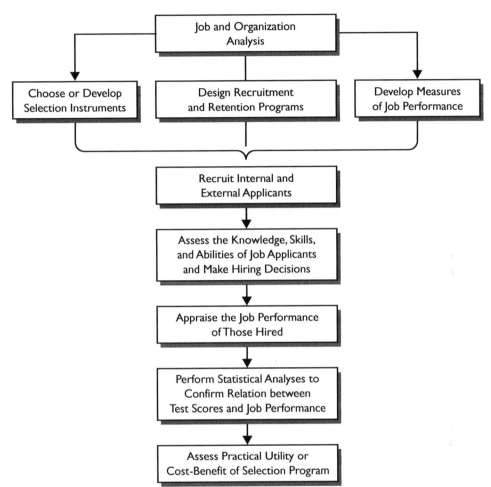

erence to their test scores, and then, on some later occasion, collects data regarding their job performance. The criterion measurement should only take place after the new hires have learned the job—that is, after orientation and training are complete and the worker is a fully contributing member of the organization. The correlation between the test data and the job performance data is then taken as evidence of criterion-related validity.

In a concurrent criterion-related validation study, the researcher collects test data and performance measures at the same time from a group of current job incumbents rather than job applicants. As in the predictive study, the correlation between

FIGURE 8.2 Task Rating Scales

A. Time spent—a measure of time spent per week doing a task relative to all other tasks within a given job.

_____ 1. Rarely do
_____ 2. Very much below average
_____ 3. Below average
_____ 4. Average (approximately 1/2 tasks take more time, 1/2 take less)
_____ 5. Somewhat more than average
_____ 6. Considerably more than average
_____ 7. A great deal more than average

B. Task difficulty—difficulty in doing a task correctly relative to all other tasks within a single job.

_____ 1. One of the easiest of all tasks
_____ 2. Considerably easier than most tasks
_____ 3. Easier than most tasks performed
_____ 4. Approximately 1/2 tasks are more difficult, 1/2 less
_____ 5. Harder than most tasks performed
_____ 6. Considerably harder than most tasks performed
_____ 7. One of the most difficult of all tasks

C. Criticality/Consequences of Error—the degree to which an incorrect performance would result in negative consequences.

_____ 1. Consequences of error are not at all important
_____ 2. Consequences of error are of little importance
_____ 3. Consequences are of some importance
_____ 4. Consequences are moderately important
_____ 5. Consequences are important
_____ 6. Consequences are very important
_____ 7. Consequences are extremely important

test and performance data is taken as evidence of the criterion-related validity of the test. Concurrent validation has been criticized because of potential differences in test-taking motivation of job applicants and job incumbents; the possibility that experience on the job affects test scores; and, perhaps most importantly, the possibility that the full range of applicant ability is not represented in a group of job incumbents. The latter problem is created by the fact that the least-qualified applicants may not have been selected in the first place, the poorest-performing individuals may have been fired, and/or the best performing individuals may have been promoted. This difficulty is referred to as the range restriction problem (discussed below). While the preference among researchers has been for the predictive criterion-related study, existing comparisons of concurrent and predictive studies have yielded small differences in validity coefficients (see Schmitt, Gooding, Noe, & Kirsch, 1984).

However, it is important to realize that validation studies are rarely conducted in the pure form in which they are described above. Sussman and Robertson (1986) identified eleven different approaches to the design of criterion-related research depending on: (1) when the selection instruments are administered, (2) how the selection decisions are made, and (3) when job performance or criteria data are collected. In the purely predictive study, tests of knowledge, skills, and ability are collected from job applicants prior to employment; selection decisions are made on a random basis; and job performance measures are collected after employees have become relatively proficient at their jobs and performance levels have stabilized.

Frequently, however, organizations do not wish to wait the considerable length of time a predictive validation effort often demands or they do not (or cannot) select employees randomly, but use an existing battery or the very same instruments that are being validated to make selection decisions. Frequently, too, existing measures of employee performance are inadequate, so special measures (often job samples or simulations) are developed to serve as criteria in the validation effort.

One of the most common problems associated with criterion-related research is the problem of *restriction of range*. As described above, organizations are understandably reluctant to hire people on a random basis. Instead, they frequently use a selection instrument before it is validated, or they use alternate methods of selection that are related to those that are the subject of a validity study. If the organization rejects low-scoring individuals, no criterion data can be collected for these persons and they cannot be included in a criterion-related validation study. As mentioned previously, in the case of concurrent criterion-related validation, it is also likely that low-performing individuals may have quit or been fired and high-performing individuals promoted away from the group being studied. The problem of restriction of range is analogous to the conduct of an experimental study with a single level of the independent variable.

Fortunately, we can correct the observed validity coefficient (the correlation between a predictor and criterion) for range restriction if we have data on the scores for all hired and rejected job applicants, and can compute the standard deviation of the applicants' scores on the selection instruments. The corrected validity coefficient is then computed using the following formula:

$$r_{xyc} = \frac{r_{xy}\,(SD_u\,/\,SD_r)}{\sqrt{1 - r_{xy}^2 + r_{xy}^2\,(SD_u^2/SD_r^2)}} \tag{8.7}$$

where r_{xyc} and r_{xy} are, respectively, the corrected and uncorrected validities, and SD_u and SD_r are, respectively, the unrestricted and restricted standard deviations. Consider a reasonably realistic situation in which the observed validity coefficient is .30 and half the applicants are accepted. With half of the applicants selected, the standard deviation of the selected group would be about 6.0 if the total applicant group's standard deviation were 10.0. With these data and the formula above, we find the corrected validity coefficient to be as follows:

$$r_{xyc} = \frac{.30(10/6)}{\sqrt{1-.09 + .09\,(100/36)}}$$

$$= \quad .5 \,/\, 1.08$$

$$= \quad .46$$

The corrected validity coefficient (.46) clearly indicates that the test has a higher functional validity than the empirically observed coefficient of .30. Such corrections may be routinely applied in making estimates of the criterion-related validity of selection instruments. Similar correction formulas are available for situations in which predictors other than those we are interested in validating are used, and for situations in which the restriction has occurred on the criterion, such as those cases in which people have been fired or promoted away from the work group. These latter corrections, however, are unlikely to result in the rather substantial increases in estimated validity that occur when direct restriction on the predictor has occurred, as in the example above.

Finally, it is important to keep in mind that the validity of a test is specific to a particular criterion, because it implies that inferences on a test can be made about an individual's standing on some specific criterion. Therefore, it is important to carefully consider the appropriate criterion measure in a validation study. Of most importance in selecting or developing criteria is their relevance to the overall objectives of the organization. For example, in an organization in which attendance is the primary determinant of successful job performance (which may be true in low-skilled, repetitive jobs in which performance is regulated by assembly line speed), perhaps the most relevant criterion is absenteeism. In another case, when training or probationary period costs are very large, perhaps training success or turnover is the most relevant job performance criterion. Most frequently, some index of the quality and quantity of performance will be judged most relevant. The selection of a particular criterion or criteria is always a judgment—one which should be taken seriously. Judgments of criterion relevance can be made by several informed judges, and their agreement as to the relevance of various criteria should be high.

In sum, criterion-related validity is a common and important part of the research process of developing and evaluating different methods of selection. The

HR Research Today box below discusses a study designed to compare the validity of two types of structured interviews.

HR RESEARCH TODAY

The Validity of Structured Interviews

As noted in Chapter 5, the employment interview is one of the most common methods of selection, and 80 years of research on the employment interview has found that "few conclusions have been more widely supported than the idea that structuring the interview enhances reliability and validity" (Campion, Palmer, & Campion, 1997, p. 655). While structured employment interviews are critical for improving interview validity, interview structure can mean many different things (Campion et al., 1997).

Elaine Pulakos and Neal Schmitt (1995) conducted a validation study to compare the validity of two types of structured interviews: the experience-based and situational interviews. The main difference between these two types of interviews is the nature of the questions. The experience-based interview asks questions about past job and life experiences that are job-relevant. For example, applicants are typically asked how they handled situations in the past that are similar to those they will face on the job. In contrast, the situational interview asks applicants to respond to questions about how they would handle or manage hypothetical job-related situations.

In order to compare the validity of the two types of structured interviews, Pulakos and Schmitt (1995) conducted a concurrent validation study. This involved first conducting a thorough task, KSA, and critical incident job analysis to develop interview questions and job performance dimensions, and included the participation of over 600 job incumbents and supervisors. At the end of the process they were able to categorize the KSAs into ten dimensions.

The researchers designed experience-based and situational questions for the following KSA categories: (1) planning, organizing, and prioritizing; (2) relating effectively with others; (3) evaluating information and making decisions; (4) demonstrating initiative and motivation; (5) adapting to changing situations; (6) meeting the physical requirements of the job; and (7) demonstrating integrity. This led to the development of sixteen experience-based and sixteen situational questions, and 7-point rating scales with very specific responses for each question.

The interview questions were administered by panels of three interviewers who were supervisory personnel in the organization and had participated in a day-long training session on how to administer the interviews. The interviewees were current job incumbents who were randomly assigned to receive the experience-based or situational interview. As well, the first-line supervisor of each job incumbent completed a behaviourally based rating scale to obtain job performance data. Recall that the behavioural dimensions of this rating scale were based on the information obtained from the job analysis.

HR RESEARCH TODAY

To determine the validity of the two structured interviews, correlations were computed between job incumbents' interview rating scores and supervisors' performance ratings.

The results indicated that the validity of the experience-based interview was significant (.32), and that of the situational interview was nonsignificant (–.02). Thus, only the experience-based interview ratings were significantly correlated with job performance. Pulakos and Schmitt (1995) concluded that "the experience-based interview was shown to be a valid predictor of job performance whereas the situational interview was not. These results thus lend support to the conclusions of Campion et al. (1994) regarding the superiority of the experience-based interview format for predicting performance" (p. 300).

Source: Based on Pulakos, E.D., & Schmitt, N. (1995). Experience-based and situational interview questions: Studies of validity. *Personnel Psychology, 48,* 289–308.

CONSTRUCT VALIDITY

The **construct validity** of a measure is the degree to which certain psychological concepts or constructs account for performance on a measure. A psychological construct is an idea that is used to organize or integrate existing knowledge about some phenomenon. Construct validity involves the testing of theoretical propositions or hypotheses concerning the construct in which we are interested. The constructs in our theory are operationalized by means of tests, observations, archival data, and so on. The hypothesized or theoretical relationships can then be assessed through the observed relationships between our tests or other observations. A way of visualizing the relationships between theoretical and observable variables is by means of a *nomological network*.

For example, a researcher may notice that some employees seek more direction than others concerning the requirements of their work. Further, the researcher's observations are that this direction-seeking behaviour occurs most frequently in those work units in which no clearly prescribed job duties exist, or in units in which the supervisors are inexperienced and not very knowledgeable about how best to use their employees. The researcher talks to employees in these units and discovers a great deal of concern about what they are supposed to do, how they stand with their supervisor, and how they can get useful information about the organization and their role in it. The researcher calls this lack of direction and unease *role ambiguity*. Role ambiguity is not directly observable, but we infer its existence through the behaviour of people.

If we were to develop a measure of role ambiguity and we wanted to establish its construct validity, we would collect a variety of pieces of information. We might conduct laboratory investigations in which we deliberately manipulate the degree to which various roles in the experimental situation are described. Responses by persons in various conditions to our measure of role ambiguity should reflect these differences in role specification. We might collect information from supervisors concerning how much direction they give their subordinates. Employees in those units in which the supervisors give a great deal of direction should experience less role ambiguity than employees in units in which little direction is given. Or, the investigator could observe the supervisors in various units and rate their direction-giving behaviour. These ratings should correlate with the role ambiguity responses in the units. Investigators may hypothesize that role ambiguity leads to stress. Hence the role ambiguity measure should correlate with self-reports of job stress, as well as other behaviours and illnesses symptomatic of stress. All of these different studies or information should converge or lead us to the conclusion that role ambiguity is a meaningful explanation or construct and that it is central in explaining the behaviour in these various studies.

A nomological network for the role ambiguity construct is illustrated in Figure 8.3. The upper portion of this figure represents our theory. We are hypothesizing that role ambiguity exists, and that it is related to supervisory skill and worker stress, but none of these constructs is directly observable. In order to study these hypothesized constructs and relationships, we must operationalize the constructs or make them observable.

The bottom half of Figure 8.3 is an illustration of one set of possible operationalizations. Supervisory skill, thought to be directly related to role ambiguity, involves the supervisor's ability to give appropriate direction regarding the work that needs to be done. One way of operationalizing this construct might be to ask the supervisors to keep a diary record of their direction-giving behaviour. Another way would be to observe their behaviour in a simulated work task and count instances of direction-giving behaviour as an index of this aspect of their supervisory skill.

You probably could identify problems with both of these operationalizations and you probably could devise several others. In spite of their problems, however, information on these different measures should converge on a single interpretation: Role ambiguity as we conceive it is responsible for observed relationships among the measured variables. Role ambiguity most frequently has been operationalized using the level of workers' agreement to several attitude statements (Rizzo, House, & Lirtzman, 1970). Stress could be operationalized physiologically by measuring blood pressure or heart rate, or we could ask the workers to report their level of perceived stress on some scale. Once the constructs are operationalized in a reliable manner, studies of the hypothesized relationships can then take place.

Thus, the process of construct validation involves three steps:

FIGURE 8.3 Illustrations of a Hypothetical Nomological Network

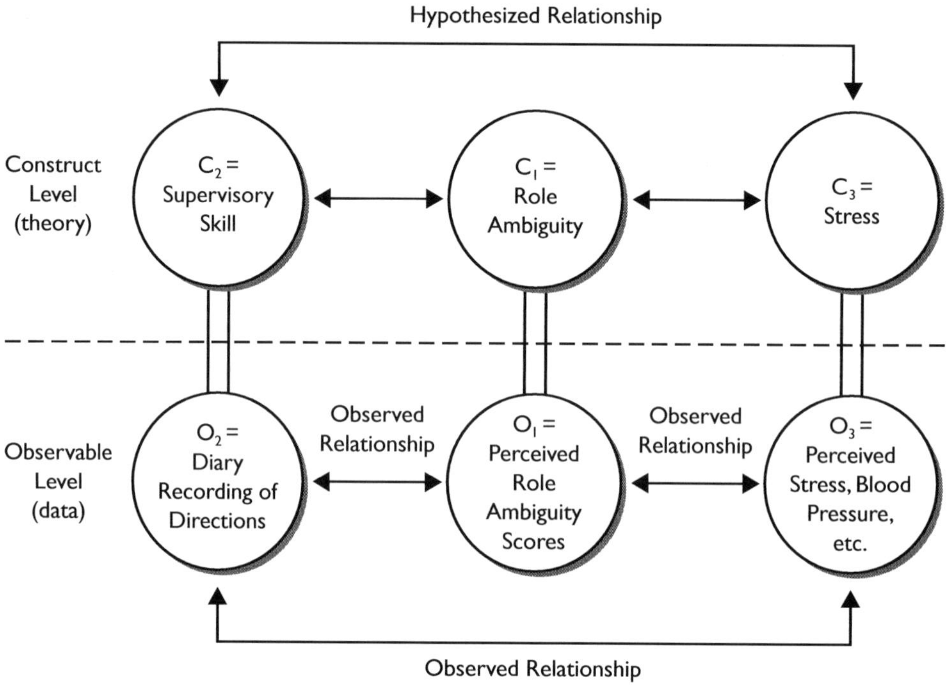

Hypothesized Relationship

Source: Adapted with permission from Walsh, W.B., and Betz, N.E. (1985). *Tests and assessments*. Englewood Cliffs, NJ: Prentice Hall.

1. The construct of interest is carefully defined, and hypotheses about the nature and extent of the construct's relationship to other variables are generated.

2. A measure is developed and its reliability is assessed.

3. Studies examining the relationship of the variable to other measures are assessed.

The method usually used to examine the relationships within the nomological network is known as the multitrait–multimethod matrix (MTMM), and is discussed in the next section.

THE MULTITRAIT–MULTIMETHOD MATRIX

The most frequently employed method used to assess the construct validity of a psychological measure has been the degree to which scores on the measure correlate with scores on other measures of the construct as well as scores on measures of dissimilar constructs. These correlations are usually summarized in a **multitrait–multimethod (MTMM) matrix**.

An example of an MTMM matrix is presented in Table 8.2. In this table, the correlations between three different measures of personality constructs assessed in three different ways are presented. If any of the three sets of scores being generated represents a meaningful construct, then it should correlate more highly with the other two measures of that construct than it does with measures of other constructs. So, for example, scores on organizational ability as measured in a situational interview should correlate highly with organizational ability as measured in the leaderless group exercise and on the questionnaire. Organizational ability scores should not correlate highly with scores on interpersonal skills measures and problem analysis measures, assuming these really are measures of different constructs.

Assessment centres are a good example of places where the MTMM is useful because they involve the systematic observation and evaluation of individuals on numerous traits through the use of a number of methods such as interviews, psychological tests, work samples, and simulations. As originally conceived, the assessment centre method is designed to measure several traits using more than one method. Therefore, it is important that the traits measured by different methods be more highly correlated with one another than they are with other traits. This

TABLE 8.2 AN EXAMPLE OF A MULTITRAIT–MULTIMETHOD MATRIX

	Situational Interview			Questionnaire			Leaderless Group Exercise		
	PA	OA	IS	PA	OA	IS	PA	OA	IS
Situational Interview									
Problem Analysis (PA)	1.00								
Organizational Ability (OA)	.41	1.00							
Interpersonal Skills (IS)	.35	.34	1.00						
Questionnaire									
Problem Analysis (PA)	(.68)	.40	.32	1.00					
Organizational Ability (OA)	.38	(.76)	.32	.36	1.00				
Interpersonal Skills (IS)	.31	.31	(.81)	.30	.29	1.00			
Leaderless Group Exercise									
Problem Analysis (PA)	(.42)	.41	.37	(.53)	.41	.28	1.00		
Organizational Ability (OA)	.37	(.45)	.36	.38	(.49)	.27	.50	1.00	
Interpersonal Skills (IS)	.29	.28	(.51)	.31	.29	(.38)	.45	.44	1.00

requires the use of the MTMM matrix to demonstrate the construct validity of the various traits.

Campbell and Fiske (1959), who first presented the MTMM matrix and described its "logic," suggested four criteria by which to judge the matrix. These criteria, and examples of their application to the matrix presented in Table 8.2, are as follows:

1. The correlations between similar traits measured by different methods (called *convergent validity*) should be both statistically significant and high enough to warrant further consideration. The values in parentheses in Table 8.2 represent convergent validities. These values are relatively good when we consider the correlations between different traits as measured in the situational interview and the questionnaire, but convergent validities involving the leaderless group exercise are only moderate in size.

2. The convergent validities should be higher than the correlations between different traits measured by different methods. This criterion is definitely met for the questionnaire and situational interview measures, but generally is not met for the leaderless group measures.

3. The convergent validities should be higher than the correlations between different traits measured by the same method. This is known as *divergent validity* or *discriminant validity*. These values are located in the *monomethod–heterotrait triangles* enclosed by solid lines in Table 8.2. Again, this appears to be true for the situational interview and questionnaire measures, but it does not hold for the leaderless group exercise measures. In fact, the correlations between the three leaderless group measures are higher than the convergent validities involving these measures.

   When the monomethod–heterotrait correlations are high, we often conclude that there is *method bias*—that is, scores on these measures are more likely a function of the method of measurement (in this case, the leaderless group exercise) than they are attributable to individual differences in the traits being measured.

4. A similar pattern of trait intercorrelations should be apparent in the monomethod–heterotrait triangles, as well as in those triangles involving both different traits and different methods (called *heterotrait–heteromethod triangles*). This criterion is generally met throughout the matrix presented in Table 8.2. Correlations between problem analysis and organizational ability are usually higher than correlations between problem analysis and interpersonal skills, and those between organizational ability and interpersonal skills. The latter two correlations are almost identical in all cases.

Measures that meet these four criteria are said to represent meaningful constructs in their own right—that is, one receives similar scores on a group of people no matter what method of measurement is used, and the trait being measured appears to be different from other psychological dimensions. While the matrix in Table 8.2 is relatively easy to interpret, matrices that include more traits and/or a larger number of methods are not as easy to interpret.

Although this process can be difficult and time-consuming, construct validation is essential in human resource research. Unless we understand the measures we use to collect data, many of the results of our studies will appear confusing and inconsistent. Construct validation is also important because the labels we attach to our measures often convey different meanings to different people, and a test with a given label may not operate the same way in all situations. For example, a measure of role ambiguity might relate to issues of the type of tasks one is expected to do or the persons to whom one must be responsible. Further, role ambiguity could be experienced within both a work organization and a family, but the same measure would not likely be useful in both contexts.

The MTMM has been used to determine the construct validity of the measures used in assessment centres. As noted earlier, assessment centres provide ratings of individuals on several skill dimensions, based on performance on various exercises. Sackett and Dreher (1982) argued that, if ratings on skill dimensions are meaningful, then ratings of the same skills obtained in different exercises should correlate highly with one another, and ratings on different skills obtained from the same exercise should not correlate highly with one another. However, Sackett and Dreher (1982) as well as several others (e.g., Turnage & Muchinsky, 1982) have reported evidence contrary to this expectation. That is, correlations among different skills obtained in the *same* exercise were high, and correlations between ratings of the same skill from *different* exercises were low. Thus, research on the assessment centre using the MTMM does not support the construct validity of the individual skill dimensions, and calls into question the construct validity of the dimensions being measured in assessment centres.

In summary, construct validity is more difficult to assess than content and criterion-related validity. It is not, however, any less important. For example, research on employment testing has shown that job applicants "fake" their responses on personality tests, a problem known as response distortion (RD). Response distortion was found not only to occur, but to influence hiring decisions and to affect the construct validity of personality measures (Rosse, Stecher, Levin, & Miller, 1998). Thus, construct validity is an important concern in employment testing, as well as content and criterion-related validity.

SUMMARY

In this chapter, the requirements for quality measures in human resource research have been described. Reliability and validity were defined, and the methods for estimating them were discussed. The importance of measurement reliability cannot be overemphasized. If the measures used in human resource research are not reliable, then we cannot conduct meaningful research, regardless of the human resource problem with which we are engaged. Furthermore, evidence that a measure is reliable must be accompanied by evidence that the measure is also a valid indicator of the construct in which we are interested. Effective human resource research and practice require measures that are reliable and valid.

Definitions

Coefficient alpha A form of internal-consistency reliability.

Construct validity The degree to which a test measures what it is supposed to measure in terms of a particular psychological construct.

Content validity The degree to which items on a test are a representative sample of the domain of interest or content area.

Content validity ratio (CVR) A summary or index of the content validity of a test or measure.

Criterion-related validity The degree to which one can make inferences about something based on test scores. Criterion validity is usually indicated by the correlation between a predictor variable and a criterion variable.

Internal consistency reliability A form of reliability based on the homogeneity or relations among the items of a test.

Interrater reliability Reliability based on the similarity of ratings made by different raters.

Multitrait–multimethod matrix (MTMM) A method used to assess the construct validity of a psychological measure that involves calculating the correlations between similar and dissimilar constructs.

Parallel/Equivalent forms of reliability Reliability based on the similarity of test scores obtained from two similar or parallel forms of a test.

Reliability The degree to which a measure is dependable, consistent, and stable.

Reliability coefficient The correlation coefficient between scores of repeated measurements of a test used to determine reliability.

Standard error of measurement Indicates the extent to which one can be confident about the accuracy of an individual's score on a test or measure.

Test–retest reliability Reliability based on the similarity of test scores from the same test when it is administered at two different points in time.

Validity   The appropriateness of the inferences and interpretations that are made from a test score.

EXERCISES

1. Review the employment interview scenario at the beginning of the chapter and answer the following questions:
   a) What do you think are some possible explanations for the lack of agreement between the raters and the failure of interview ratings to predict job performance?
   b) What would you do in order to understand what the problem is and to improve the employment interview?
   c) Explain how you would calculate the reliability and validity of the employment interview. For each type of reliability and validity, explain how you would proceed. What type(s) of reliability and validity would be most practical and meaningful in this situation?

2. Contact a member of a human resource department and ask her/him about the reliability and validity of the measures used in selection. Using the information provided in Chapter 5 about research interviews, develop a series of interview questions to learn about the reliability and validity of selection methods being used by the organization. For example, do they have information on the reliability and validity of their selection measures? If

so, what type of reliability and validity information do they have? How was reliability and validity determined? What is the reliability and validity of their selection methods?

3. In the last several years, emotional intelligence (EI) has become a hot topic. According to Daniel Goleman (1995), author of *Emotional Intelligence*, EI consists of a number of domains, including knowing one's emotions, managing emotions, motivating oneself, recognizing emotions in others, and handling relationships. Proponents of this view argue that EI affects many aspects of one's life, including health, relationships, as well as careers. Not surprisingly, some organizations have begun to consider testing employees for EI as part of the selection process, and test makers have begun to market tests that purport to measure EI.

   If management in your organization asked you to consider purchasing a test to measure EI for selection purposes, what would be your response? Based on the information provided in this chapter, what would you do to determine whether your organization should purchase a test that measures EI for use in selection?

References

Campbell, D.T., & Fiske, D.W. (1959). Convergent and discriminant validation by the multitrait–multimethod matrix. *Psychology Bulletin, 56,* 81–105.

Campion, M.A., Palmer, D.K., & Campion, J.E. (1997). A review of structure in the selection interview. *Personnel Psychology, 50,* 655–702.

Goleman, D. (1995). *Emotional intelligence.* New York: Bantam Books.

Lawshe, C.H. (1975). A quantitative approach to content validity. *Personnel Psychology, 28,* 563–575.

Levine, E.L. (1983). *Everything you always wanted to know about job analysis.* Tampa, FL: Mariner Publishing Co.

Mussio, S.J., & Smith, M.K. (1972). *Content validity: A procedural manual.* Minneapolis, MN: Civil Service Commission.

Pulakos, E.D., & Schmitt, N. (1995). Experience-based and situational interview questions: Studies of validity. *Personnel Psychology, 48,* 289–308.

Rizzo, J.R., House, R.J., & Lirtzman, S.I. (1970). Role conflict and ambiguity in complex organizations. *Administrative Science Quarterly, 15,* 150–163.

Rosse, J.G., Stecher, M.D., Levin, R.A. & Miller, J.L. (1998). The impact of response distortion on preemployment personality testing and hiring decisions. *Journal of Applied Psychology, 83,* 634–644.

Sackett, P.R., & Dreher, G.F. (1982). Constructs and assessment center dimensions: Some troubling empirical findings. *Journal of Applied Psychology, 67,* 401–410.

Schmitt, N., Gooding, R.Z., Noe, R.A., & Kirsch, M.P. (1984). Meta-analyses of validity studies published between 1964 and 1982 and the investigation of study characteristics. *Personnel Psychology, 37,* 407–422.

Sussman, M., & Robertson, D.U. (1986). The validity of validity: An analysis of validation study designs. *Journal of Applied Psychology, 71,* 461–468.

Turnage, J.J., & Muchinsky, P.M. (1982). Transituational variability in human performance within an assessment center. *Organizational Behavior and Human Performance, 30,* 174–200.

Wanous, J.P., Reichers, A.E., & Hudy, M.J. (1997). Overall job satisfaction: How good are single-item measures? *Journal of Applied Psychology, 82,* 247–252.

9

Individual Measurement Techniques

◆ ◆ ◆
INTRODUCTION

Measurement in human resources often involves the measurement of individuals' traits, behaviours, and outputs. Many techniques have been developed to measure individual-level variables. Over the years, the goal has been to uncover the best technique or scale. However, it is important to note at the outset that no one technique has been found to be the best, even for a given purpose. In fact, some have argued that looking for the perfect scale or instrument is not a fruitful way of dealing with the issue of improving quality (Landy & Farr, 1980). The focus of this chapter is the variety of methods and techniques used in human resource research to measure individual level variables.

After reading this chapter, you should be able to:

- Describe the different options for individual measurement in human resources.

- Understand the meaning and use of objective output measures.

- Know how to use ratings and the different types of rating scales.

- Understand how to use various personnel comparison systems.

- Describe the advantages and disadvantages of different sources for individual measurement.

- Discuss the major forms of rating biases and errors.

- Describe the different approaches for improving measurement of individuals.

◆ ◆ ◆
MEASURING INDIVIDUALS

To start, it is important to consider which aspects of individuals are measured or rated in human resource research. Some years ago, Campbell and his associates (Campbell, Dunnette, Lawler, & Weick, 1970) described the numerous options open to human resource specialists regarding the content or substance of assessments at the individual level. They suggested that measurement programs can emphasize person, process, or products.

By *person* they meant that a rating can focus on evaluating the personal traits or qualities that are felt to be important in employees. Thus, an effective employee is one who has or exhibits key attributes, such as initiative, loyalty, dependability, and so on. Despite its popularity and the documented preference of people to use trait categories in relating to one another, Campbell et al. (1970) and others (Bernardin & Beatty, 1984) argue strongly against this type of orientation. Making trait assessments is quite difficult, even for individuals trained as specialists (psychologists). Traits are not tangible or clearly defined entities. They must be inferred from what people do or say. Yet, arguments can be made for the use of trait-based assessment programs under certain circumstances.

Process data refer to job-relevant behaviours. Instead of emphasizing personal qualities, this approach focuses on what a person does or does not do on the job. The attention to job-relevant behaviour appears to have at least three advantages. First, behaviour is observable. We can see and record it with some reliability. Second, it is likely to be under the control of the individual. It is something for which individuals can be held accountable. Finally, it can usually be changed or modified. This is related to the second point. Dysfunctional or inappropriate behaviour patterns, when isolated, may be useful as examples in programs designed to bring about improvement in effectiveness.

Getting at relevant processes can present quite a challenge if what is truly important is how a person thinks or makes decisions in contrast to any particular job behaviours. In this case the phenomenon of interest is mental, and cannot be observed or noticed under normal conditions. Thus, we may have to rely on self-reports of how a problem is approached intellectually (through interviews or diaries), or develop observable indicators of the underlying mental processes. For example, Martin and Klimoski (1990) had managers speak aloud under controlled circumstances while they conducted an evaluation of their employees. This provided information regarding their mental processes on this task. These data, in turn, could be evaluated for correctness or effectiveness. Similarly, cognitive psychologists have devised procedures to allow for the measurement of mental processes through such observable behaviours as decision time, the way people search for information as they solve problems, or the choices that they make (Ford, Schmitt, Schechtman, Hults, & Doherty, 1989). Finally, some worker-oriented job analysis techniques do attempt to get at the relevance and importance of on-the-job thinking and decision making as it relates to work effectiveness.

Alternatively, measurement ratings may stress what have been called *products*. Guion (1965) labels the product of effort or work a secondary outcome. These are the things accomplished or produced as part of one's job. Sometimes they are referred to as outcomes. The attraction of indexing effectiveness in terms of "number of units produced," "commissions earned," "scrap levels," and so forth, stems in large part from the apparent objectivity involved. Such things can be counted or measured directly. But, as pointed out in the discussion of criterion contamination in Chapter 7, these indicators, too, have their problems. Sometimes a criterion measure is used just because it is easy to measure. Such measures often are deficient and contaminated. As well, the objective nature of these types of criteria is frequently overstated. Subjectivity and human judgment enter into the measurement process at many points (Smith, 1976).

To appreciate the distinction between person, process, and product, consider the following example, in which we want to evaluate a manager's dependability:

Person	*Process*	*Product*
Judged on dependability	Observed tendency to review own work and the work of subordinates daily	Percent of deadlines achieved

As you can see, while the concept of dependability is retained in each case, the operational indicators are different. Current thinking among human resource specialists is that there are advantages to using job-related behaviours (process data) as the substance of effectiveness measures. However, each approach appears to have features that may make it attractive under certain circumstances. For example, trait measurement would be appropriate and even necessary if the purpose were to select individuals for new or different assignments (Bernardin & Beatty, 1984). Evaluating individuals on the basis of behaviour would seem useful for the planning of training or development activities or for evaluating training programs (Wexley & Latham, 1981). Outcome measures may be appropriate as a basis for administrative decisions such as compensation (Carroll & Schneier, 1982).

Regardless of the choice of person, process, or product, it should be kept in mind that the problems of contamination, deficiency, reliability, and so on, must still be dealt with. To put it another way, the purpose for the measurement of individuals should determine which approach(es) should be used. In the remainder of this chapter, different techniques for rating individuals are presented.

◆ ◆ ◆
OBJECTIVE OUTPUT MEASURES

To measure variables at the individual level, many organizations and researchers prefer to use work products or output measures as discussed above. This is done in the belief that such indicators are less subjective and less prone to errors and biases. Moreover, these indicators are attractive to many managers because they can be more easily translated into a dollar value, which is a measure that most people can understand and use. The "amount of goods produced" or "customers serviced" is the stuff that industry is built on.

The use of any output measure for indexing the effectiveness of individuals, however, requires some basis for comparison. Several options exist. A person's performance can be assessed relative to his or her past performance, the performance of others, some established standard, or a set or an implied goal (Carroll & Schneier, 1982). Of these possibilities, the one that is most widely used involves the determination and use of engineered standards.

The application of performance standards has a rich tradition in industry, deriving from the scientific management movement. Thus, it is not surprising that a variety of techniques for their derivation has been invented. For example, historical (typical) performance levels are used as standards in this way. The most common techniques to establish standards are *time study* and *work sampling*. Both involve the systematic observation of workers as they perform the job or elements of the job. Job behaviours and activities are then classified and timed. As a result of this developmental work, the specialist can estimate fairly accurately the amount of time it takes the typical worker to do the tasks that make up a job and, consequently, how much work can be performed in a period of time (e.g., an hour or a day).

Output data can be gathered in any number of ways. A supervisor may count the products produced, the worker may do this, or it might be done automatically. The U.S. Navy, for example, employs many civilians whose job it is to enter information into military computers at seven centres throughout the country. Recently they have come to emphasize the "number of keystrokes per hour" as an output measure of the effectiveness of personnel. One advantage of this measure is that these data can be recorded directly by the computer being fed the information. A standard of 9000 strokes per hour has been established as reasonable for entering data, and a somewhat higher rate is expected for the verification of data.

To index a worker's effectiveness, one can look at their performance relative to a standard. Usually this is done by computing an efficiency index (EI) and comparing employees on this basis. An efficiency index is created by dividing the person's output, in units, by the standard, in units, for some unit of time (e.g., an hour) and then multiplying by 100 as follows:

$$\text{Efficiency index} = \frac{\text{Output in units}}{\text{Standard in units}} \times 100 \qquad (9.1)$$

Productive efficiency or productivity, then, is a function of the employee's efficiency index and the number of hours worked relative to the number authorized or expected.

It may not be obvious from this brief description that a great number of choices or decisions have to be made in order to come up with such objective indices of effectiveness. For example, the analyst has to choose the method for studying the job, a "typical" group of workers has to be selected and observed, levels of effort exerted by these people must be estimated, and so forth. As Smith (1976) points out, human judgment enters into every performance measure.

HR RESEARCH TODAY

Objective and Subjective Measures of Employee Performance

In human resource research, job performance is the most widely studied criterion or out-come variable. Not surprisingly, the construct validity of job performance measures is criti-cal. The most common way to distinguish measures of job performance is in terms of objective and subjective measures.

Objective measures of job performance are defined as "direct measures of countable behaviours or outcomes" (Bommer et al., 1995, p. 588). Subjective measures usually refer to supervisor ratings of job performance. The use of these two types of measures in job performance research raises an interesting question: How similar are objective and subjec-tive measures of job performance, and are they interchangeable? This is an important research question because different measures of job performance are often treated syn-onymously.

To answer this question, Bommer et al. (1995) conducted a meta-analysis of studies that included both objective and subjective measures of employee job performance. The purpose of their meta-analysis was to assess the relationship between objective and sub-jective performance measures. They also tested for several moderator variables including job type, rating method, rating format, and the objective measure's content (i.e., quantity or quality).

The meta-analysis included a total of 40 articles that resulted in 50 correlations between objective and subjective measures of job performance. The overall correlation between objective and subjective performance measures was .39. The results of the mod-erator analysis revealed that the correlation between objective and subjective measures was higher when the objective measure reflected performance *quantity* (.38) rather than *quality* (.24). Thus, the relationship between objective and subjective performance measures was stronger for objective measures of performance quantity.

On the basis of these results, Bommer et al. (1995) concluded that objective and sub-jective measures should not be used interchangeably. However, they also noted that, in the case of objective indicators of production quantity, subjective measures are likely to be a reasonable approximation.

Source: Based on Bommer, W.H., Johnson, J.L., Rich, G.A., Podsakoff, P.M., & Mackenzie, S.B. (1995). On the inter-changeability of objective and subjective measures of employee performance: A meta-analysis. *Personnel Psychology*, 48, 587–605.

Output measures frequently reflect factors outside the worker's control (they are contaminated criteria). The rate of work may be determined by product demand more than by worker ability or motivation. Even for jobs that lend themselves to such measurement, it is inappropriate to think of them as capturing the worker's true value to the organization (they are deficient criteria). The worker's output may vary in quality or there may be requirements to help co-workers that are not part of the productivity measure. To the extent that such measures are available, they must be scrutinized before being used for purposes for which they were not originally designed.

While output measures provide an objective indicator of an individual's performance and behaviour, their use is limited to those jobs that result in measurable objective outputs. Most jobs do not result in clear, objective outcomes. As a result, other types of measures are needed to measure individual behaviour. However, as noted in the HR Research Today box on page 232, other more subjective measures of employee performance do not necessarily measure the same thing.

◆◆◆
RATINGS

Ratings are perhaps the most prevalent technique for measuring individual-level variables. In fact, the term "rating" is almost synonymous with the measurement of individual behaviour. In this technique, managers are asked to form an impression of an employee's performance or effectiveness relative to some standard of excellence. Usually the standard is with regard to certain expectations held for anyone in that job. Thus, ratings are assumed to involve what are called *absolute judgment*. Ratings reflect how much effectiveness there is. Inasmuch as it is felt that the particular scale used for recording these judgments also plays a role in their formulation (DeNisi, Cafferty, & Meglino, 1984), a great deal of attention has been given to scale format.

GRAPHIC SCALES

The **graphic scale** is the oldest and perhaps most popular type of rating scale. It is also one of the simplest. In its most basic form, the scale takes the shape of a line upon which the rater places a mark at the point that best reflects his or her judgment. However, the continuum is usually broken into a number of parts or segments (called *scale points*), each representing a discrete level or degree of effectiveness. A wide variety of graphic scales can be seen in Figure 9.1.

It is clear from Figure 9.1 that graphic scales can differ in the number of scale points used to reflect effectiveness. At a minimum, a scale might have just two points or levels. A person may be judged "good" or "bad" at some behaviour, judged to have or not to have a trait or quality, and so on. Most of the time, however, there are more than two levels. It also has been discovered that managers don't like to be forced into making such simple assessments, so more scale points are typically used. On the other hand, too many points on a continuum can cause problems with reliability.

FIGURE 9.1 Alternative Scale Formats

a) Quality   High |_____|_____✓_____|_____|_____| Low

b) Quality   High |_____|_____✓_____|_____|_____| Low
                    5   4   3   2   1

c) Quality |_____|_____✓____|_____|_____|

| Exceptionally high-quality workmanship | Work usually done in a superior way | Quality is average for this job | Work contains frequent flaws | Work is seldom satisfactory |

d) Quality

| Too many errors | About average | Occasional errors ✓ | Almost never makes mistakes |

e) Quality   5   (4)   3   2   1

f) Quality

Performance Factors	Performance Grade			
	Consistently Superior	Sometimes Superior	Consistently Average	Consistently Unsatisfactory
Quality: Accuracy Economy Neatness	☐	☒	☐	☐

g) Quality

1 2 3 4 5	6 7 8 9 10	11 12 13 14 15	16 17 18 19 20	21 22 23 24 25
▯▯▯▯	▯▯▯▯▯	▯▯▯▯▯	☒▯▯▯▯	▯▯▯▯
Poor	Below Average	Average	Above Average	Excellent

h) Quality of Work

     15   13   (11)   9   7   5   3   1

| Rejects and errors consistently rare | Work usually OK: errors seldom made | Work passable: needs to be checked often | Frequent errors and scrap: careless |

i) Quality of Work   Judge the amount of scrap; consider the general care and accuracy of his or her work; also consider inspection record.

                 Poor. 1–6;   Average. 7–18;   Good. 19–25.   __20__

Source: Reprinted with permission from Guion, R.M. (1965). *Personnel testing.* New York: McGraw-Hill.

FIGURE 9.2   The Best Scale Anchors for a Five-Point Summated Scale

a) When Assessing Frequency: "How often does this worker turn in work on time?"

1	2	3	4	5
Never	Occasionally	Fairly many times	Very often	Always

b) When Assessing Amount: "How much potential for management does this worker have?"

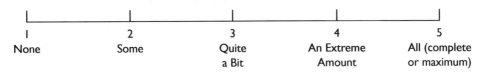

1	2	3	4	5
None	Some	Quite a Bit	An Extreme Amount	All (complete or maximum)

Source: Adapted with permission from Bass, B. M., Cascio, W. F., and O'Connor, E.J. (1974). Magnitude estimations of expressions of frequency and amount. *Journal of Applied Psychology, 59*, 313–320.

Simply put, you are asking the rater to make discriminations that are too fine-grained and unrealistic, given the limits of human nature. While we may conceive of 100 levels or degrees of some construct, we simply cannot make this level of differentiation with any degree of reliability.

Over the years, several studies have been conducted to establish the appropriate number of scale points (e.g., Bass, Cascio, & O'Connor, 1974; Lissitz & Green, 1975). For most purposes, five to nine levels are recommended, as shown in Figure 9.2.

Graphic scales differ in the way that the scales and scale points are labelled or anchored. The attribute or factor to be rated may simply be listed or attached to each scale, or short paragraphs may be provided. Similarly, the scale points may be defined by numbers, adjectives, adverbs, or more elaborate descriptive phrases. As you will see shortly, the trend in the construction of scales is to make use of more complete descriptions employing behaviours as anchors. Ultimately, even these latter variations will have implicit or explicit numerical values. Thus, a person's score on the graphic scale becomes the sum or total number of points produced by the choice of scale location.

SUMMATED SCALES/BEHAVIOUR OBSERVATION SCALES

This format is also simple to use, and builds on features of graphic scales. Based on a job analysis, a large number of statements related to work behaviour are generated.

Using various forms of item analyses, a subset is retained for scale use. If the instrument is to get at several dimensions of effectiveness (e.g., customer relations, technical knowledge), multiple items can be used to define each dimension. In any event, each statement becomes a stimulus to which a rater must respond.

In the **summated scale** format, possible response continua include frequency, degree of goodness, and amount or intensity. Thus, the scale points (regardless of their number) would be anchored according to the type of judgment desired. Figure 9.2 shows the results of one study (Bass et al., 1974) that identified the best words to use to anchor a continuum of frequency or amount for a scale involving five points. The Bass et al. (1974) study could be consulted if you wanted the optimal anchors for various numbers of scale points.

To use the resulting summated scale, raters place a mark at an appropriate place on the continuum associated with each item. An employee's overall score is the sum of the values represented by the scale points given.

Latham and Wexley (1981) have presented a type of summated scale called the **behaviour observation scale (BOS)**. A key feature of BOS development is a careful job analysis. The items are specific, job-relevant descriptions of behaviour. The manager is required to indicate the frequency with which each occurs on the job. In practice, several items are used to measure effectiveness in a particular area. Numerous dimensions are required for most jobs. An example of a BOS scale used by managers to measure effectiveness in the area of dealing with organizational change is presented in Figure 9.3.

Part of the appeal of the BOS approach is that it is likely to produce higher-quality ratings by making appraisals less difficult to perform. Only basic judgments of frequency are called for and few inferences are required. Moreover, the fact that the statements are so job-related promotes the impression that the scale is appropriate and valid (which it should be, if developed properly). And this, in turn, encourages conscientious effort in the conduct of the appraisal.

WEIGHTED CHECKLIST

The scales described to this point have a common feature in that the person completing them has a pretty clear idea of the score he or she is awarding to someone being rated. The values of the various scale points are usually obvious. Thus, should the manager want to, it would be easy to give someone a score that is unwarranted (too high or too low). In many organizations this generally means inflated ratings. **Weighted checklists** are thought to reduce this possibility by not giving the rater scale value information.

When originally introduced in the 1940s (Knauft, 1948), the items in a checklist were adjectives, statements, or phrases. Today, they more often are short descrip-

FIGURE 9.3 An Example of a Behaviour Observation Scale

Example of One BOS Criterion or Performance Dimension for Evaluating Managers

I. Overcoming Resistance to Change*

    1. Describes the details of the change to subordinates.

        Almost Never   1   2   3   4   5   Almost Always

    2. Explains why the change is necessary

        Almost Never   1   2   3   4   5   Almost Always

    3. Discusses how the change will affect the employee.

        Almost Never   1   2   3   4   5   Almost Always

    4. Listens to the employee's concerns.

        Almost Never   1   2   3   4   5   Almost Always

    5. Asks the employee for help in making the change work.

        Almost Never   1   2   3   4   5   Almost Always

    6. If necessary, specifies the date for a follow-up meeting to respond to the employee's concerns.

        Almost Never   1   2   3   4   5   Almost Always

Total = _____

Below Adequate	Adequate	Full	Excellent	Superior*
6–10	11–15	16–20	21–25	26–30

*Scores are set by management.

Source: Latham, G.P., and Wexley, K.N., *Increasing productivity through performance appraisal*, 2nd edition, p. 85. Copyright 1994, 1981 Addison-Wesley Publishing Company Inc. Reprinted by permission.

tions of behaviour, not unlike BOS items (Bernardin & Beatty, 1984). To construct this type of scale, a large number of items are generated by people familiar with the job in question. Participants are asked to recall specific examples of on-the-job behaviours that reflect something that is noteworthy because it was something either very good or very poor. These descriptions of incidents are edited down to short phrases. Job experts are then asked to scale the items in this large pool according to the level of effectiveness they reflect. One way to do this is to use the method of equal-appearing intervals developed in attitude measurement research. Using this method, the items are sorted into eleven piles or categories, each representing distinguishable levels of effectiveness. Items for which there is a consensus are then selected for use on the rating instrument. Their value becomes the mean of the scores obtained from the scaling that was conducted.

The final appraisal instrument that is presented to raters consists of a series of short behaviour descriptions. Usually, the items are mixed up with regard to the level of effectiveness they convey and, in the case of a multidimensional instrument, the areas of effectiveness as well. In all cases, the scale values of the items are not given. To use the instrument, the rater is required to check off those items that are felt to be descriptive of the employee being assessed. The score received by that employee is a function of the sum of the scale values of the items selected or the median of these items. In practice, the rater presumably would not have access to the weights, so the scores might be computed by someone in the human resource department.

FORCED CHOICE SCALES

In some respects, **forced choice scales**, in which the rater is forced to make a choice of statements about an employee from a group of potential statements, represent an extension of the weighted checklist approach. They were developed mainly because of a growing dissatisfaction with the way evaluations were being made and recorded on more conventional scales. Wherry (1952) is credited with creating them with the goal of reducing error of leniency and increasing accuracy. Initial evidence has confirmed that, compared to graphic scales, ratings on these scales are more normally distributed. Not all individuals are given high evaluations. The key seems to lie in the fact that, as in the case of the checklist, the rater does not know the scale values of the items, and they are hard to discern intuitively.

In the forced choice format, items are grouped so that they have equal desirability in the eyes of the rater. He or she is required, or forced, to choose one or more items from each cluster that best describe the employee. The scale value of the items selected (unknown to the rater) then becomes the employee's score.

To understand this approach, it is important to know the procedure used to create, scale, select, and cluster the items. Items usually are generated by job experts and edited into short phrases. They are then scaled for and arranged by two properties. The first is referred to variously as *importance* or *favourability*. This is the extent to which the attribute or behaviour reflected in the item is attractive or makes a person manifesting it look good. The second property is referred to as *discriminability*. This is the appropriateness of the item for describing a truly superior employee. In a sense, it is the item's validity. Statements are arranged so that, in a cluster of two or four, all would have about the same importance or favourability; however, only one might truly reflect effectiveness.

Constructed this way, the scale is resistant to carelessness or deliberate distortion. Checking a statement at random should not introduce a particular bias into a score. More importantly, a person who wanted to give an employee a very high (or low) evaluation when one was not warranted would have a difficult time. He or she would not be able to use the apparent favourability as a clue to which ones to select.

There are several ways to scale statements for favourability and discriminability, but there is no conclusive evidence that one might be better than another (Bernardin & Beatty, 1984). On the other hand, there seems to be a professional consensus that the use of clusters of four favourable or positive items, two of which have some relation to effectiveness and two of which do not, is the format to be preferred (Berkshire & Highland, 1953). In this situation, the rater is required to select two of the four that he or she feels is appropriate. The ratee's score then becomes the number of valid statements chosen.

Research on this type of scale appears to have been carried out in two "waves" of activity—when it first was invented (e.g., Sisson, 1948) and more recently (King, Hunter, & Schmidt, 1980). While there seems to be a fair amount of data to support the view that its use does result in ratings that have higher psychometric quality, the extent to which it is liked or accepted by users is not so clear. Some managers resent not being able to talk about the kind of evaluation they have just given their subordinate. In fact, some supervisors have attempted to outwit the system by keeping good records of their ratings and relating these to what evaluations come out of human resources for their employees. Others have tried to do this by not actually rating the person they are supposed to rate. Instead, if they wished to give an overly favourable evaluation they might imagine the most effective worker they have known on the job and complete the form with her or him in mind. In theory, at least, this should increase the likelihood that they would select the valid items.

BEHAVIOURALLY ANCHORED RATING SCALES (BARS)

Smith and Kendall (1963) introduced **behaviourally anchored rating scales** with a great deal of optimism that they would deal with many of the factors that reduced the quality of ratings (Campbell, Dunnette, Lawler, & Weick, 1970). Behaviourally anchored rating scales (BARS), or behavioural expectations scales (BES), have been heavily researched in the last thirty years. While the evidence is not clear enough to make firm conclusions at this time, it seems safe to say that BARS represents, at most, only a small advance in scale technology (Bernardin & Beatty, 1984).

There have been several versions of BARS. With one important exception (the way in which they are actually used), they have a lot in common. In contrast to other approaches (e.g., the forced choice method) that have tended to look for ways to outsmart or trick the rater into giving good quality evaluations, the philosophy behind the development and use of BARS has been to help the rater be accurate. In particular, every effort is made to be certain that potential scale users provide a lot of input into the critical features of the scales design.

Behaviourally anchored rating scales are usually constructed for a particular job or cluster of jobs that have a great deal in common (e.g., college teaching). They employ a multistep procedure that involves participation of several groups of supervisors or employees at critical points. While in practice these could vary, the steps outlined below follow those presented in the original version (Bernardin & Beatty, 1984):

1. Because effectiveness in most jobs is multifaceted, the performance dimensions must be identified and defined. This is usually done by having a group of future scale users meet to discuss the job in question and to reach a consensus. This same group is asked to write statements clarifying what is meant by being high or low on each dimension.

2. A second group of future users is then given the dimensions with these general anchors. Their task is to come up with a large number of behavioural examples for each dimension. They may be instructed in the use of the critical incident framework for structuring this activity in order to keep focused on job effectiveness and to come up with the necessary number of examples.

3. The examples are usually edited by the human resource specialist conducting the project into short behavioural phrases. These are then given to another group. They receive the list of dimensions and the behavioural examples produced so far, but the latter are deliberately mixed up with regard to dimensions. This group's task is to match each example with its appropriate dimension to double-check the work of their predecessors. Usually, an agreement of 80 percent is required for a given statement to be assigned to a dimension.

4. Still another group is then asked to rate or scale the examples that have survived to this point. This group is to indicate the extent to which each example reflects effectiveness on the dimension to which it has been assigned (usually on a 1-7 scale). This is done independently by each person. A standard deviation is then computed on the scores given to each example. Those examples with a large standard deviation are rejected. This reflects a lack of agreement among raters due to the level of effectiveness described by that example.

5. Examples are placed as anchors at appropriate points on the score of effectiveness for each dimension. Usually, this is done for only some of the points along the continuum, but in a manner that still covers the full range of effectiveness. An example of the final scale for college professors is presented in Figure 9.4.

The "retranslation" step in number 3 is important, and is a unique aspect of BARS methodology. It sometimes uncovers dimensions that were overlooked in the earlier steps, because it is discovered that there are some examples "left over" that also seem to go together. On the other hand, the importance or relevance of dimensions that arise from this process with none or very few examples is questionable. The requirement for a high degree of consensus also eliminates examples that might

FIGURE 9.4 A Behaviourally Anchored Rating Scale for College Professors

Organizational skills: A good constructional order of material slides smoothly from one topic to another; design of course optimizes interest; students can easily follow organizational strategy; course outline followed.

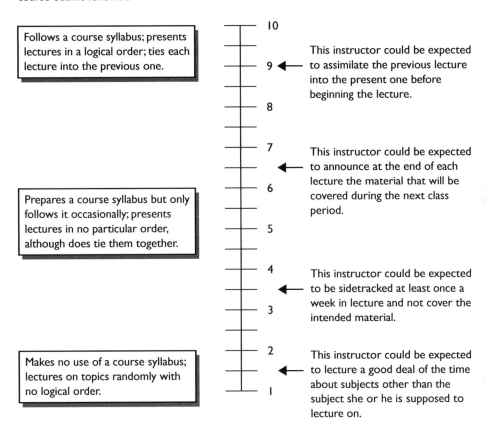

Source: Reprinted with permission from Berardin, H.J. (1977). Behavioral expectation scales versus summated scales: A fairer comparison. *Journal of Applied Psychology, 62,* 422–427.

be appropriate for more than one dimension, thus reducing the potential for halo error (see discussion of rating errors later in this chapter) when they are used as anchors in the final scale. In a sense, these steps in the BARS development process tend to ensure that the concepts and language of the scale will be accepted and understood by everyone.

The actual way BARS are used or applied appears to have evolved somewhat since it was invented (Bernardin & Smith, 1981). Originally, the scales were to serve as a structure for systematic observation and record keeping by managers prior to making ratings. That is, over some period of time managers were to notice the job behaviour of a person due for a review, and to record examples of good or poor performance on the relevant scale dimension. This was to be done at an appropriate point on the continuum. They were expected to use the scaled anchors to make this judgment. Later, they would review these entries and make a summary rating on each dimension. These then would become an employee's scores.

More recently, however, BARS have not been used in this future-oriented or prospective manner. Instead, much like any rating scale, it is completed at the time an appraisal is required. The manager is expected to reflect on the employee's behaviour in a particular performance domain during the period of time in question, integrate this information in the form of a judgment, then record this impression on the scale at a point he or she feels is correct. The scale definition, description, and the behavioural anchors presumably help to do this accurately.

◆ ◆ ◆

PERSONNEL COMPARISON SYSTEMS

Despite the diversity apparent in the various scales just described, they all represent formats in which the person doing the assessment makes judgments with regard to job-relevant or absolute standards. A poor worker, for example, is thought to be poor because he or she cannot or will not do the job. In general, this is a property of ratings. In contrast, personnel comparison systems are based on a different set of assumptions. As a group, their advantage is that the distribution of scores is "spread out." A discussion of various personnel comparison systems follows.

PERSONNEL RANKINGS

All of us are familiar with the concept of ranking. We see it every day in the popular press or hear it used in conversation. When applied to personnel evaluations, **personnel rankings** involve the ordering of employees on a continuum so that individuals who are placed higher are felt to be better than those who are ranked lower. Because it is an easily understood and straightforward way of evaluating and recording evaluations, it is very popular.

When there are a fairly large number of workers to consider (say, over ten), it is sometimes difficult to differentiate among them, especially in the middle ranges of effectiveness. Thus, Guion (1965) recommends that a variation of this method, known as *alternation ranking*, be used. In this approach, the manager works from a list of employees. He or she first selects the most effective and the least effective persons on the list. These are then given the first and last place (rank) respectively. Their names are taken off the initial roster and the choice of first and last place is again made with regard to the people who are left. These are assigned the second-best and the second-worst ranks. Then their names are dropped from the list. This process is continued until the list is exhausted. Alternation ranking is based on the premise that it is easier to make extreme judgments. It is sometimes called the "peel-off method," because the process resembles peeling away layers.

If more than one manager is in a position to provide ranking information on a group of workers, it is feasible to average the data that they provide. However, if this is done, it is unlikely that the resulting numbers will be whole integers (e.g., the top person might get an average rank of 1.7). Moreover, with more than one set of rankings, it is also possible for two or more individuals to have the same average rank score. In any event, the appropriateness of averaging ranks should be carefully considered insofar as the different judges may not be equivalent in opportunity or capacity to evaluate employees.

FORCED DISTRIBUTION METHOD

Ranking requires that each individual be given a unique position in the ordering. There are times, however, when all that is desired is some notion of how groups of workers compare in a relative sense. In the **forced distribution method** the manager is only expected to place workers into five or seven groups or categories of effectiveness, usually in specified proportions. Thus, in a five-category system, 10 percent of the workers are to be assigned to the extreme high and low clusters, 20 percent are to be placed into the next highest and lowest categories, and the remaining 40 percent are to be clustered in the middle.

It is no coincidence that the distribution described above approximates a normal distribution. The use of the forced distribution method is most appropriate when one is willing to assume that the true levels of effectiveness of the workers are, in fact, distributed in this way. This should be the case when fairly large numbers of employees are being evaluated. Even when it is not the case, the final arrangement of people must conform to this pattern. Hence the technique is also called a *forced distribution*. It would be possible, however, to force placements into something other than a normal distribution, if that were believed to be fair given what is known about the people being evaluated (e.g., they may all be competent and experienced workers, so one may not want to use the whole effectiveness continuum). In general, however, forced distribution systems do not appear suitable when only a small number of employees is to be evaluated.

This approach is sometimes used to narrow the field of workers for future consideration. For example, under such circumstances, the 10 percent in the topmost category might then be ranked individually in order to determine the person most deserving of some honour (e.g., a teaching award).

It is clear that both simple ranking and the forced distribution method require that individuals be placed in some kind of order of effectiveness, even when it may not be warranted. These methods may not allow for the possibility that two or more individuals are equally effective. Moreover, they only provide what is essentially ordinal data. We know that a person ranked fourth is better than one ranked fifth, but we don't know how much better. Similarly, we cannot rely on differences between ranks at different parts of the distribution to reflect equivalent differences in effectiveness. For example, Figure 9.5 shows a situation in which a decision to promote the top two candidates based only on rank information would unfairly disenfranchise the next runner up, who is, in fact, barely distinguishable from one who would be chosen. While the next method to be described, the paired comparison method, does not deal with the issue of forcing differences, it does provide a mechanism for deriving some insight into the magnitude of the differences in effectiveness of the individuals who are compared.

FIGURE 9.5 **When Rank Order Information Is Misleading**

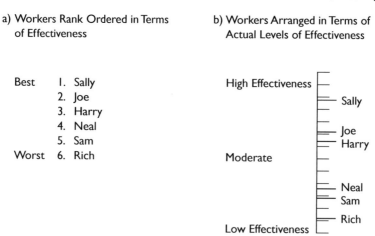

a) Workers Rank Ordered in Terms of Effectiveness

b) Workers Arranged in Terms of Actual Levels of Effectiveness

PAIRED COMPARISON METHOD

The **paired comparison method** systematically compares all workers with regard to their effectiveness. A formula for determining how many judgments are required of a manager is as follows:

$$[N(N-1)]/2 \qquad (9.2)$$

Thus, if you had five subordinates you would make $5 \times 4/2$, or 10 paired comparison judgments. More specifically, a list of all workers, taken two at a time and in all possible combinations, would be prepared. The supervisor then would indicate which person of each pair was the more effective. In determining someone's score, the supervisor analyzes the proportion of judgments in which the employee is chosen over all the others. Those proportions are frequently standardized/normalized, yielding interval data. Thus, one can also tell by what degree each worker differs in judged effectiveness, although these scores are also based on the assumption that individual performance is distributed normally.

Despite the apparent simplicity of this approach, as in the case of rankings and forced distributions, when work groups are large it is quite tedious to use. In fact, research has been conducted to discover modifications that can be made so that the number of pairs to be evaluated can be reduced and yet result in a valid coverage of employees (McCormick & Bachus, 1952). However, a principal concern with regard to this method remains: it asks for a global or overall judgment of effectiveness, one that is not well defined or anchored. This makes it difficult to know on what basis the judgments have been made (Bernardin & Beatty, 1984).

An additional feature of the paired comparison method is also true for personnel comparison appraisal systems. It is very difficult, except under unusual circumstances, to compare evaluations across departments or organizational divisions. The best person in one area may not be as effective as a person ranked at the middle of the distribution in another work group. Thus, it would be rare to see these techniques used when there is a need for system-wide data.

◆ ◆ ◆
SOURCES OF INDIVIDUAL MEASUREMENT

Throughout this chapter, reference has been made to the manager, supervisor, or human resource professional as the agent responsible for rating individuals. This reflects the reality of how these programs are carried out in most organizations. However, it is possible to obtain evaluations from a number of sources, including the employee (self-ratings), co-workers (peer ratings), superiors, or subordinates. Moreover, there is evidence that the quality of ratings may be related to their source under different circumstances. As well, there will be times when we will want information from multiple sources for maximum appraisal validity.

Wexley and Klimoski (1984) stress that four factors should be considered when selecting the person to conduct evaluations. The person must: (1) be in a position to observe the performance and behaviour of the individual, (2) be knowledgeable about what constitutes effectiveness, (3) have an understanding of the measures to be used, and (4) be motivated to be accurate.

A great deal of accumulated evidence has established that evaluations made from these various perspectives are different and should not be considered interchangeable (Borman, 1974; Klimoski & London, 1974; Holzbach, 1978). However, while they may be different, it is possible for each to be valid, at least under various circumstances. In particular, the five potential sources of appraisal data listed above are in positions that encourage somewhat different definitions of effectiveness, allow for different opportunities for observation, and imply different levels of motivation to be accurate (Carroll & Schneier, 1982).

Superiors, of course, should have a good understanding of what constitutes effective job performance, but they may not always be in a position to see a subordinate's behaviour in key areas. Co-workers can observe a person's day-to-day activities, yet when it comes to what is desirable behaviour, may have a limited perspective. One must assume that self-ratings are made with the benefit of insight as to what the worker actually does on the job, but, characteristically, they are inflated and reflect a great deal of halo. The fact is, each perspective has certain strengths and weaknesses, as shown in Table 9.1.

One of the most critical factors to influence the appropriate choice of a rater is the purpose for which the rating is being made (Wexley & Klimoski, 1984). This is because of the impact that purpose appears to have on the motivation of the different agents to be accurate. In general, assessments being made exclusively for research tend to generate the least anxiety and resistance (and hence distortion) from all of the sources. However, if the assessments are to be used for administrative action (e.g., for salary recommendations), there is reason to avoid having peers (DeNisi & Mitchell, 1978) or the employee (Thornton, 1980) supply the information.

Subordinate ratings of an employee are best used when the goal is to improve the latter's effectiveness. However, there is some evidence that peers are good at describing a colleague's strengths and weaknesses (Greller, 1980; Kane & Lawler, 1978). Thus, it is not surprising that both peer and subordinate ratings of performance are becoming more common in organizations (Maurer, Raju, & Collins, 1998). Maurer et al. (1998) recently tested the equivalence of peer and subordinate ratings in a study in which managers were rated by two of their peers and two subordinates in terms of their team-building skills. The results indicated the existence of measurement equivalence of peer and subordinate ratings. In other words, the underlying characteristics being measured by both groups were the same and are therefore comparable.

The use of peer appraisals appears to be especially important for self-managing work groups because of the absence of a traditional manager or supervisor. In fact, a recent study found that developmental peer appraisals in self-managing work groups have a positive effect on group member perceptions of open communication, group task focus, group viability, and member relationships (Druskat & Wolff, 1999).

Self-appraisals also appear to have good potential especially when used for developmental purposes (Mabe & West, 1982). In fact, Klimoski (1983) reports a

TABLE 9.1 STRENGTHS AND WEAKNESSES OF MEASUREMENT SOURCES

	Strengths	Weaknesses
Supervisors	Legitimate authority; Controls rewards, punishments; Knowledge of subordinates' job responsibilities	Subject to self-interest; Poorly motivated to be accurate
Peers	Knowledge of co-workers' duties; Opportunity to observe co-workers closely	Frequently in competition; Subject to collusion; Subject to friendship bias; May not see full range of colleagues' responsibilities
Subordinates	Opportunity to observe supervisor closely; Can evaluate personnel management component of supervisor's job	Subject to intimidation; Subject to loyalty forces
Self	Intimate knowledge of intentions, effort; Knowledge of job performance; Encourages self-development	Subject to self-serving bias
Personnel Specialist	No vested interest in rating outcome; Well trained and practised; Able to get information from multiple sources	May not have adequate opportunity to observe performance; May take away legitimate responsibility from supervisor

Source: Adapted with permission from Carroll, S.J., & Schneier, C.E. (1982). *Performance appraisal and review systems.* Glenview, IL: Scott Foresman.

project involving a municipal agency in which a combination of self, peer, and subordinate ratings was used successfully to provide data on the developmental needs of managers. These then served as the basis for an individualized training program designed to increase the manager's effectiveness as a supervisor of workers.

When it comes to research conducted in artificial settings or laboratories, the investigator has the full range of options as to the choice of agent. Subjects in laboratory studies who are being observed may be evaluated by other subjects or by assistants to the researcher, or they themselves may provide data. The main difference between laboratory and field settings, however, is how well the investigator can ensure that the rater has the opportunity to observe, and how well the essential dynamics of the roles are, in fact, operating. However, regardless of the source of the ratings, rating errors are a serious problem that can lead to inaccurate ratings.

◆ ◆ ◆
RATING ERRORS

The quality of a measure is based on the extent to which it reflects the characteristics or behaviour of an individual in the areas defined by our construct. As discussed in previous chapters, this is largely a function of how a measure was developed and of its reliability and validity. However, measurement requires human judgment and is therefore subject to human error and bias. Therefore, it should not be assumed that, just because a measure has been properly developed and has a high degree of reliability and validity, it will be used properly. In human resources, there are a number of known rating errors or biases that can result in measurement problems. Among these are: (1) central tendency and range restriction; (2) leniency and severity; (3) halo effects; (4) order and contrast effects; and (5) unfair bias and discrimination. Each of these is described below.

CENTRAL TENDENCY

Central tendency is a pattern in which scores on a measure cluster at or near the middle of the distribution of potential scores. In the case of ratings, managers would not use the extremes of the scales, and all workers would be described as average. Central tendency is viewed as an error or as a manifestation of poor data because it is believed that this is not really the true state of affairs in most work situations. Some employees are bound to be better or more effective than others. When there are large numbers of people being evaluated, we might expect that the distribution of their evaluations should resemble a normal distribution.

Central tendency errors frequently occur when managers don't really know the people being evaluated, or when managers do not believe the appraisals to be important. In the latter case, rather than working at making valid assessments or running the risk of alienating some workers by giving them a (perhaps warranted) low evaluation, managers give everyone the same middle score. The end result is low discriminability, since the measurement program fails to differentiate between employees. Such data are not particularly useful for most purposes.

Notice that we are making assumptions when we say that obtained scores with limited variability clustered about the middle of the distribution are in error and that we have low-quality data. None of the measures of range restriction or central tendency can tell us if, in fact, this is not the correct distribution. In some contexts (e.g., when we have a preselected group) it might be the case. Thus, it is not an error if it reflects the true state of affairs. Whether or not measurements are appropriate or are in error must be determined through additional analyses.

LENIENCY AND SEVERITY

Leniency and **severity** also refer to the tendency of people to use only a limited part of the scale of a measurement system. However, this time evaluations are represented as universally high (lenient) or universally low (severe). This is an error or reflection of questionable data because, once again, it is presumed to be an inaccurate picture of the true situation. It is unlikely that all individuals are truly great or really poor.

The causes of leniency and severity effects are numerous and complex. In some cases they may be a function of the personal style of the manager doing the evaluations—some have tougher standards than others. Far more likely causes though, are forces in the measurement situation that promote this type of distortion. For example, leniency is frequently observed when the evaluations are not to be used as input to any important decisions, when the supervisor is not self-confident, and desires the positive regard of the people being measured (who are likely to see their scores), or when the supervisor believes that low appraisals reflect badly on his or her own ability to manage. Under all these circumstances, the motivation of the manager to be accurate is low and the desire to be discriminating weak. The result is poor-quality data.

HALO EFFECTS

A **halo effect** is the tendency to evaluate a person in an undifferentiated manner so that he or she is regarded as equally effective or ineffective in all domains. While the general notion is clear, how or why halo comes about is not. For instance, we might manifest halo because we get a global or overall impression and we let this affect our judgments in the specific areas to be evaluated; we might not have enough opportunity to observe the person being evaluated; or it might occur because we let our (possibly accurate) assessment in one area of effectiveness determine our evaluations in the others.

The fundamental assumption that underlies the notion of halo as an error must always be questioned. That is, in a given circumstance, can we assume that a person is all good or all bad? We must always be sensitive to the possibility that the extremely high scores across various dimensions might reflect reality. We might have a group of truly effective (or ineffective) individuals.

ORDER AND CONTRAST EFFECTS

Order effects occur when the sequence in which we receive information alters or distorts our perceptions and evaluations. The first performance data or cues about a person that we become aware of are frequently given too much weight in our thinking. This is referred to as a **primacy effect** (Latham, Wexley, & Purcell, 1975). On the other hand, under certain circumstances, evaluations may be biased by something that has just happened. This is referred to as a **recency effect**. Recency effect can also refer to a situation in which events that happened some time before a manager does a performance review are forgotten or at least given little weight in the evaluation. In theory, our impressions will reflect a balance of both tendencies. It seems clear that first impressions do a great deal to set up certain expectations or cognitive structures that have direct effects on what we attend to later (Feldman, 1981; DeNisi et al., 1984).

It is also true that our judgments of a person's effectiveness are influenced by the performances of others doing the same kind of work. This is referred to as the **contrast effect** (Landy & Farr, 1980). In their study, Grey and Kipnis (1976) discovered that a manager gave unusually high recommendations to an employee when he or she was a good performer in a work group made up largely of poor performers. Presumably, the former stood out in contrast to peers. This phenomenon has also been found in selection interviews in which an interviewer must meet with and evaluate a large number of applicants in quick succession. The quality of preceding candidates can cause a bias in impressions, especially at the end of the day (Schmitt, 1976). As a result, the ratings and evaluation that job applicants receive are, in part, due to the quality of those candidates who were interviewed before them.

UNFAIR BIAS AND DISCRIMINATION

All too often in organizations, the ratings and evaluations that individuals receive are subject to biases and prejudices. For example, interview evaluations or performance appraisals could be influenced by the interviewer's bias toward members of particular racial or ethnic groups. Personal prejudice and bias should not enter into the evaluation of individuals.

Data that systematically reflect lower scores for employees belonging to particular groups may be the result of bias or prejudice. The actual detection of unfair bias is difficult. Often, researchers and managers compare the psychometric properties of scores (e.g., means and standard deviations) for known groups. Thus, ratings given to visible minorities and whites might be compared to see if the former are systematically lower than the latter. More sophisticated analyses involve the careful examination of patterns of relationships among indicators of effectiveness or the presumed correlates of effectiveness.

◆◆◆
IMPROVING INDIVIDUAL MEASUREMENT

Given the many factors that can bias the measurement of individuals, researchers have been interested in finding ways to improve the accuracy and quality of measures. In this regard, there are some general rules or principles to follow. When it comes to the use of subjective measures, there are ways other than changing techniques that can improve the quality of data. These include the opportunity to observe, capability to evaluate, motivation to be accurate, research motivation, and rater training. In fact, some would argue that these alternatives are more likely to make an impact on quality than the choice of scale.

OPPORTUNITY TO OBSERVE

This rule appears straightforward. Only those who have an adequate opportunity to see the employee in job-related settings and over a suitable period of time should be used to evaluate them. Sometimes formal reporting relationships can be deceiving in this regard. One would normally expect the immediate supervisor to be in a good position to supply evaluations. However, in highly decentralized systems this may not be the case. Opportunity to observe needs to be verified. Conversely, a second opinion regarding an employee should not be given weight if it comes from someone who is quite removed from the day-to-day functioning of the employee.

CAPABILITY TO EVALUATE

Not all individuals are able to do a quality job of rating individuals and supplying data. There is some evidence that reliable individual differences exist in this regard (Borman, 1977; Taft, 1955). The key here is to find a way to identify who these individuals are in a given context. Alternatively, individuals' capabilities might be enhanced by their involvement in the careful development and application of evaluation tools or instruments. Finally, managers responsible for rating individuals might have their capability increased by training programs designed for this purpose (see discussion below on training raters).

MOTIVATION TO BE ACCURATE

Several of the biases or errors that we detect in effectiveness data stem from the fact that managers frequently lack the motivation to be accurate in their data gathering and reporting. There is some evidence that this factor may account for the greatest amount of variance in the quality of data. This, too, implies careful attention to the process of program implementation.

251

It is well known that people are frequently uncomfortable with the responsibility of completing performance evaluations (McGregor, 1957). Most managers realize that it is a part of their job, but they also know that it can affect the nature of their relations with subordinates. It emphasizes the power differences and frequently places two people in an adversarial relationship when they should normally be working closely together as a team.

In general, people try to avoid giving negative or unpleasant information to others (Blumberg, 1972; Tesser & Rosen, 1975). Thus, Stone (1973) reports that a majority of managers surveyed dislike giving negative evaluations. Several laboratory studies have documented the tendency of evaluators to raise the evaluations of poor performers and to give more positive feedback to subordinates than is warranted (Ilgen & Knowlton, 1980; Fisher, 1979). In some cases, this tendency has been viewed as subconscious or perceptual (Weary, 1979). However, many writers conclude that people do recognize poor performance when it occurs, but do not record it as such (Ilgen & Knowlton, 1980; Larson, 1984). They are simply not motivated to rate accurately.

In terms of organizational practices, there are several things that can be done to change this. Most fundamentally, senior management can create the climate for high-quality assessments. This means attending to the perspective and needs of the managers who use the system, understanding the views of employees, and being certain that the performance measurement program is consistent with other policies and practices.

MOTIVATION IN RESEARCH

Researchers who are gathering data for research purposes have to be concerned about the motivation of those who are supplying the data. If the research is being conducted in field settings, the motivation of those involved will be strongly affected by the way in which the study is introduced to participants, the degree to which the integrity of the data will be maintained, and the credibility of the research team.

To the extent that the study is presented and accepted as important, the data are only to be used for research, the sources of the data are confidential (or anonymous), and the existence of the data cannot come to hurt the participants (raters and employees), the researcher is more likely to get cooperation and expect acceptable levels of motivation. As in the case of observations and interviews, the establishment and maintenance of trust between the researcher and respondents is very important.

When data are gathered in artificial or laboratory settings, the researcher usually has the capacity to seek out individuals to conduct ratings for research purposes. However, even in this case, issues of motivation should not be overlooked. In particular, it is quite common to conduct research in a laboratory in which undergraduate students are used as raters, and their behaviours (ratings) are the focus of attention.

But, often, motivation is assumed to be consistent and relatively high for all subjects, across all conditions, and over the period of the session. Procedures need to be implemented as part of the investigation so that high motivation does indeed occur. For example, being paid for participation might help. Alternatively, creating accountability forces might be warranted (Klimoski & Inks, 1990). In any event, it would also be prudent, as a matter of practice, to check on the level of motivation of research participants who are providing data.

TRAINING RATERS

As indicated earlier, sources responsible for rating individuals can have their capability increased by training programs designed for this purpose. The traditional approach to rater training has been to offer a workshop to potential users in which the philosophy of the measurement program is reviewed and the forms and expected "paper flow" are outlined. But the core of traditional training has been to emphasize the nature of potential bias and errors (e.g., leniency, central tendency, halo, etc.). Usually, these are defined and examples provided. The raters are told to avoid these errors if at all possible (Levine & Butler, 1952; Wexley, Sanders, & Yukl, 1973). Instruction is usually in a lecture/discussion format. The training itself might last from an hour to a day.

When these training programs have been rigorously evaluated, however, there has been little evidence that they had the desired effects (Bernardin, 1978; Spool, 1978). Although managers might have come away with an understanding of what the appropriate forms are and might be able to define errors, their actual evaluations continued to show poor quality. It seems clear that merely imparting knowledge is not a sufficient basis for rater training (Wexley & Latham, 1981).

In the last fifteen years, however, there has been something of a revolution in the area. In fact, it represents a good example of how advances in theory have contributed greatly to changes in professional practice. Much of the credit is due to individuals whose research has led to a more complete understanding of the social judgment process. As outlined earlier in this chapter, we now know much more about the causes of rating bias and distortion. Developments in training theory and technology have also occurred. Thus, both training content and training process have been affected.

The best evidence is that rater training should focus on improving observation and categorization skills (Bernardin & Beatty, 1984), and stressing accuracy (Bernardin & Pence, 1980), using a training format that requires active participation and practice on the part of trainees (Latham et al., 1975).

Frame of reference training has been suggested as a useful approach to increasing the accuracy of observations (Bernardin & Beatty, 1984; Borman, 1979). In this approach, individuals are taught which job behaviours to look for when assessing employees and how to evaluate differing behaviour patterns. In particular, trainees are allowed opportunities to make and record their own observations and to learn how their processing and use of information differ from those of others. In a sense, the training attempts to make explicit the performance schemes and prototypes actually held by the trainees, and to highlight those felt to be more appropriate. The desired schema thus becomes a common frame of reference to be used by everyone.

There also is some evidence that the quality of data can be enhanced if rater training includes an emphasis on a more systematic approach to documenting and recording observations of relevant job behaviours. Bernardin (1978) recommends the use of a diary to do this. In a study involving the measurement of teaching effectiveness, some student raters were trained to keep a diary of critical incidents in instructor behaviour throughout the school term. It was found that ratings of this group had less leniency and halo than those of another group of student raters who did not receive this training. The trained group found the diary very helpful in making their ratings (Bernardin & Walter, 1977). It also should be recalled that one of the strengths of the BARS method as originally developed was that it helped structure on-the-job observations of workers. Raters were to record these on the actual instrument to be used later when appraisal judgments were required.

A final point is worth mentioning with regard to advances in the technology of rater training. As mentioned, more successful programs require a great deal of active participation on the part of trainees. In particular, they receive practice making ratings of people in a very standardized context. Usually, they will make ratings of workers (actors) who are portrayed on videotape. Not only does this provide a constant stimulus for all trainees, but, because it has been scripted in a particular manner (e.g., to represent a poor performer), it is also possible to assess and give feedback on the accuracy of ratings. Unlike most rating situations, there is a true score to serve as the basis for examining the quality of the ratings supplied by trainees and for providing feedback to them (Ivancevich, 1979; Warmke & Billings, 1979). It appears that information regarding observational errors at this level of specificity and detail is what is needed by trainees to improve the quality of their ratings (Nemeroff & Cosentino, 1979; Thornton & Zorich, 1980).

◆ ◆ ◆
SUMMARY

Research in human resources almost always involves measuring some aspect of individual traits, behaviours, and/or outputs. Therefore, understanding the various techniques of individual measurement is an essential requirement for research in human resources. This chapter has described the various techniques available for individual measurement, as well as the different sources that can be used to provide individual-level data. Rater biases and errors were also described, as well as the ways to reduce these problems and improve the quality of data.

Definitions

Behaviourally anchored rating scales (BARS)   Rating scales that consist of specific examples of effective and ineffective behaviour for each dimension that is rated.

Behaviour observation scale (BOS)   A type of summated scale that consists of job-relevant descriptions of behaviour; the respondent indicates the frequency with which each behaviour occurs.

Central tendency   A rating error in which scores on a measure cluster at or near the middle of the distribution of potential scores.

Contrast effect   An effect in which the rating of an individual is influenced by the ratings given to others, such as when the ratings and evaluation that a job applicant receives are influenced by the quality of those candidates who were previously interviewed.

Forced choice scale   The rater is forced to choose from a group of statements those that best describe the individual being assessed.

Frame of reference training   A type of training that is used to increase the accuracy of raters' observations by teaching them which job behaviours to look for when assessing employees and how to evaluate different behaviour patterns.

Graphic scale   A type of rating scale in which the rater places a mark at the point that best reflects his/her judgment of an individual.

Personnel rankings   The ordering or ranking of employees on a continuum of overall effectiveness.

Forced distribution method   Workers are placed into five or seven groups or categories of effectiveness, usually in specified proportions.

Halo effect   The tendency to evaluate an individual in an undifferentiated manner so that he/she is regarded as equally effective or ineffective in all areas or domains.

Leniency and severity   Rating errors in which the rater uses only a limited part of the scale, and rates all individuals at the high end (lenient) or at the low end (severity).

Order effects   Rating errors in which the sequence in which one receives information may alter or distort ratings.

Paired comparison method   Involves systematically comparing all workers with regard to their effectiveness.

Primacy effect   An order effect in which early information about an individual is given too much weight in the rating.

Recency effect   An order effect in which the most recent information about an individual is given too much weight in the rating.

Summated scale   A type of rating scale in which statements describing work behaviour are rated in terms of frequency, degrees of quality, amount, or intensity.

Weighted checklist   A series of short behaviour descriptions in which the rater is required to check off those items that are felt to be descriptive of the individual being assessed.

EXERCISES

1. Obtain a copy of the evaluation form used at your school for course evaluations. Describe and comment on the measurement technique used for rating course instructors.

   Develop a measure for evaluating course instructors using each of the following measurement techniques (if class time is limited, groups may be formed and assigned one of the methods):
   a) Objective output measures
   b) Graphic scales
   c) Summated scales/Behaviour observation scales
   d) Weighted checklist
   e) Forced choice scales
   f) Behaviourally anchored rating scales (BARS)
   g) Personnel rankings
   h) Forced distribution method
   i) Paired comparison method

   Based on the above, which rating method do you think is the most practical in terms of: (i) design, (ii) implementation, and (iii) the quality and usefulness of the evaluation information? If it were up to you, which of the individual measurement techniques would you recommend for evaluating instructors and courses. Why?

2. Describe the measurement technique used to evaluate your job performance in your current or a previous job. What type of measurement technique is (was) used and how effective and fair do you feel it is (was) for measuring your job performance? What measurement technique do you think would be more effective and fair? Why?

References

Bass, B.M., Cascio, W.F., & O'Connor, E.J. (1974). Magnitude estimations of expressions of frequency and amount. *Journal of Applied Psychology, 59,* 313–320.

Berkshire, J.R., & Highland, R.W. (1953). Forced-choice performance rating: A methodological study. *Personnel Psychology, 6,* 355–378.

Bernardin, H.J. (1978). Effects of rater training on leniency and halo errors in student ratings of instructors. *Journal of Applied Psychology, 63,* 301–308.

Bernardin, H.J., & Beatty, R.W. (1984). *Performance appraisal: Assessing human behavior at work.* Boston, MA: Kent.

Bernardin, H.J., & Pence, E.C. (1980). Rater training: Creating new response sets and decreasing accuracy. *Journal of Applied Psychology, 65,* 60–66.

Bernardin, H.J., & Smith, P.C. (1981). A clarification of some issues regarding the development and use of behaviorally anchored rating scales. *Journal of Applied Psychology, 66,* 458–463.

Bernardin, H.J., & Walter, C.W. (1977). Effects of rater training and diary keeping on psychometric error in ratings. *Journal of Applied Psychology, 62,* 64–69.

Blumberg, H.H. (1972). Communication of interpersonal evaluations. *Journal of Personality and Social Psychology, 23,* 157–162.

Bommer, W.H., Johnson, J.L., Rich, G.A., Podsakoff, P.M., & Mackenzie, S.B. (1995). On the interchangeablility of objective and subjective measures of employee performance: A meta-analysis. *Personnel Psychology, 48,* 587–605.

Borman, W.C. (1974). The rating of individuals in organizations: An alternative approach. *Organizational Behavior and Human Performance, 12,* 105–124.

Borman, W.C. (1977). Consistency of rating accuracy and rating errors in the judgment of human performance. *Organizational Behavior and Human Performance, 20,* 238–252.

Borman, W.C. (1979). Format and training effects on rating accuracy and rater errors. *Journal of Applied Psychology, 64,* 410–421.

Campbell, J.P., Dunnette, M., Lawler, E.E. III, & Weick, K.E. (1970). *Managerial behavior, performance, and effectiveness.* New York: McGraw-Hill.

Carroll, S.J., & Schneier, C.E. (1982). *Performance appraisal and review systems.* Glenview, IL: Scott Foresman.

DeNisi, A.S., Cafferty, T.P., & Meglino, B.M. (1984). A cognitive view of the performance appraisal process: A model and research propositions. *Organizational Behavior and Human Performance, 33,* 360–396.

DeNisi, A. S., & Mitchell, J.L. (1978). An analysis of peer ratings as predictors and criterion measures and a proposed new application. *Academy of Management Review, 3,* 369–374.

Druskat, V.U. & Wolff, S.B. (1999). Effects and timing of developmental peer appraisals in self-managing work groups. *Journal of Applied Psychology, 84,* 58–74.

Feldman, J.M. (1981). Beyond attribution theory: Cognitive processes in performance appraisal. *Journal of Applied Psychology, 6,* 127–148.

Fisher, C.D. (1979). Transmission of positive and negative feedback to subordinates: A laboratory investigation. *Journal of Applied Psychology, 64,* 533–540.

Ford, J.K., Schmitt, N., Schechtman, S.L., Hults, B., & Doherty, M.L. (1989). Process tracing methods: Contributions, problems, and neglected research questions. *Organizational Behavior and Human Decision Processes, 43,* 75–117.

Greller, M.M. (1980). The nature of subordinate participation in the appraisal interview. *Academy of Management Journal, 12,* 646–658.

Grey, R.J., & Kipnis, D. (1976). Untangling the performance appraisal dilemma: The influence of perceived organizational context on evaluative processes. *Journal of Applied Psychology, 61,* 329–335.

Guion, R.M. (1965). *Personnel testing.* New York: McGraw-Hill.

Guion, R.M., & Gottier, R.F. (1965). Validity of personality measures in personnel selection. *Personnel Psychology, 18,* 49–65.

Holzbach, R.L. (1978). Rater bias in performance ratings: Superior, self, and peer ratings. *Journal of Applied Psychology, 63*, 579–588.

Ilgen, D.R., & Knowlton, W.A. (1980). Performance attributional effects on feedback from superiors. *Organizational Behavior and Human Performance, 25*, 441–456.

Ivancevich, J.M. (1979). Longitudinal study of the effects of rater training on psychometric error in ratings. *Journal of Applied Psychology, 64*, 502–508.

Kane, J.S., & Lawler, E.E. (1978). Methods of peer assessment. *Psychological Bulletin, 85*, 555–586.

King, L.M., Hunter, J.E., & Schmidt, F.L. (1980). Halo in a multidimensional forced-choice performance appraisal scale. *Journal of Applied Psychology, 65*, 507–516.

Klimoski, R.J. (1983). Needs assessment for management development. *Personnel Selection and Training Bulletin, 4*(1), 7–17.

Klimoski, R.J., & Inks, L. (1990). Accountability forces in performance appraisals. *Organizational Behavior and Human Decision Processes, 45*, 188–206.

Klimoski, R.J., & London, M. (1974). Role of the rater in performance appraisal. *Journal of Applied Psychology, 59*, 445–451.

Knauft, E.B. (1948). Construction and use of weighted checklist rating scales for two industrial situations. *Journal of Applied Psychology, 32*, 63–70.

Landy, F.J., & Farr, J.L. (1980). Performance rating. *Psychological Bulletin, 87*, 72–107.

Larson, J. (1984). The performance feedback process: A preliminary model. *Organizational Behavior and Human Performance, 33*(1), 42–76.

Latham, G.P., & Wexley, K.N. (1981). *Increasing productivity through performance appraisal.* Reading, MA: AddisonWesley.

Latham, G.P., Wexley, K.N., & Purcell, E.D. (1975). Training managers to minimize rating errors in the observation of behavior. *Journal of Applied Psychology, 60*, 550–555.

Levine, J., & Butler, J. (1952). Lecture vs. group decision in changing behavior. *Journal of Applied Psychology, 36*, 29–33.

Lissitz, R.W., & Green, S.B. (1975). Effect of the number of scale points on reliability: A Monte Carlo approach. *Journal of Applied Psychology, 60*, 10–13.

Mabe, P.A., III, & West, S.G. (1982). Validity of self-evaluation of ability: A review and meta-analysis. *Journal of Applied Psychology, 67*, 280–296.

Martin, S., & Klimoski, R.J. (1990). Use of verbal protocols to trace cognitions associated with self and supervisor evaluations of performance. *Organizational Behavior and Human Decision Processes, 46*, 17–25.

Maurer, T.J., Raju, N.S., & Collins, W.C. (1998). Peer and subordinate performance appraisal measurement equivalence. *Journal of Applied Psychology, 83*, 693–702.

McCormick, E.J., & Bachus, J. (1952). Paired comparison ratings: The effect on ratings of reductions in the number of pairs. *Journal of Applied Psychology, 36*, 123–127.

McGregor, D. (1957). An uneasy look at performance appraisal. *Harvard Business Review, 35*, 89–94.

Nemeroff, W.F., & Cosentino, J. (1979). Utilizing feedback and goal setting to increase performance appraisal skills of managers. *Academy of Management Journal, 22*, 566–576.

Schmitt, N. (1976). Social and situation determinants of interview decisions: Implications for the employment interview. *Personnel Psychology, 29*, 79–101.

Sisson, E.D. (1948). Forced choice: The new army rating. *Personnel Psychology, 1*, 365–381.

Smith, P.C., & Kendall, L.M. (1963). Retranslation of expectations: An approach to the construction of unambiguous anchors for rating scales. *Journal of Applied Psychology, 47,* 149–155.

Smith, P.E. (1976). Management modeling training to improve morale and customer satisfaction. *Personnel Psychology, 29,* 351–359.

Spool, M.D. (1978). Training programs for observers of behavior: A review. *Personnel Psychology, 31,* 853–888.

Stone, J.H. (1973). An examination of six prevalent assumptions concerning performance appraisal. *Public Personnel Management, 5,* 408–414.

Taft, R. (1955). The ability to judge people. *Psychology Bulletin, 52,* 1–23.

Tesser, A., & Rosen, S. (1975). The reluctance to transmit bad news. In L. Berkowitz (Ed.), *Advances in experimental social psychology* (vol. 8). New York: Academic Press.

Thornton, G.C. (1980). Psychometric properties of self-appraisals of job performance. *Personnel Psychology, 33,* 263–271.

Thornton, G.C., & Zorich, S. (1980). Training to improve observer accuracy. *Journal of Applied Psychology, 65,* 351–354.

Warmke, D.L., & Billings, R.S. (1979). Comparison of training methods for improving the psychometric quality of experimental and administrative performance ratings. *Journal of Applied Psychology, 64,* 124–131.

Weary, G. (1979). Self-serving attributional biases: Perceptual or response distortions? *Journal of Personality and Social Psychology, 37*(8), 1418–1420.

Wexley, K.N., & Klimoski, R.J. (1984). Performance appraisal: An update. In K. Rowland and G.R. Ferris (Eds.), *Research in personnel and human resources management* (vol. 2). Greenwich, CT: JAI Press.

Wexley, K.N., & Latham, G.P. (1981). *Developing and training human resources in organizations.* Glenview, IL: Scott Foresman.

Wexley, K.N., Sanders, R.E., & Yukl, G.A. (1973). Training interviewers to eliminate contrast effects in employment interviews. *Journal of Applied Psychology, 57,* 233–236.

Wherry, R.J. (1952). *The control of bias in rating: A theory of rating.* Washington, DC: Department of the Army, Personnel Research Section.

10

Group and Organization Measurement Techniques

INTRODUCTION

The previous chapter discussed measurement techniques for individuals, which have traditionally been the focus of human resource research. In recent years, however, groups have become increasingly more common in organizations. Further, as discussed in Chapter 1, human resource management has important consequences for organizational performance and effectiveness. Therefore, research in human resources often involves the measurement of group and organization-level variables. This chapter focuses on defining and measuring group and organizational variables, and serves to complement the measurement of individual variables.

After reading this chapter, you should be able to:

- Understand the need and importance of measuring group and organization-level variables in human resource research.

- Describe the different work group factors and how to measure them.

- Describe the different organization-level variables and how to measure them.

- Describe the different organization-level outcome variables and how to measure them.

- Understand and explain the special considerations and issues associated with measuring group and organization-level variables.

Why should we be interested in group and organization-level measures? For both practical and theoretical reasons, the manager or researcher frequently will find that the focus on the individual level is inappropriate. In particular, there are many instances in which the nature of the work requires individuals to work together in groups or teams. In fact, organizations are increasingly made up of groups of workers who interact and work together as a team rather than on their own. Therefore, there is an increasing need to measure group-related variables in the study of human resources.

As well, recall that in Chapter 1 it was noted that human resource practices have been linked to organizational outcomes and measures of effectiveness. Furthermore, there is increasing pressure on the human resource function to demonstrate its value-added to organizational effectiveness. Therefore, human resource research demands the measurement of group and organization-level variables in addition to individual-level variables. This requires an understanding of the methods and approaches to measuring group and organization-level phenomena.

◆◆◆
DEFINING AND MEASURING GROUP-LEVEL VARIABLES

Because group functioning is a complex process and involves numerous components, a framework is helpful to guide us in the definition and measurement of group behaviour and effectiveness. Figure 10.1, adapted from Hackman (1986), will be used to guide our understanding of group-level variables and their measurement.

According to the framework portrayed in Figure 10.1, to understand group functioning we need to be able to characterize certain aspects of the group itself, the group dynamics that take place (and critical intermediate factors), as well as group outcomes. Put another way, we must attend to input variables and process variables if we are to understand group outcome variables.

FIGURE 10.1 The Nature of Group Effectiveness

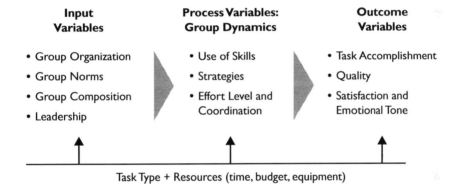

Input Variables	Process Variables: Group Dynamics	Outcome Variables
• Group Organization	• Use of Skills	• Task Accomplishment
• Group Norms	• Strategies	• Quality
• Group Composition	• Effort Level and Coordination	• Satisfaction and Emotional Tone
• Leadership		

Task Type + Resources (time, budget, equipment)

Source: Adapted with permission from Hackman, J.R. (1986). The design of work teams. In J. Lorsch (Ed.), *Handbook of organizational behavior.* Englewood Cliffs, NJ: Prentice Hall.

GROUP INPUT FACTORS

According to the framework in Figure 10.1, group functioning will be strongly influenced by a number of input variables. Four of these are identified as follows:

1. *Task organization (or group structure).* Task organization refers to how the work to be done is divided up among group members. It implies a division of labour with regard to duties and activities. It also includes the notion of responsibility and authority. That is, task organization will subsume issues as to who has the

power and final authority to make decisions. Finally, the concept of task organization reflects group size. Discussions regarding the division of labour inevitably include an examination of how many people are needed to get the job done. Do we need five or twenty-five individuals in the group? It is important to point out that while task group structure sometimes derives from or is dictated by the essential properties of the task itself, in most contexts decision makers have a lot of discretion in this area. They can decide just what work will be performed by which group members.

2. *Group norms.* Group norms are the informal rules that groups develop or adopt to regulate members' behaviour. Norms exist and are enforced by group members in order to facilitate working together and to make the behaviour of group members more predictable. To the extent that norms clarify what is expected of individuals, they are felt also to be important to group survival (Feldman, 1984). Finally, the existence of group norms increases the likelihood that groups can effectively regulate members' behaviour by rewarding conformity and punishing deviance (Hackman, 1976).

   Norms derive from a number of sources. Critical events in a group's history may determine expectations for key behaviours well into the future (e.g., with regard to vigilance or reliability). Indeed, there is often a carry-over into the current situation of "lessons learned" from the past experiences of individual group members. But it also turns out that norms may be shaped by the behaviours and statements of important or respected group members. Thus, managers, supervisors, and leaders will have an impact on what will become normative for the group (Feldman, 1984).

3. *Group composition.* The nature of the individuals making up the group constitutes group composition, or the mix of types of people in the group. In the theory and research on groups, quite a large number of composition variables have been explored (Shaw, 1981). Thus, group composition may refer to the proportion of males and females in the group, the age distribution of the people involved, and the mix of members' abilities or their personalities. In some contexts, even the distribution of height (as in basketball teams) or weight (for hot-air balloon crews) may be relevant.

4. *Leadership.* Group leadership includes both the formal assignment of leadership duties and the actual, informal, and ad hoc attempts at influence that take place in the group. While there is no agreed-upon system for classifying leaders and leader behaviours, a number of approaches are available (Yukl, 1989). For example, it is common to describe leadership in groups in terms of the extent to which it is centralized or shared, or whether leadership efforts are aimed at task accomplishments (e.g., efforts at structuring, clarifying, summarizing), group mainte-

nance (supporting and harmonizing), or both (Cartwright & Zander, 1968; Shaw, 1981; Yukl, 1989). Group input variables are important because they set the stage for process and outcomes. A particular combination of group organization, norms, composition, and leadership will have predictable consequences. The wrong combination will retard group accomplishments. It may even produce a disaster!

The definition and measurement of input factors are not well developed. This means that the manager/researcher will frequently be challenged to innovate and improvise. In instances in which organization or structure is of interest, it is useful to start with a consideration of the way the manager/researcher has set up the division of labour within the group. This may be reflected in the description of the group's task or in the job titles given to specific individuals. Of course, when studying ad hoc laboratory groups, the most direct way to index the task structure is to uncover what had been created by way of task properties.

In most cases, however, the structure of within-group activities relative to the division of labour must be assessed by some means other than a review of position descriptions. Investigators frequently will use interviews or questionnaires to assess group member perceptions of group structure. Finally, group organization may be indexed by careful observation of the group members as they work. Thus, the techniques for process measurement described below will be found useful.

The measurement of group norms is also problematic. While the concept of norms has been around for many years, it is only recently that the elements of norms have been articulated (Hackman, 1976). Thus, Jackson (1965) identifies the importance of indexing norms in terms of both the pattern and intensity of approval and disapproval associated with various possible behaviours. Jackson's (1965) theory predicts that group member behaviour will be regulated to the extent that expectations have been crystallized—that is, when there is a high degree of consensus among group members regarding what should or should not be done. This will be moderated by the intensity of feelings held by group members with regard to deviance from expectations. When there are both crystallized expectations and strong feelings, group members will be very likely to expect conformity from one another.

Group norms may be measured by obtaining reports from group members using questionnaires and/or individual or group interviews. However, because of the emotions or affect usually associated with norms, these approaches might prove to be too obtrusive. Direct questions might prompt distortion or concealment. Thus, once again, norms may be best measured by careful observations of actual behaviour, with the goal of capturing norm-relevant influence attempts. As in the case of indexing group organization, we must rely on inferences from careful observation and attention to group process.

In contrast, the measurement of composition factors lends itself to a direct approach. In fact, composition is often a variable of interest in group research so it becomes a measured or manipulated variable.

To illustrate, Tziner and Eden (1985) experimentally varied the composition of three-man military tank crews to assess its effects on performance. Specifically, both crew members' ability and motivation were assessed, and crews were made up on the basis of the scores obtained. The ability index was a composite of performance on an intelligence test, level of formal education achieved, Hebrew language proficiency (the study was conducted in the Israeli army), and ratings derived from a semi-structured interview. Motivation levels were estimated from answers to items embedded in a questionnaire. A given soldier was designated as either high or low (relative to the median) on the two composition factors. Then the tank crews were configured to allow for all possible combinations of crew types. In this study it was found that ability and motivation levels had additive effects on crew performance. But ability levels were more important. Not surprisingly, crews composed of uniformly high ability outperformed the typical crew.

The measurement of leadership in groups usually has relied on process approaches (see below). However, since it relates to its status as an input factor, it seems reasonable to characterize the existence and nature of formal leadership roles. Groups may or may not have a formal leader. This would be important to index. Moreover, if there is a formal leader, research has pointed out that it is relevant to note and record how that person came to the role (assigned, elected, through personal effort, etc.). This is related to the characteristics that the formal leader possesses: experience, power, authority, even gender. All of these have been found to be relevant to group processes and outcomes (Shaw, 1981).

When it comes to both composition and leader input variables, the issue is usually not one of how to measure variables, but what one is to measure. While basic research on groups can provide some guidance, appropriate choices will depend on knowledge of such factors as the task and the social or organizational context in which the group will be functioning.

In thinking of group effectiveness, then, it seems appropriate to consider (and even measure) these input factors. To put it another way, an effective group may be defined as one that is organized, staffed, and led appropriately to get the job done.

GROUP PROCESS FACTORS

Group process refers to the behaviours that take place in the group, the patterning of those behaviours (across individuals and across time), and the immediate consequences of these behaviours and patterns (Steiner, 1972). While a review of all group process theory is not feasible, it does seem useful to highlight a few concepts, since they help clarify potential process indicators of group effectiveness.

Three factors associated with or caused by levels of effectiveness in group process include: group member effort, skills utilization, and strategies.

1. *Group member effort*. For group effectiveness, group members need to demonstrate an appropriate level and pattern of effort directed toward the task. It is important to note here that this does not imply giving extraordinary effort all the time or the same levels of effort (beyond a minimum) for everyone. Moreover, effort levels will be affected by group norms, the perceived importance of the group task, and group leadership. Clearly, group members' behaviours toward one another will also have a significant impact (Hackman, 1976).

2. *Group member skills utilization*. Even when the group is composed of individuals with the requisite skills and abilities, it is possible for the group to make ineffective use of them. Group process can determine if those people with the best knowledge are allowed to contribute to group functioning or, alternatively, to promote a waste of time by those who have little of substance to offer (Hoffman, 1965).

3. *Work group strategies*. There seems to be ample evidence that how the group approaches the job to be done has important consequences for ultimate group success (Vroom & Yetton, 1973). While work group strategies will be affected by the input variables of structure and composition, they still are superimposed on these. At a minimum, work group strategies, as the plan to be followed by group members, must be compatible with these variables.

A focus on group process recognizes that it is important to the prediction and to the understanding of ultimate group success. It also provides the manager or researcher with an intermediate way of defining effectiveness. Thus, an effective work group is not only one that is appropriately composed (via input factors), but one that allows or encourages critical processes to unfold.

In essence, group process refers to the series of actions or operations that take place in a group as they relate to some goal or end (Steiner, 1972). Thus, process is reflected in behaviours. In attempting to measure group processes, it is important to realize that it is probably impossible to produce a complete or total description of all that occurs in a group. Such a description would have to include an enormous number of variables, some of which may only be manifest in the thoughts of the people involved. But we rarely even try to do this. Instead, we are interested in certain fragments of process.

In general, we seek to detect and record such things as who acts and how often, to whom the acts are directed, what the acts are made of, when the acts occur, and why the acts occur. Thus, while it is possible that an investigator might approach the study of group process without any preconceived notion of what to look for, most of us go into an examination of group process with some framework in mind.

The heart of any framework is a set of variables of interest and a system for recording them. The preferred technique for measuring group process is to observe groups (in real time or as recorded on audio or videotape). The system of recording often includes rules for observation as well (i.e., what to look for).

Explicit records of our observations imply some attention to detail. As a rule, the value of process data stems from the richness of detail that it provides. The challenge to investigators of group process is to settle on what level of detail to attend to and record. In this regard, it is useful to distinguish between narrative systems and checklists.

Narratives can take the form of anecdotes. These are descriptions of behavioural episodes written in some detail. A type of narrative that has been found useful in applied work is the critical incident. A specimen record is a second type of narrative that is more continuous in nature. As written, it is a sequential description of behaviour along with some contextual material. It is the sort of thing that we generate when we are setting up a story in a conversation. When used in the measurement of group process, these materials would constitute the raw material for content or thematic analysis.

In contrast, checklists provide greater structure to the measurement of process. Checklists often provide for the characterization of the setting of interest. This might include the number of people involved, the physical context (e.g., office or conference room), and the task or problem at hand. Action checklists describe behaviours rather than settings. Activity logs focus on clusters of activities as they relate to some purpose or goal.

One of the best-known checklist systems for describing and measuring group process derives from the work of Bales (1950). During interactions, the acts initiated and received by group members are recorded according to a format pictured in Figure 10.2. Once the frequencies of acts are recorded, they are converted to percentages. Not only does this allow for a description of events, but the scores can then be used according to a scheme for interaction process analysis to infer levels of individual and group phenomena (leadership, conflict, conformity, cohesiveness).

As mentioned in Chapter 5, when it comes to the use of the observation method, a critical choice relates to the frequency with which to observe and record. In this regard, the nature of the study (its goals and the resources available) will dictate whether or not to use a sampling strategy. However, in most cases the amount of process data accumulates so rapidly that continuous records are rare. It should also be recalled that the process of observation and recording can be obtrusive. Thus, an investigator should consider the likely consequences of passive, participative, or hidden observation plans.

Group process data can be obtained by using techniques other than direct observation. Usually this involves getting information from the group participants

FIGURE 10.2 A System for Measuring Group Process

Social-Emotional Area: Positive A	1	*Shows cohesion*, raises other's status, gives help, reward						
	2	*Shows tension release*, jokes, laughs, shows satisfaction						
	3	*Agrees*, shows passive acceptance, understands, complies						
Task Area: Neutral B	4	*Gives suggestions*, direction, implying autonomy for others						
	5	*Gives opinion*, evaluation, analysis, expresses feelings, wish						
	6	*Gives orientation*, information, repetition, confirmation						
C	7	*Asks for orientation*, information, repetition, confirmation						
	8	*Asks for opinion*, evaluation, analysis, expression of feeling						
	9	*Asks for suggestion*, direction, possible ways of action						
Social-Emotional Area: Negative D	10	*Disagrees*, shows passive rejection, formality, withholds help						
	11	*Shows tension*, asks for help, withdraws out of field						
	12	*Shows antagonism*, deflates other's status, defends or asserts self						

a) problems of communication (6, 7)
b) problems of evaluation (5, 8)
c) problems of control (4, 9)
d) problems of decision (3, 10)
e) problems of tension reduction (2, 11)
f) problems of reintegration (1, 12)

A. Positive reactions
B. Attempted answers
C. Questions
D. Negative reactions

Source: Bales, R.F. (1950). *Interaction process analysis*. Reading, MA: Addison-Wesley.

themselves. In this regard, most of the methods described in the chapter on qualitative methods in this text could be considered as potentially useful (e.g., individual and group interviews, diaries). Similarly, process information often can be accessed through the use of retrospective questionnaires. Thus, group members may be asked to respond to questions as to what happened in group sessions. Such questionnaires may be completed immediately after group sessions or after some time lapse. Further, group members can be forewarned that they will be filling out such an instrument before they meet as a group or afterwards. Each of these options has advantages and disadvantages, since they imply the potential for bias and memory lapses and thus affect the quality of information the investigator will receive.

The setting or context will also have an effect on the kind of group process that can be obtained and what methods are appropriate. A contrived setting is one created by the manager or investigator for specific purposes (in this case, to understand group process). A contrived setting may be set up in a behavioural sciences laboratory. However, training and development contexts, assessment centre contexts, or specially called committee meetings all provide an opportunity to study group process. In general, contrived settings will present greater opportunities for direct and systematic observation. In field (organizational) contexts, we are more likely to have to rely on alternative techniques (e.g., questionnaires).

In assessing the effectiveness of group process, the investigator attempts to use any of the techniques reviewed in order to index the extent to which group member and leader actions and behaviours are, indeed, appropriate for the group, its members' attributes (knowledge, abilities, needs, etc.), the task at hand, and the resources available. Because there will be no single system for selecting the particular behaviours that are likely to promote or inhibit group member skills, effort levels or performance strategies, and so on, the manager or researcher needs to use professional judgment in order to select or develop the behaviour recording system that will have the necessary content (or construct) validity.

GROUP OUTCOME FACTORS

When defining group effectiveness, we are usually thinking in terms of how well the group has been able to accomplish certain **group outcomes**. This commonsense notion will be retained in this chapter. The following is a set of various outcome factors based on the theoretical and empirical studies in the area.

1. *Objective group performance.* In some instances, a case can be made that an appropriate measure of *group effectiveness* can be derived from counting what the group has produced or accomplished. For example, the effectiveness of most sports teams is defined in terms of the number of games won, points earned, and so forth. Similarly, in military settings, objective performance indicators may be available for use. For example, Tziner and Eden (1985) looked at the effects of crew composition on tank crew performance. In their study, tank crew performance was measured in terms of accuracy of gun fire, time lapse between target sighting and firing, and number of equipment failures attributed to poor maintenance. In a study of 100 different sales teams, Gladstein (1984) used actual sales revenue as an effectiveness measure.

   Objective performance data may be collected explicitly for the purpose of a study, or may be taken from records already being kept by the group or the organization of which the group is a part. In the Tziner and Eden (1985) tank study, the latter strategy was used. Similarly, effectiveness indicators built on operational measures may make use of historical or archival records or observations. Gladstein (1984) made use of both current and archival data in her study.

   As in the case of individuals, objective group performance may be couched in terms of absolute measures (e.g., "number of targets destroyed"), relative scores ("team performance is ranked third out of eight teams"), or with reference to standards. In Gladstein's (1984) research, one effectiveness measure was the dollar amount of commissions that was earned by each sales team, where commissions were based on the revenue the team brought in above a specified objective (standard) determined at the start of each year.

2. *Subjective group performance.* In defining and measuring group performance, it is not uncommon to obtain and use *subjective assessments,* in which individuals with the opportunity to observe group outputs are asked to share or record their impressions. At times these individuals are managers or leaders. They may be the group members themselves or they may be experts or staff convened for the purpose of effectiveness measurement. In their tank crew study, Tziner and Eden (1985) asked military unit commanders to provide subjective performance rankings of crews. Gladstein (1984) asked sales team members to rate their own performance. She and her colleagues also made their own ratings based on interviews and extensive observations. Katz (1982), in his study of research and development project teams, interviewed each department manager and laboratory director to obtain his or her subjective assessment of the overall technical performance of all projects with which he or she was familiar. Finally, Pritchard, Jones, Roth, Stuebing, and Ekeberg (1988) reported a very elaborate group performance measurement system based on the subjective assessment of the output of military maintenance and repair teams. In their system, a score of zero would mean that personnel were just meeting expectations; their productivity was neither particularly good nor bad. The more positive the score, the more the teams were exceeding these expectations.

3. *Efficiency.* There are cases in which group effectiveness has been conceptualized in terms of efficiency. While productivity is thought of as an index of what has been accomplished, *efficiency* refers to accomplishments relative to the resources utilized. Thus, efficiency is an output to input ratio (Pritchard et al., 1988). As in the case of productivity, efficiency indicators of effectiveness may be built around subjective or objective measurements. Thus, Katz (1982) used a seven-point rating scale to get at lab managers' impressions of a team's cost/performance ratios. In contrast, in a laboratory experiment examining the effects of task properties and interdependence, Shiflett (1972) was able to compute an efficiency score for each of the groups studied based on the number of units produced per unit of time.

   More recently, Banker, Field, Schroeder, and Sinha (1996) studied the impact of work teams on labour productivity, which was measured as a ratio of the number of units produced to total production hours. Their results indicated that labour productivity improved following the formation of work teams.

4. *Quality.* Several authors (e.g., Maier & Solem, 1962; Vroom & Yetton, 1973) have argued that many group decisions and tasks require solutions that have a

high quality component. Thus, it is not sufficient to produce something that is good enough to get the job done. The idea, product, or service must meet certain additional criteria—it must possess quality. While it is possible to index quality with reference to objective standards, on many occasions a quality determination must involve subjective assessments. These, in turn, may be obtained through ratings. Alternatively, inferences of quality may be made from the way group members behave relative to the group's decision or product. Thus, the speed and enthusiasm with which group decisions are implemented could serve to reflect the quality of group decisions (see White, Dittrich & Lang, 1980).

The research by Banker et al. (1996) on the impact of work teams on labour productivity also included a measure of quality, which was simply the percentage of total units that were defective. Their results indicated that quality also improved following the formation of work teams.

5. *Group emotional tone.* Most theories of group functioning imply that an effective group is one that meets or satisfies group member needs (Hackman, 1976, 1986; Shaw, 1981). Thus, a reasonable indicator of an effective group can be found in the *emotional tone* of intragroup relations. More operationally, assessments of this tone can be made with reference to the group or to its members.

Indices of emotional tone focused at the group level can be obtained using a number of techniques. For example, Gersick (1988) observed and recorded meetings of groups over numerous sessions. She then had transcripts made that allowed her to create a group-level indicator of energy spent on the task. Wicker, Kirmeyer, Hanson, and Alexander (1976) analyzed recordings of the interplay between members of their four-person laboratory groups in order to develop an index of comfort level. In a study of church groups, Wicker and Kauma (1974) recorded church service attendance levels over time to infer levels of satisfaction. Blumberg (1980) measured satisfaction in work groups that had gone to a new style of worker development (job rotation) in a coal mining company. He created an index of job-switching behaviour based on company records, and determined that this switching index did reflect anxiety and satisfaction levels in the work groups made up of people with particular job classifications.

Frequently, however, researchers attempt to get at estimates of emotional tone by interviewing or otherwise obtaining subjective assessments from individuals who belong to the groups under study. Group scores are thus created by aggregating or averaging individual scores.

6. *Group member commitment.* In decision-making settings, not only is it important to know that the quality of the solutions generated is good, it is also important to determine if the solutions will be adopted or implemented. To put it another way, an important outcome variable is group member commitment.

To illustrate, White et al. (1980) were interested in the impact produced by three different types of group meeting procedures. In their study with a sample of nursing supervisors, they found that a structured method of conducting a meeting to deal with work-related problems produced a significantly greater rate of implementing group-derived solutions. This was true for both simple and complex problems. In contrast, unstructured discussions had a lot less impact in solution implementation back on the job. The authors speculate that the structured approach allowed for a more balanced participation on the part of group members. This involvement, in turn, was felt to increase commitment to implementing the solutions on the job.

Finally, in doing research on groups, or when group data are to be analyzed, it is important to keep in mind that the unit of analysis is the group. Thus, the *sample size* is the number of groups involved in the investigation. This simple notion is sometimes forgotten, however, as the actual data often are generated by group members. A case in point occurs when satisfaction is a variable of interest. We usually obtain measures of satisfaction by asking individuals to complete a survey. If our study involves comparing the impact of two programs on satisfaction, it would be important first to compute team or group averages. To aggregate across all individuals exposed to one or the other program and use this as a basis for comparison would be inappropriate.

It is not uncommon for the manager or researcher to think in terms of cause and effect. Thus, our study might examine the impact of group communication patterns (a cause) on group member satisfaction (the effect). However, the nature of group dynamics is such that feedback loops are quite numerous and tend to operate quickly (Hackman, 1976). Consequently, what is an effect might indeed become the cause. In the example offered here, this would mean that the levels of satisfaction felt by group members (initially the result of communication patterns) would, in turn, quickly influence the nature and amount of communication. Relationships in which variables may be both cause and effect are often referred to as instances of **reciprocal causation**.

These dynamics imply that it might be best to study group phenomena in contrived settings in which we can take fine-grained measurements. The researcher would be able to capture the sequences of the cause-and-effect forces involved. In any context, these reciprocal dynamics would seem to require some type of longitudinal research design (Gersick, 1988).

In summary, work groups and teams are increasingly becoming the focus of work and research. The functioning of groups and the many factors involved make it difficult to study and measure groups. Fortunately, researchers have made substantial progress in this area, as reported in the following HR Research Today box.

HR RESEARCH TODAY

A Study of Work Team Characteristics and Effectiveness

An important research area on the topic of teams is understanding what characteristics make teams most effective. The results of research along these lines have important practical implications for designing effective work teams in organizations. Based on a review of the literature, Campion, Medsker, and Higgs (1993) developed a framework that consists of five major themes of team characteristics. Each of the themes consists of key characteristics and includes the following:

- Job design (self-management, participation, task variety, task significance, task identity).
- Interdependence (task interdependence, goal interdependence, and interdependent feedback and rewards).
- Composition (heterogeneity, flexibility, relative size, preference for team work).
- Context (training, managerial support, communication/cooperation between teams).
- Process (potency, social support, workload sharing, and communication/cooperation within the team).

These themes/characteristics are predicted to be related to effectiveness criteria, which include productivity, satisfaction, and manager judgments of effectiveness.

In a recent study to test the model, Campion, Papper, and Medsker (1996) studied 60 teams of professional workers. They collected data on the characteristics and criteria of the Campion et al. (1993) model and used multiple sources. In particular, data on team characteristics were obtained from employees and managers, and data on team effectiveness were obtained from employees, managers, and archival records. It is also important to realize that the group was the level of analysis.

The results indicated that the work team characteristics were significantly related to team effectiveness. The job design characteristics and interdependence were related to most of the effectiveness criteria; context characteristics were related to many criteria; and composition characteristics were related to only a few criteria. However, the process characteristics were the most strongly related to the effectiveness criteria, perhaps because they are closer to the criteria than the other team characteristics, which are really the inputs.

Based on their results, Campion et al. (1996) provide the following suggestions for designing effective work teams:

- Design motivating jobs.
- Make the team members interdependent.
- Create a supportive context for the team.
- Monitor and encourage positive team processes.

FIGURE 10.3 Themes and Characteristics Related to Work Team Effectiveness

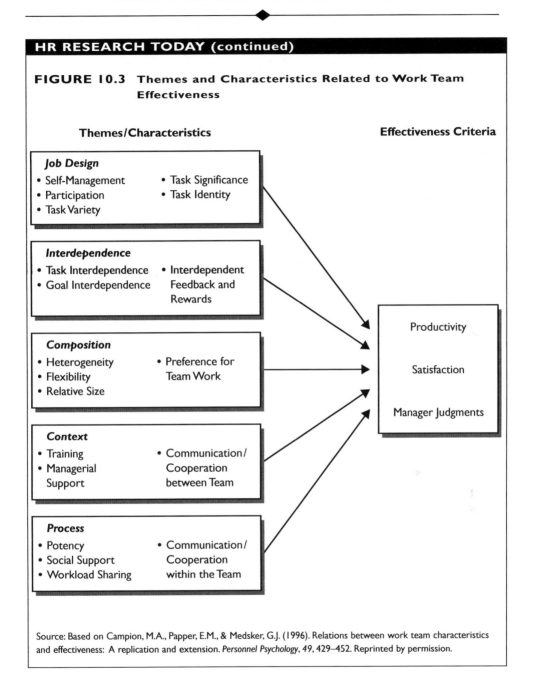

Themes/Characteristics

Effectiveness Criteria

Job Design
- Self-Management
- Participation
- Task Variety
- Task Significance
- Task Identity

Interdependence
- Task Interdependence
- Goal Interdependence
- Interdependent Feedback and Rewards

Composition
- Heterogeneity
- Flexibility
- Relative Size
- Preference for Team Work

Context
- Training
- Managerial Support
- Communication/ Cooperation between Team

Process
- Potency
- Social Support
- Workload Sharing
- Communication/ Cooperation within the Team

Productivity

Satisfaction

Manager Judgments

Source: Based on Campion, M.A., Papper, E.M., & Medsker, G.J. (1996). Relations between work team characteristics and effectiveness: A replication and extension. *Personnel Psychology, 49*, 429–452. Reprinted by permission.

◆◆◆
DEFINING AND MEASURING
ORGANIZATION-LEVEL VARIABLES

As is the case with groups, organizations are extremely complex by nature. Thus, it is not surprising that there are a number of perspectives with which to approach the definition and measurement of organization-level variables. In this section, a number of these approaches are presented. Once again you will discover that there is no single best way to think of organizations. Appropriate use of concepts and measures will depend on informed judgment.

Human resource research at the organization level is often concerned with the relation between particular organizational characteristics and the effectiveness of the organization. Organization-level variables that are treated as predictors or independent variables are often based on the following: organizational structure, human resource systems, and organizational development.

ORGANIZATIONAL STRUCTURE

Organizations are often characterized in terms of their structure. Traditionally, this has meant that writers have focused on the formal configuration of roles, rules, and procedures that already exist. The emphasis has been on lines of authority regarding the integration of work tasks under a common manager (who reports to whom), and the amount of discretion individuals have as they do their jobs (Dow, 1988).

Structure is often described in terms of the following concepts (James & Jones, 1976):

1. *Interdependence*—how the work flows from one department or unit to another.

2. *Centralization of decision making*—the location where important decisions are made.

3. *Specialization*—the division of labour as it relates to whether the job duties are unique or shared.

4. *Standardization*—the extent to which the tasks to be done are specified in detail.

5. *Formalization*—how explicit or codified the procedures are.

6. *Configuration*—the shape of the organization as determined by the nature of differentiation (specialization) that exists, the number of people working in the organization, the number of people typically reporting to a manager, and the number of levels of authority that are operative.

Thus, to characterize an organization in terms of its structure, the researcher would attempt to create, develop, or adopt measures of each of these factors. Recently, however, the concept of structure has been augmented to refer to the particular patterns of activities and behaviour that take place in the organization (Ranson, Hinings, & Greenwood, 1980).

Writers have argued that the formal or prescribed frameworks described in organizational charts are only weakly related to what people actually do. In fact, most positions and job descriptions are only loosely defined. People are constantly interpreting and improvising as they fulfill their work roles. Individuals affect what other individuals do. And one group's functioning will have consequences for several others. It's not that the formal design of the organization isn't important; it's just that it should be viewed as merely setting the stage for what goes on there, perhaps even constraining actions somewhat. Thus, the operative structure is emergent and changing, rooted in the behaviours of individuals, and in the interpretations of events or the sense-making processes of the people involved (Dow, 1988; Ranson et al., 1980).

To understand this realized configuration (as contrasted to the prescribed configuration), writers with this view argue that a researcher cannot rely on formal organization charts or company documents. Instead, one would have to attend to and measure key behaviours and activities of individuals and groups involved.

HUMAN RESOURCE SYSTEMS

As indicated in Chapter 1, an increasing body of research has tested the relations between human resource practices, policies, and systems with organizational effectiveness measures. Arthur (1994), for example, found that human resource policies and practices used by steel mini-mills could be categorized as being commitment or control systems. Commitment human resource systems emphasized the development of employee commitment, and control human resource systems emphasized efficiency and the reduction of labour costs.

Huselid (1995) examined high-performance human resource work practices and identified two major dimensions. The first dimension he called *employee skills and organizational structures* and included the following practices:

1. Formal information-sharing program.
2. Formal job analysis.
3. Internal hiring.
4. Attitude surveys administered on a regular basis.
5. Quality of work life programs, quality circles, and labour–management participation teams.
6. Incentive plans, profit-sharing plans, and/or gain-sharing plans.
7. Hours of training received by employees.
8. Formal grievance procedures and/or complaint resolution system.
9. Use of employment tests for hiring.

Huselid (1995) called the second dimension of high-performance systems *employee motivation*. It includes the following practices that recognize and reinforce desirable employee behaviours:

1. Performance appraisals used to determine compensation.
2. Use of formal performance appraisals.
3. Use of merit or performance ratings versus seniority for promotion decisions.
4. Number of qualified applicants per position.

Delery and Doty (1996) identified seven strategic HR practices that have been linked to organizational performance:

1. *Internal career opportunities*—the use of internal labour markets.
2. *Training*—the amount of formal training that employees receive.
3. *Results-oriented appraisals*—appraisals can focus on behaviours of individuals or the consequences of behaviours.
4. *Profit sharing*—linking pay to performance.
5. *Employment security*—a formal or informal policy of employment security.
6. *Participation*—formal grievance systems and participation in decision making.
7. *Job descriptions*—the extent to which jobs are tightly or narrowly defined or not clearly defined.

Delery and Doty (1996) developed this list of practices based on the existing literature, and consider them to be critical characteristics of employment systems in organizations. As well, they suggest that the seven practices can be used to describe two types of employment systems: a market-driven system and an internal system. Table 10.1 presents the measures of the seven HR practices and the characteristics of the two systems. Based on the results of their study, Delery and Doty (1996) concluded that "differences in HR practices are associated with rather large differences in financial performance" (p. 825).

In a study of the relationship between human resource practices and performance in manufacturing firms, Youndt, Snell, Dean, and Lepak (1996) measured what they considered to be the most recognized areas of HRM:

1. *Staffing practices*—selectivity in hiring and selection for manual and physical skills, technical skills, and problem-solving skills.
2. *Training practices*—comprehensiveness, policies and procedural training, and training for technical and problem-solving skills.
3. *Performance appraisal*—developmental focus, results-based focus, and behaviour-based focus.

TABLE 10.1 CHARACTERISTICS AND MEASURES OF EMPLOYMENT SYSTEMS

HR PRACTICES	MARKET-TYPE SYSTEM	INTERNAL SYSTEM	MEASURES*
Internal career opportunities	Hiring almost exclusively from outside the organization. Very little use of internal career ladders	Hiring mainly from within the organization. Extensive use of well-defined career ladders	Individuals in this job have clear career paths within the organization. Individuals in this job have very little future within this organization (reverse-coded). Employees' career aspirations within the company are known by their immediate supervisors. Employees in this job who desire promotion have more than one potential position they could be promoted to.
Training	No formal training provided. Little if any socialization taking place within the organization	Extensive formal training provided. Great amount of socialization within the organization	Extensive training programs are provided for individuals in this job. Employees in this job will normally go through training programs every few years. There are formal training programs to teach new hires the skills they need to perform their jobs. Formal training programs are offered to increase employees' promotability in this organization.
Results-oriented appraisals	Performance measured by quantifiable output or results-oriented measures. Feedback in the form of numbers and for evaluative purposes	Performance measured by behaviour-oriented measures. Feedback more for developmental purposes	Performance is more often measured with objective, quantifiable results. Performance appraisals are based on objective, quantifiable results.
Profit sharing	Profit sharing used extensively	Few incentive systems used. Very little use of profit sharing	Individuals in this job receive bonuses based on the profit of the organization.
Employment security	Very little employment security given	Great deal of employment security among those who make it through initial trial period. Extensive benefits to those "outplaced". Formal dismissal policies	Employees in this job can expect to stay in the organization for as long as they wish. It is very difficult to dismiss an employee in this job. Job security is almost guaranteed to employees in this job. If the bank were facing economic problems, employees in this job would be the last to get cut.
Participation	Employees given little voice in the organization	Employees likely have access to grievance systems. Employees more likely to participate in decision-making	Employees in this job are allowed to make many decisions. Employees in this job are often asked by their supervisor to participate in decisions. Employees are provided the opportunity to suggest improvements in the way things are done. Superiors keep open communications with employees in this job.
Job descriptions	Jobs are not clearly defined. Job definitions are loose	Jobs very tightly defined	The duties of this job are clearly defined. This job has an up-to-date job description. The job description for this job contains all of the duties performed by individual employees. The actual job duties are shaped more by the employee than by a specific job description (reverse-coded).

*Response scale: 1 = Strongly disagree, 2 = Disagree, 3 = Slightly disagree, 4 = Neither agree nor disagree, 5 = Slightly agree, 6 = Agree, 7 = Strongly agree.

Source: Adapted from Delery, J.E., & Doty, D.H. (1996). Modes of theorizing in strategic human resource management: Tests of universalistic, contingency, and configurational performance predictions. *Academy of Management Journal, 39*, 809, 834. Reprinted by permission of the publisher via Copyright Clearance Center Inc.

4. *Compensation systems*—type of pay (hourly, salary, skill-based), incentives (individual and group), and equity (individual and external).

Youndt et al. (1996) combined these HR practices into two indexes that they labelled the *administrative HR system* and the *human-capital-enhancing HR system*. They found that HR practices influence firm performance when the practices are aligned with an organization's strategy.

Finally, Delaney and Huselid (1996) studied the impact of human resource management practices on perceptions of organizational performance. Their measures of HRM practices included the following:

1. *Improving employee skills*—selectivity in hiring and employee training.

2. *Enhancing employee motivation*—incentive compensation and grievance procedures.

3. *Structure of jobs and work*—decentralized decision making.

4. *Internal labour market*—opportunities for promotion and job security.

Based on the results of their study, Delaney and Huselid (1996) concluded that "progressive HRM practices, including selectivity in staffing, training, and incentive compensation, are positively related to perceptual measures of organizational performance" (p. 965).

In summary, research on human resource practices, policies, and systems has tended to focus on a number of key HR practices. While some of these practices are universally considered to be related to organizational performance, some appear to be more appropriate in organizations with particular business strategies. Therefore, organization-level research on human resources should focus on the types of practices described in this section. Unfortunately, as the reader probably has noted from the research described in this section, the measurement of HRM practices across studies is not consistent. This is a serious problem, and, as noted by Delaney and Huselid (1996), the development of reliable and valid measures of HRM systems is needed to advance research in this important area.

ORGANIZATIONAL DEVELOPMENT PERSPECTIVE

Organizational development (OD) is a process of planned and systematic change to improve the functioning of organizations. The goal is to bring about what might be considered a healthy organization and to improve the well-being of individuals and groups. This often involves improving work and interpersonal processes within organizations such as communication, decision making, problem solving, and leadership.

Organizational development seeks to develop appropriate or desirable processes that promote the physical, psychological, and social welfare of individuals (both managers and workers) employed by the organization and the organization itself. In order to successfully achieve this, a diagnosis of the organization is required. This is in effect a rigorous research process that is designed to identify the organization's strengths and weaknesses. According to Levinson (1994), "Organizational diagnosis is a systematic method for gathering, organizing, and interpreting information about organizations for the purpose of helping them anticipate or ameliorate their adaptive problems" (p. 27).

In order to conduct a diagnosis, investigators must gather data about organizational processes, as well as groups and individuals. Many of the research methods discussed earlier are used to conduct an organizational diagnosis, including interviews, observations, surveys, and archival data such as organizational papers and documents. Interviewing members of an organization is the most common method (Burke, 1994).

One approach to organizational diagnosis is the Burke-Litwin model of organizational performance and change. The model indicates the various elements that need to be measured when diagnosing an organization and identifying the changes needed to improve individual and organizational functioning (Burke, 1994). Using the Burke-Litwin model, the diagnosis would involve gathering information on the following variables (Burke, 1994):

1. *External environment*—factors that can influence organization performance.
2. *Mission and strategy*—central purpose of the organization and how the organization achieves its purpose.
3. *Leadership*—executive values, practices, and behaviour.
4. *Culture*—the rules, values, and principles that guide behaviour.
5. *Structure*—structural work arrangements of functions and people.
6. *Management practices*—the practices and behaviours of management.
7. *Systems*—policies, mechanisms, and organizational systems.
8. *Climate*—members' relations with one another and with supervisors.
9. *Task requirements and individual skills/abilities*—skills and knowledge required for task accomplishment.
10. *Individual needs and values*—individual psychological feelings of desire and worth.
11. *Motivation*—desire to achieve goals and attain high standards of performance.
12. *Individual and organizational performance*—outcomes or results of individuals and the organization.

According to Burke (1994), the use of a model such as the Burke-Litwin model enables the investigator to categorize the data according to the variables in the model, and to provide clues regarding what action is necessary to improve the organization and to determine the most appropriate intervention. While there are many such models in the organizational development literature, the focus is usually on formal and informal organizational processes and systems. The research process of gathering data to perform an organizational diagnosis is a critical activity for improving organizations. For more information about the use of the Burke-Litwin model for data gathering and analyses, the reader should consult Burke (1994).

◆◆◆
ORGANIZATIONAL OUTCOMES

The previous section of this chapter focused on the independent variables in organization-level research: organization structure, human resource systems, and organizational processes. Usually, the researcher will want to study the relations between these variables and organizational outcomes.

Organizational outcomes can vary widely depending on the goals and purpose of the research. Steers (1975) reviewed seventeen studies that looked at or measured organizational effectiveness. He paid particular attention to the criteria used. He discovered that there was very little overlap among studies with regard to what the authors had chosen to measure. Table 10.2 summarizes the frequency of use of the fourteen different constructs. Steers (1975) also points out that, without exception, the authors of the studies stated a priori what was good, desirable, or required for effectiveness. Thus, it is an area of research in which the theoretical orientation or the personal values of the investigator play a key role.

Goodman, Atkin, and Schoorman (1983) highlighted several unfortunate trends in the area of organizational effectiveness research. Specifically, all too often researchers tend to rely on single indicators of effectiveness and to ignore the relationships among multiple measures. When they do use appropriate measures they do not address the time frame implied by the criterion. The fact is, some measures of effectiveness (e.g., changes in market share) take longer to unfold than others (changes in worker attitudes). Goodman et al. also argue that there is an unfortunate tendency to apply particular criterion concepts or to use effectiveness indicators across dissimilar organizations without regard for their appropriateness.

In the section below, four general approaches to the definition and measurement of organizational effectiveness are described: organizational goal attainment measures, employee outcome measures, human resource outcome measures, and system outcome measures.

ORGANIZATIONAL GOAL ATTAINMENT MEASURES

In light of the fact that organizations exist in order to accomplish some objective or achieve some goal, it seems reasonable that the definition and measurement of effec-

TABLE 10.2 ALTERNATIVES IN THE DEFINITION OF ORGANIZATIONAL EFFECTIVENESS

Concept	Frequency of Use (Out of 17)
Adaptability / Flexibility	10
Productivity	6
Satisfaction of Employee	5
Profitability	3
Resource Acquisition	3
Absence of Strain	2
Control over the Environment	2
Development of Employees	2
Efficiency	2
Employee Retention	2
Growth	2
Integration	2
Open Communications	2
Survival	2
All Others	1

Source: Adapted with permission from Steers, R.M. (1975). Problems in the measurement of organizational effectiveness. *Administrative Science Quarterly, 20,* 546–558.

tiveness should centre on goal attainment (Georgiou, 1973). Most authors using this approach recognize that a goal perspective requires that attention needs to be given to resolving just which goals (e.g., publicly stated or operative goals) or whose goals (e.g., company owners or top management) are to be pursued before efforts at measurement can be undertaken.

The last point notwithstanding, many writers would grant that organizations need to produce a product or service and make a profit. The following are some specific indicators that reflect this orientation.

1. *Profit and Profit-Related Indices.* Profit is the amount of revenue from sales left after all costs and obligations are met. Percent return on investment, percent return on assets, and measured operating income are *profit-related indices.* Price and Mueller (1986) refer to these indices as *financial viabilities* and argue that they are quite compatible with goal approaches to effectiveness. A variety of financial indicators such as profit margin, return on assets, and return on equity are commonly used to draw inferences regarding effectiveness by the financial community. In his study on the impact of human resource practices, Huselid (1995) used several measures of corporate financial performance, including a measure of the gross rate of return on capital.

2. *Productivity.* Productivity is usually defined as the quantity or volume of the major product or service that the organization provides. This concept and its measurement at both the group and individual levels have already been noted. Usually, archival records are utilized to develop appropriate scores. Sometimes this is expressed as a rate (productivity per worker or per unit of time). Price and Mueller (1986) recommend an index of cost per unit of output. In addition to measuring corporate financial performance, Huselid (1995) also measured productivity in terms of sales per employee.

3. *Quality.* Quality usually refers to the attributes of the primary product or service provided by the organization. It would have to be operationalized carefully in light of the specific product or service. The restaurant and hospitality industries use surveys of customers or clients to get data on perceptions of quality. In the specialty retail business and in banking, trained observers may "shop" company and competitor stores and take notes to index quality of service delivery.

4. *Growth.* Growth refers to an index of such variables as plant capacity, assets, sales, profits, market share, or number of new products introduced. While it could be argued that growth is not always desirable, it is often viewed as a hallmark of effectiveness.

5. *Efficiency.* In most cases, we think of efficiency in terms of a ratio that reflects a comparison of some aspect of performance relative to the costs incurred for that performance. Indices of efficiency can be derived from archival records. Damanpour and Evan (1984) created three efficiency measures in their study of libraries (e.g., circulation/size of holdings). Glisson and Martin (1980) calculated an efficiency measure for mental health professionals as "the number of clients served per week per $10,000 budget" (p. 28). Hoy and Hellriegel (1982) distinguished between internal and external efficiency in small business operations. However, most writers appear to feel that efficiency is an insufficient (deficient) indicator of effectiveness (Katz & Kahn, 1978).

6. *Perceptual Measures of Goal Attainment.* Although accounting data and financial measures are often used to measure the outcomes discussed in this section, perceptual measures have also been used to measure performance, growth, and quality-related outcomes. For example, in their study on the impact of human resource management practices, Delaney and Huselid (1996) designed two perceptual measures of firm performance. First, they measured *perceived organizational performance* by asking respondents to compare their organization's performance on the following seven dimensions over the past three years with other organizations that do the same kind of work:

   a. Quality of products, services, or programs.
   b. Development of new products, services, or programs.

c. Ability to attract essential employees.

d. Ability to retain essential employees.

e. Satisfaction of customers or clients.

f. Relations between management and other employees.

g. Relations among employees in general.

They also measured *perceived market performance* by asking respondents to compare their organization's performance over the past three years in terms of marketing, growth in sales, profitability, and market share to other organizations that do the same kind of work.

In defence of their use of perceptual measures of organizational performance, Delaney and Huselid (1996) note that measures of perceived organizational performance have been shown to be positively related to objective measures of firm performance. However, when using such measures one has to consider the potential limitations of self-report data and perceptual measures, as discussed in previous chapters.

EMPLOYEE OUTCOME MEASURES

Although organizational goal attainment outcomes are often an important outcome measure, it is important to realize that there are many factors, both internal and external to the organization, that can influence these types of outcomes. As well, such outcomes are somewhat removed from other outcomes that are more directly influenced by human resource practices. For example, recall that in Huselid's (1995) study on the impact of human resource management practices, the impact of such practices on corporate financial performance was due in part to their influence on employee turnover and productivity.

Thus, these more immediate outcomes (e.g., employee performance, turnover) tend to be more directly influenced by human resource practices, and are also likely to precede and influence organizational goal attainment outcomes. The following are some of the most important employee outcomes that are measured at the organization level.

1. *Employee Performance/Productivity.* In order for organizations to be successful and profitable, their employees need to achieve high levels of performance or productivity. Therefore, it is important to measure the relative level of employee performance or productivity. For example, one of the most widely used measures of productivity, and the one used by Huselid (1995), is sales per employee.

2. *Absenteeism.* Absenteeism is nonattendance when an employee is scheduled to come to work. It is common to distinguish between voluntary and involuntary

absenteeism, where the former involves a choice on the part of an individual. More operationally, it usually is measured as time lost, and the frequency and number of short-term absences. Absenteeism can be a costly expense for organizations and is related to other outcomes such as lower job performance (Johns, 1997).

3. *Tardiness.* Tardiness reflects absenteeism for a period of time shorter than a day. When employees are regularly late for work or take longer breaks and lunches, this can amount to many hours of lost work and productivity. Like absenteeism, tardiness can also be a costly and avoidable expense for organizations. A recent meta-analysis found that lateness behaviour is strongly related to absenteeism and turnover behaviour, and moderately related to work attitudes and performance (Koslowsky, Sagie, Krausz, & Singer, 1997).

4. *Turnover.* Turnover refers to employees voluntarily or involuntarily leaving the organization. Turnover can be extremely costly to organizations, and for those industries in which there is a shortage of skilled labour, it can be difficult to replace employees who quit. As a result, many organizations have implemented human resource practices to lower turnover. In his study on human resource practices, Huselid (1995) measured organizations' average annual rate of turnover, and found that certain human resource practices are associated with lower employee turnover.

There are many potential indices of turnover, and one may be more suitable or appropriate for a given investigation, depending on the availability of data (Schmittlein & Morrison, 1983). However, Price and Mueller (1986) recommend quit rate and average length of service. *Quit rate* is the ratio of the number of employees who leave voluntarily during a given period to the average number of employees working for that same period. In contrast, the *average length of service* measure is the median length of service of all employees who leave voluntarily during a period.

5. *Accidents and work-related illnesses (both physical and emotional).* The quality of work life is thought to have an effect on the physical and mental well-being of employees. The number, rate, and severity of accidents will have economic consequences for an organization in terms of insurance premiums, medical expenses, lost wages, temporary replacement costs, and even fines imposed by government agencies. Thus, measures of the frequency and severity of accidents and, increasingly, stress-related illnesses are important outcomes.

6. *Grievances, strikes, and work stoppages.* These related events usually occur when individuals working under collective bargaining agreements feel that management practices or policies violate provisions of their agreement or that the workplace is unsafe. They can be variously indexed in terms of number, frequency,

severity, or duration. In any event, these manifestations of poor work life quality can be readily related to costs or expenses beyond what would normally be incurred in doing business.

In summary, the outcomes described in this section are important for at least two reasons. First, these are employee-related outcomes, and as such they are most directly influenced by human resource practices. For example, improved recruitment and selection practices, as well as employee training and development and incentive programs are likely to have some influence on most, if not all, of the outcomes discussed above. Second, these outcomes (e.g., employee productivity, turnover, absenteeism) can influence the organizational goal attainment outcomes discussed in the previous section. As such, they are important organization-level outcomes in human resource research and practice.

HUMAN RESOURCE OUTCOMES

While employee outcomes such as turnover and absenteeism are often used as key outcome measures in human resource research, they represent measures that are not always directly the result of human resource systems. In other words, they are not human resource outcomes per se, although human resource practices and systems are often implemented with the goal of having some influence on them, and as already noted, they do have an impact.

With this in mind, it is important to consider outcomes that are more directly related to human resource practices. These "**human resource outcomes**" are generally associated with particular human resource practices. For example, consider the possible outcomes of recruitment activities. Breaugh (1992) presents over a dozen criteria that are possible outcomes of recruitment. For example, *global criterion measures* include such things as the number and/or percentage of jobs filled, jobs filled in a timely fashion, jobs filled with above-average performers, and so on. *Recruiter-oriented criterion measures* include the number of interviews conducted, number of minorities and women recruited, and cost per hire. *Recruitment method–oriented criterion measures* include the number of applications generated, time required to generate applicants, and the quality of employees hired. These are just some of the many possible outcomes of recruitment.

Human resource outcomes tend to be specific to a particular function or activity. For example, training criteria usually include measures of trainees' reactions, learning, behaviour, and organization results (Kirkpatrick, 1994). Training outcomes may also include such things as the number of employees trained, average number of hours of training received by employees, and so on. Obviously, the outcomes will depend on the human resource activity or system under investigation, and the needs and goals of the organization. More examples of outcomes for specific human resource functions, including recruiting, selection, performance appraisal, and compensation, can be found in Phillips (1996).

OPEN-SYSTEMS PERSPECTIVE

Organizations are open systems, and as such there is often an interest in the organizational processes and functioning that are required for organizations to achieve their goals. The processes of interest are those involved in the various subsystem activities and functions within organizations. That is to say, to the extent that an organization is designed, structured, and managed to fulfill these functions, the open-systems proponent would argue that it is an effective organization.

Some open-systems effectiveness indicators that have been identified in the literature include survival, conflict, acquisition of resources, flexibility/adaptation, innovation, and distinctive competence.

1. *Survival.* Strictly speaking, survival could be viewed as an outcome variable. It is also the ultimate criterion of an open system. Reimann (1982) studied twenty organizations over nine years using a survival criterion. Interestingly, he found that growth, decline, and disappearance could be predicted years before the fact on the basis of data obtained in interviews with key managers.

2. *Conflict.* Conflict over goals, values, and resources among organizational units is usually dysfunctional. High levels of conflict would, therefore, imply ineffectiveness. Cameron (1986) measured conflict with a questionnaire administered to school personnel, whereas Webb (1974) used structured interviews.

3. *Acquisition of Resources.* Acquisition of resources (e.g., capital, energy) follows directly from open-systems theory. Yuchtman and Seashore (1967) and Cameron (1986) used this as a criterion variable. Opinions of senior staff were used in the Cameron (1986) study to create an index of effectiveness in the acquisition of resources.

4. *Flexibility/Adaptation.* Flexibility/adaptation refers to the organization's capacity to change its operating procedures in light of environmental demands. While questionnaires have been used, it is possible to use interviews or observations to get at the speed and nature of response to threats or opportunities (Pettigrew, 1979).

5. *Innovation.* Innovation is the extent to which changes are intentionally introduced into the organization (Price & Mueller, 1986). While it is somewhat related to adaptation, innovation implies a certain proactivity that may allow an organization to preempt threats or take advantage of opportunities. Some authors distinguish between administrative and technological innovation (Damanpour & Evan, 1984). All agree, however, that the notion implies the successful implementation of new ideas.

6. *Distinctive Competence.* Distinctive competence refers to those things that an organization does well relative to its competitors (Selznick, 1957). This is not just what an organization can do, but what it does particularly well (Andrews, 1971). As an aspect of systems effectiveness, it may be thought of as an analogue to establishing an ecological niche. Snow and Hribiniak (1980) measured distinctive competencies in terms of the perceptions of top managers with regard to various organization functions (e.g., research and development, production, marketing) in four industries and found them to be related to the overall strategies that these managers were following.

In summary, the open-systems perspective of organizations suggests a number of important organizational outcomes in addition to those associated with organizational goal attainment and employee outcome measures. The different perspectives suggest the many possible outcome measures available. However, it is important to remember that the goals and objectives of the research should guide the selection of organizational outcomes that need to be measured in any particular study.

◆ ◆ ◆
SPECIAL CONSIDERATIONS FOR MEASURING GROUP- AND ORGANIZATION-LEVEL VARIABLES

Measures of group and organization-level variables require consideration of a number of important issues. When measuring variables at these levels, the researcher needs to consider the level of analysis, aggregation, sample size, and a number of issues associated with the type of criteria and data.

Writers differ with regard to the level of analysis appropriate for measuring organizational effectiveness (Cameron, 1978). Katz and Kahn (1978) argue that effectiveness must be viewed from the perspective of the supra system (larger society). Thus, agents or entities outside the organization should be the basis for effectiveness data. Others prefer to look at the subunit (division or strategic business unit) as the appropriate level for analysis (e.g., Pennings & Goodman, 1977). Ultimately, the goals and interest of the researcher and sponsors of the research should determine the appropriate level of analysis.

The above point notwithstanding, when studying organization-level phenomena, it is not unusual to obtain data from (or on) individuals, groups, departments, divisions, and so forth. The ways in which the data are combined can have an impact on the validity of the measure and the results. Therefore, the researcher needs to be sure of what the appropriate **level of aggregation** should be. This depends on the purpose and focus of the study.

For example, in a study on the influence of the work environment on the transfer of training, Tracey, Tannenbaum, and Kavanagh (1995) measured the climate and culture of 52 supermarkets, and considered three levels of aggregation: individual, group, and store. Their results indicated that both the transfer climate and a continuous-learning culture were related to post-training behaviours, and that both the group and store levels of aggregation were most appropriate. This study demonstrates the importance of giving special consideration to the appropriate level of aggregation. Different levels of aggregation can lead to different results.

A related issue is sample size. For research on groups and organizations, one needs to sample and study reasonable numbers of groups and organizations. For example, to study the influence of the work environment on transfer of training, Tracey et al. (1995) had to study 52 stores of a supermarket chain. Campion, Papper, and Medsker (1996) studied 60 teams in their research on team characteristics and effectiveness. The difficulty associated with gaining access to reasonable numbers of groups and organizations should not be underestimated.

We often characterize organizations in terms of their primary product or service (schools, hospitals, etc.). The fact is, these different types of organizations will present different challenges and opportunities for defining and measuring effectiveness. In some cases (e.g., manufacturing organizations), there is some consensus regarding indicators of effectiveness. In other cases (e.g., schools), there is a greater need for the researcher to define and create measures of effectiveness (Cameron, 1978; Damanpour & Evan, 1984). In the latter case, this produces the unfortunate state of affairs in which the results from different investigations may be hard to compare. It may be desirable, then, to attempt to use measures from prior investigations whenever possible.

The various measurement options described in this chapter reflect a mixture of objective and subjective data. Each has strengths and weaknesses with regard to reliability and validity. An investigator has to determine the level of confidence to place in each. In particular, when both types of data are used, differing qualities may provide difficulties of inference (Cameron, 1978). Campbell (1977) takes the extreme position that, in the final analysis, effectiveness criteria should always reflect human judgments. But this still raises the question of who should provide such judgments (Cameron, 1978).

Given the current state of affairs, it appears that there is no single conceptual model of group or organization effectiveness. But there is no shortage of possibilities either. The investigator interested in measuring effectiveness at the group or organization level clearly needs to make choices.

SUMMARY

This chapter has discussed issues of measurement at the group and organization levels of analysis. Organizations are increasingly implementing teams to perform the work in organizations, and human resource practices are increasingly being linked to organization-level outcomes. As a result, the need to measure group and organization-level variables in human resource research can be expected to become increasingly important and relevant. The information provided in this chapter should prove useful for understanding and measuring group and organization-level variables and to supplement the individual-level measurement techniques discussed in Chapter 9.

Definitions

Employee outcome measures   Measures that focus on employee-related outcomes and behaviours, such as performance and productivity, absenteeism, tardiness, turnover, and grievances.

Group input factors   The factors that are associated with the design and structure of a group, such as task organization, group composition and norms, and leadership.

Group outcome factors   The outcomes or consequences of group effort and goal accomplishment, such as group performance, efficiency, quality, emotional tone, and group member commitment.

Group process factors   The behaviours that take place in the group, the patterning of these behaviours, and the immediate consequences of these behaviours and patterns.

Human resource outcomes   Measures that focus on the outcomes of specific human resource programs and practices that are specific to the various human resource function areas.

Human resource systems   The nature and structure of human resource practices, policies, and procedures.

Level of aggregation   The level at which the data are combined for the purpose of developing measures and analyses.

Level of analysis   The level at which the researcher chooses to measure organizational effectiveness, such as individual, group, or organization.

Open-systems outcomes   Measures that focus on organizational processes and functioning, such as survival, conflict, resource acquisition, flexibility/adaptation, innovation, and distinctive competence.

Organizational development   The process of planned and systematic change to improve the functioning of organizations and the well-being of individuals.

Organizational goal attainment measures   Measures that focus on the goals or outcomes of organizations, such as profit, productivity, quality, growth, and efficiency.

Organizational structure The formal configuration of roles, rules, and procedures and the lines of authority regarding the integration and coordination of work tasks in organizations.

Reciprocal causation Relationships in which variables may be both a cause and effect.

EXERCISES

1. Joan Chan was recently hired as an assistant to the director of human resources in a large manufacturing company. During the past several years, the organization has begun to redesign work by forming teams. While there was a great deal of controversy and difficulty in changing to a team-based organization, many believed that it would eventually result in positive consequences for employees and the organization. However, many employees and managers are beginning to question the effectiveness of the teams, and some are even considering reversing the trend. In an effort to address these concerns, the director of human resources has given Joan an important assignment: Conduct a research study on team effectiveness.

   What variables should Joan measure, and how should she proceed? What information should she try to obtain, and why?

2. Using the measures of human resource practices in Table 10.1, measure the practices in your organization or the last organization for which you worked. Describe the HR practices in your organization. Based on your results and Table 10.1, determine the type of HR system in your organization. Using Delaney and Huselid's (1996) perceptual measures of organizational performance (pages 284–285), measure your organization's performance. Finally, based on all of the above, what can you say about human resource practices, systems, and performance in your organization?

3. The outcomes used in research on human resources are often specific to the particular human resource activity or system being studied. For each of the following human resource areas, prepare a list of five possible outcome measures:
   a) selection
   b) orientation and socialization
   c) performance appraisal
   d) compensation

RUNNING CASE: THE VP OF HUMAN RESOURCES—PART 6

Describe which variables you will measure as part of your effort to demonstrate the value-added of the HRM department and its programs to the organization. Will you measure individual, group, and/or organization-level variables? Which independent and dependent variables will you measure? Be specific about the variables you choose to measure within each level and why. What are the advantages and disadvantages of measuring variables at each level?

References

Arthur, J.B. (1994). Effects of human resource systems on manufacturing performance and turnover. *Academy of Management Journal, 37,* 670–687.

Andrews, K.R. (1971). *The concept of corporate strategy.* Homewood, IL: Irwin.

Bales, R.F. (1950). *Interaction process analysis.* Reading, MA: Addison-Wesley.

Banker, R.D., Field, J.M., Schroeder, R.G., & Sinha, K.K. (1996). Impact of work teams on manufacturing performance: A longitudinal field study. *Academy of Management Journal, 39,* 867–890.

Blumberg, M. (1980). Job switching in autonomous work groups: An exploratory study in a Pennsylvania coal mine. *Academy of Management Journal, 23,* 287–306.

Breaugh, J.A. (1992). *Recruitment: Science and practice.* Boston, MA: PWS-Kent.

Burke, W. W. (1994). Diagnostic models for organization development. In Ann Howard and Associates (Eds.), *Diagnosis for organizational change* (pp. 53–84). New York: The Guilford Press.

Cameron, K. (1978). Measuring organizational effectiveness in institutions of higher education. *Administrative Science Quarterly, 23,* 604–632.

Cameron, K. (1986). A study of organizational effectiveness and its predictors. *Management Science, 32,* 87–112.

Campbell, J.P. (1977). On the nature of organizational effectiveness. In P.S. Goodman, J.M. Penning, and Associates (Eds.), *New perspectives on organizational effectiveness.* San Francisco: Jossey-Bass.

Campion, M.A., Medsker, G.J. , & Higgs, A.C. (1993). Relations between work group characteristics and effectiveness: Implications for designing effective work groups. *Personnel Psychology, 46,* 823–850.

Campion, M.A., Papper, E.M., & Medsker, G.J. (1996). Relations between work team characteristics and effectiveness: A replication and extension. *Personnel Psychology, 49,* 429–452.

Cartwright, D., & Zander, A. (1968). *Group dynamics: Research and theory* (3rd ed.). New York: Harper & Row.

Damanpour, F., & Evan, W.M. (1984). Organizational innovation and performance: The problem of organizational lag. *Administrative Science Quarterly, 29,* 392–409.

Delaney, J.T., & Huselid, M.A. (1996). The impact of human resource management practices on perceptions of organizational performance. *Academy of Management Journal, 39,* 949–969.

Delery, J.E., & Doty, D.H. (1996). Modes of theorizing in strategic human resource management: Tests of universalistic, contingency, and configurational performance predictions. *Academy of Management Journal, 39,* 802–835.

Dow, G.K. (1988). Configurational and coactivational views of organizational structure. *Academy of Management Review, 13*, 53–64.

Feldman, D.C. (1984). The development and enforcement of group norms. *Academy of Management Review, 9*, 47–53.

Georgiou, P. (1973). The goal paradigm and notes towards a counter paradigm. *Administrative Science Quarterly, 18*, 291–310.

Gersick, J.G. (1988). Time and transition in work teams: Toward a new model of group development. *Academy of Management Journal, 31*, 9–41.

Gladstein, D.L. (1984). Groups in context: A model of task group effectiveness. *Administrative Science Quarterly, 29*, 499–517.

Glisson, C.A., & Martin, P.Y. (1980). Productivity and efficiency in human service organizations as related to structure, size, and age. *Academy of Management Journal, 23*, 21–37.

Goodman, P.S., Atkin, R.S., & Schoorman, F.D. (1983). On the demise of organizational effectiveness studies. In K.S. Cameron & D.A. Whetten (Eds.), *Organizational effectiveness: A comparison of multiple models* (pp. 163–183). New York: Academic Press.

Hackman, J.R. (1976). Group influences on individuals in organizations. In M.D. Dunnette (Ed.), *Handbook of industrial and organizational psychology*. Chicago: Rand-McNally.

Hackman, J.R. (1986). The design of work teams. In J. Lorsch (Ed.), *Handbook of organizational behavior*. Englewood Cliffs, NJ: Prentice Hall.

Hoffman, L.R. (1965). Group problem solving. In L. Berkowitz (Ed.), *Advances in experimental social psychology* (vol. 2). Orlando, FL: Academic Press.

Hoy, F., & Hellriegel, D. (1982). The Kilmann and Herden model of organizational effectiveness: Criteria for small business managers. *Academy of Management Journal, 35*, 308–322.

Huselid, M.A. (1995). The impact of human resource management practices on turnover, productivity, and corporate financial performance. *Academy of Management Journal, 38*, 635–672.

Jackson, J. (1965). A conceptual and measurement model for norms and roles. In I.D. Steiner & M. Fishbein (Eds.), *Current studies in social psychology*. New York: Holt.

James, L.R., & Jones, A.P. (1976). Organizational structure: A review of structural dimensions and their conceptual relationships with individual attitudes and behavior. *Organizational Behavior and Human Performance, 16*, 74–113.

Johns, G. (1997). Contemporary research on absence from work: Correlates, causes and consequences. In C.L. Cooper and I.T. Robertson (Eds.), *International Review of Industrial and Organizational Psychology*, vol. 12 (pp. 115–173). Chichester: John Wiley & Sons Ltd.

Katz, R. (1982). The effects of group longevity on project communication and performance. *Administrative Science Quarterly, 27*, 81–104.

Katz, D., & Kahn, R.L. (1978). *The social psychology of organizations*. New York: Wiley.

Kirkpatrick, D.L. (1994). *Evaluating training programs*. San Francisco, CA: Berrett-Koehler Publishers.

Koslowsky, M., Sagie, A., Krausz, M., & Singer, A.D. (1997). Correlates of employee lateness: Some theoretical considerations. *Journal of Applied Psychology, 82*, 79–88.

Levinson, H. (1994). The practitioner as diagnostic instrument. In Ann Howard and Associates (Eds.), *Diagnosis for organizational change* (pp. 27–52). New York: The Guilford Press.

Maier, N.R.F., & Solem, A.R. (1962). Improving solution by turning choice situations into problems. *Personnel Psychology, 15*, 151–157.

Pennings, J.M., & Goodman, P.S. (1977). Toward a workable framework. In P.S. Goodman & J.M. Pennings (Eds.), *New perspectives on organizational effectiveness*. San Francisco: Jossey-Bass.

Pettigrew, A.M. (1979). On studying organizational cultures. *Administrative Science Quarterly*, *24*, 570–581.

Phillips, J.J. (1996). *Accountability in human resource management*. Houston, TX: Gulf Publishing Company.

Price, J.L., & Mueller, C.W. (1986). *The handbook of organizational measurement*. Marshfield, MA: Pitman Publishing.

Pritchard, R.D., Jones, S.D., Roth, P.L., Stuebing, K.K., & Ekeberg, S.E. (1988). Effects of group feedback, goal setting and incentives on organizational productivity. *Journal of Applied Psychology*, *73*, 337–358.

Ranson, S., Hinings, R., & Greenwood, R. (1980). The structuring of organizational structures. *Administrative Science Quarterly*, *25*, 1–17.

Reimann, B.C. (1982). Organizational competence as a predictor of long run survival and growth. *Academy of Management Journal*, *25*, 323–334.

Schmittlein, D.C., & Morrison, D.G. (1983). Modeling and estimation using job duration data. *Organizational Behavior and Human Performance*, *32*, 1–22.

Selznick, P. (1957). *Leadership in administration*. New York: Harper & Row.

Shaw, M.E. (1981). *Group dynamics: The psychology of small group behavior* (3rd ed.). New York: McGraw-Hill.

Shiflett, S.C. (1972). Group performance as a function of task difficulty and organizational interdependence. *Organizational Behavior and Human Performance*, *7*, 442–456.

Snow, C.C., & Hribiniak, L.G. (1980). Strategy, distinctive competence and organizational performance. *Administrative Science Quarterly*, *25*, 317–336.

Steers, R.M. (1975). Problems in the measurement of organizational effectiveness. *Administrative Science Quarterly*, *20*, 546–558.

Steiner, I.D. (1972). *Group process and productivity*. New York: Academic Press.

Tracey, J.B., Tannenbaum, S.I., & Kavanagh, M.J. (1995). Applying trained skills on the job: The importance of the work environment. *Journal of Applied Psychology*, *80*, 239–252.

Tziner, A., & Eden, D. (1985). Effects of crew composition on crew performance: Does the whole equal the sum of its parts? *Journal of Applied Psychology*, *70*, 85–93.

Vroom, V.H., & Yetton, P.W. (1973). *Leadership and decision making*. Pittsburgh, PA: University of Pittsburgh Press.

Webb, R.J. (1974). Organizational effectiveness and the voluntary organization. *Academy of Management Journal*, *17*, 663–677.

White, S.E., Dittrich, J.E., & Lang, J.R. (1980). The effects of group decision-making process and problem-situation complexity on implementation attempts. *Administrative Science Quarterly*, *25*, 428–440.

Wicker, A.W., & Kauma, C.E. (1974). Effects of a merger of a small and a large organization on members' behaviors and experiences. *Journal of Applied Psychology*, *59*, 24–30.

Wicker, A.W., Kirmeyer, S., Hanson, L., & Alexander, D. (1976). Effects of manning levels on subjective experiences, performance and verbal interaction in groups. *Organizational Behavior and Human Performance*, *17*, 251–274.

Youndt, M.A., Snell, S.A., Dean, J.W., Jr., & Lepak, D.P. (1996). Human resource management, manufacturing strategy, and firm performance. *Academy of Management Journal*, *39*, 836–866.

Yuchtman, E., & Seashore, S.E. (1967). A system resource approach to organizational effectiveness. *American Sociological Review*, *32*, 891–903.

Yukl, G.A. (1989). *Leadership in organizations* (2nd ed.). Englewood Cliffs, NJ: Prentice Hall.

11

Statistical
Evaluation

◆◆◆
INTRODUCTION

Previous chapters of this text have described different approaches to research design, as well as the measurement of individual, group, and organizational variables. Once a research project has been completed, the emphasis turns to evaluation. This involves the ways in which the research data will be used and analyzed to interpret the results of the research. Evaluation is at the centre of human resources research. Ultimately, we want to find out how effective an intervention or program is for achieving some outcome(s). There are, of course, many ways of doing this.

This chapter describes methods of evaluation that involve statistical analysis of research data. These data analysis techniques include basic descriptive indices, as well as statistics that allow us to make statements about the relation or correlation between variables and the effects of human resource interventions.

After reading this chapter, you should be able to:

■ Describe and understand individual differences and the normal distribution.

■ Calculate measures of central tendency, variability, and standard scores.

■ Understand, analyze, and interpret descriptive data.

■ Conduct *t*-tests to test for differences between groups of individuals and tests of significance.

■ Understand and explain the use of analysis of variance for testing differences between groups of individuals.

■ Understand and explain measures of association, and calculate correlation coefficients and tests of significance.

■ Describe the different types of correlation coefficients and when they are used.

■ Understand and explain the purposes of multiple regression analyses.

■ Know how to conduct a meta-analysis review as a function of the average correlations and mean differences, and the role and meaning of moderator analyses.

◆◆◆
THE NORMAL DISTRIBUTION

To say that people are different is something that most people would agree with. *Why* people differ has been the major interest of various social science researchers. As an example, consider your reaction to a human resource management class or training experience you have had in the past. Some of your classmates would undoubtedly think that the experience was one of the best they had ever had. Others would be just as adamant that much of their time and effort had been wasted. Why?

One explanation might be the family background of the individuals in the class—did their parents work as supervisors or managers or union employees? Another explanation might be their work experience—have they had work experiences that might help them relate to the problems discussed in this course? A large number of other factors may also influence trainees' or students' reactions to a course: the age and personality of the instructor, the format in which the course is offered, the time of day it is offered, the grading policy, to name but a few.

The aim of behavioural research is to explain or account for these individual differences. In research projects, it is important that the measures we use be sensitive to individual differences. If there are no differences in reactions to a training program, or no differences in the level of pay satisfaction, then we have nothing to explain.

Sometimes a lack of differences among individuals is the result of how we measure some behaviour, opinion, or skill. For example, a human resource manager might evaluate a training program only on the basis of whether the participants would want to attend future sessions. Perhaps the participants say they would want to attend because the training content is useful to them or because they enjoy being away from their usual work routine. However, a serious and much more useful training evaluation might allow for questions that yield more than simple yes/no responses about the desirability of future training. While all or most of the trainees might want to go again, some might not be very enthusiastic about the program as a whole. Using a scale that allowed responses from 1 ("the worst program I ever attended") to 5 ("the best program I ever attended") might reveal differences in opinions about the program. These differences might relate to the background of the trainees or to their opinions about various aspects of the training (such as the trainer's presentations, audiovisuals, physical surroundings, perceived relevance of training to work, etc.).

While this example refers to the use of survey or questionnaire instruments, the importance of variability in persons also applies to experimental research. In either experimental research or in research in which we are simply interested in measuring and relating two or more variables, it is assumed that individual differences exist and that it is the task of the researcher to adequately measure and capture the full extent of those differences. Therefore, this chapter will describe the ways in which researchers summarize the data they collect and how they analyze that data to make appropriate interpretations or reach justifiable conclusions about human resources.

While behavioural researchers assume the existence of individual differences in ability and attitudes, they also assume that individual differences are **normally** distributed. This assumption implies that a relatively small number of individuals represent the extreme scores on tests or attitude measures, and that most of the individuals' scores lie in the middle of the distribution. The exact form of this normal distribution is illustrated in Figure 11.1.

FIGURE 11.1 **The Normal Distribution**

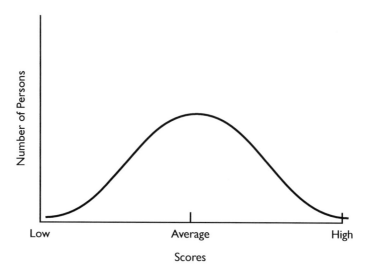

The basis for the assumption of normality lies in the distribution of physical characteristics, such as height and weight, that can be measured directly and that are distributed normally in the adult population. We assume, by analogy to measures of physical characteristics, that various psychological variables are also normally distributed. We do not measure characteristics such as intelligence, personality, or attitude directly as we do height and weight. We assume a certain degree of intelligence when a person answers the verbal, perceptual, and quantitative items that appear in intelligence tests. To produce the desired assumed normal distribution of scores on psychological measures, we either choose test items whose summed responses produce a normal distribution, or we transform individuals' scores in a way that produces a normal distribution. As discussed below, this normality assumption is useful when we begin to summarize and draw conclusions from the data. Normally distributed data have interval properties that allow the computation of various useful descriptive and inferential statistics outlined below.

When we collect data or try to interpret the data someone else has collected, we compute or request access to summary measures that allow us to make interpretive statements about given cases. For example, if we know that a retail store clerk makes sales totaling $4000 in a given week, it helps to know the average clerk's sales for the same week. After you learn the average, usually the next question concerns the range of the weekly sales figures; or, if you have been exposed to statistical data, you may realize the importance of the standard deviation. The sales figure of $4000 would be positive and impressive if the store average were $3500 and the range of sales figures were $2800–$4000. You would be much less impressed if the average was $4500 and the range of sales figures was $3800–$5200.

The average is one type of **central tendency** measure; the range is a measure of **variability**. Very often we are also interested in the degree to which the means or averages of one group of individuals differ from those of another group.

Therefore, the following sections of this chapter will describe measures of central tendency and variability, discuss how to determine whether groups of individuals are different on some variable, and explain how to determine whether two or more variables are related to one another.

◆ ◆ ◆
MEASURES OF CENTRAL TENDENCY

The arithmetic **mean** or average of a set of data as described above is a measure of central tendency that is strictly appropriate only when the data collected have interval or ratio properties.

If we have only ordinal data, we correctly report the **median**, which is the middle score in a rank-ordered distribution of scores, as the measure of central tendency. The median of income statistics is commonly reported, because a few millionaires in a group of people, most of whom have salaries around $30 000, would significantly distort the average. Even in large organizations, the computation of a mean annual salary might be a deceptive index of the earning power of organizational members, since the chief executive officers' salaries sometimes approach or exceed a million dollars, while the great bulk of employees make much less.

The **mode** is the appropriate index of central tendency when one has only nominal data. If one is trying to decide at what height to construct tables and chairs at a preschool building, and the mean height of the people is used to construct the chairs and tables, the teachers will find them too small and the children will find them too large. In this case, two sets of chairs and tables will be necessary.

Table 11.1 presents a distribution of scores obtained on a measure of pay satisfaction, along with the computation of the mean, median, and mode.

◆ ◆ ◆
MEASURES OF VARIABILITY

After we know our score on a test and the class average, we are usually interested in the highest and/or lowest scores—or the variability of the score distribution. We

TABLE 11.1 MEASURES OF CENTRAL TENDENCY AND VARIABILITY

Person	Level of Pay Satisfaction	Summary Statistics*
A	4	Mean = Total of Individual Scores / Number of
B	5	Persons = 220/20 = 11.0
C	7	Median = Middle score in the ranked distribution
D	7	= 10.5‡
E	8	
F	8	Mode = Most frequently occurring score = 10
G	9	
H	10	Range = 4 – 17
I	10	
J	10	Standard deviation = $\sqrt{\Sigma(X_i - M)^2 / N}$
K	11	
L	12	$= \sqrt{282/20}$
M	13	$= 3.75$
N	13	
O	14	where X_i are the individual scores, M is the mean,
P	14	N is the number of scores, and Σ indicates the sum
Q	15	of the squared $X_i - M$ values.
R	16	
S	17	
T	17	
Total	220	

*The mean, median, and mode of a distribution of scores are equal only when the distribution of scores is normal, as in Figure 11.1

‡ When there is an even number of scores, then the median is usually represented as the average of the two middle scores, in this case 10 and 11.

know intuitively that a score two points above the mean is more impressive when the range of scores is 16 to 20 than when the range of scores is 0 to 20. When we have interval data, however, we usually compute an arithmetically more complex measure of variability called the **standard deviation**.

The standard deviation computed in Table 11.1 is particularly useful because of its relationship to the normal curve depicted in Figure 11.1. The percentage of cases falling in any portion of the normal curve are known and are presented in tabular form in statistics books. For example, we know that a person whose score lies one standard deviation below the mean score lies below approximately 84 percent of the other individuals and above 16 percent. Most persons (about 96 percent) will have scores within plus or minus approximately two standard deviations of the mean score. In Table 11.1, this would mean that most scores would lie between 3.5 and 18.5 (11 ± 2 [3.75]). The probability of scores falling outside this range is relatively low.

When behavioural scientists are interested in determining whether they have produced a real change, or whether two variables are really related, or the conclusions from a set of observations can be explained by chance alone, they compute a form of the standard deviation called the *standard error* to form confidence intervals beyond which it is unlikely to observe some value computed in a sample. Confidence intervals are computed to tell us how likely it is that the value of some statistic computed in a sample falls within a certain range. Usually, this range includes scores approximately two standard errors above and below the sample statistic in which we are interested.

◆ ◆ ◆
STANDARD SCORES

Standard deviations are also useful in the computation of standard scores with which we can compare scores from different tests or performance ratings given by two different raters. An example of ratings coming from two different raters whose ratings differ both in terms of mean and standard deviation is presented in Table 11.2.

Assuming there are no real differences between the two units of employees, and if we want to compare Employee A with Employee I (or any other pair of employees across supervisory units), we must take into account the fact that Supervisor 1 gives ratings close to the centre of the seven-point scale and that these ratings vary little. Supervisor 2 tends to give somewhat lower ratings but, in addition, uses the entire 1–7 point scale. By expressing the scores in terms of **standard scores** (distance from the mean score divided by the standard deviation), we remove the differences between raters in the mean and standard deviation of their ratings, and can make direct comparisons of individuals in different supervisory units. Note that standard score distributions have a mean of zero and standard deviation of 1.00.

◆ ◆ ◆
ANALYSIS OF DESCRIPTIVE DATA

In Chapter 3 on survey research methods, it was noted that analyzing and interpreting the results of survey data usually begins with an examination of descriptive statistics such as means, standard deviations, and frequencies. This can also involve comparisons of basic descriptive data which are usually conducted and are necessary to make the results meaningful and useful for initiating appropriate policy

TABLE 11.2 RATINGS FROM TWO SUPERVISORS THAT ARE NOT DIRECTLY COMPARABLE

	Supervisor 1			Supervisor 2	
Employee	Raw Score	Standard Score	Employee	Raw Score	Standard Score
A	3	−1.14	I	2	−.49
B	4	.38	J	7	1.67
C	4	.38	K	1	−.92
D	3	−1.14	L	6	1.27
E	5	1.89	M	5	.81
F	4	.38	N	1	−.92
G	4	.38	O	2	−.49
H	3	−1.14	P	1	−.92
Mean =	3.75		Mean =	3.13	
SD =	.66		SD =	2.32	

$$\text{Standard score} = \frac{(\text{Raw Score} - \text{Mean})}{\text{Standard Deviation}}$$

changes. As well, it was noted that at least four types of comparative data are possible: (1) comparisons of different departments, locations, occupational groups, etc., within an organization; (2) comparisons with similar groups in other organizations; (3) comparisons of the responses of similar groups across time; and (4) comparisons of the same group to different aspects of some content area, such as a training program or work situation.

Table 11.3, part A, presents survey responses of people in different divisions of an organization. One question that presents itself is whether the mean differences and percentile differences are meaningful. Statistical tests of significance can address the question of whether differences this large could be attributable to chance, but equally important (especially when the sample sizes are very large) is the practical significance of the difference. This is a more difficult determination to make and almost always involves a value judgment. Here, it may be a judgment as to whether the relatively low job satisfaction in manufacturing and maintenance is a significant problem for the organization. Are these groups characterized by abnormally high rates of turnover, product sabotage, absenteeism, or grievances? If so, then the organization would want to further explore the reasons for low job satisfaction. Or perhaps there is no evidence that this low job satisfaction is being translated into unproductive behaviour, but the organization is interested in positive work reactions among its employees.

TABLE 11.3 VARIOUS POSSIBLE COMPARISONS OF DESCRIPTIVE DATA

A) Comparisons Across Departments within an Organization

Employee Job Satisfaction

Department	N	X	SD	Percentile (Corporate Wide)
Sales	78	3.8	5.3	
2) Research & Development	22	21.7	6.	
3) Manufacturing	238	0.2	4.3	
4) Maintenance	39		5.7	
5) Finance	8	8.7	0.	

B) Comparisons of Similar Units Across Different Organizations

Research & Development

	N	X	SD	
Organization A	22	21.7	6.	
Organization B	3	23.2	7	
Organization C	48	8.6	5.7	
Organization D	38	9.8	6.3	

Manufacturing

	N	X	SD	
Organization A	238	0.2	4.3	
Organization B	417	3	3.7	
Organization C	321	9.8	3.7	
Organization D	62	0.5	4.	

C) Comparisons Across Time: Job Satisfaction

Research & Development (Percentiles Based on Responses of R & D Only n Various Organizations)

	N	X	SD	
997	8	9.8	5.7	
998	21	20.7	6.3	
999	22	21.7	6.	

Manufacturing (Percentiles Based on Manufacturing Personnel Only n Various Organizations)

	N	X	SD	
997	321	4.	5.	
998	281	3.8	6.0	
999	238	0.2	4.3	

D) Comparison of Responses of Manufacturing Group to Specific Job Satisfaction Dimensions

Satisfaction with	N	X	SD	Percentiles Based on Manufacturing Personnel n Various Organizations
Work	321	2.2	5.	
Coworkers	328	3	5.3	
Pay	325	8.7	3.2	
Supervision	323	76	4.0	
Promotions	322	0.5	4.7	

These questions of practicality can be better answered when other types of comparative data are also available. For example, Table 11.3, part B, contains comparative data for the research and development and manufacturing units in similar organizations. As can be seen, the figures from the research and development unit in organization A don't look very good in these comparisons, and figures from the manufacturing area don't appear to be very negative. Both groups appear relatively average compared with similar groups in organizations B, C, and D.

Further comparisons of the research and development and manufacturing groups' responses indicate that the research and development group has remained relatively stable over the period during which surveys were conducted, while the manufacturing group has experienced a relatively sizable decline in job satisfaction. In this case, the job satisfaction instrument contained items related to various aspects of work as depicted in the Job Description Inventory (Smith, Kendall, & Hulin, 1969). This allowed for the comparisons in Table 11.3, part D, which indicate that the manufacturing respondents' dissatisfaction relates primarily to supervision and pay. The survey, then, has identified a potential problem area, and the organization must now proceed to develop more concrete notions of the nature of the problem and to develop interventions that provide solutions to these problems.

Several aspects of these hypothetical data analyses are important. First, data have meaning only by virtue of relevant comparisons. To allow these comparisons to take place, one must plan for them by asking appropriate questions of the respondents (i.e., their department, work group, tenure, gender, ethnic status, job classification, etc.). Second, data can be much more useful if there is a large comparative database collected over a period of time. Changes can be noted and, in some instances, related to specific events. For example, it appears as though the manufacturing work force in organization A is declining (see the sample sizes in Table 11.3, part D). This decline in the work force may be the reason (direct or indirect) for the lower levels of satisfaction with supervision and pay. Finally, Table 11.3 should serve as an illustration that pictorial data can be very useful in communicating research results.

Once the researcher has analyzed the descriptive data, he or she will want to learn more about the effects and relations among the variables. In particular, the researcher will want to test the study hypotheses. This almost always involves testing the mean differences between groups and the correlations between variables.

◆ ◆ ◆

TESTING MEAN DIFFERENCES BETWEEN GROUPS OF INDIVIDUALS

When evaluating the effects of human resource interventions, the researcher is usually interested in comparing the attitudes or performance of different groups of workers. In an experimental research design, this usually means making comparisons between experimental and control groups. For example, a researcher might be interested in performance differences between trained and untrained groups, men and women, individuals who were recruited using different methods, workers being paid on a piece-rate basis versus those on a salary, and so on. When we are interested in comparing the mean differences between two groups, the statistical technique employed is the t-test. When more than two groups are being compared, it is necessary to use a technique called analysis of variance.

T-TESTS

In this section, an example is presented using the *t-test* to compare two groups' job evaluation ratings. In the example, the researcher used a point method to obtain evaluations of two jobs (forklift operator and secretary) by four different groups of men and women. One group of each gender evaluated both jobs. In the point method of job evaluation, jobs are graded as to their skill requirements (education, experience, initiative, and ingenuity), effort requirements (physical demand, mental or visual demand), responsibility requirements (equipment or process, material or product, safety of others, and work of others), and job conditions (normal working conditions, hazards), most frequently on a five-point scale. Each of these factors can be given different degrees of importance or weight, depending on the job. The weighted factor scores are added up to give each job an economic value rating. These values are then translated into dollar amounts, depending on the total pool of money available. The data set we are using in our example consists of the evaluations of two jobs by 32 people using this system.

The researcher wanted to know whether men and women evaluating jobs that are typically held by one gender or the other (forklift operators by males, secretaries by females) would produce evaluations of jobs that differ from one another. Specifically, the data presented in Table 11.4 were used to address three questions: (1) Do men and women's job evaluations differ? (2) Do the evaluations of forklift operator and secretary differ? and (3) Is there some combination of job and gender of evaluator that results in different evaluations? The latter possibility would reflect what was referred to in Chapter 1 as an *interaction*. For example, it may be that men evaluate jobs that are usually performed by men higher than do women and higher than they evaluate other jobs typically performed by women. The first two of these questions are addressed first using the t-test.

In Table 11.4, we see that the mean of the men's job evaluations was 41.82, while the women averaged 37.82, Given the evaluative and subjective nature of these judgments, we would not expect these two averages to be exactly the same. But are these two judgments different enough that if we asked another sample of 16

TABLE 11.4 JOB EVALUATIONS BY DIFFERENT GROUPS OF MEN AND WOMEN FOR TWO DIFFERENT JOBS

Forklift Operator Job		Secretary Job	
Men	Women	Men	Women
A. 39	I. 36	Q. 44	Y. 35
B. 41	J. 39	R. 43	Z. 40
C. 49	K. 41	S. 41	AA. 39
D. 39	L. 40	T. 38	BB. 44
E. 41	M. 35	U. 37	CC. 36
F. 44	N. 34	V. 45	DD. 40
G. 46	O. 38	W. 39	EE. 37
H. 47	P. 36	X. 36	FF. 35
Total 346	299	323	306
Mean ($\bar{X}$) 43.25	37.38	40.38	38.25

$\bar{X}_{women} = 37.82, \bar{X}_{men} = 41.82, \bar{X}_{FLO} = 40.32, \bar{X}_{SEC} = 39.32$

$SD_{women} = 2.67, SD_{men} = 3.66, SD_{FLO} = 4.21, SD_{SEC} = 3.22$

men and 16 women to perform similar judgments we would expect men's evaluations to be higher than those of women? In addressing this question, researchers typically express their confidence in experimental results in terms of a probability statement. That is, after evaluating the difference between men and women, we want to say that we would (or would not) expect to observe a difference this large between 16 men and 16 women more than 5 (or 1 or 10, etc.) percent of the time given that there is *no real* difference between men's and women's judgments. In the jargon of scientific research, we seek to test the **null hypothesis** that there are no male–female differences in job evaluations. We reject the null hypothesis if the observed mean difference is so large that it is improbable (less than 5 percent or 1 percent are the two usual levels of probability used) that the null hypothesis is correct.

To test the null hypothesis implicit in the first research question, we compute a *t*-value as follows:

$$t = (\bar{x}_{women} - \bar{x}_{men})/\sqrt{(SD_{women}{}^2/N_{women} - 1) + (SD_{men}{}^2/N_{men} - 1)} \qquad (11.1)$$

where $\bar{x}$, SD, and N refer to the mean, standard deviation, and sample size of the two groups.

Numerically, $t = (37.82 - 41.82) / \sqrt{(2.67^2/15) + (3.66^2/15)}$
$t = -4/1.17$
$t = -3.42, df = 30, p < .05$

In this computation, the difference between the mean evaluations of men and women is divided by a value that is the standard error of the mean mentioned above. This is the standard deviation of the differences between means that we would expect if, in fact, there were no real differences between men and women. The observed mean difference must be significantly greater than the standard error for us to conclude that there is a real difference.

The t-value is referred to a statistical table that gives the probabilities of achieving a given value of t when no difference is present. In this case, we refer to the tabled value for 30 (number of persons minus the number of groups) degrees of freedom (df), which indicated that any value greater than 2.04 had a probability value less than .05. This .05 is referred to as the **significance level**. Since this t-value was highly improbable, our conclusion is that men do, indeed, rate jobs higher than women.

Computation of the t-value necessary to test the significance of the null hypothesis that there are no differences in the evaluation of forklift operator and secretary jobs yields the following:

$t = (40.32 - 39.32)/ \sqrt{(4.21^2/15) + (3.22^2/15)}$
$t = 1.00/1.37$
$t = .73, df = 30, p > .05$

In this instance, the probability of achieving a t-value of .73 is quite high, higher than .05; hence, we do not conclude that evaluations of these two jobs are significantly different since the results support the null hypothesis.

However, as you have probably guessed, these two tests do not give us the answer to our third question. In fact, the lack of consideration of the type of job and gender of the evaluator in the same analysis may hide the real explanation for some of the variability in these job evaluations. To assess the effect of these two variables in combination, researchers often use a technique called analysis of variance.

ANALYSIS OF VARIANCE

Research designs are sometimes more complex than the one in our example, and as a result the comparisons that a researcher wants to make involve more than detecting differences that might exist between two groups. In some research designs, there are more than two independent variables and more than two levels of each independent variable. For example, in research on realistic job previews (RJPs), the author compared the effects of a written RJP, a verbal RJP, and a general job preview (Saks & Cronshaw, 1990). This required the use of a statistical technique called **analysis of variance** to determine if differences existed between the three conditions.

Analysis of variance is also required when there are two or more independent variables. For example, in the study on gender and job evaluations, there are two levels of each of the two independent variables: gender (male and female) and job type (forklift operator and secretary). To answer the third question above about the possible interaction between gender and job type, analysis of variance is used because it can analyze data from more than one independent variable and test the effects of each independent variable (i.e., male versus female, forklift job versus secretary job), as well as the interaction effects between the independent variables.

Therefore, in our example, an analysis of variance would be used to provide a test of the significance of the effect of job, the effect of gender of the evaluator, and a test for the interaction effect. An **interaction effect** occurs when the effect of one independent variable (e.g., gender of evaluator) on the dependent variable (job evaluation) varies as a function of the effect of the other independent variable (job type).

Analysis of variance is much more complicated then the *t*-test, and is best conducted using a statistical software package such as SPSS. For detailed descriptions of analysis of variance and the calculations involved, the interested reader should consult a book on statistics.

◆ ◆ ◆
MEASURES OF ASSOCIATION

The statistical tests discussed above are used to compare the mean differences on dependent variables between different groups. As such, they are most often used to evaluate the results of experimental research. However, for survey research the objective of the researcher is to observe how variables relate to one another. One frequently wants to know how two variables *vary* together as we observe them in the workplace. Or, we may want to know what we can expect to observe concerning one variable when we know the value of a second.

For example, if we know the scores of a set of employees on a number of tests, can we predict their job performance? Or, knowing the job performance of employees, can we predict their job satisfaction? Assessment of the degree to which variables *co-vary* involves the computation of a correlation coefficient. Similar measures of association are computed from analyses of variance, though correlations are probably the most frequently used measure of association. Observation of a sizable and statistically significant correlation will allow us to predict one variable from another. In this section, the calculation of some measures of association (correlation) are described, as well as how this knowledge might be useful in making predictions.

PEARSON PRODUCT–MOMENT CORRELATION

Correlation coefficients indicate the extent to which two variables co-vary, or the extent to which change in one variable is associated with change in another variable. Correlations can range from –1.00 to 1.00. Both negative and positive correlations are equally useful in prediction, but they describe a different type of relationship. A zero coefficient describes an absence of relationship between two variables or a relationship between two variables that is nonlinear. Nonlinear relationships, for example, may indicate that, as values of one variable increase, the values of a second variable first increase, then decrease, or the reverse.

The **Pearson product–moment correlation**, described below, is a summary of the relationship between linearly related variables (increasing values on one variable are directly related to increases or decreases on a second variable). Most of the relationships we observe in human resource research are linear and of the magnitude of .00 to .60. Cohen (1988) classifies correlations of .10 as small, correlations of .30 as modest, and correlations of .50 as large.

The Pearson product–moment correlation is the most frequently encountered correlation coefficient, and is used with interval-level data. It is usually designated simply as r and its simplest computational form is as follows:

$$r_{xy} = \frac{\Sigma(Z_x Z_y)}{N} \qquad (11.2)$$

where Z_x equals the standard score of an individual on variable X; Z_y equals the standard score of an individual on variable Y; Σ indicates that we sum all the $Z_x Z_y$ products for the group of cases for which the correlation is being computed; N is the number of persons available for the computation of the correlation; and r_{xy} is the correlation between two variables designated as x and y.

A formula for the computation of r from raw scores and an example of its use is provided in Table 11.5 for a set of hypothetical data on job satisfaction and worker productivity. To determine the correlation between job satisfaction and productivity, we are looking for a number of things: if all the values of X and Y pairs tend to be similar—that is, high positive Xs are associated with high positive Ys and high negative Xs are associated with high negative Ys,—then the sum of products will be at its maximum, and the correlation will be high. When positive Xs are consistently paired with negative Ys, the correlation coefficient will be negative.

As shown in Table 11.5, the correlation between job satisfaction and productivity is .44. But how do we know if this is significant? As was the case for t-tests, we also want to determine if the correlation between two variables is significant. This requires the use of a statistical test. In collecting data on any project, we set out to discredit the notion that there is no relationship between two variables, or that the true correlation is .00. As in the case of our hypothesis above that there were no

311

TABLE 11.5 EXAMPLE OF THE COMPUTATION OF A CORRELATION COEFFICIENT USING RAW SCORES AND STANDARD SCORES

Job
Satisfaction Productivity

	(X)	(Y)	X^2	Y^2	XY	Z_x	Z_y	Z_xZ_y
Kevin	6	4	36	16	24	.1	−.3	−.03
Abigail	8	5	64	25	40	.8	.1	.08
Dan	10	7	100	49	70	1.5	.8	1.20
Mei	9	10	81	100	90	1.1	2.0	2.20
Marcy	7	3	49	9	21	.4	−.7	−.28
Bob	4	2	16	4	8	−.6	−1.1	.66
Kabir	3	6	9	36	18	−.9	.5	−.45
Sue	2	7	4	49	14	−1.3	.8	−1.04
Cheri	7	3	49	9	21	.4	−.7	−.28
Rick	1	1	1	1	1	−1.6	−1.5	2.40

$\Sigma X = 57$ $\Sigma Y = 48$ $\Sigma X^2 = 409$ $\Sigma Y^2 = 298$ $\Sigma XY = 307$ $\Sigma Z_xZ_y = 4.46$

Standard Score Formula:

$r_{xy} = \Sigma Z_xZ_y/N = 4.46/10 = .44$

Raw Score Formula:

$$r_{xy} = \frac{N\Sigma XY - (\Sigma X)(\Sigma Y)}{\sqrt{[N\Sigma X^2 - (\Sigma X)^2][N\Sigma Y^2 - (\Sigma Y)^2]}}$$

$$r_{xy} = \frac{(10 \times 307) - (57 \times 48)}{\sqrt{[(10 \times 409) - (57)^2][10(298) - 48^2]}}$$

$= .44$

mean differences in the evaluation of jobs, this is called a **null hypothesis**. In our example, a **test of statistical significance** tells us the confidence with which we can say, based on our ten observations in Table 11.5, that the satisfaction–performance correlation is greater than zero. If we find that the probability of observing a correlation of .44 in a group of 10 is less than 5 times out of 100 (.05), we say that the correlation of .44 is statistically significant.

The test of significance in this case again involves the computation of t and referral of this value to a table that tells us the value of t for a sample size of 10 at the .05 level of significance. In this case, t is given by this formula:

312

$$t = (r \sqrt{N-2}) / \sqrt{1-r^2} \qquad\qquad (11.3)$$
$$= (.44 \sqrt{10-2}) / \sqrt{1-.44^2}$$
$$= 1.39, \, df = 8, \, p > .05.$$

The critical value of t needed for statistical significance with eight $(N-2)$ degrees of freedom is 2.31; hence, we conclude that the correlation of .44 between satisfaction and productivity is nonsignificantly different from zero.

If the correlation is significantly different from zero, it can be negative or positive. If the researcher has reason to hypothesize that the correlation is positive (or negative), the probability value is doubled (i.e., .10) and the test is called a **one-tailed test**. The t-value needed for statistical significance at the .10 level is 1.86 in our example. Our obtained t is smaller than 1.86 and nonsignificant, even in the event that we had formulated a one-tailed hypothesis.

Another method of presenting correlation coefficients is by means of a scattergram. A **scattergram** is a plot of the relationship between two variables. In Figure 11.2, scatterplots represent a variety of possible relationships between two variables. A correlation coefficient is actually a summary measure of the degree of scatter one observes in a scatterplot. If all the dots in the scatterplot formed a straight line, the correlations computed by either of the formulas in Table 11.5 would equal 1.00 or –1.00. Maximum dispersion of the dots in a scatterplot occurs when $r = .00$.

OTHER CORRELATIONS

In Chapter 7, it was noted that there are four different levels of measurement, and that the level of measurement influences the type of statistics that can be used to test for statistical relationships. The Pearson product–moment correlation is used primarily for variables that have been measured using interval data. However, there are times when we want to know the correlation between variables that were measured using other levels of measurement, such as nominal or ordinal scales. For these types of measures, there are specific types of correlation coefficients.

For example, with two nominal variables, the measure of association is a correlation called the **phi-coefficient**. An example of the calculation of this coefficient is presented in Table 11.6. The data in Table 11.6 pertain to high school graduation and turnover, and can be used to answer the following question: Is high school graduation associated with job turnover? Simple examination of this table and the numbers in it would lead us to believe that high school graduation is related to turnover; that is, individuals with high school diplomas are more likely to leave their job within one year. The computation of the phi-coefficient gives us a summary measure of the relationship between these two measures—in this case, .60. The phi-coefficient is a special case of the Pearson product–moment correlation.

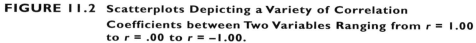

FIGURE 11.2 **Scatterplots Depicting a Variety of Correlation Coefficients between Two Variables Ranging from *r* = 1.00 to *r* = .00 to *r* = −1.00.**

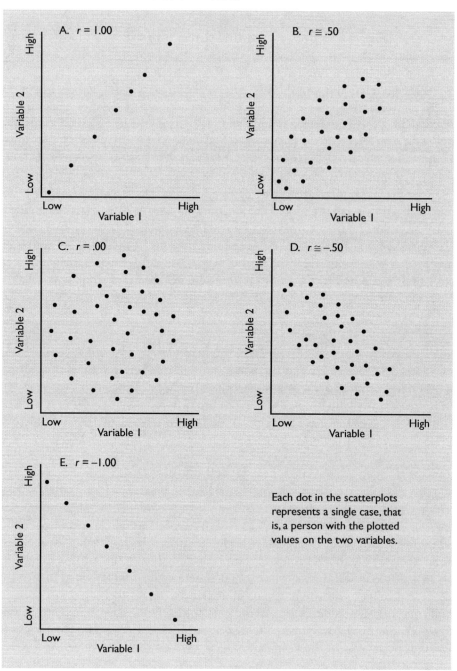

Each dot in the scatterplots represents a single case, that is, a person with the plotted values on the two variables.

TABLE 11.6 AN EXAMPLE OF THE COMPUTATION OF A PHI-COEFFICIENT

		Turnover within One Year		
		No	*Yes*	*Total*
High School	NO	40 (A)	10 (B)	50
Graduation	YES	10 (C)	40 (D)	50
		50	50	

$$\text{Phi-coefficient} \quad = \quad \frac{(A \times D) - (B \times C)}{\sqrt{(A + B)(C + D)(A + C)(B + D)}}$$

$$\text{Phi-coefficient} \quad = \quad \frac{(40 \times 40) - (10 \times 10)}{\sqrt{50 \times 50 \times 50 \times 50}}$$

$$= \quad \frac{1500}{2500}$$

$$= \quad .60$$

Occasionally, researchers are interested in the association between nominal variables that have more than two categories. For example, we might be interested in coding various nonverbal behaviours of interviewers to determine if such behaviours have any effect on applicant reaction to the interview situation. In this case, one important question is whether people who are asked to record the nonverbal behaviour of the interviewer can agree as to the exhibited behaviour. This agreement is a critical measure of the quality of our measure of nonverbal behaviour. Table 11.7 presents the agreement between two coders on the type of nonverbal behaviour exhibited in 1000 time intervals each 10 seconds in duration.

As one index of agreement, we could calculate the percentage of times the coders indicated that the same behaviour occurred; in this case, 78 percent ((450 + 138 + 192) /1000). However, the percent agreement is not a good index because it is dependent on the frequency of the use of the three categories. With large use of a single category (nods were recorded in just over half of the cases), percent agreement may be high by virtue of chance. An index called **Kappa** (Cohen, 1960, 1968) is used to calculate agreement between raters above and beyond the agreement that occurs simply as a function of chance. As you can see at the bottom of Table 11.7, we would expect the raters to agree almost 39 percent of the time, purely by chance. Corrected for the probability of chance agreement, Kappa indicates these two coders agreed 64 percent of the time, which is a reasonable level of Kappa.

Finally, sometimes the data one has obtained are ordinal; that is, the data consist of a ranking of pairs of variables. For example, recall from Chapter 7 that the

TABLE 11.7 INTERCODER AGREEMENT ON THE CATEGORIZATION OF NONVERBAL BEHAVIOUR

		Rater A				
		Nods	Frowns	Leans Back	Totals	Percent
	Nods	450	52	10	512	51.2
	Frowns	73	138	31	242	24.2
Rater B	Leans Back	18	36	192	246	24.6
	Totals	541	226	233	1000	
	Percent	54.1	22.6	23.3		

$\text{Kappa} = (P_0 - P_c) / (1 - P_c)$

where P_0 = proportion of times the two raters agreed on the behaviour exhibited by the interviewer, which equals 78% here.

P_c = proportion of times that agreement would occur by chance, which is equal to the sum of the product of corresponding row and column proportions (i.e., percent/100).

P_c = $(.512 \times .541) + (.242 \times .226) + (.246 \times .233) = .277 + .055 + .057$

= .389

Kappa = $(.78 - .389) / (1 - .389)$

= .64

Organization Culture Profile, which is used to measure work values of individuals and organizations, consists of a ranking of values from most to least important. The correlation between rankings for individuals and organizations is calculated and treated as a measure of values congruence. Correlations between variables that have been measured using ordinal scales are calculated using a **rank order correlation**.

The data used to calculate a rank order correlation consist of pairs of variables that are ranked from lowest to highest. For example, if you were to rank the 40 values of the Organizational Culture Profile (see Table 7.1) from least to most characteristic of you, and then ranked the values in a similar manner for your organization (i.e., least to most characteristic), you would have two sets of rankings for each of the 40 values. What you would want to determine, in effect, is the similarity of the rankings or the correlation between them—that is, how similar is your ranking of the values that are most characteristic of you relative to those that are most characteristic of your organization? Obviously, the more similar the rankings of the values, the more highly correlated they will be.

An example of a rank correlation is the *Spearman rank correlation*, which is calculated as follows:

$$r_s = 1 - \left[\frac{6(\Sigma_i D_i^2)}{N\,(N^2 - 1)} \right] \qquad (11.4)$$

where D is the difference between the paired ranks (e.g., the difference in ranking of your values and the organization values for each value), N is the number of pairs in the sample (e.g., 40 in the case of the Organizational Culture Profile), and r_s is the Spearman rank correlation coefficient (Hays, 1981).

◆◆◆
REGRESSION ANALYSIS

Correlations are useful for describing the type of relationship that exists between two variables, but very often in human resources we want to predict an individual's scores on one variable based on their scores on one or more other variables. The procedure for developing prediction equations is called **regression analysis** and the result is a prediction or **regression equation**.

To illustrate, let's say we are interested in predicting the turnover of employees in an organization. In this instance, the organization wants to know how likely it is that their employees will quit. This information would be helpful in planning interventions to decrease turnover among competent and desirable employees, and in making plans to replace these individuals if they cannot be retained. We would then be interested in the correlation between turnover of employees and some important predictor variable, such as job satisfaction. Predictions of the likelihood of an employee's quitting could then be made on the basis of his or her job satisfaction.

In most situations involving human behaviour, it is likely that several different factors or measured variables will be useful in making predictions. For example, when trying to predict a job applicant's potential performance on a job, we often collect information about a variety of knowledge and skill requirements, using numerous selection techniques such as an ability test, a personality test, and job interview ratings. Therefore, the regression equation would be used to predict job performance using job applicants' scores on each of these tests.

When we attempt to write regression equations involving two or more variables, the equations become increasingly complex, but the principles underlying prediction with three or more predictors are identical to the two-predictor case. How well two or more predictors combined improve the predictability of some behaviour of interest depends on their relationship to one another, as well as their relationship to the variable being predicted. If two predictors do not correlate with each other, but both are correlated to some outcome or criterion variable, we could depict their relationship as in the set of circles in Figure 11.3(a). In this figure, the central circle represents the variable we are predicting (the criterion); the degree of overlap of the criterion with the two predictor circles is representative of their relationship with the criterion or validity. The combined relationship between two or more predictors and a criterion is called the **multiple correlation (R)**. The multiple correlation coefficient, when the predictors are uncorrelated as in Figure 11.3(a), is expressed as follows:

$$R = \sqrt{r_{y1}^2 + r_{y2}^2} \qquad (11.5)$$

where r_{y1}^2 and r_{y2}^2 are the correlations between variable 1 and 2 with the criterion.

Let's compute R for the case in Figure 11.3(a) in which the two predictors are uncorrelated, assuming the predictor validities are .60 for variable 1, and .40 for variable 2:

$$
\begin{aligned}
R &= \sqrt{.6^2 + .4^2} \\
&= \sqrt{.36 + .16} \\
&= .72
\end{aligned}
$$

As you can see, the multiple R is greater than the simple correlations for each of the variables. If variables 1 and 2 represented an ability test and a personality test, and the criterion was job performance, then this result would indicate that both tests combined would be more effective for predicting job performance than either test used alone.

In most cases, however, two valid predictors also are correlated with each other. The diagram relating the three appears in Figure 11.3(b). Note that the interrcorrelation between the two predictor variables, or r_{12}, is not .00. While each predictor is valid and predicts some unique portion of the criterion variable, all three variables overlap to some degree, which means that the two predictors are predicting some of the same criterion variance. Under these conditions, the multiple correlation must be expanded to include consideration of the intercorrelation between the variables, as follows:

$$R_{y.12} = \sqrt{(r_{y1}^2 + r_{y2}^2 - 2r_{y1}r_{y2}r_{12}) / (1 - r_{12})^2} \qquad (11.6)$$

Assuming that the intercorrelation between the two predictor variables is .40, the multiple R would be calculated as follows:

$$
\begin{aligned}
R &= \sqrt{(.6^2 + .4^2 - 2 \times .4 \times .6 \times .4) / (1 - .4^2)} \\
&= \sqrt{(.36 + .16 - .192) / .84} \\
&= .62
\end{aligned}
$$

As is apparent from these calculations, it is best to have unrelated predictor variables. R decreased from .72 to .62 when the intercorrelation between the two

FIGURE 11.3 **Diagrams Illustrating the Case of Uncorrelated and Correlated Predictor Variables**

a)

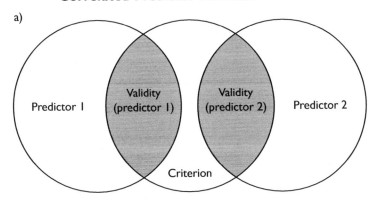

b)

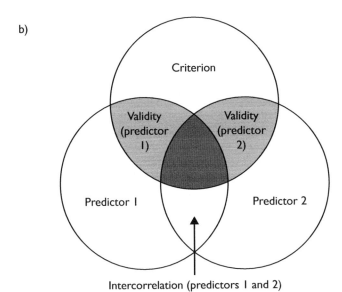

predictors was .40. A commonsense interpretation and an example of this phenomenon might read as follows: Given a test of cognitive ability, we would likely learn
more about a group of job applicants if we added a personality test than if we added
another test of cognitive ability. This may be true even though the second test of cognitive ability is just as valid as the first cognitive ability test and more valid than the
personality measure.

Finally, as was the case with correlation analysis involving just two variables, we can test the significance of the multiple correlation computed in multiple regression. For the overall multiple correlation, we compute the following F-value:

$$F = (R^2(n - k - 1))/((1 - R^2)k), \, df = k, \, n - k - 1 \qquad (11.7)$$

where n equals the number of subjects and k equals the number of predictors. For the numerical example presented above, assuming $n = 100$,

$$F = (.62(100 - 2 - 1))/((1 - .62^2)2)$$
$$F = 48.89, \, df = 2, 97, \, p < .05$$

We would consult a table with a distribution of F values to determine if our F-value exceeded the established probability value ($p < .05$). In this case, it did, so we conclude there is a significant relationship between this combination of the two predictors and the criterion.

In sum, multiple regression analysis is a powerful statistical procedure for testing the relationships between multiple predictors and criterion measures. In addition, multiple regression analysis is also useful for testing some of the relations discussed in Chapter 1, such as interactions between predictor variables or moderating variables (in which the relationship between a predictor and criterion variable depends on the level of a third variable); mediating or intervening variables (when the relation between a predictor variable and a criterion variable can be explained in whole or in part by a third variable); as well as nonlinear relationships. For more information about multiple regression analyses, the interested reader should refer to a text on the topic, such as that by Pedhazur (1997).

◆ ◆ ◆
CALCULATING EFFECT SIZES IN META-ANALYSIS

In this chapter, statistical tests have been described that test the mean differences between groups and calculate correlations between variables. However, recall from Chapter 6 that a meta-analysis involves the cumulation of these statistics from many studies in a particular area. The result of a meta-analysis is an effect size that represents the strength of a relationship between variables or the effect of a human resource intervention on some dependent variable(s). Thus, effect sizes can be calculated as an average of correlations or as a function of the mean differences across studies. The final section of this chapter describes the calculation of these effect sizes.

EFFECT SIZES EXPRESSED AS A FUNCTION OF THE AVERAGE OF CORRELATIONS

The actual estimates of effect size in meta-analytic reviews are easily obtained. When the effect size is expressed as a function of the average correlation, the average correlation across studies is usually weighted by the sample size in the study that produced the correlation as follows:

$$\bar{r} = \Sigma[N_i r_i]/\Sigma N_i \qquad (11.8)$$

where r_i is the correlation recorded from study i, Σ represents a summation over the total number of r_i, and N_i is the sample size in study i. The variance of the observed relationships across studies is given as follows:

$$\sigma_r^2 = \Sigma[N_i\,(r_i - \bar{r})^2]/\Sigma N_i \qquad (11.9)$$

Notice in the first formula, r_i is weighted by the sample size. This will prove to be a better estimate of the population correlation, except in those instances in which a single or small number of large sample size studies come from populations in which the effect size is different than in small sample size studies. We can check for this problem by doing separate analyses for the two sets of studies, or by correlating sample size with effect size. In the event of differences or an effect size–sample size correlation, however, there are no guidelines as to what procedure to follow. Perhaps the best one can do is to report the problem so that other researchers are aware that the results of studies differ in this way.

An example of a set of ten studies is presented in Table 11.8, with the calculations for $\bar{r}$ and σ_r^2. For these hypothetical data, half the studies were conducted when the weather was fair, the other half when it was stormy. In this case, the researcher had an a priori hypothesis about the effect of weather conditions on the size of the satisfaction–absenteeism relationship. The weighted average correlation is .38, and its variance across studies is .0076. However, Hunter, Schmidt, and Jackson (1982) point out that, in most cases, some of that variability is due to actual differences in population correlations and some is due to sampling error. To estimate the actual variance in population correlations, the value of σ_r^2 must be corrected for sampling error. The variance of the sampling error is given as follows:

$$\sigma_e^2 = [(1 - \bar{r}^2)^2 K]/\Sigma N_i \qquad (11.10)$$

where K is the number of studies. This formula uses $\bar{r}$ as an estimate of the population correlation. In the hypothetical data set, the estimate of the variance of sampling error is .0033, leaving .0043 as the estimate of actual variability in the satisfaction–absenteeism relationship. The value of .0043 is obtained by subtracting the variance of sampling error (.0033) from the total observed variance in the validity coefficient (.0076).

TABLE 11.8 AN APPLICATION OF META-ANALYTIC FORMULAS TO THE SATISFACTION–ABSENTEEISM* RELATIONSHIP

Study	Year	Weather	N	r	Nr	$r_i-\bar{r}$	$N_i(r_i-\bar{r})^2$
1	1952	Stormy	57	.38	21.66	.00	.00
2	1971	Fair	72	.19	13.68	−.19	2.60
3	1968	Fair	98	.23	22.54	−.15	2.21
4	1973	Stormy	212	.41	86.92	.03	.19
5	1958	Fair	70	.23	16.10	−.15	1.58
6	1984	Stormy	580	.39	226.20	.01	.06
7	1979	Stormy	320	.50	160.00	.12	4.61
8	1956	Fair	79	.26	20.54	−.12	1.14
9	1981	Fair	412	.31	129.58	−.07	2.02
10	1983	Stormy	291	.47	136.77	.09	2.36
			2191		833.99		16.77

$$\bar{r} = (833.99) / 2191 = .38$$
$$\sigma_r^2 = 16.77 / 2191 = .0076$$
$$\sigma_e^2 = 7.3 / 2191 = .0033$$

*Absenteeism is coded so that it really represents those who were at work. A positive correlation means that those who came to work tended to be more satisfied with the work situation.

Schmidt, Hunter, and their colleagues list a variety of other artifacts that may produce variability in estimated coefficients, such as unreliability in the measured variables, differences in the variability of one or more measured variables across studies, differences in the factors measured across studies, and reporting errors. Schmidt, Hunter, and colleagues (Schmidt & Hunter, 1981; Schmidt, Hunter, Pearlman, & Hirsh, 1985) have argued that the largest portion of variability in effect sizes in selection research is due to sampling error. However, the portion of variability due to sampling error also is clearly dependent on the sample size of the studies reviewed (McDaniel, Hirsh, Schmidt, Raju, & Hunter, 1986). With small sample sizes, more of the variability will be accounted for by sampling error; as sample size increases, a smaller proportion of the variability will be accounted for by sampling error. Given that actual data on these artifacts are frequently unavailable and that their effect is likely minimal for most of the sample sizes encountered, it may be best to settle for corrections due to sampling error only. However, correction formulas do exist, and for those research areas in which they are applicable and reasonable estimates exist, it would certainly be prudent to correct the σ_r^2 for these artifacts as well.

The remaining variance (.0043) in the estimates of the satisfaction–absenteeism relationship depicted in Table 11.8 can be used to compute a credibility interval regarding our expectation of satisfaction–absenteeism relationships in other situations. Taking the square root of the remaining variance leaves .066. The 95 percent credibility interval then would be .38± 1.96 (.066) or .25 to .51. This credibility interval means that we would expect to find a nonzero relationship between satisfaction and absenteeism when organizational conditions similar to those in the studies reviewed prevail.

Computation of credibility intervals is more complicated when corrections are made for other artifacts (e.g., lack of reliability and range restriction). Hunter et al. (1982) supply these more complex formulations.

It should be noted that when corrections for range restriction and/or criterion unreliability are made to the estimate of the population correlation, these corrections also must be made to the estimate of the standard deviation of this estimate (Schmidt, Gast-Rosenberg, & Hunter, 1980). In validity generalization work, one is normally interested in how consistently a test–job performance relationship would be observed across situations. To answer this question, we would compute the credibility interval.

Schmidt, Hunter, and colleagues usually report the lower bound of the 90 percent credibility value, which, for our example, would be .30 (.38 – 1.28 (.066)). This credibility interval tells us whether moderators are likely to produce zero test–criterion relationships in some situations. Tests of the significance of an average observed correlation from a meta-analysis require the computation of a confidence interval (as distinguished from the credibility interval described above). Standard errors for the computation of confidence intervals in cases in which it is concluded that there are or are not moderators are provided in Schmidt, Hunter, and Raju (1988).

EXAMINING POTENTIAL MODERATOR EFFECTS

Computation of the total variance (.0076) in the validity coefficients and the variance attributable to sampling error (.0033) leaves a relatively large amount of remaining variability (.0043), and the resultant credibility interval (.25 to .51) is relatively large. The remaining variance may be due to other artifacts in the studies reviewed, or it may be due to some moderator variable that causes differences in the correlations between two variables. If the remaining variance were close to .00, then any apparent moderator effects would be totally explained by sampling error.

In the hypothetical data presented in Table 11.8, the authors suspected that satisfaction and absenteeism from work were more highly correlated during stormy weather. Their rationale was that individuals who were unhappy with work would use the weather as an excuse to stay home, thereby increasing the satisfaction–absenteeism relationship. When the weather was fine, no excuse existed and satisfaction and absenteeism would be less highly correlated. To evaluate this moderator hypothesis, the researchers gathered archival data regarding weather conditions on the dates

TABLE 11.9 SUMMARY OF MODERATOR ANALYSIS FOR THE ABSENTEEISM–SATISFACTION RELATIONSHIP

Fair Weather	Stormy Weather
$\bar{r}$ = .28	$\bar{r}$ = .43
σ_r^2 = .0019	σ_r^2 = .0022
σ_e^2 = .0063	σ_e^2 = .0028
σ_p^2 = −.0044	σ_p^2 = −.0008

*σ_p^2 indicates the population variability.

on which absenteeism data were collected, and classified the weather as fair or stormy.

If weather were a real moderator, we would expect the average correlations for studies done in fair versus stormy conditions to be different, and the corrected variance averages to be lower in the two subsets of data than in all ten studies. A summary of the data relevant to this question is contained in Table 11.9.

The average correlation of satisfaction and absenteeism in stormy weather (.43) is different from the same average correlation in fair weather (.28). Further, within each subset of the data, sampling error accounts for more variance than is actually present in the observed correlations. This frequently occurs when the number of studies included in the review is small, and is referred to as *second-order sampling error*. In any event, the data presented in Table 11.9 are consistent with the hypothesis that weather moderates the relationship between satisfaction and absenteeism.

EFFECT SIZES EXPRESSED AS A FUNCTION OF MEAN DIFFERENCES

Frequently, evaluations of human resource programs produce results that are not reported in correlational form. For example, experimental methods usually produce data regarding control and experimental group means and standard deviations, and tests of the significance of the differences in group means. In these cases, a d statistic is computed indicating the effect size of the experimental intervention compared with a control group.

Glass, McGaw, and Smith (1981) and Hunter et al. (1982) provide the formulas and a discussion of meta-analyses of program effects when the effect size is d. Glass et al. (1981) compute d as follows:

$$d = \frac{\bar{X}_e - \bar{X}_c}{SD_c} \tag{11.11}$$

where $\overline{X}_e$ and $\overline{X}_c$ are the experimental and control group means and SD_c is the standard deviation of the control group. The reason for using SD_c is that the experimental treatment may have affected the standard deviation as well as the mean. Hunter et al. (1982) agree with this precaution but prefer, instead, to use the within-group standard deviation because it has the least sampling error.

Assume we have gathered the effect sizes from a group of experimental evaluations of a human resource intervention (e.g., diversity training program); then we would estimate $\overline{d}$ using the following formula:

$$\overline{d} = \Sigma[N_i d_i]/\Sigma N_i \qquad (11.12)$$

where $\overline{d}$ is the average effect size,
N_i is the number of subjects in the study i, and
d_i is the effect size in study i.

The variance of the effect sizes across studies can be calculated as follows:

$$\sigma_d^2 = \Sigma[N_i(d_i - \overline{d})^2]/\Sigma N_i \qquad (11.13)$$

Finally, the sampling error across studies is given by:

$$\sigma_e^2 = \{4[(1 + \overline{d}^2)/8]K\}/\Sigma N_i \qquad (11.14)$$

where K is the number of studies, and ΣN_i is the number of subjects in all studies. The variance of effect size corrected for variability due to sampling error is the difference between σ_d^2 and σ_e^2. These formulas parallel those given previously for the cumulation of correlational data. When appropriate, and when adequate estimates are available, d and variability in d can be corrected for other artifacts just as we can correct for correlational data.

An example of a meta-analysis conducted on a set of studies evaluating the number of accidents per year by experimental and control groups after an accident prevention training program was conducted in the experimental group is presented in Table 11.10. In this case, as in the example above in which cumulated effect sizes expressed as correlations were calculated, the average weighted effect size ($\overline{d}$ = –.59), the variance of this effect size (σ_d^2 =. 0634), and the variance attributable to sampling error (σ_e^2 = .0061) can be calculated. In our example, there is substantial remaining variance; that is, $\sigma_d^2 - \sigma_e^2$ = .0573. If we take the standard deviation (.24) of this value and compute the 95 percent credibility interval, we get –.12 to –1.06. The lower bound of the 90 percent credibility value would be –.28 [–.59 + 1.28 (.24)]. This value has been frequently used in meta-analytic research. It represents the value below which we can expect 10 percent of the validity coefficients. The conclusion in this case is that the accident prevention training does have an effect. However, less than 10 percent of the variance in effect sizes is explained by sampling

TABLE 11.10 EXAMPLE OF A META-ANALYSIS OF STUDIES EVALUATING ACCIDENT PREVENTION TRAINING PROGRAMS

Study	N_i*	$\bar{X}_c$	SD_c	$\bar{X}_e$	SD_e	d_i†	$N_i d_i$	$d_i - \bar{d}$	$N_i(d_i - \bar{d})^2$
1	100	18	8	15	5	−.45	−45.0	.14	1.96
2	50	20	10	19	6	−.12	−6.0	.47	11.05
3	30	12	5	13	5	.20	6.0	.79	18.72
4	120	20	6	16	8	−.57	−68.4	.02	.05
5	240	18	8	12	8	−.80	−192.0	−.21	10.58
6	90	16	6	10	6	−1.00	−90.0	−.41	15.13
7	150	14	5	12	6	−.36	−54.0	.23	7.94
8	180	17	6	13	7	−.61	−109.8	−.02	.07
9	60	22	10	16	8	−.44	−24.4	.15	1.35
10	80	12	4	8	6	−.78	−62.6	−.19	2.89
	1100						−646.2		69.74

$$\bar{d} = -646 / 1100 = -.59$$
$$\sigma_d^2 = 69.74 / 1100 = .0634$$
$$\sigma_e^2 = \{4[(1 + .59^2)/8]10\} / 1100 = .0061$$

* N in the experimental and control group are assumed equal.

† In computing d, SD_w was used.

error. The remaining variance could be due to variability in other artifacts or to some moderator of the effect of the training. Unfortunately, this example includes no other characteristics of the studies, the situations in which the studies were conducted, or the type of subjects studied, so moderator analyses cannot be carried out.

◆ ◆ ◆
SUMMARY

This chapter began with a discussion of individual differences and the normality of the distribution of those differences. This was followed by a description of the ways in which we summarize our observations about groups of individuals, and the degree to which we can use our observations on a sample to make inferences about some population. The summary measures discussed included measures of central tendency and variability. The chapter then described *t*-tests and analyses of variance as methods for evaluating the effects of human resource interventions by comparing mean scores between groups. Correlation coefficients and regression analyses were described as methods for evaluating the relationships between variables. Finally, examples of meta-analyses of hypothetical correlational and experimental data were provided. The material presented in this chapter should enable the reader to statistically evaluate many programs and relationships of interest to human resource researchers and practitioners. It will also allow the reader to better understand and interpret the research literature in human resource management.

Definitions

Analysis of variance   Procedure for testing the statistical significance of differences between the means of different groups of observations.

Central tendency   The value that is typical of an observation from a particular sample.

Interaction effect   The effect of two variables on a third variable that represents an effect greater or lesser than the sum of the effect of either variable alone.

Kappa   An expression of the degree of relationship between nominal variables corrected by the level of agreement that would obtain if they were related only by chance.

Linear relationship   A relationship in which a unit change in one of two variables results in constant change in a second variable.

Mean   The sum of the values of observations in a sample divided by the number of observations; the arithmetic average.

Measures of association   Measures of the degree to which values of one variable change as a function of values of a second variable.

Median   Value of the middle observation in a set of ranked observations in a sample.

Mode   The value of the most frequently occurring observation in a sample.

Multiple correlation   The combined relationship between two or more predictor variables and a criterion.

Normal distribution   A distribution of the values of observations that has a single mode, is symmetric and bell-shaped, and has limits of positive and negative infinity.

Null hypothesis   Statement of the absence of a relationship between variables or the absence of an effect for some experimental manipulation.

One-tailed test   Test in which only one alternative hypothesis is considered; for example, that the nature of relationship between two variables is positive.

Pearson product–moment correlation   A measure of the degree to which values of one variable are associated with the values of another variable; a summary of the relationship between linearly related variables.

Phi-coefficient   Product–moment correlation expressing the degree of relationship between two variables when both are dichotomies.

Rank order correlation   Correlations between variables that have been measured using ordinal scales.

Regression analysis A powerful statistical procedure for testing the relationships between multiple predictors and criterion measures.

Regression equation An equation that is developed through a regression analysis that indicates the relation between predictor variables and some criterion variable.

Scattergram Pictorial representation of the relationship between two variables.

Significance level Probability of rejecting the null hypothesis when it is true; probability of making a Type I error.

Standard deviation Measure of variability of the values of observations; square root of the average of the squared differences between the observation's value and the mean.

Standard score The value of an observation minus the mean of the observations divided by the standard deviation of observations; also called a z score.

Test of significance Test carried out to determine the probability of a given set of observations given that the null hypothesis is correct.

T-test Statistical procedure for comparing the mean differences between two groups.

Variability The degree to which the values of observations of a variable differ from one another.

EXERCISES

1. Complete the Organizational Culture Profile provided in Chapter 7 (see Table 7.1) as follows:

   a) Sort the 40 values into nine categories by asking yourself the following question: "How characteristic is this attribute of me?" Using a scale of least characteristic to most characteristic, sort the values into the following nine categories, beginning with the two most and least characteristic, then the three most and least characteristic and so on as follows:

   Least Characteristic 2, 3, 4, 7, 8, 7, 4, 3, 2 Most Characteristic

   When you are finished, rank your values by allocating them a value from 1 (least characteristic) to 9 (most characteristic).

   b) Do the same as the above for your organization or the last organization that you worked for, this time asking yourself the following question: "How characteristic is this attribute of my organization?"

   c) Calculate a Spearman rank correlation between your values and your organization's values. If this correlation is an indication of the congruence between your values and your organizations, what does it tell you?

   d) Complete the job attitudes measures provided in Chapter 3, Table 3.2 (i.e., job satisfaction, organizational commitment, and intentions to quit). Calculate your average score for each variable and then submit these along with your values congruence score to your instructor, who can then organize and feed back the scores for the entire class. With the data from your class, calculate the correlations between values congruence and job satisfaction, organizational commitment, and intentions to quit, and interpret the results.

2. Refer to Table 11.3 and perform *t*-tests to answer the following questions:

   a) Is employee satisfaction in the manufacturing department significantly lower than in the other departments?

   b) Is employee satisfaction in the manufacturing department of Organization A significantly different from that in the manufacturing departments of Organizations B, C, and D?

   c) What interpretations and conclusions can you make based on the *t*-tests you have performed?

3. Review several recent issues of the *Journal of Applied Psychology* and *Personnel Psychology* and find an article that compares the mean differences between groups of individuals and one that includes measures of association. Answer the following questions about the articles:

   a) What are the independent and dependent variables?

   b) What are the statistical techniques used to compute the mean differences and the measures of association? What variables are compared and what variables are tested for association?

   c) What are the major findings of the studies?

   d) What interpretations and conclusions are made by the authors?

   e) What are some of the practical implications of each study?

4. Refer to the model of turnover presented in Chapter 1 (see Figure 1.3). Describe the statistical procedures you would use to test the relationships shown in the model.

References

Cohen, J. (1960). A coefficient of agreement for nominal scales. *Educational and Psychological Measurement, 20*, 37–46.

Cohen, J. (1968). Weighted kappa: Nominal scale agreement with provision for scaled disagreement of partial credit. *Psychological Bulletin, 70*, 213–220.

Cohen, J. (1988). *Statistical power analysis for the behavioral sciences*. Hillsdale, NJ: Erlbaum.

Glass, G.V., McGaw, B., & Smith, M.L. (1981). *Meta-analysis in social research*. Beverly Hills, CA: Sage.

Hays, W.L. (1981). Statistics (3rd ed.) New York, NY: Holt, Rinehart and Winston.

Hunter, J.E., Smidth, F.L., & Jackson, G.B. (1982). *Meta-analysis: Cumulating research findings across studies.* Beverly Hills, CA: Sage.

Iaffaldano, M.T., & Muchinsky, P.M. (1985). Job satisfaction and job performance: A meta-analysis. *Psychological Bulletin, 97,* 251–273.

McDaniel, M.A., Hirsh, H.R., Smidt, F.L., Raju, N.S., & Hunter, J.E. (1986). Interpreting the results of meta-analytic research: A comment on Schmitt, Gooding, Noe, and Kirsch (1984). *Personnel Psychology, 39,* 141–148.

Pedhazur, E.J. (1997). Multiple regression in behavioral research: Explanation and prediction (3rd ed.). Fort Worth, TX: Harcourt Brace College Publishers.

Saks, A.M., & Cronshaw, S.F. (1990). A process investigation of realistic job previews: Mediating variables and channels of communication. *Journal of Organizational Behavior, 11,* 221–236.

Smith, P.C., Kendall, L.M., & Hulin, C.L. (1969). *The measurement of satisfaction in work and retirement: A strategy for the study of attitudes.* Chicago, IL: Rand McNally.

Schmidt, F.L., Gast-Rosenberg, Il, & Hunter, J.E. (1980). Validity generalization results for computer programmers. *Journal of Applied Psychology, 65,* 643–661.

Schmidt, F.L., & Hunter, J.E. (1981). Employment testing: Old theories and new research findings. *American Psychologist, 36,* 1128–1137.

Schmidt, F.L., Hunter, J.E., Pearlman, K., & Hirsh, H.R. (1985). Forty questions about validity generalization and meta-analysis. *Personnel Psychology, 38,* 697–798.

Schmidt, F.L., Hunter, J.E., & Raju, N.S. (1988). Validity generalization and situational specificity: A second look at the 75% rule and Fisher's z transformation. *Journal of Applied Psychology, 73,* 665–672.

12

Financial Evaluation

of Human

Resources

INTRODUCTION

As discussed in Chapter 1, there is increasing pressure for human resource professionals to demonstrate the value-added of their programs. As well, one of the reasons that human resource departments have been treated as expenses and burdened with tight budgets "has been their inability to communicate with management in the language of business" (Fitz-enz, 1995, p. xv). Thus, it is important for human resource departments to be able to evaluate the costs and benefits of human resource practices in financial terms. This chapter describes several procedures for conducting such an evaluation. As you will see, the evaluation of human resources in terms of costs and benefits can be readily applied to most, if not all, human resource programs, and provides important information to be used when making decisions about human resource interventions and practices.

After reading this chapter, you should be able to:

- Discuss the relevance, reasons, and importance of evaluating human resources in terms of costs and benefits.

- Explain the application and approaches of human resource accounting, and why this approach has not been used on a larger scale by organizations.

- Know how to calculate the return on investment of human resource programs.

- Explain how utility analysis is conducted, and calculate the utility of human resource programs.

- Understand the research issues and concerns that have been expressed about utility analyses.

Human resource researchers have often reported significant validity coefficients (relating scores on a selection procedure to measures of job performance) as proof of a test's usefulness, or significant mean differences between employees who attended a training program and employees who did not as evidence of the program's effectiveness. The assumption was that managerial decision makers would see the importance of human resource programs. Unfortunately, management must compare the assertions of human resources experts with those of organizational members who typically document their claims and requests in monetary terms rather than statistical terms. For example, a production manager requests new machinery, supporting the request with projected increases in productivity and resultant decreases in unit production costs. A sales manager supports his or her request for a new centralized computer system with figures concerning the amount of salesperson time that would be saved and estimates of the increased amount of sales that could be generated. Thus, a human resource manager must compete for scarce organizational resources in the same language as his or her colleagues. The recommendation that human resource professionals learn and use the language of economists has been voiced repeatedly over the years (Cascio, 1991; Fitz-enz, 1995).

In addition to being able to compete with other members of the organization, it is also important that human resource professionals have better information concerning the relative costs and benefits of various human resource efforts, such as training, selection, recruitment, career development, and so on. As well, it is important to be able to provide information concerning the relative costs and benefits of making different kinds of choices when confronted with conflicting goals regarding human resource allocation.

Some may object to evaluating human resources in dollar and cents terms. However, by failing to consider our actions in these terms, especially at a time when human resources are increasingly being outsourced, we are saying that the values underlying the decisions currently being made are acceptable and are ensuring the maintenance of the status quo. All decisions, even a decision to leave things as they are, are based on a set of values. Therefore, isn't it best that all parties clearly articulate their values so that fully informed debate about which values are to be maximized can take place? Use of cost evaluation promotes clear statements about values. As noted by Pfeffer (1994, p. 57),

> In a world in which financial results are measured, a failure to measure human resource policy and practice implementation dooms this to second-class status, oversight, neglect, and potential failure.

The remainder of this chapter will present several approaches to evaluating human resource programs and practices in financial terms. These approaches include human resource accounting; costs, benefits, and return on investment; and utility analysis.

◆ ◆ ◆
HUMAN RESOURCE ACCOUNTING

In the United States in the 1970s, there was discussion and debate regarding what came to be called quality of work life (Lawler, 1982). *Quality of work life (QWL)* refers to workplace practices such as democratic supervision, safe working conditions, and employee involvement in their work (Lawler, 1982; Davis & Cherns,

1975). It also implied working conditions in which individuals experience personal satisfaction and growth.

One distinguishing feature of the QWL approach is that it involved a concern for organizational effectiveness in terms of productivity and profitability. Thus, the creation of a satisfied and committed workforce was also felt to have financial or economic consequences for the organization. A number of writers attempted to establish measurement techniques to demonstrate such linkages (Likert & Bowers, 1969). Specifically, investigators tried to determine the financial impact of worker behaviours that were felt to occur as a consequence of high or low quality of work life environments. This led to the belief that human resources could be treated as organizational assets similar to other assets found in accounting statements. This idea stemmed from the fact that, even though organizations made investments in human resources through recruiting, selection, training and development, and so on, conventional accounting practices considered the costs of these programs to be expenses, thereby assuming that they did not have any real value to the organization (Brummet, Pyle, & Flamholtz, 1969). Likert and Bowers (1969) argued that ignoring human resources in an organization's records of financial performance would result in serious inadequacies and errors.

Human resource accounting (HRA) uses standard accounting practices to index and report an organization's human assets in economic terms. It involves calculating the costs incurred by an organization to recruit, select, hire, train, develop, and retain employees. The first such approach was taken by the R.G. Barry Corporation in 1967 (Cascio, 1991). The company determined the costs of individuals, based on such factors as recruitment and formal training, and amortized these costs over individuals' expected working lives. This approach is an example of an *asset model* of accounting, because it considers the costs associated with the organization's employees to be investments (Cascio, 1991).

During the 1970s, several approaches to HRA were developed. As indicated above, human resource expenses associated with initiatives such as selection and training were treated as investments rather than expenses, and the value of employees was based on the investments made to recruit, select, train, and develop them. A second approach involves determining the value of employees in terms of the costs associated with having to replace them (Cascio, 1991). An approach known as *present value of future earnings* determines an individual's future contribution as an indicator of his or her present value (Cascio, 1991).

Other approaches to HRA have attempted to link the investments made in human resources to outcomes such as leadership and job attitudes to productivity and earnings, using measures such as job performance as indicators of an employee's value to the organization (Cascio, 1991; Latham & Whyte, 1994).

For example, Brummet et al. (1969) designed a human resource accounting model to extend capital budgeting concepts to an organization's human resources. The idea was to consider the anticipated return of organization investments such as training and development programs. Such returns, or "end-result variables," could then be expressed in terms of a **return on investment**. As an example, they noted how a $75 000 investment in an organizational development program that results in changes valued at $93 750 produces a return on investment of 25 percent. In terms of accounting procedures, the current value would be based on discounting the estimated future end results.

While human resource accounting set the stage for treating human resource initiatives as investments and employees as assets, interest in HRA began to wane by the end of the 1970s. Some writers criticized the idea of equating investments in people with their competence, and others argued that human resources are not assets because they are not purchased and sold. Others noted the difficulty of attaching a monetary value to all aspects of an individual's job performance and knowing what portion of performance is the result of individual inputs or other factors such as technology. In the end, HRA practices were not well accepted by managers or accounting firms, and were perceived by many to be impractical (Latham & Whyte, 1994; Rhode, Lawler, & Sundem, 1976).

While HRA has received more academic than practical interest over the years, some organizations have made use of HRA (Appelbaum & Hood, 1993; Latham & Whyte, 1994; Phillips, 1996). As well, with the increased attention to the value of human resources, some writers have suggested that the time for HRA has finally come, and that more organizations will begin to list the financial value of their human resource assets on financial statements (Appelbaum & Hood, 1993; Phillips, 1996).

◆◆◆
COSTS, BENEFITS, AND RETURN ON INVESTMENT

Over the years, many writers have developed models to calculate the return on investment of human resource programs. The basic approach is to calculate the cost of a program, such as recruitment or training, and to determine the benefit in dollar terms of results such as improved productivity or a reduction in absenteeism, accidents, and turnover. Examples of how to determine the costs and benefits of various human resource areas such as staffing, compensation, training and development, employee attitudes, and employee assistance and wellness programs have been well documented (Cascio, 1991; Phillips, 1996).

In an early attempt to demonstrate the value of positive job attitudes, Mirvis and Lawler (1977) demonstrated how the relationship between job attitudes and employee behaviours could be calculated in financial terms, using a sample of bank tellers in twenty branches. In particular, they showed that an improvement in job attitudes resulted in lower employee absenteeism and turnover. Next, they calculated the costs of each of these behaviours to the organization, and the costs associated with different levels of job attitudes. Their results showed that more positive job attitudes resulted in lower costs associated with a reduction in turnover and absenteeism. Overall, an increase of .5 standard deviations in employee job attitudes was estimated to result in an annual savings of $17 664.

Training and development programs have often been used to develop models of costs and benefits. A good example is provided by Robinson and Robinson (1989). They reported on a wood plant that implemented a training program to improve the quality of wood panels, housekeeping, and the number of preventable accidents. Plant managers and supervisors attended a training program on performance management, interpersonal skills, and work habits. The costs of the training program were calculated in terms of five cost categories: direct costs, indirect costs, development costs, overhead costs, and compensation costs. The total cost of the training program was calculated to be $32 564.

The benefits of the training program were calculated in terms of the improvement in the quality of the panels and the reduction in preventable accidents. After training, there were 360 less panels rejected per day, which was calculated as saving $172 800 per year. They also reported a decrease of eight accidents per year, a cost savings of $48 000 per year. The total savings to the organization was $220 800.

To calculate the return on the investment (ROI) of an HR program such as training, one needs to calculate the total costs and benefits of a program using the following formula (Phillips, 1996):

$$ROI = \frac{Net\ Benefits}{Program\ Costs} \qquad (12.1)$$

Therefore, the return on the investment for the training program in the above example is $220 800/$32 564 = 6.8 (68 percent), or $188 236 per year ($220 800 − $32 564). Thus, the key to calculating the ROI is to calculate the costs and benefits of a human resource program. However, in other cases it is much more difficult to calculate the benefits. This is because "soft" measures such as communication, interpersonal skills, and so on, are much more difficult to quantify in dollar terms than "hard" measures such as accidents, productivity, and absenteeism.

One outcome measure that is often used in calculating the costs and benefits of human resources is employee turnover. Turnover is very costly for organizations, and in many companies the rate of turnover is exceedingly high (Cascio, 1991). As a result, calculating the cost of turnover to organizations, as well as the benefits associated with programs to reduce turnover, is of considerable importance.

Estimating the economic consequences of turnover is quite complex. A large number of factors must be considered and many assumptions must be made. Some of these factors include:

1. Dollar value of the productivity of the individuals who leave.
2. Salary costs of the people who leave.
3. Cost of benefits of the people who leave.
4. Recruiting costs.
5. Salary costs of the replacements.
6. Cost of benefits for replacements.
7. Costs associated with training replacements.
8. Dollar value of the lower levels of productivity of the replacements.
9. Speed with which replacements reach desired levels of productivity.
10. Coordination costs associated with the need for experienced employees to adjust their work pace to that of replacements.

From this list it can be inferred that the economic costs of turnover will vary greatly depending on the circumstances. Turnover of high performers who are hard to replace and train reflects a poor state of organizational effectiveness. Lawler and Rhode (1976) reported a situation in which the costs associated with replacing a below-average-performance sales associate was $31 600, and the cost to replace an effective sales manager was $185 000. The cost of turnover for a salesperson in the retail automobile industry averages over $18 000 (Cascio, 1991). On average, the annual turnover rate is reported to be 12 percent (Cascio, 1991). For some organizations, this can mean substantial costs. For example, as reported by Cascio (1991), Corning Glass Works found that turnover was costing the company $16 to $18 million a year.

Due to the high cost of turnover, human resource programs that reduce turnover can result in considerable benefits, and calculating these benefits is becoming increasingly important. Cascio (1991) provides a detailed procedure for identifying and measuring turnover costs. According to Cascio (1991), there are three major cost categories associated with turnover: separation costs, replacement costs, and training costs.

Separation costs include a number of expenses that occur during the period in which an employee leaves an organization, such as administration costs, separation pay, unemployment tax, and the cost of conducting exit interviews. *Replacement costs* are those costs involved in replacing employees. These costs cover such activities as:

communication of job availability, pre-employment administrative functions, entrance interviews, testing, staff meetings, travel/moving expenses, postemployment acquisition and dissemination information, and employment medical exams. *Training costs* for new employees include informational literature, instruction in a formal training program, and instruction by employee assignment. One final factor that also has to be considered is what Cascio (1991) refers to as *Difference in Performance (DP)*, which refers to differences in performance between employees who leave and their replacements.

Therefore, the total cost of turnover is the sum of the separation, replacement, and training costs plus the difference in performance. Calculating these costs is important because it provides information to determine if some action should be taken to lower the rate and cost of turnover. Cascio (1991) provides several examples of programs to manage and lower turnover, including realistic job previews, psychological and performance tests, prehire payback agreements, changes in compensation, and job enrichment.

Consider the use of realistic job previews (RJPs). As noted by Cascio (1991), research on RJPs has found that they lower turnover by approximately 9 percent. Consider an organization in which the average cost of turnover is $7000 per employee. For every 100 employees, the use of RJPs would result in savings of $63 000 (Cascio, 1991). Of course, the savings would be considerably greater for organizations with higher rates of turnover, or in which the cost per employee turnover is higher. To calculate the ROI, it would be necessary to determine the cost of the RJP, which is usually very low unless it involves the production of a video.

For example, consider an organization with a turnover rate of 12 percent per year. If we assume that the organization employs 1000 employees, then we would expect 120 employees to quit each year. However, with the implementation of RJPs, the turnover rate should be reduced from 12 percent to 3 percent. Therefore, if we assume that each turnover costs approximately $10 000, then the total savings to the organization would be the original cost of turnover or $1 200 000 (120 × $10 000) per year minus the cost of turnover following implementation of RJPs or $300 000 (30 × $10 000) per year, which equals $900 000 per year.

The cost of the RJP would include the design and printing of a written RJP or about $5000. The ROI would be $900 000/$5000 = 180. This ROI is, of course, extremely high, and it is important to realize that the reduced turnover rate will only result for individuals who received the RJP. However, the overall turnover rate for the organization will remain close to 12 percent, since the majority of the 1000 employees will have been hired without the use of an RJP. Thus, it is important to realize that this ROI is based on a situation in which all employees have received an RJP.

However, if we consider the first year following implementation of an RJP with a turnover rate of 12 percent, each year the organization must replace 120 employees. Therefore, of the first 120 employees hired using the RJP, we would expect 3 percent, or 3.6 of them, to quit, compared to the 12 percent, or 14.4, who would be expected to quit without the RJP. This results in a savings of $108 000 (10.8 × $10 000) in the first year, and an ROI of $108 000/$5000 = 21.6. Thus, the return on investment in the first year as a result of the use of a new RJP is still very high, and, of course, is a more realistic estimate.

While the calculation of ROI in the evaluation of human resources is a powerful way to demonstrate the value-added of human resource systems, the fact is that very few organizations actually evaluate human resources in this manner (Davidson, 1998). However, as noted elsewhere in this text, this situation is likely to change. According to several authors, evaluating the costs and benefits of human resources is more important than ever and likely to become much more common (Davidson, 1998; Fitz-enz, 1995; Phillips, 1996). For more detailed and complex examples of calculating the costs, benefits, and ROI of human resources, the reader should refer to readings devoted to these topics (Cascio, 1991; Fitz-enz, 1995; Phillips, 1996).

◆ ◆ ◆
UTILITY ANALYSIS

Utility analysis is a method of forecasting the net financial benefits that result from human resource programs, such as selection, performance appraisal, training, and turnover (Whyte & Latham, 1997). It involves procedures in which validity coefficients and effect sizes (see Chapter 6 on meta-analysis) can be translated into dollar and cent values. One of the first approaches to utility analysis was provided by Brogden (1946), who showed that the validity coefficient is a direct index of utility. He assumed that both predictor and criterion are continuous (not discretely categorized), that predictor and criterion distributions are the same, and that the relationship between predictor and criterion is linear. When these conditions are met, a test with a validity of .50 could be expected to produce 50 percent of the gain in utility that would result if we had a test of perfect validity, or a test of validity equal to .25 would have half the utility of a test with a validity of .50. So, if an organization had turnover costs of $500 000 a year, a test with a correlation of .50 with turnover could be used to make turnover predictions that would save the company $250 000 annually, or half the amount saved if perfect prediction of turnover could be achieved.

Brogden (1946) also showed how the selection ratio (the number of employees hired from the existing applicant pool) and the standard deviation of job performance in dollars (SD_y) influence the utility of a selection procedure. The change in utility per person selected is equal to the product of (1) the validity of the test; (2) the standard deviation of job performance expressed in dollars; and (3) the mean standard score on the test of those persons selected. (Note that the lower the selection ratio, the higher will be the average test score of the persons selected.) Multiplying this number by the number of persons hired yields the total annual gain, which accrues from the use of the test.

A critical feature of this analysis is the standard deviation of job performance in dollar terms. For jobs in which the contribution of individual employees to the organization is widely different, valid testing will result in large dollar gains. In those situations in which individual contributions are relatively similar, even a valid testing procedure and a low selection ratio will not result in large dollar gains. Validity is related linearly to increases in the standard score on the criterion. Recall that the standard score is expressed in terms of the number of standard deviations a given score is away from the mean. Hence, we must know the value of the standard deviation of performance differences in order to make estimates of utility.

Brogden (1949) also addressed the role of information-gathering costs in the determination of utility and pointed out that, for very low selection ratios, an organization incurs tremendous testing costs, since many applicants are tested to hire relatively few people. With high selection ratios, we are testing many applicants to reject a few. In both situations, the SD_y must be large or the net gain in utility becomes negative.

In 1979, Schmidt, Hunter, McKenzie, and Muldrow reported a pilot study in which they derived estimates of SD_y for budget analysts. Supervisors were asked to judge the worth of their budget analysts, since they were thought to have had the best opportunities to observe actual performance and output differences among employees. Schmidt et al.'s (1979) method for estimating employee worth was based on the following reasoning: If job performance in dollar terms is normally distributed (see Chapter 11 for a description of the normal distribution), then the difference between the value to the organization of the products and services produced by an average employee and the products and services produced by an employee at the 85th percentile (one whose performance is as good or better than 85 percent of the employees) is equal to SD_y.

Similarly, the estimated difference between the average performer and the person who performs at the 15th percentile (as good as or better than only 15 percent of the employees) should be equal to SD_y. The 15th and 85th percentiles are approximately one standard deviation below and above the average, or 50th, percentile. The supervisors of budget analysts were asked to estimate the contribution of employees at both the 50th (average) and 85th percentile, and these values were averaged over 62 supervisors. The average SD_y was $11 327 for the budget analyst position.

Since the introduction of the Schmidt et al. (1979) method for estimating utility, a great deal of work on utility estimation has been conducted. Most researchers have concluded that the Schmidt et al. (1979) method provides a reasonable approximation of the variability in employees' organizational worth. The next section describes examples of the application of utility analysis to various human resource programs.

◆◆◆
APPLICATION OF UTILITY ANALYSIS TO HUMAN RESOURCE PROGRAMS

Most utility estimations have been done in the context of selection, but the concepts can be usefully applied to other human resource interventions as well. This section describes examples of the application of utility analysis to estimate the costs and benefits of selection tests, training programs, and performance evaluations.

SELECTION

Schmidt, Mack, and Hunter (1984) presented utility estimates for the selection of park rangers in the U.S. National Park Service using a test with an estimated validity of .51 as opposed to an unstructured interview for which validity was estimated as .14. They also estimated the utility that would result when different modes of test use were employed: (1) top-down selection, (2) random selection of those persons scoring above the mean, and (3) random selection of those persons who meet a minimum score equal to one standard deviation below the mean. Their estimate of the standard deviation of the dollar contribution of park rangers was $4450.74, based on the average of two estimates from the responses of 114 head rangers. Directions to these rangers required that they make dollar estimates of the contribution of an average ranger, of a ranger working at the 85th percentile, and of a ranger working at the 15th percentile. Two standard deviations were then computed, as described above, and averaged to arrive at the $4450.74 estimate.

Utilities were estimated by the following equation:

$$\Delta U = [TN_s\,(r_1 - r_2)\,(\phi/p)] - [N_s\,(C_1 - C_2)/p] \qquad (12.2)$$

where

ΔU	=	the gain in productivity in dollars from using the test for one year
T	=	tenure in years of the average selectee
N_s	=	number selected per year
r_1	=	the validity of the test (.51)
r_2	=	the validity of the interview (.14)
C_1	=	per applicant cost of the test
C_2	=	per applicant cost of the interview
SD_y	=	the standard deviation of the dollar contribution ($4450.74)
p	=	proportion selected

ϕ/p = average standardized test score for those selected. For those in which only the top persons were selected (10 percent in this case), this value was 1.758. It was .7978 when random selection above the mean was employed, and .2877 when the minimum test score of one SD below the mean was applied.

If 80 people are selected per year using the test, and their average tenure is five years and we select the best 10% of the applicants, assuming that the expense of administering the test and the interview is approximately equal, then the expected change in utility would be as follows:

$$\Delta U = [(5 \times 80) \, (.51 - .14) \, (\$4450) \, (1.758)] - [80 \, (0)/.10] = \$1 \; 157 \; 819.$$

The Schmidt et al. (1984) analysis and others like it show that the economic benefits of valid selection procedures can be quite substantial. They also show that the way a test is used can affect the utility realized. For example, if a cutoff score is set at the mean of the test, and we select randomly from those above the mean, and we are still interested in hiring 10 percent of the applicants, the utility gained drops from the $1 157 819 computed above to just over $525 000. If a very low cutoff is used (e.g., one standard deviation below the mean), then utility drops to $190 000 over the average five-year tenure of the 80 selected candidates. Of course, if the selection procedure remains in use, and the organization continues to employ 80 new applicants per year, then the utility associated with each of these new cohorts also would be realized. While additional complications arise in estimating the utility of human resource programs, the Schmidt et al. (1979) procedure represented a significant breakthrough in this area and has stimulated a remarkable number of additional research studies.

TRAINING

The second example of the estimation of benefits accruing from human resource activities involves estimating the effects of a training program. In a typical evaluation study, the performances of a control group and an experimental group are compared using a t-test or analysis of variance that tells us whether group differences are statistically significant. The significance test, however, doesn't tell us the dollar value of the impact of the training program. Schmidt, Hunter, and Pearlman (1982) provide a hypothetical example of the evaluation of a training program for computer programmers in which 100 employees are in the training or experimental group and 100 employees are in the control group. The cost of training was $500 per person. Supervisors were not told who had received training, but they were asked to rate the quality of the programs produced by each employee each month for a six-month period. The six-month composites were standardized against the control group performance so that mean performance equalled 50 and the standard deviation 10.

The following formula was used to estimate the utility of the training program:

$$\Delta U = TNd_t\, SD_y - NC \qquad (12.3)$$

where

ΔU	=	the dollar value of the program
T	=	the number of years the training has a continued effect on performance
N	=	the number trained
d_t	=	the true difference in job performance between the average trained and untrained employee in standard deviation units
SD_y	=	the standard deviation of job performance in dollars of the untrained group
C	=	the cost of training each programmer

In the example, the mean of the trained group was 55, so d equaled .5 ((55 – 50)/10). Schmidt et al. (1982) further corrected d for unreliability in the performance ratings used. Their estimate of reliability was .60; hence d_t = .65 (.50/$\sqrt{.60}$). Occasionally, d is estimated from a meta-analysis of previous studies in which the only data presented are significance tests or correlations. Schmidt et al. (1982) provide formulas by which these statistics can be converted to d.

The SD_y can be estimated using procedures described above. The appropriate reference group in making those estimates would be untrained employees. Schmidt et al. (1982) used a previously derived estimate of the SD_y of computer programmers equal to $10 413. The length of time an organizational intervention lasts must be estimated. In this example, the estimate was two years.

Using the formula above to assess the economic benefit of the training program results in the following:

$$\Delta U= 2(100)(.65)(\$10\ 413) - 100(\$500)$$
$$\Delta U= \$1\ 303\ 690$$

The expected return on this training program for each 100 employees trained is over $1 million. For those cases in which we can derive estimates of d for an organizational intervention, these procedures can be readily used to estimate the degree to which a particular program is worth pursuing. Kopelman (1986) and Guzzo, Jette, and Katzell (1985) provide comprehensive reviews of various types of human resource interventions from which d may be estimated.

PERFORMANCE EVALUATION

A third application of utility analysis is for performance evaluation and feedback (Landy, Farr, & Jacobs, 1982). The Schmidt et al. (1984) formula has been modified to estimate the utility of a performance evaluation and feedback program as follows:

$$\Delta U = Nd_f\, SD_y - NC \qquad (12.4)$$

where

ΔU = the benefit of the program

N = the number of persons receiving evaluation and feedback

d_f = the true difference in performance for the average person in the experimental group and the average person in the control group

C = the cost of the evaluation and feedback program for each employee

Landy et al. (1982) present the following estimates of the parameters of this equation for a large manufacturing firm that employs 500 middle-level managers. SD_y was estimated at $20 000. They estimated the cost of delivering the performance evaluation system at $700 per manager. Their cost estimate included development of the program, the time required to train supervisors to implement the program, and the actual time required of supervisors and subordinates in giving and receiving feedback. Finally, their review of the performance evaluation and feedback literature suggested a correlation of .30 to .50 between feedback and subsequent job performance. This value was transformed to d_f using a formula provided by Schmidt et al. (1982).

Using these values and the formula presented above yields the following:

$$\Delta U = 500(.64)\ (\$20\ 000) - (500 \times 700)$$
$$= \$6\ 050\ 000$$

Given that the estimates above are reasonable, the economic advantage of an effective performance evaluation and feedback program can be considerable.

In conclusion, examples of the application of utility concepts to three different areas of human resource management—selection, training, and performance appraisal—have been described. Clearly, these are tools with wide applicability that human resource managers and researchers should have at their disposal.

◆◆◆
RESEARCH ON UTILITY ANALYSIS

Research on utility analysis has identified a number of issues that need to be considered when calculating the utility of human resource programs. For example, Boudreau (1983a) argued that the Schmidt et al. (1979) model should include economic considerations that are applied to other management decisions, such as variable costs, taxes, and discounting. *Variable costs* occur when the cost of producing a unit varies either positively or negatively with productivity. *Taxes* also increase with a firm's level of net profit; hence, in order to compute a firm's tax liability, we must know their marginal tax rate. *Discounting* refers to the fact that present monetary values can't be directly equated with future values. A benefit received two years from now must be decreased by the percentage of interest one could earn with that money were one to receive it now. So, a promise of $1000 in two years is really worth only about $826, assuming 10 percent interest can be earned on the money $\{[1 / (1 + .10)^2] (\$1000)\}$. Applying all three of the Boudreau modifications to the utility of the training program example above reduced the utility estimate from $1 303 690 to $584 937. While Boudreau (1983a) was making armchair estimates of each of these values, it is clear that their impact on utility estimates can be substantial and that they must be considered in utility calculations.

Boudreau (1983b) also examined utility when a program is instituted, continued over a number of years, and applied to several sets of employees. His formulations show that even when discounting, taxes, and variable cost problems are included, the benefits of human resource programs are likely higher than earlier estimates by Schmidt et al. (1982, 1984). These earlier estimates had extended utility estimates for one set of employees over some estimate of the number of years of their tenure, but they ignored the estimate of the impact of the program being extended to new sets of employees every year.

Another complication in applying utility analyses has been described by Murphy (1986). He pointed out that previous utility formulations assumed that when a job offer was made to a group of applicants, they accepted the offer. Because some offers are declined, they must be extended to other lower-scoring individuals, and the average ability of those selected will be correspondingly lower. Murphy (1986) developed formulas and considered three separate possibilities: (1) cases in which offers are declined at random, (2) cases in which the highest-scoring applicants decline, and (3) cases in which test scores are related, but imperfectly so, to the probability of accepting an offer.

Murphy (1986) used an example previously presented by Hunter and Schmidt (1982) in which they had estimated the utility of a test to select 2000 budget analysts at $8 133 012 in a single year. If 10 percent of the original offers are declined, utility drops to $7 248 147 under case 1 conditions, to $5 973 859 under case 2 conditions, and to $6 881 152 when case 3 conditions apply. If half of the original offers are declined, corresponding figures are $2 416 049, $0.00, and $1 617 019 for cases 1, 2, and 3 respectively. Clearly, rejected offers have a huge impact on the utility of a selection procedure.

Murphy (1986) claims that, under realistic circumstances, utility formulas that do not take account of rejected offers overestimate utility gains by 30 to 80 percent. Rejected offers may be minimized if special efforts are made to recruit a more highly qualified labour pool, or if special efforts are made to get those persons first offered a job to accept. These efforts, however, will cost money, and those expenditures should be included in estimates of the recruiting and selection process. Boudreau and Rynes (1985) have developed utility formulas that explicitly include recruitment costs and the effects of different recruitment strategies.

Where do all these modifications leave us with respect to the use of utility analysis in human resource evaluation? As it turns out, even conservative estimates of the utility of most human resource efforts have produced very favourable estimated returns. Furthermore, when a program is continued over a number of years or repeated, such as a training program or selection test, the benefit accruing from additional cohorts of employees should be estimated, since this will add further gains and returns on the investment.

Finally, and perhaps most importantly, Rauschenberger and Schmidt (1987) have begun to consider how best to communicate the results of these utility estimates on human resource programs to other members of the organization. This particular problem deserves much more attention if human resource professionals are to make maximum use of the procedures described in this chapter. Recall that one of the reasons for evaluating human resources in this way is to provide information to management and the rest of the organization in a common language: dollars and cents. Thus, it is important to know whether managers do in fact respond favourably to utility analysis information. For some surprising answers to this question, see the HR Research Today box below.

HR RESEARCH TODAY

Managers' Reactions to Utility Analysis Information

Although utility analysis provides an effective means of evaluating the financial benefits of human resource programs, this is only one of the objectives of using utility analysis. As noted by Latham and Whyte (1994), a primary purpose of utility analysis "is to assist managers in deciding whether to invest in human resource management systems such as selection tools, performance appraisal processes, or training programs" (p. 33). This is based on the assumption "that managers emphasize and rely heavily on rational analysis in the management of organizations" (p. 33).

In order to test the assumption that managers would use utility analysis information to make decisions about human resource systems, Gary Latham and Glen Whyte of the University of Toronto conducted an experiment in which some managers received standard validity information, and some managers received utility analysis information about a selection system. The managers were requested to imagine that they were the vice-president of a large multinational corporation and that they had the authority to decide if they should implement a selection system proposed to them by a psychologist. The utility information included an explanation of utility analysis and the utility equation, as well as the calculation of the utility of the proposed selection system. The managers then answered questions about whether they would implement the selection system.

Latham and Whyte (1994) found a significant difference between conditions, but not in the direction expected. Managers who received standard validation information were

HR RESEARCH TODAY (continued)

more likely to implement the selection system than those in the utility analysis condition. As noted by the authors, "The managers in this study did not base their decisions on the quantifiable costs and benefits contained in a utility analysis ... the psychologist's recommendations were viewed most favourably when the information presented was confined to straightforward validation procedures" (p. 41).

In a second study, Whyte and Latham (1997) included a videotaped presentation from an expert on utility analysis, who explained the logic and benefits of utility analysis. The expert, Steven Cronshaw of the University of Guelph, then appeared live during the experiment to answer questions about the video presentation and utility analysis. This, however, did not change the results. Once again, the managers were more likely to accept the advice of the psychologist when they were provided with validity information rather than utility information. The authors concluded that their results "do not support the use of utility analysis as a tool to assist managerial decision making" (p. 608).

Sources: Based on Latham, G.P., & Whyte, G. (1994). The futility of utility analysis. *Personnel Psychology, 47,* 31–46; Whyte, G., & Latham, G. (1997). The futility of utility analysis revisited: When even an expert fails. *Personnel Psychology, 50,* 601–615.

◆ ◆ ◆
SUMMARY

In this chapter, methods to evaluate human resource programs in financial terms were described. After discussing the importance of financial evaluation for human resources, the chapter described human resource accounting as a way to treat human resource programs as investments and human resources as assets. This was followed by a discussion of the costs and benefits of human resource practices, and how to calculate the return on investment. Finally, utility analysis techniques were described, and several examples of the application of utility analyses for different human resource interventions were presented.

While these techniques continue to receive more attention in research than in practice, this is likely to change in the near future with increasing demands to demonstrate the value-added of human resource initiatives and expenditures. Furthermore, describing the return on investment, cost reductions and savings, and the utility that results from human resource programs is likely to improve human resource decision making and to place the human resource department on a level playing field with the rest of the organization.

Definitions

Human resource accounting (HRA)   An approach that is used to index and report an organization's human assets in economic terms, using standard accounting practices.

Return on investment (ROI)   The financial benefit of a human resource program relative to the costs of the program; calculated as a ratio of the net benefits of a program to the cost of the program.

Utility analysis   A method used to forecast the net financial benefits that result from human resource programs.

EXERCISES

1. Using HRA practices, consider your value as an asset to your organization based on the following:
   a) your replacement cost
   b) the total value of investments your organization has made in you in terms of recruitment, selection, training, etc.
   c) your future contribution as an indicator of your present value.

   Do you think that these approaches adequately indicate your value to the organization?

2. Based on the information provided in this chapter about the study by Mirvis and Lawler (1977) on the financial impact of employee attitudes, consider the following: If an organization implemented a bonus plan to improve job attitudes, what would be the return on investment if job satisfaction increased by 1.5 standard deviations, and the costs of the program were as follows:
   a) Cost of developing and implementing the program: $5000
   b) Cost of the bonuses: approximately $10 000 per year
   c) Cost of management and administration of the program: $5000 per year

   How much of an improvement in job attitudes would be required in order for the program to return more than it costs? How much of an increase in yearly bonuses can the organization afford to provide in order for the program to break even?

3. After conducting a true experiment to test the effects of a training program to improve customer service, Jack Manojlovic found a significant difference in customer service between the training and the control group six months after the training program. As the director of human resources, he was eager to inform the president about these results. In his report, Jack noted that the performance of the training group in terms of their customer service averaged 8.5, compared with the control group, which had an average of 6.5. The president, however, was not very excited about these results and sent Jack a memo in which

he stated: "These numbers don't mean a thing to me. Is this all you can tell me about the effects of the training program?" How should Jack respond? What should he do and how should he proceed?

4. Refer to the HR Research Today box (page 346–347) on Latham and Whyte's research on managers' reactions to utility analysis information. Why do you think that the managers were more likely to accept the selection system when they were provided with standard validation information rather than utility analysis information? What are the implications of this for the use of utility analysis for evaluating human resource systems?

References

Appelbaum, S.H., & Hood, J. (1993). Accounting for the firm's human resources. *Managerial Accounting Journal, 8*(2), 17–24.

Boudreau, J.W. (1983a). Economic considerations in estimating the utility of human resource productivity improvement programs. *Personnel Psychology, 36,* 551–576.

Boudreau, J.W. (1983b). Effects of employee flows on utility analysis of human resource productivity improvement programs. *Journal of Applied Psychology, 68,* 396–406.

Boudreau, J.W., & Rynes, S.L. (1985). Recruitment effects on staffing utility analyses. *Journal of Applied Psychology, 70,* 354–366.

Brogden, H.E. (1946). On the interpretation of the correlation coefficient as a measure of predictive efficiency. *Journal of Educational Psychology, 37,* 65–76.

Brogden, H.E. (1949). When testing pays off. *Personnel Psychology, 2,* 171–183.

Brummet, R.L., Pyle, W.C., & Flamholtz, E.G. (1969, July-August). Human resource accounting in industry. *Personnel Administrator,* 34–46.

Cascio, W.F. (1991). *Costing human resources: The financial impact of behavior in organizations.* Boston, MA: Kent.

Davidson, L. (1998, September). Measure what you bring to the bottom line. *Workforce,* 34–40.

Davis, L.E., & Cherns, A.B. (1975). *The quality of working life* (vols. 1 & 2). New York: The Free Press.

Fitz-enz, J. (1995). *How to measure human resources management.* New York: McGraw-Hill.

Guzzo, R.A., Jette, R.D., & Katzell, R.A. (1985). The effects of psychologically based intervention programs on worker productivity: A meta-analysis. *Personnel Psychology, 38,* 275–291.

Kopelman, R.E. (1986). *Managing productivity in organizations.* New York: McGraw-Hill.

Landy, F.J., Farr, J.L., & Jacobs, R.R. (1982). Utility concepts in performance measurement. *Organizational Behavior and Human Performance, 30,* 15–40.

Latham, G.P., & Whyte, G. (1994). The futility of utility analysis. *Personnel Psychology, 47,* 31–46.

Lawler, E.E., III. (1982). Strategies for improving the quality of work life. *American Psychologist, 37,* 486–493.

Lawler, E.E., III, & Rhode, J.G. (1976). *Information and control in organizations.* Santa Monica, CA: Goodyear.

Likert, R., & Bowers, D.G. (1969). Organization theory and human resource accounting. *American Psychologist, 24*, 585–592.

Mirvis, P.H., & Lawler, E.E., III. (1977). Measuring the financial impact of employee attitudes. *Journal of Applied Psychology, 62*, 1-8.

Murphy, K.R. (1986). When your top choice turns you down: Effect of rejected offers on the utility of selection tests. *Psychological Bulletin, 99*, 133–138.

Pfeffer, J. (1994). *Competitive advantage through people: Unleashing the power of the work force.* Boston, MA: Harvard Business School Press.

Phillips, J.J. (1996). *Accountability in human resource management.* Houston, TX: Gulf Publishing Company.

Rauschenberger, J.M., & Schmidt, F.L. (1987). Measuring the economic impact of human resource programs. *Journal of Business Psychology, 2*, 50–59.

Rhode, J.G., Lawler, E.E., III, & Sundem, G.L. (1976). Human resource accounting: A critical assessment. *Industrial Relations, 15*, 13–25.

Robinson, D.G., & Robinson, J. (1989). Training for impact. *Training and Development Journal, 43*(8), 34–42.

Schmidt, F.L., Hunter, J.E., McKenzie, R., & Muldrow, T. (1979). Impact of valid selection procedures on workforce productivity. *Journal of Applied Psychology, 64*, 609–626.

Schmidt, F.L., Hunter, J.E., & Pearlman, K. (1982). Assessing the economic impact of personnel programs on workforce productivity. *Personnel Psychology, 35*, 333–347.

Schmidt, F.L., Mack, M.J., & Hunter, J.E. (1984). Selection utility in the occupation of U.S. park ranger for three modes of test use. *Journal of Applied Psychology, 69*, 490–497.

Whyte, G., & Latham, G. (1997). The futility of utility analysis revisited: When even an expert fails. *Personnel Psychology, 50*, 601–615.

13

Evaluation of Human Resource Systems

In the previous two chapters, statistical and financial evaluation of human resources were described. While both of these methods of evaluation are common and important, they are limited in a number of ways. The major limitation of these two approaches is that they are best suited for evaluating particular human resource programs or practices. For example, statistical evaluation can be used to evaluate a training program or, perhaps, a selection test. Financial evaluation is useful for evaluating the return on investment or utility of the same training program or selection test. Another drawback is that both forms of evaluation usually involve a limited number of outcome or dependent variables. For example, both statistical and financial evaluation might involve evaluating the effects of a training program on job performance. Thus, both statistical and financial evaluation are very useful for evaluating particular HRM practices or programs on some outcome variable(s) of interest.

However, these two forms of evaluation are generally not as capable of evaluating the entire human resource system or particular HRM functional areas. This, however, is increasingly the type of evaluation that is required by human resource departments and organizations. Therefore, in this chapter the focus is on evaluating human resource systems through the use of auditing procedures and benchmarking.

After reading this chapter you should be able to:

- Describe the use and objectives of auditing as a technique for evaluating human resource systems.

- Understand and describe the stages of the HRM auditing process.

- Describe how to perform an HRM audit using the key indicators, multiple-constituency, and strategic approaches.

- Describe the use and objectives of benchmarking as a technique for evaluating human resource systems.

- Understand and describe the stages of the HRM benchmarking process.

- Understand and describe HRM best practices and how they can be used in the benchmarking process.

◆ ◆ ◆
HUMAN RESOURCE AUDITING

Human resource auditing is a systematic, formal process of gathering data across human resource functions (Gómez-Mejía, 1985; Rothwell & Kazanas, 1988). Much like a financial audit, a human resource audit is a diagnostic process for evaluating how well human resource functions, policies, and systems are performing. In this respect, the audit is a process of evaluating the effectiveness of the entire human resource system (Gómez-Mejía, Balkin, & Cardy, 1995; Phillips, 1996).

One can also think of the audit as a method for making sure that the human resource function is achieving its goals. One of the goals of a human resource audit is to identify the strengths and weaknesses within the HR system (Rothwell & Kazanas, 1988). Shortfalls and problem areas can be identified, and action can be taken for improvement. For example, an audit of recruitment activities might indicate that applicants from some recruitment sources do not have job-related qualifications. Audits can also provide information in areas such as absenteeism, turnover, accidents, and so on. An increase in the rate of turnover might be investigated by focusing on audit information from various functional areas in order to determine some possible causes.

Human resource audits are most useful when they involve all functional areas and track them over a period of time. In this way, it is possible to develop a more complete evaluation of the HRM system across time. This is important, since activities in the functional areas tend to be related and interconnected to one another, and changes in one area can have ramifications for other areas.

According to Phillips (1996), the use of human resource audits has been increasing. As a form of evaluation, they can be a very effective tool for assessing how well human resource functions are performing. The scope of human resource audits, as well as the type of information collected, has also been expanding.

Although the general idea of auditing is to assess how well human resource functions and systems are functioning, there are actually a number of different approaches for conducting a human resource audit. In effect, each of these approaches aims to evaluate HRM, but they differ in terms of the benchmark or criterion of effectiveness. For example, the **key indicators** approach focuses on objective and quantitative indicators of effectiveness, such as training hours per employee. The **multiple-constituency** approach focuses on the satisfaction of **stakeholders** or individuals that affect or are affected by human resource activities and functions. And the **strategic** approach focuses on the extent to which HRM practices and policies support the organization's corporate strategy and objectives (Gómez-Mejía et al., 1995).

In summary, the primary objective of the human resource audit is to evaluate the strengths and weaknesses of the human resource system and to develop and implement action plans to improve human resource policies, activities, programs, and functions. In particular, a human resource audit might serve any of the following objectives:

1. Comparative effectiveness of HRM relative to internal or external standards.
2. Compliance with employment laws and regulations.
3. Contribution of HRM to organizational goals and strategic objectives.
4. Stakeholder satisfaction with HRM products and services.
5. HRM contributions to organizational effectiveness.

Before discussing the different approaches for conducting an HRM audit, it is useful to first understand the auditing process.

◆◆◆
THE HRM AUDITING PROCESS

As indicated above, the HRM auditing process is a systematic and formal evaluation of an organization's human resource practices, programs, and policies (Rothwell & Kazanas, 1988). Like any systematic and formal process, HRM auditing consists of a number of sequential steps. Therefore, it is helpful to have a model or framework that can be used as a guide throughout the auditing process. Rothwell and Kazanas (1988) have developed just such a model, which is presented in Figure 13.1. Following is a review of the model as described by Rothwell and Kazanas (1988).

In the first step, the HRM auditor must determine which issues will be the focus of the audit, and how extensive it will be. In this respect, there are three general categories. First, the audit can be *comprehensive* and focus on the entire HRM system and its interactions with the organization. A comprehensive human resource audit is conducted to determine how well the entire system is functioning and achieving department and organization goals. Comprehensive audits are important for strategic planning because they deal with the entire human resource system. Second, an audit may be *programmatic* and focus on specific HRM areas such as recruitment, training, compensation, and so on. Programmatic audits are conducted to determine how well a particular functional area is operating and are useful for developing new policies and strategies in a particular HRM area.

Third, an HRM audit might be *restricted* and focus on single issues of concern such as turnover, absenteeism, accident rates, and so on. Thus, many organizations want to keep track of turnover and absenteeism rates to ensure that they are at

FIGURE 13.1 A Model of the HR Auditing Process

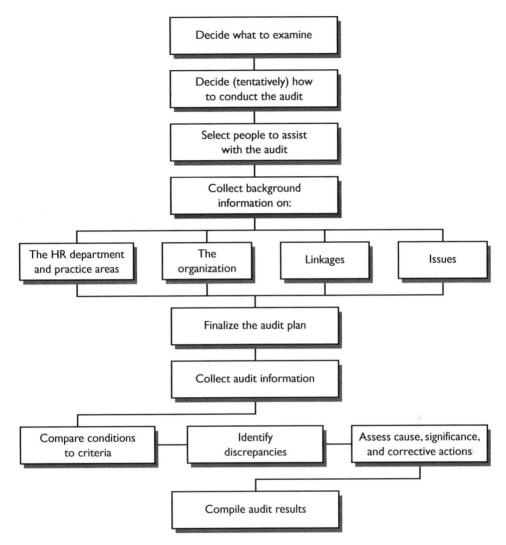

Source: Rothwell, W.J., & Kazanas, H.C. (1988). *Strategic human resources planning and management.* Englewood Cliffs, NJ: Prentice Hall.

acceptable levels. The results of this type of audit are useful for the development of programs and policies to improve problem areas such as turnover and absenteeism.

The auditor must also identify the basis upon which to determine strengths and weaknesses. For example, the auditor might want to compare the organization's

HRM programs with those in other organizations. This type of comparative analysis is generally known as benchmarking and will be discussed later in the chapter.

In some cases, an organization will hire an external consultant to conduct the audit, and he or she will determine problem areas and weaknesses and then provide recommendations for improvement based on his or her expertise. A restricted audit will usually focus on ratios/measures of things such as performance, turnover, absenteeism, and/or accident rates. In this way, the auditor can identify discrepancies between actual and desired levels of these variables.

A compliance analysis focuses on compliance with laws, rules, and regulations with respect to employment equity, health and safety, and pay equity. This type of audit is designed to ensure that an organization's human resource policies and practices are in keeping with government laws and regulations. The results of a compliance analysis should indicate areas in which human resource policies or programs are not in compliance with laws or regulations, as well as potential legal problems if some corrective action is not taken (Segal & Quinn, 1989).

A good example of a compliance analysis was recently conducted by Eastman Kodak Co. in response to concerns raised about pay inequity. The results of an internal audit indicated that some 2000 female and minority workers were underpaid. As a result, Kodak said it would pay about $10 million (U.S.) to adjust the inequities and give pay raises to the underpaid women and minority factory workers (Volpe, 1999).

Finally, the basis of the audit could be to identify the extent to which HRM practices and policies are meeting objectives. Thus, an auditor will want to compare any objectives with the current state of things and identify discrepancies. For example, some organizations guarantee their employees a specific number of hours of training each year. Therefore, an audit of the training function would include information on whether this objective is being met or if there is a discrepancy.

In the next step of the auditing process, plans have to be made regarding how to conduct the audit. This tentative audit plan is simply an informal description of what the audit will look at, the type of information that it will contain, and the resources required to conduct it. During this step, the auditor will want to obtain the information needed to make the type of comparisons discussed above. For example, what are the HRM practices in other organizations? What are the state-of-the-art practices in each area of HRM? What are the appropriate ratios/measures for things such as turnover and absenteeism? What are the government laws and regulations that impact HRM? What are the HRM department goals and objectives?

Audits are usually conducted by a team, so it is important that a team be selected to conduct the audit. The members of the team can include individuals in the HRM department, organizational members from other departments in the organization, or individuals from outside the organization. The key is that the team consist of members who have the knowledge and skills required to conduct an audit, such as knowledge about the organization, the HRM department, HRM practices, and methods of data collection and analyses.

In the next step, background information that will help guide the audit process must be gathered. For example, what is the purpose of the audit? Who are the interested parties? What do they expect to get out of the audit? An important part of this step is to be clear about who needs the information and what it will be used for. Thus, the audit team must be clear about the purpose of the audit, what information will be required, what issues need to be examined, and what is expected. As indicated in Figure 13.1, background information should be collected on the HR department and particular functional areas, linkages between the HRM department and the organization, and the specific issues of concern to the organization.

Before conducting the audit and collecting information, it is important to finalize the audit plan. Therefore, at this stage the tentative audit plan is finalized and becomes the guide for conducting the audit. Rothwell and Kazanas (1988) suggest that the audit plan contain the following information:

1. A list of the tasks to be performed.
2. The estimated time frames expressed as days, weeks, or months.
3. The tasks to be performed by each member of the team.
4. The time and resources required to conduct the audit.

The most important and time-consuming stage of the audit process is collecting the audit information. The audit team must collect the information required as stated in the audit plan. The nature of the data collected will depend on a number of factors. First, as indicated earlier, it will depend on the scope or extensiveness of the audit and whether it is to be comprehensive, programmatic, or restrictive. Second, it will also depend on the focus or basis of comparison, as explained earlier. Third, the audit itself can take the form of a number of different approaches, namely, the key indicators, multiple-constituency, or strategic approach. Each of these approaches will be described in the next section of this chapter.

The methods used to collect the information have already been discussed in this text. That is, a human resource audit may consist of interviews, surveys, observations, archival data, and of course existing literature, if the purpose is to make comparisons with state-of-the-art practice and theory. Interviews and surveys, however, are the most common and effective approaches (Phillips, 1996). One other method of particular importance, however, is the review of documents used for the administration of human resource policies and programs. This would include such things as an employee handbook, supervisor policy and procedure manuals, collective bargaining agreements, personnel records, employment equity targets and programs, job applications, performance appraisal forms, turnover statistics, and so on (Segal & Quinn, 1989).

Organizational members in different functional areas and different levels of the organization may be interviewed and surveyed about the strengths and weaknesses of HRM practices and programs. Interview and survey questions may be developed to focus on the general strengths and weaknesses of the HRM department, as well as the practices and programs of particular functional areas. Table 13.1 provides an example of an interview guide for assessing the strengths and weaknesses of an HRM department. Of course, as indicated, human resource documents and records are also an important source of information, especially for data pertaining to performance, absenteeism, turnover, accident rates, grievances, and so on. Once the information is collected, comparisons can be made, discrepancies noted, the reasons for such discrepancies identified, and corrective actions can then be planned and implemented.

In the final stage of the audit process, the audit team will usually prepare an oral and/or verbal report in which they present the results of the audit. The report should provide a summary of the strengths and weaknesses of the HR department, functional areas, programs, and practices; explain the discrepancies that were found in the aforementioned areas; and provide suggestions for corrective action in order to address the discrepancies.

TABLE 13.1   INTERVIEW GUIDE FOR ASSESSING THE STRENGTHS AND WEAKNESSES OF THE HR DEPARTMENT

1. In your opinion, what is the chief strength of the HR department in
   a. Contributing to achievement of organizational strategic plans?
   b. Contributing to the achievement of your department's objectives? Operations?
2. In your opinion, what is the chief weakness of the HR department in
   a. Contributing (or not contributing) to achievement of organizational strategic plans?
   b. Contributing (or not contributing) to achievement of your department's objectives? Operations?
3. What has the HR department been doing exceptionally well?
4. What should the HR department be doing that it is not doing at present?
5. What has the HR department been doing rather poorly?
6. What should the HR department *not* do that it has been doing?
7. In what ways do you feel that the HR department could contribute most effectively to achievement of organizational plans?
8. In what ways do you feel that programs of activities of the HR department impede achievement of organizational plans?

Source: Rothwell, W.J., & Kazanas, H.C. (1988). *Strategic human resources planning and management* (p. 116). Englewood Cliffs, NJ: Prentice Hall.

While the audit process is designed to evaluate the human resource system, it is important to realize that the results of the audit are highly dependent on the criteria for success. For example, while employees might be receiving the designated 40 hours of training per year, an outcome that would be regarded as satisfactory, employees and managers might perceive the training as ineffective and a waste of time and money. Therefore, it is important to understand that the strengths and weaknesses are relative to the criteria chosen for comparison. In this respect, it is necessary to consider the different approaches to conducting an HRM audit.

◆ ◆ ◆

HRM AUDIT APPROACHES

As indicated earlier, there are several different approaches to conducting an HRM audit. While the process for conducting the audit does not change, the type of information collected will largely depend on the HRM audit approach. In effect, this is driven by what the organization wishes to evaluate with respect to the HRM system and its functions. In this respect there are three approaches for conducting an HRM audit. These approaches differ in that the focus of evaluation is based on one of the following: (1) quantifiable indicators of HRM, (2) stakeholder or customer satisfaction with HRM, or (3) the strategic fit between organization objectives and HRM practice.

KEY INDICATORS APPROACH

The best-known and most common and established approach to HRM auditing is the **key indicators** approach (Gómez-Mejía et al., 1995; Phillips, 1996). This is a quantitative approach in which specific measures, or "key indicators," are used within each of the major topic areas of HRM.

For example, a key indicator of training is the number of hours of training employees receive per year; a key indicator of staffing is the ratio of acceptances to offers made. Key indicators are similar to the human resource outcome measures discussed in Chapter 10. At that time, several examples of recruitment outcomes were noted, such as the number and/or percentage of jobs filled, jobs filled in a timely fashion, jobs filled with above-average performers, and so on. These are, in effect, key indicators of the recruitment function.

This approach requires that key indicators of importance to the HRM department and organization be identified, and then measures of them developed (Gómez-Mejía et al., 1995). A comprehensive audit of an HRM department may include key indicators from any number of functional areas, including HR policies and procedures, recruitment, selection, training, planning, performance reviews, job analysis and design, compensation, benefits, health and safety, equal employment, labour relations, organizational development, employee assistance, and information systems (Rothwell & Kazanas, 1988; Segal & Quinn, 1989). Table 13.2 presents key indicators for different HRM functions.

TABLE 13.2 SELECTED KEY INDICATORS USED IN HR EVALUATION

Staffing

Average days taken to fill open requisitions

Ratio of applicants to requisitions per job family

Ratio of offers made to number of applicants

Ratio of acceptances in offers made

Ratio of minority/women applicants to representation in local labour market

Average days between application and formal response

Per capita recruitment costs

Average years of experience/education of hires per job family

Average test scores (where available) for hires

Equal Employment Opportunity

Ratio of EEO grievances to employee population

Ratio of EEO suits to employee population

Minority representation by EEO categories

Rejection rates of minorities by job categories

Minority turnover rate

Training

Percentage of employees participating in training programs per job family

Percentage of employees completing training programs per job family

Percentage of employees receiving tuition refunds

Training hours per employee

Training dollars per employee

Employee Appraisal and Development

Distribution of performance appraisal ratings

Reliability of appraisal ratings

Careers

Ratio of promotions to number of employees

Percentage promoted by demographic category

Ratio of open requisitions filled internally to those filled externally

Percentage of employees transferred between divisions and/or geographically

Average years/months between promotions

Wage and Salary Administration

Ratio of payroll problems to number of employees

Ratio of "equal pay" complaints to number of employees

Per capita (average) merit increases

Ratio of recommendations for reclassification to number of employees

TABLE 13.2 SELECTED KEY INDICATORS USED IN HR EVALUATION (continued)

Ratio of exit interviewees citing pay as a reason for termination to number of employees

Average merit increase per performance level

Ratio of protected classes' wages to non-protected classes' wages

Percentage of overtime hours in straight time

Ratio of average salary offers to average salary in community

Ratio of average salary to midpoint by grade level

Benefits

Average unemployment compensation payment (UCP)

Average workers' compensation payment (WCP)

Benefit cost per payroll $

Percentage of sick leave to total pay

Average annual premium for unemployment and workers' compensation insurance

Cost of employee benefits as a percentage of hourly base rates

Average length of time taken to process claims

Work Environment / Safety

Frequency/severity ratio of accidents

Safety-related expenses per $1000 of payroll

Plant security losses per square foot (fires, burglaries, etc.)

Ratio of OSHA citations to number of employees

Labour Relations

Ratio of concerted activities to number of employees

Ratio of grievances by pay plan to number of employees

Frequency and duration of work stoppages

Percentage of grievances settled

Average length of time to settle grievances

Overall Effectiveness

Ratio of personnel staff to employee population

Turnover rate

Absenteeism rate

Ratio of per capita revenue to per capita cost

Net income per employee

Source: Tsui, A., Gómez-Mejía, L.R. (1988). Evaluating human resource effectiveness. In L. Dyer (Ed.), *Human resource management: Evolving roles and responsibilities.* Washington, DC: Bureau of National Affairs.

In one of the first attempts to identify the major dimensions to include in an HRM audit and their relation to organizational outcomes, Gómez-Mejía (1985) designed a survey with 37 audit indicators, as well as measures of employee attitudes and executive perceptions of effectiveness. The survey was distributed to employees and senior executives of a large electronics manufacturing organization. Analysis of the 37 items resulted in nine audit dimensions: manpower flows; staffing; compensation and rewards; managerial behaviour; labour relations; health and safety; career training and development; performance appraisal; and policies and procedures. Furthermore, the nine dimensions were significantly related to a number of outcome measures, including executives' judgments of organizational performance, employees' satisfaction with human resource services, and profitability. For example, staffing, compensation, and rewards were most predictive of employee satisfaction with the human resource department. Gómez-Mejía (1985) suggests that these findings support the use of audits for diagnosing and improving the performance of human resource functions. Furthermore, the audit can be used not only for diagnostic and evaluative purposes, but also for identifying those activities that have the greatest impact on employee and management perceptions.

The major strength of the key indicators approach is that it provides objective and quantifiable data. Therefore, it enables comparisons, across time, with HRM goals and industry averages. As a result, it is possible to evaluate HRM functions against any comparative criteria and to identify strengths and weaknesses and areas that require corrective action. The major disadvantage of the key indicators approach is that the data are in and of themselves just numbers. That is, they don't say very much about the reasons or causes for problems but only the symptoms (Gómez-Mejía et al., 1995.).

For example, the key indicators approach might indicate that the ratio of job acceptances to job offers is very low. However, it would not indicate why this was the case. As a result, the key indicators approach requires a great deal of interpretation in order to understand the results. It is also likely that more in-depth research will be required to better understand the results of the key indicators approach. For instance, if the results indicate an increase in turnover rates, exit interviews or an attitude survey will be required to better understand the reasons for the increase. While the key indicators approach might provide some clues (e.g., average test scores of new hires are low), it would be difficult to know for sure what the reasons are without further research. Nonetheless, it does serve to provide a picture of the strengths and weaknesses of the HRM system and functions relative to whatever comparative criteria are of concern.

MULTIPLE-CONSTITUENCY APPROACH

Some years ago, Friedlander and Pickle (1968) conducted a study of organizational effectiveness in which specific measures taken from stockholders, workers, managers, suppliers, and customers were found to be only moderately related to one another. They pointed out that perceptions of effectiveness may reflect one's vantage point. More recently, this observation has been developed into a fairly cogent framework for conceptualizing effectiveness (Connolly, Conlon, & Deutsch, 1980; Zammuto, 1984).

Zammuto (1984) argues that we should think of organizations as entities that come into existence and are maintained in order to satisfy the needs and views of diverse groups of people. What happens in organizational life, then, is the result of the intersection of the decisions, actions, and behaviours of the various constituencies involved. Whether an organization is effective will depend on who wants what and how important it is that a demand be satisfied.

The measurement of effectiveness in a multiple-constituency framework requires that the investigator establish the stakeholders in an organization. These are the individuals and groups whose viability is affected by organizational actions or decisions. Establishing the stakeholders might be done through analysis or field interviews. Some typical stakeholders include the following:

1. The owners of the business (private company).
2. The stockholders/shareholders (public company).
3. Workers.
4. Unions.
5. Managers.
6. Customers/clients.
7. Suppliers.
8. The people and officials in the community (especially small communities).
9. Appropriate government officials (in the case of large corporations).

Anne Tsui has done a considerable amount of research in developing a multiple-constituency approach in human resources. Tsui and Milkovich (1987) were among the first to use the multiple-constituency approach to analyze the tasks and activities of HR departments. According to Tsui (1987), **constituencies** refer to those parties, customers, or clients who depend on the HR department and have a stake in its activities. These include groups at the operating level, such as managers and employees who are involved in the design and delivery of products or services, as well as those at the business/corporate or strategic level, such as executives and senior management. The basic premise of the multiple-constituency approach is a marketing concept in which "an important criterion for effectiveness is the extent to which the constituencies' needs and expectations are satisfied by the Human Resource department" (Tsui, 1987). Furthermore,

> *According to the multiple constituency approach, effectiveness is defined as the extent to which the department meets constituency expectations. Since constituency expectations may vary, their opin-*

ions regarding a department's effectiveness may also diverge if the department is not able to satisfy different expectations simultaneously. (Tsui & Milkovich, 1987, p. 535)

Tsui (1987) conducted a series of studies to identify the activities and criteria considered to be of importance to the multiple constituencies, and to compare the different constituencies on these dimensions. Information was obtained from members representing eight constituencies. First, Tsui (1987) found that there were seventeen activities that were considered to be most important. They included routine administrative services such as benefit enrollment, as well as consultative activities such as providing advice to management on staffing strategies. Table 13.3 presents the seventeen most important activities.

Second, Tsui (1987) identified twelve criteria that were considered to be the most important for evaluating the effectiveness of the HR department. These included subjective criteria such as employees' trust and confidence in the HR department, as well as objective criteria such as the average time taken to fill requisitions. Most of the criteria relate to how well the HR department responds to stakeholders' needs in terms of service quality and quickness. Table 13.4 presents the twelve most meaningful criteria for evaluating the effectiveness of the HR department.

Third, based on the perspectives of managers and nonmanagement employees, Tsui (1987) identified the most important dimensions of human resource activities. Respondents were asked to indicate how important it is that each activity listed be performed by the human resource department. The results indicated that the following eight dimensions were considered to be the most important:

1. Staffing/Human Resource Planning.
2. Organization/Employee Development.
3. Compensation/Employee Relations.
4. Employee Support.
5. Legal Requirements/Compliance.
6. Labour/Union Relations.
7. Policy Adherence.
8. Administrative Services.

Administrative services and compensation/employee relations activities were rated as the most important activities, and labour/union relations as the least important.

Fourth, Tsui (1987) identified the criteria for evaluating the effectiveness of human resource departments that the constituencies considered to be most meaningful. Respondents were asked to indicate how meaningful it is that the human

TABLE 13.3 THE SEVENTEEN MOST IMPORTANT HUMAN RESOURCE DEPARTMENT ACTIVITIES

1. Provide advice and counsel to management on individual employee problem identification and solution (e.g., deal with adverse or difficult personnel situations such as absenteeism).
2. Communicate to management the philosophy, legal implications, and strategy relating to employee relations.
3. Provide advice and counsel to management on employee relations problems.
4. Ensure consistent and equitable treatment of all employees.
5. Administer grievance procedure according to policy (e.g., identify and analyze problems, review deviations and exceptions, resolve problems).
6. Provide advice and counsel to management on staffing policy and related problems.
7. Coordinate the hiring procedure (e.g., establish starting salaries, send offer letters, follow up to obtain acceptance, administer medical questionnaires).
8. Communicate compensation/benefits programs to management (e.g., interpret/explain compensation policies and procedures, inform management of legal implications of compensation practices).
9. Process enrollments and communicate benefits program to employees.
10. Resolve benefits administration problems.
11. Process benefits claims (e.g., health, worker's compensation, pension, unusual or unique claims).
12. Assist management in resolving salary problems involving individual employees (e.g., salary equity issues).
13. Maintain employee and organization files (e.g., keep files orderly and systematic).
14. Ensure compliance with Federal and State Fair Employment Practices.
15. Communicate sexual harassment policy and other communications of general EEO philosophy and objectives.
16. Consult with management on the practical implications of corporate human resources programs.
17. Keep up with HR programs developed at the corporate or central personnel departments.

Source: Tsui, A.S. (1987). Defining the activities and effectiveness of the human resource department: A multiple constituency approach. *Human Resource Management (26)*, 41. Reprinted by permission of John Wiley & Sons, Inc.

resource department be evaluated on each of the criteria listed. The following five dimensions were identified:

1. Responsiveness to constituent needs.
2. Managing cost and negative performance.

> ### TABLE 13.4 TWELVE MOST MEANINGFUL CRITERIA FOR EVALUATING THE EFFECTIVENESS OF THE HUMAN RESOURCE DEPARTMENT
>
> **Subjective criteria:**
> 1. Level of cooperation from personnel department
> 2. Line managers' opinion of personnel department effectiveness
> 3. Degree to which the department is open and available to all employees to deal with problems or explain company policies
> 4. Employees' trust and confidence in the personnel department
> 5. Quickness and effectiveness of responses to each question brought to the personnel department
> 6. Rating of quality of service provided by the personnel department to other departments
> 7. Rating of quality of information and advice provided to top management
> 8. Satisfaction and dissatisfaction of clients—managers and employees
>
> **Objective criteria:**
> 9. Degree to which the department has a strategy to support local management business plans in relation to human resources
> 10. Affirmative action goal attainment
> 11. Average time taken to fill requisitions
> 12. Efficiency—personnel department budget / population served
>
> Source: Tsui, A.S. (1987). Defining the activities and effectiveness of the human resource department: A multiple constituency approach. *Human Resource Management (26)*, 42. Reprinted by permission of John Wiley & Sons, Inc.

3. Proactivity and innovativeness.

4. Training and development.

5. Affirmative action accomplishments.

The results indicated that both managers and employees considered responsiveness to client needs and proactivity and innovativeness to be the most important criteria for evaluating the effectiveness of the HR department.

Finally, Tsui (1987) compared the responses of the different constituencies on the activities and criteria and found some important differences. For example, employees rated organization/employee development and employee support activities as more important than managers. Overall, however, the ratings of activities and criteria by managers and employees were very similar. More substantial differences were found between the operating level and those at the corporate or strategic level. For example, constituencies at the operating level have a strong preference for administrative services and employee support activities. Corporate level constituencies place more importance on strategic activities that have implications for the entire organization. While there were some differences in ratings of effectiveness criteria, developing a positive company image among employees was most important for all constituencies.

Thus, it appears that an important issue that arises in the multiple-constituency approach is the existence of incompatibility and conflict in the expectations that are held by the multiple constituencies. This raises a number of important questions regarding which constituencies are most important, and which should be the focus of an HRM audit. These are difficult issues to resolve. However, it seems that there are really two broad concerns that can be addressed by the HRM audit and the HR department. As noted by Tsui (1987), the multiple-constituency approach is most useful at the operating level of the organization, since it is at this level that the HR department provides services for employees and managers. However, for those at the corporate or strategic level, where the concern rests primarily on strategic planning and development activities, a more strategic approach to HRM auditing may be undertaken, as discussed in the next section.

Finally, the results of the multiple-constituency approach to HRM auditing can have important practical implications for HRM practice. By conducting a multiple-constituency audit, the HRM department is able to diagnose how effectively it is meeting the needs and expectations of its most important constituencies. Besides learning how to understand and manage the conflicting demands that might exist (Tsui & Milkovich, 1987), the HRM department can take corrective action in order to better fulfill the needs and expectations of its constituencies.

Rosik (1991) has described how the HRM department can become more customer-oriented through both research and action by understanding and responding to customers' needs. The first step involves preparing for and conducting a multiple-constituency audit, and involves the following steps:

1. Create a customer list of all individuals considered to be important customers of the HRM department (i.e., multiple constituencies).

2. Classify each listed individual in terms of position level and function.

3. List the services and activities offered by the HRM department.

4. Design a questionnaire to assess customers' perceptions of the importance of each service/activity to their business goals and their satisfaction with each service/activity. In addition, the questionnaire should inquire about new services desired by customers, current services no longer needed, and the two or three most important services the HRM department can provide to help customers achieve their business goals.

5. Print and distribute the questionnaire.

The second stage involves analyzing the survey results and developing plans for responding to the results through follow-up actions to better meet customers' needs. This involves the following steps:

1. Establish customer segments based on customers' service and product needs.

2. Outline possible activity changes for each group based on what is most important to the group and those services considered to be a priority.

3. Review the results with customers in each group to reach agreement on conclusions and to discuss potential actions for improvement.

4. Incorporate customers' ideas into planned actions for improvement.

5. Communicate progress and results to inform customers of the HR department's efforts to meet their needs and business goals.

6. Develop follow-through processes to measure and evaluate progress and make any necessary changes and/or modifications. This might, at some point, involve administering the customer survey again to measure overall progress.

Thus, Rosik's (1991) approach effectively combines the audit process with HRM actions and initiatives for improvement. An important part of this process is the development of a partnership between the HRM department and its customers, and regular communication with customers to maintain a high level of customer awareness of HRM efforts to meet and support customers' needs and goals. This approach is based on a customer-oriented HRM department in which the HRM department helps customers achieve their business goals through the use of HRM products and services. Therefore, the audit serves as a key tool for identifying how well the HRM department is meeting customers' needs, and for determining what actions and activities can be undertaken to improve customer satisfaction.

The importance of this approach to HRM auditing for research evaluation and practice can be seen in the dramatic turnaround of Continental Airlines. In 1994, Continental Airlines was one of the least-respected airlines, according to the company's vice president of corporate communications (Flynn, 1997). Employee job satisfaction and morale were extremely low, customer satisfaction was low, the company was rated at the bottom among major carriers in on-time performance, complaints in baggage handling were common, and a survey of 3000 employees ranked human resource services in the bottom 50th percentile. A new management team implemented a number of programs, including employee involvement, incentive plans, and new channels of communication.

Furthermore, as part of the revamping of the company, and in response to the low ratings of the HR department's service, the HR department was completely restructured, and members of the department were given new assignments. Another major change was the decentralization of HR, which had previously been centralized.

As a result, HR skills were placed in areas in which they were needed most, and employees now had greater access to HR services. HR executives also redesigned the training and development program for front-line managers, based on a number of areas of core competencies. In 1994, when 48 training courses were offered, attendance was as low as 200 people. By 1996, after the courses had been trimmed down to seven in the core competencies areas, attendance was as high as 5000 (Flynn, 1997).

Since the changes in 1995, Continental has been ranked as the number one major airline in customer satisfaction for flights of 500 miles or more, and has also reported its most profitable years in the airline's 63-year history. Employee morale and job satisfaction have also increased, and the HR department received standard or above reviews in 18 out of 20 human resource areas in a recent employee survey. Thus, the auditing of human resources resulted in major changes to the HR department and an improvement of services.

Finally, for an example of how an audit of customer service satisfaction can be used to improve a particular area of human resources, see the HR Research Today box below on assessing and improving managers' satisfaction with staffing services.

STRATEGIC HRM APPROACH

The **strategic approach** to HRM auditing focuses primarily on the extent to which the HRM system and each functional area are supportive of and consistent with the strategy of HRM and the organization. As well, a strategic focus is also concerned with how the various functional areas of HRM are consistent and compatible with one another (Gómez-Mejía et al., 1995; Rothwell & Kazanas, 1988).

Clearly, this is an increasingly important area of HRM auditing and evaluation, although it is also probably the least used of the three approaches (Gómez-Mejía et al., 1995). However, this is likely to change. Recall from Chapter 1 that the role of the human resource function in organizations is becoming increasingly more strategic, and human resource professionals in many organizations are involved in the strategic planning process. This involves the development and implementation of human resource practices and policies that will help the organization achieve its goals and objectives by supporting and reinforcing its business strategy. A strategic human resources approach also requires that human resource practices be consistent with one another and carefully aligned with the organization's corporate goals (Gómez-Mejía et al., 1995).

Therefore, strategic audits will become an increasingly important method of HRM evaluation. This will require knowledge of an organization's major strategic objectives and their implications for HRM strategy and specific HRM functions. For example, most business strategies will have implications for recruitment, selection, socialization, training, compensation and rewards, and performance appraisal.

HR RESEARCH TODAY

Assessing and Improving Managers' Satisfaction with Staffing Services

HRM systems are not always customer-focused. In fact, survey data in the public sector indicate generally low opinions of the HRM function's overall service delivery and effectiveness, particularly in the area of staffing services. Heneman, Huett, Lavigna, and Ogsten (1995) designed a survey to assess managers' satisfaction with staffing services delivered to them by the State of Wisconsin's Department of Employment Relations. Focus groups of line and HR managers were used to gather data to identify and define the relevant content for a tailor-made Staffing Service Delivery Satisfaction Survey. The results of the focus groups were used to develop a survey containing 53 items grouped into the following five dimensions of staffing-service delivery:

1. *Communication*—How well are you kept informed of the staffing process? "Staffing process" includes recruitment, examination, and selection.
2. *Timeliness*—How do you feel about the speed of recruitment, examination, and selection services?
3. *Candidate quality*—How do you feel about the quality of the job candidates on employment lists? "Quality" means the extent to which the candidates possess the required knowledge and skills for the job.
4. *Test quality*—How do you feel about the quality of the civil service exams (e.g., paper-and-pencil tests, work samples, oral boards, etc.)?
5. *Service focus*—To what extent do you believe that your personnel/staffing representatives are committed to providing high-quality service?

The survey was then distributed by e-mail to line managers and managers in the HR function. They were asked to respond to each item using a scale where 1 = very dissatisfied and 5 = very satisfied. Analysis of the survey results indicated support for the five dimensions and reasonable levels of reliability. As well, line managers were significantly less satisfied than HR managers with all five dimensions of staffing service. This finding demonstrates the importance of the need to assess the satisfaction of the service users and not just the service providers.

The survey results were fed back to HR managers, who were then responsible for communicating the results in their agencies. The results were then used as input for deciding on changes and improvements in staffing-services. For example, a new training program and an electronic job vacancy information system were developed to improve communication. In addition, special recruitment/selection programs have been developed for entry-level professionals and for critical vacancy positions that are hard to fill in order to improve timeliness and candidate quality. These programs have reduced the average time to produce a list of qualified candidates from 70 to under 40 days. These programs also help managers to attract a more qualified pool of initial applicants and to provide more timely job offers to qualified job applicants. Finally, a walk-in candidate testing program was developed in order to improve timeliness and candidate quality for positions that require written tests. The program eliminated advance application to take tests and reduced the average time needed to produce a list of qualified applicants by 35 days.

The results of this study demonstrate how customer service satisfaction surveys can be tailor-made to particular HRM areas, and how the results can be used as input in the development and implementation of new programs to improve HRM service. In this study, new programs to improve staffing service delivery resulted in an increase in the speed of service delivery, elimination of paperwork, higher applicant quality, and positive applicant reactions.

Source: Based on Heneman, H.G., III, Huett, D.L., Lavigna, R.J., & Ogsten, D. (1995). Assessing managers' satisfaction with staffing services. *Personnel Psychology, 48,* 163–172.

Therefore, an HRM strategy should ensure that these activities are driven by and supportive of the organization's strategic objectives.

A worksheet can be used to provide a clear picture of an organization's strategies and how HRM practices support them. Gómez-Mejía et al. (1995) suggest a number of steps to follow when performing a strategic audit that one can use as a guide in setting up an HRM strategic audit worksheet:

1. Identify the organization's major strategies, goals, and objectives.

2. Determine HRM policies, procedures, programs, and activities within each functional area that will be required to support the organization's major strategies, goals, and objectives.

3. Identify the organization's current HRM policies, procedures, programs, and activities within each of the functional areas, and compare them with those indicated in the previous step.

4. Modify, design, and implement HRM policies, procedures, programs, and activities within each functional area as indicated in step 2, consistent with the organization's overall business strategies.

As an example, consider an organization that has developed a strategy of superior customer service and satisfaction. How will this strategy impact each of the major HRM functions? First, it will require recruitment and selection programs that produce an applicant pool and new hires who have good interpersonal and communication skills required for superior customer service. Second, socialization and training programs will be required to socialize new hires into the organization's service culture and to train them in the behaviours required to provide superior customer service. At Starbucks, for example, the company imprints its obsession with customer service during orientation, at which time employees learn about the company's mission statement and do customer service role-plays, and then attend a rigorous training program that includes sessions on "retail skills," "coffee knowledge," and "customer service" (Gruner, 1998; Reese, 1996).

Third, performance reviews will need to be designed in order to evaluate customer service behaviour and performance, and reward and incentive programs will need to be designed to recognize and reward superior customer service performance. As you can see, failure to align HRM practices with the organization's strategy of superior customer service will limit the organization's success in achieving its goals and objectives.

There are a number of other approaches to conducting a strategic HRM audit. For example, notice that the interview guide in Table 13.1 includes several questions that assess how an HRM department contributes to an organization's strategic plans. As well, recall from Chapter 3 that employee attitude surveys can be used to measure the strategic objectives of an organization (Schneider, Ashworth, Higgs, & Carr, 1996). The survey asks employees questions about organization practices and policies in terms of the organization's strategic goals. While the purpose of the survey is to find out the extent to which an organization is carrying out its strategic objectives, it might be used to measure the extent to which HRM practices support and reinforce strategic objectives.

The major disadvantage of the strategic HRM audit is that it is somewhat subjective in that those who are involved in the audit are required to judge the extent to which HRM policies and practices are consistent with the organization's strategic objectives (Gómez-Mejía et al., 1995). Therefore, it is important that members of the organization who are familiar with and knowledgeable of the organization's strategic planning and human resource strategy be involved in the process.

COMBINED APPROACHES

Although each of the approaches to HR auditing is distinct, it is important to realize that there is a certain amount of overlap between them, and in many cases an HR audit includes aspects of each of the approaches. For example, you might have noticed that a number of questions in Table 13.1 ask about the HR department's contribution to strategic plans. As well, the research conducted by Gómez-Mejía (1985) on audit dimensions consisted of items that are key indicators (e.g., average selection ratios) and customer satisfaction items (e.g., satisfaction with training/development). In addition, the multiple-constituency approach often includes items that measure the contribution of the HR department to organization goals and objectives.

Another example of the overlap between the three approaches is a framework developed by Monica Belcourt on the five ways (the 5 Cs) in which HR practices can make a difference for organizations (Belcourt, 1996/97):

1. *Compliance*—Ensuring that organizational practices are in compliance with employment laws and regulations, such as health and safety, employment equity, and pay equity.

2. *Client Satisfaction*—Improving customer satisfaction with the HR department.

3. *Culture Management*—Developing a culture that fosters desired behaviours and improves levels of performance.

4. *Cost Controls*—Reducing employee costs in areas such as turnover, absenteeism, and occupational injuries and illness.

5. *Contribution*—Demonstrating the impact of HR practices on employee and organizational performance.

Therefore, on the basis of this model, an HR audit would focus on the 5 Cs and, in the process, develop action plans to strengthen each of them. While each of the 5 Cs includes numerous measures, in combination they take into account the key measures of the three major approaches to HR auditing.

◆◆◆
HRM BENCHMARKING

Benchmarking involves comparing an organization's HRM practices and services to the best practices provided by other organizations (Gómez-Mejía et al., 1995; Phillips, 1996). The intent is to improve an organization's HRM practices and services by adopting the best practices of other organizations. Benchmarking practices were first used as part of the quality movement, and have recently begun to be used to evaluate HRM practices (Phillips, 1996). An increasing number of organizations are benchmarking their HRM practices in response to global competition and other external and internal pressures (Glanz & Dailey, 1992).

Benchmarking HRM practices serves a number of important purposes. First, organizations can gauge their own practices against those in excellent organizations and get an idea of how they compare and how well they are doing. Second, benchmarking enables organizations to learn from other organizations about effective HRM practices and services. Third, benchmarking can help create and initiate the need for change because it identifies what an organization needs to do to improve relative to how excellent companies deliver HRM practices. Fourth, organizations that benchmark the best practices of other organizations can adopt those practices and potentially improve the success of their organization. Fifth, the benchmarking process allows organizations to identify which HRM practices used by other organizations have the greatest value-added and are therefore worth adopting. Finally, benchmarking HRM practices enables organizations to monitor and track performance and improvements over time through the systematic identification and implementation of best practices (Glanz & Dailey, 1992; Ulrich, Brockbank, and Yeung, 1989).

As indicated earlier in this chapter, benchmarking can be considered a special case of HRM auditing. For the most part, benchmarking involves the comparison of HRM activities, processes, and outcomes with those in other organizations, particularly those known for their "best practices." Thus, it is really a more extensive form of auditing, because it includes numerous organizations. While there is some similarity in the auditing and benchmarking processes, because the focus of benchmarking is on best practices and involves the participation of a number of partner organizations, there are some important differences between the benchmarking and audit processes, as discussed next.

THE BENCHMARKING PROCESS

Phillips (1996) has provided a detailed description of benchmarking for HRM evaluation purposes. According to Phillips (1996), benchmarking is a logical and systematic process that consists of seven key phases. Following is a brief overview of the seven phases of the benchmarking process based on Phillips's (1996) description:

1. *Determine what to benchmark.* The first step involves identifying exactly what the organization wants to benchmark. For example, an organization might want to benchmark product or service features, work processes, particular HRM functions, HRM performance measures, or HRM strategies and goals. Factors that are chosen for benchmarking should be those considered most important and critical for an organization's success and overall effectiveness. Once this is done, it is possible to identify the items to measure across organizations.

   Many of the items will be similar to those used in the key indicators audit such as training cost, cost per hire, training hours, turnover percentage, trainee hours, offer-to-acceptance ratio, and so on (Phillips, 1996). However, benchmarking may also include HRM outcomes or broad productivity measures such as defections per employee; HRM practices such as selection methods or compensation systems; stakeholder expectations; or competencies of HRM professionals (Glanz & Dailey, 1992). Glanz and Dailey (1992) discuss how Digital Equipment Corporation benchmarked HR outcomes and how United Technologies Corporation used internal customers' perceptions of HR services as a benchmark. United Technologies designed a customer service survey (see Table 13.5) to find out how internal customers and HR professionals perceived HR performance.

2. *Build a benchmarking team.* Because of the amount of work required to conduct a benchmarking evaluation, it is best to use a team approach. Teams may be composed of individuals from different HRM functions, line managers, or individuals

who volunteer to participate in the benchmarking process. The team should have a leader who is a champion of the benchmarking process and will take responsibility for the effective implementation and management of the project.

3. *Identify benchmark partners*. Partners must be identified for participation in the benchmarking process. Benchmark partners should be those with "best practices," and may include internal units, competitors, noncompetitors in the same industry, organizations in the same geographic location, organizations in the same country, or international organizations. Once potential partners have been identified, they need to be contacted and asked to participate in the benchmarking process. It is also important during this phase to define what is meant by "best practices," since it can mean a number of different things.

4. *Collect benchmarking data*. Once organizations have indicated their willingness to participate in the benchmarking process, data need to be collected from each of the benchmarking partners. Benchmarking data are most often obtained through telephone interviews, personal meetings during a site visit, questionnaires, and/or public documents. Phillips (1996) recommends that a combination of approaches be used and consideration be given to the quality of information, cost of data collection methods, time considerations of survey respondents, and intended use of the information in choosing a method(s).

   Digital Equipment Corporation used public information as well as visits to companies with excellent HR practices. Some of the companies they visited included Federal Express, Hewlett Packard, 3M, General Electric, Motorola, and Xerox (Glanz & Dailey, 1992).

5. *Analyse the data*. Once the data have been collected, it must be analyzed and interpreted. According to Phillips (1996), this is most often done with the use of a spreadsheet on which the partner organizations are listed on the left side, and the headings representing the type of data are listed across the top. It is also useful to calculate averages and percentages and to look for trends in the data. The data analysis at Digital Equipment Corporation involved the identification of major themes and underlying principles for effective HR practice (Glanz & Dailey, 1992).

6. *Distribute the information to benchmarking partners*. Following the analysis of the data, a report that describes the benchmarking project and the major findings should be prepared and distributed to all of the benchmarking partners.

7. *Initiate improvement and action plans*. The final phase of the benchmarking process involves the development of action plans to improve HRM programs and practices. This involves calculating performance gaps or deviations between the way things are and the desired or best practice. Performance gaps for every benchmarked item should be identified. Action plans are then developed to

TABLE 13.5 UNITED TECHNOLOGIES HUMAN RESOURCES PRACTICES SURVEY

In this short questionnaire, you will be asked to comment on the human resource organizations which have served your area of immediate business responsibility. Your responses will be more valuable if they reflect your assessment of human resources as a total organization, not the senior human resources executive. Some questions will be easier to answer than others because of your degree of exposure to the human resources unit. However, please answer all of the questions, giving your perception or best judgment if necessary.

Always	Usually	Sometimes	Rarely
1	2	3	4

To what extent does the Human Resource organization ...

Score

_____ 1. Understand where the business is headed and what management is trying to accomplish.

_____ 2. Stand up for the human resource perspective on business issues.

_____ 3. Staff the HR organization with competent professionals.

_____ 4. Participate actively in the business planning process.

_____ 5. Take appropriate risks.

_____ 6. Respond in a timely manner.

_____ 7. Develop human resource objectives in the context of business priorities.

_____ 8. Do its homework.

_____ 9. Provide competent advice and support.

_____ 10. Explore alternative solutions to problems.

_____ 11. Find ways to balance its functional interests with other needs of the business.

_____ 12. React quickly to changes in the needs of the business.

_____ 13. Anticipate business problems.

_____ 14. Help more than hinder the organization in attaining its business objectives.

_____ 15. Have people seek its advice.

_____ 16. Set high standards for evaluating its own effectiveness.

_____ 17. Bring a competitive global perspective to the HR function.

_____ 18. Design solutions to business problems that meet the needs of the business.

Source: Glanz, E.F., & Dailey, L.K. (1992). Benchmarking. *Human Resource Management* (*31*), 19. Reprinted by permission of John Wiley & Sons, Inc.

address the performance gaps and to implement the best practices in each area in which a performance gap has been identified. A report should then be prepared for members of the organization, indicating the benchmarking process, the major findings, performance gaps, and action plans.

United Technologies identified performance gaps by comparing managers' and HR professionals' perceptions of HR performance. This was followed by a conference of the organization's HR professionals from around the world and some line managers who completed the survey. The result was the development of action plans for improvement and plans for the HR professionals to become strategic partners. At Digital Equipment Corporation, action plans and measures to monitor progress were developed, based on the major themes and principles identified in the data analysis. The benchmarking process is now institutionalized, and the company participates in ongoing benchmarking activities as part of a process of continuous improvement (Glanz & Dailey, 1992).

In sum, the benchmarking process enables organizations to compare their HRM practices with the best practices in other organizations. Once performance gaps are identified, action plans for improvement can be developed, and best practices implemented as part of a process of continuous evaluation and improvement. Thus, benchmarking can be used as an effective tool for evaluating an organization's HRM practices, for setting new standards, and for constantly improving HRM programs and practices that can impact an organization's financial performance. As noted by Phillips (1996), benchmarking should be part of a continuous, long-term process of improvement, and an integral part of HRM evaluation. For a more a detailed discussion of the phases of the benchmarking process, the reader should refer to Phillips (1996).

◆◆◆
HRM BEST PRACTICES

One of the most important issues in HRM benchmarking is identifying or defining what constitutes "best practices." This affects not only the content and items of the benchmarking instrument as well as the action plans for improvement, but also the ability to establish a common model or framework that will allow comparisons across organizations (Ulrich et al., 1989).

Ulrich et al. (1989) conducted a study in which they presented and tested a model for benchmarking human resource practices. The model consisted of six domains of HRM practices that can be used by organizations to accomplish three major purposes. Each purpose is accomplished by two HRM practices. The first purpose, "generating competencies," has to do with ensuring that employees have the knowledge, skills, and abilities to help the organization achieve its goals and objectives. This can be accomplished through HRM practices of staffing and development. The second purpose, "reinforcing competencies," involves improving and strengthening employee skills through performance appraisals and rewards. The third purpose is "sustaining competencies," which involves the institutionalization of the competencies through organization design and communication.

Ulrich et al. (1989) suggested that by setting benchmarks for these six HRM practices it would be possible for organizations to compare their HRM practices with national norms. Therefore, they developed measures for each of the practices, and asked HRM professionals in 91 organizations to indicate the extent to which their organization focused resources (i.e., time and money) on each of the HRM practices.

Their results indicated that more attention was given to generating competencies (i.e. staffing and development) and sustaining competencies (i.e., performance appraisal and rewards) than reinforcing them (i.e., organization design and communication). They also found differences in the attention paid to HRM practices in terms of industry, function, organizational role, and level in the organization. The fact that HRM practices vary by industry has important implications for the design and implementation of HRM practices. As noted by Ulrich et al. (1989), "to design HR practices without understanding the industry conditions and criteria would result in companies implementing HR practices appropriate in one setting, but not in another." (pp. 331–332). They concluded that these results provide a useful benchmark that also can be used as standards for the design and delivery of HRM practices.

Since Ulrich et al. (1989) conducted their study, a number of other studies have presented what are considered to be HRM best practices. In fact, a number of these studies were discussed in Chapter 10 on the topic of human resource systems. For example, Huselid's (1995) study of high-performance human resource work practices resulted in a dimension of employee skills and organizational structures, and employee motivation. Youndt, Snell, Dean, and Lepak (1996) focused on staffing, training, performance appraisal, and compensation, and combined them into two indices they labelled the "administrative HR system" and the "human-capital-enhancing HR system."

In his book, *Competitive Advantage through People*, Jeffrey Pfeffer (1994) argues that the main factor that differentiates organizations today is their work force. The most successful organizations are those that effectively manage their employees. According to Pfeffer (1994), sustained competitive advantage and organizational effectiveness are increasingly related to the management of human resources. Based on a review of the popular and academic literature, Pfeffer (1994) identified the following sixteen practices that characterize effective companies that have achieved competitive success through the management of their human resources:

1. *Employment security.* The successful companies provide their work force with employment security. This signals the organization's long-term commitment to the work force.

2. *Selectivity in recruiting.* They use a rigorous selection process and extensive screening in order to hire the best employees.

3. *High wages.* They pay their employees wages that are above average. This enables them to attract and retain the best people, and sends the message that employees are valued.

4. *Incentive pay.* They reward individual and/or team performance with contingent compensation. Incentive programs, such as profit sharing, are positively related to productivity.

5. *Employee ownership.* Employees have ownership interests in the organization. This aligns employees' goals with those of the organization and its shareholders.

6. *Information sharing.* They share important information with employees so that employees have the information that they need to be successful.

7. *Participation and empowerment.* Lower-level employees are given autonomy and control over their own work processes. Participation increases employee satisfaction and productivity.

8. *Teams and job redesign.* They make use of team work arrangements rather than the traditional organizational hierarchy. The teams have autonomy and authority to manage themselves.

9. *Training and skill development.* The successful organizations have a strong commitment to training and skill development.

10. *Cross-utilization and cross-training.* Employees are multiskilled and are able to do multiple jobs. This makes the work more interesting, and changes in staffing needs can be more easily made.

11. *Symbolic egalitarianism.* Successful organizations use symbols or signals that communicate the existence of comparative equality within the organization in order to avoid an "us" versus "them" mentality.

12. *Wage compression.* A compressed distribution of wages exists, which leads to greater cooperation and less interpersonal competition. Members of the organization fare comparably in terms of the rewards they receive.

13. *Promotion from within.* Successful organizations use promotion from within, which binds workers to employers and provides a sense of fairness and justice in

the workplace. It also perpetuates the organization's culture and ensures that those running the organization know the business and the organization.

14. *Long-term perspective.* The practices required for managing people effectively take time to implement and for the results to materialize. The successful organizations have a long-term perspective.

15. *Measurement of the practices.* The successful organizations measure their practices and evaluate their efforts. Measurement of their efforts is a critical part of the overall process.

16. *Overarching philosophy.* The practices that are used by the successful organizations are held together by a philosophy and set of values about how to manage people.

Although successful organizations do not necessarily do all sixteen of these practices, successful organizations do tend to do more of them than less successful organizations. As well, there are examples of successful organizations that do all of them. Thus, as noted by Pfeffer (1994), it would be useful for organizations to grade themselves against the sixteen practices. However, it should be recognized that those practices that are most important for a particular organization will depend on things such as strategy and technology. According to Pfeffer (1994),

> *The specific implementation of the practices, and the form they may take, are obviously contingent not only on strategy but also on other contextual factors such as location, nature and interdependence of the work, and so forth. Of course, one can achieve competitive success on the basis of things other than people. However, particularly because many of the other bases of success are more readily imitated (e.g., it is easier for someone to copy a low-wage, low-skill, low-commitment work system), only at one's potential peril should one refuse to at least consider using these practices. (p. 65)*

Thus, there is now a considerable amount of research on what are considered to be best HRM practices. While this literature provides useful information for benchmarking, it is important to keep in mind that best practices might depend on organizational factors such as industry and strategy. That is, the HRM system must be aligned with and supportive of an organization's strategic objectives. In this regard, benchmarking and implementing best practices that are carefully matched to an organization's context can have economic effects on firm performance (Becker & Gerhart, 1996). According to Becker and Gerhart (1996),

> *Research is just beginning to establish the plausible range of these effects, but early work indicates that reasonable changes in an HR system can affect a firm's market value by $15,000–$45,000 per employee and can affect the probability of survival for a new firm by as much as 22 percent. Other research has established strong HR effects on intermediate outcomes that are consistent with an ultimate bottom line effect. In sum, at multiple levels of analysis there is consistent empirical support for the hypothesis that HR can make a meaningful difference to a firm's bottom line. (p. 797)*

Thus, the identification and implementation of best HRM practices through the benchmarking process can have a substantial impact on an organization's financial performance.

◆ ◆ ◆
SUMMARY

This chapter described the process of HRM auditing and benchmarking, and the different approaches to auditing. While statistical and financial evaluation are extremely useful for evaluating specific HRM activities, practices, and programs, HRM auditing and benchmarking are necessary for determining the effectiveness of the overall HRM system. An HRM audit can be used to determine if the HRM department is achieving its goals, supporting the organization's strategic objectives, and meeting the needs of its stakeholders. Benchmarking allows the HR department to evaluate its programs and policies relative to the best practices in other organizations. Ultimately, what is key to auditing and benchmarking is the identification of problem areas and weaknesses, and the subsequent design and implementation of new programs and policies to improve the functioning and effectiveness of the HR department. Therefore, auditing and benchmarking provide a valuable method for HRM evaluation and practice.

Definitions

Benchmarking   A process of comparing an organization's HRM practices and services to the best practices provided by other organizations.

Constituencies   Those parties, customers, or clients who depend on the HR department and have a stake in its activities.

Human resource auditing   A systematic and formal process of gathering data across human resource functions as part of an evaluation of how well human resource functions, policies, and systems are performing.

Key indicators audit   An approach to human resource auditing that focuses on objective and quantitative indicators of effectiveness within each major area of HRM.

Multiple-constituency audit   An approach to human resource auditing that focuses on the satisfaction of stakeholders or individuals who affect or are affected by human resource activities and systems.

Stakeholders   Individuals and groups whose viability is affected by organizational actions and decisions.

Strategic audit   An approach to human resource auditing that focuses on the extent to which HRM practices and policies support the organization's corporate strategy and objectives.

EXERCISES

1. Contact the human resource department of a number of organizations until you find one that conducts HR audits and is willing to discuss its auditing process with you. You can use your own organization if it conducts HR audits. Design a series of questions to learn about the auditing process. In particular, be sure to gather information concerning each of the following steps of the auditing process using Figure 13.1 as a guide:

   a) Describe the scope of the audit. Is it comprehensive, programmatic, or restrictive? What HR areas, functions, and issues are included in the audit and why?

   b) What is the basis upon which the organization identifies a strength or weakness? Is the analysis comparative, external, statistical, compliant, or strategic?

   c) What methods are used to obtain the information for the audit, and who is involved in gathering the information? Is an audit team used to conduct the audit and, if so, who are the members of the team and what are their roles?

   d) Describe the approach used to conduct the audit. Is it the key indicators, multiple-constituency, or strategic approach? What is the nature of the information collected (e.g., what key indicators, constituencies, etc.)?

e) How were the data analyzed and interpreted, and who did the analysis and interpretation? What were the major findings of the analysis?

f) Was a report of the audit project and results prepared? Describe the content of the report and how it was communicated to others.

g) Were action plans developed on the basis of the auditing project? What problems or weaknesses were found, and what action plans were developed to address them? What changes and HR practices were implemented and why?

h) What has been the effect of the auditing process and the action plans? What has changed in the organization, and how have employees and managers reacted? Has there been an improvement in HRM practices, programs, or services?

i) Has the organization continued to conduct HR audits, and does it monitor and track progress and improvements? If so, how is this done and how often?

2. Conduct a human resource audit using the interview guide in Table 13.1 for assessing the strengths and weaknesses of an HRM department. First, find a partner in your class and take turns conducting the interview. Second, interview several people in your organization. If possible, try to interview people in different departments and levels in the organization, including members of the HR department. After completing your interviews, consider the following:

a) How effective do you feel an interview is as a method for conducting an HR audit?

b) Analyze the results of your interviews. What conclusions can you make about the human resource department? Do the results differ as a function of respondents' department and level in the organization? Are there differences between members of the HR department and the rest of the organization? Describe these differences as well as any similarities.

c) What recommendations would you make to the human resource department based on your results?

3. Conduct a multiple-constituency audit in your organization as follows:

a) Create a customer list of all individuals considered to be important customers of the HR department.

b) Classify each listed individual in terms of position level and function.

c) List the services and activities offered by the HR department.

d) Design a questionnaire to assess customers' perceptions of the importance of each service/activity to their business goals and their satisfaction with each service/activity. The questionnaire should also include questions about new services desired by customers, current services no longer needed, and the two or three important services that, if provided by the HR department, would help customers achieve their business goals.

e) Distribute the questionnaire to members of your organization who represent the company's various constituencies, including members of the HR department, employees, and managers.

f) Analyze the results in terms of customer segments based on customers' service and product needs; identify differences in ratings of importance and satisfaction among constituencies.

g) Outline possible changes and suggest action plans based on what is most important to the groups and those services considered to be a priority.

4. Conduct a strategic HR audit by developing an HRM strategic audit worksheet that includes the following information:

a) Identify your organization's major strategies, goals, and objectives.

b) Determine HR policies, procedures, programs, and activities within each functional area that will be required to support the organization's major strategies, goals, and objectives.

c) Identify the organization's current HR policies, procedures, programs, and activities within each of the functional areas and compare them with those indicated in the previous step.

d) Discuss the changes that you would recommend in order to modify or change the organization's current HR policies, procedures, programs,

and activities in each functional area in order to be consistent with the organization's overall business strategies.

5. Contact the human resource department of a number of organizations until you find one that has participated in a benchmarking project and is willing to discuss the project with you. You can use your own organization if it has been part of a benchmarking project. Design a series of questions to learn about the benchmarking project and process. In particular, be sure to gather information concerning each of the seven steps of the benchmarking process:

a) Find out exactly what was benchmarked and why (e.g., product or service features, work processes, particular HR functions, HR performance measures, HR strategy, etc.).

b) Describe the benchmarking team. Who were the team members, what did they do, how or why were they chosen, and who was the team leader?

c) Who were the benchmarking partners, and how and why were they chosen? Were the partners from internal units, competitors, noncompetitors in the same industry, organizations in the same geographic location, organizations in the same country, or international organizations?

d) How were the benchmarking data collected and what were the reasons for using a particular method?

e) How were the data analyzed and interpreted, and who did the analysis and interpretation? What were the major findings of the data analysis? What were the "best practices"?

f) Was a report of the benchmarking project and results prepared for the partner organizations? Describe the content of the report and how it was distributed.

g) Were action plans developed on the basis of the benchmarking project? What performance gaps or deviations were found, and what action plans were developed to address them? What best practices were implemented and why?

h) What has been the effect of the benchmarking process and the action plans? What has changed in the organization, and how have employees and managers reacted? Has there been an improvement in HR practices, programs, or services?

i) Has the organization continued to participate in benchmarking projects, and does it monitor and track progress and improvements? If so, how is this done and how often?

6. Conduct a benchmarking evaluation in your organization using the Human Resources Practices Survey in Table 13.5. Try to get a number of people who represent different groups such as managers, employees, and the HR department. Make sure that respondents indicate their department and position on the survey. After you have distributed and collected the surveys, calculate a mean score for each item and the total survey score for each group. Compare and contrast the results and describe differences and similarities between the groups. Based on your findings, what are your interpretations and conclusions? What recommendations for action plans would you make based on your conclusions?

RUNNING CASE: THE VP OF HUMAN RESOURCES—PART 7

What type of evaluation would you use to demonstrate the value-added of the HRM department? If you were to conduct a statistical evaluation, what would you use it for and what type of statistic would you use? Would you conduct a financial evaluation? If you were to perform a financial evaluation, what would you use it for and what type of financial information would you employ? What are the advantages and disadvantages of statistical and financial evaluation?

Describe how you would conduct an HR audit and benchmarking to demonstrate the value-added of the HRM department and its programs to the organization. Be sure to discuss the audit approach you would use, how you would conduct the audit and benchmarking process, and what type of information and data you would collect. Based on your answer to the above, would you conduct an HR audit or benchmarking in order to demonstrate the value-added of HRM to your organization? What are the advantages and disadvantages of doing so?

References

Becker, B., & Gerhart, B. (1996). The impact of human resource management on organizational performance: Progress and prospects. *Academy of Management Journal, 39*, 779–801.

Belcourt, M. (1996/97, December/January). Making a difference ... and measuring it with the 5 C's. *Human Resources Professional*, 20–24.

Connolly, T., Conlon, E.J., & Deutsch, S.J. (1980). Organizational effectiveness: A multiple-constituency approach. *Academy of Management Review, 5*, 211–217.

Flynn, G. (1997, July). A flight plan for success. *Workforce, 76*(7), 72–78.

Friedlander, F., & Pickle, H. (1968). Components of effectiveness in small organizations. *Administrative Science Quarterly, 13*, 534–540.

Glanz, E.F., & Dailey, L.K. (1992). Benchmarking. *Human Resource Management, 31*, 9–20.

Gómez-Mejía, L.R. (1985). Dimensions and correlates of the personnel audit as an organizational assessment tool. *Personnel Psychology, 38*, 293–308.

Gómez-Mejía, L.R., Balkin, D.B., & Cardy, R.L. (1995). *Managing human resources*. Englewood Cliffs, NJ: Prentice Hall.

Gruner, S. (1998, July). Lasting impressions. *Inc.*, 126.

Heneman, H.G., III, Huett, D.L., Lavigna, R.J., & Ogsten, D. (1995). Assessing managers' satisfaction with staffing services. *Personnel Psychology, 48*, 163–172.

Huselid, M.A. (1995). The impact of human resource management practices on turnover, productivity, and corporate financial performance. *Academy of Management Journal, 38*, 635–672.

Pfeffer, J. (1994). *Competitive advantage through people: Unleashing the power of the work force*. Boston: Harvard Business School Press.

Pfeffer, J. (1994). Producing sustainable competitive advantage through the effective management of people. *Academy of Management Executive, 9*, 55–72.

Phillips, J.J. (1996). *Accountability in human resource management*. Houston, TX: Gulf Publishing Company.

Reese, J. (1996, December 9). Starbucks: Inside the coffee cult. *Fortune*, 190–200.

Rosik, P. (1991, October). Building a customer-oriented HR department. *36*, 64–66.

Rothwell, W.J., & Kazanas, H.C. (1988). *Strategic human resources planning and management*. Englewood Cliffs, NJ: Prentice Hall.

Schneider, B., Ashworth, S.D., Higgs, A.C., & Carr, L. (1996). Design validity, and use of strategically focused employee attitude surveys. *Personnel Psychology, 49*, 695–705.

Segal, J.A., & Quinn, M.A. (1989, May). How to audit your HR programs. *Personnel Administrator*, 67–70.

Tsui, A. S. (1987). Defining the activities and effectiveness of the human resource department: A multiple constituency approach. *Human Resource Management, 26*, 35–69.

Tsui, A.S., & Milkovich, G.T. (1987). Personnel department activities: Constituency perspectives and preferences. *Personnel Psychology, 40*, 519–537.

Ulrich, D., Brockbank, W., & Yeung, A. (1989). Beyond belief: A benchmark for human resources. *Human Resources Management, 28,* 311–335.

Volpe, N. (1999, May 4). Kodak underpaid minorities, women, audit shows. *National Post* (Reuters), C9.

Youndt, M.A., Snell, S.A., Dean, J.W., Jr., & Lepak, D.P. (1996). Human resource manage-ment, manufacturing strategy, and firm perfor-mance. *Academy of Management Journal, 39,* 836–866.

Zammuto, R.F. (1984). A comparison of multi-ple constituency models of organizational effec-tiveness. *Academy of Management Review, 9,* 606–616.

14

The Future of
Human Resource
Research

♦♦♦
INTRODUCTION

If you have made it to this final chapter, you have already learned a great deal about how to conduct research in human resources. You should now be familiar with the different research designs and levels of measurement, and the evaluation of research data and information. The purpose of this chapter is to provide you with some perspective regarding human resource research. First, the changes facing the field of human resources will be reviewed with respect to the research implications that stem from them. Second, an integrative framework will be presented that combines research designs, measures, and evaluation procedures. Third, a brief overview will be provided on how to write a research report. Finally, innovations in HR research will be discussed.

After reading this chapter, you should be able to:

- Understand and explain the research implications that stem from the main issues facing the field of human resources today.

- Explain and apply the integrated framework of HR research, measurement, and evaluation.

- Understand and explain how to write a research report.

- Understand the role of research in developing new and innovative research methods.

♦♦♦
HUMAN RESOURCE RESEARCH AND PRACTICE

This book began with a discussion of the merits of a research- versus intuition-based approach to human resource management. By now, the virtues of research and the important link between research and practice in human resources should be evident. As noted in the Human Resource Research and Practice Model in Chapter 1, the identification of problems and solutions, as well as the design, implementation, and evaluation of effective HRM practices depends on sound and rigorous research.

The importance of research in human resources is now more evident than ever. In fact, in many ways we are entering a new period of human resources in which the role of research is being recognized as a fundamental and necessary part of the human resource system. Nowhere is this more evident than in the increasing number of organizations that have become involved in benchmarking projects, the search for best practices, and the study of the impact of best practices and high-performing HR systems on employees and organizations.

Consider again some of the issues first introduced in Chapter 1 and the research, measurement, and evaluation implications of these issues. Human resource practices have now been shown to be related to a number of organizational outcomes, including both objective and subjective measures of organizational performance. As indicated in Chapter 13, changes in the human resource system can improve an organization's market value and the probability of survival for new firms (Becker & Gerhart, 1996). The research implications of this should be clear. Research is required to identify and measure best practices and to monitor and evaluate them once they have been implemented. This requires survey research and the measurement of human resource systems and employee and organizational outcomes. Evaluation can be statistical or financial, or it can involve auditing and benchmarking.

In an increasingly competitive environment, organizations are demanding accountability on the part of all functional areas within an organization. This, of course, includes the human resource department. The need to adequately demonstrate accountability will become a common and necessary part of life for human resource professionals. This means that research will need to be conducted to demonstrate that human resource efforts and programs are sound and effective. This can be aided through experimental research and the results of meta-analysis, which indicate the effectiveness of the programs implemented by the human resource department. Measurement may involve individual, group, and/or organizational outcomes, and evaluation may be statistical or involve benchmarking to demonstrate that best practices are being designed and implemented.

The increasing role played by human resources in strategic planning brings with it new requirements for research. As discussed in Chapter 13, human resource policies and practices must be aligned with organizational strategies. This requires research to identify the extent of alignment, and the development of new policies and programs to improve the fit between HR and the organization's strategic initiatives. Research along these lines would involve the use of surveys or interviews. Measurement of human resource practices and systems would be necessary. Evaluating the alignment between HR and strategy can be done by a multiple-constituency or strategic HR audit.

One of the most important issues facing human resources is the need to demonstrate the value-added of the human resource department and its programs. Ulrich (1997) believes that the time has come for HR to focus on outcomes and the results of HR efforts. As was discussed in previous chapters, this inevitably involves some form of financial evaluation in order to demonstrate the value of human resource efforts and investments. Thus, this will require experimental research that tests the effectiveness of human resource programs, the measurement of individual or group outcomes, and the calculation of return on investments or utility analysis. Benchmarking can also be used in order to provide an organization with HR programs that are recognized as best practices. As well, a multiple-constituency HR audit can also be used to demonstrate the value-added of the HR department and its programs in terms of stakeholders' satisfaction.

In sum, it should be clear that the success of the changes that are facing the human resource function and profession today will be highly dependent on sound and rigorous research. As well, the type of research, the variables that need to be measured, and the nature of the evaluation will vary and, in part, depend on the particular issue at hand. Therefore, to put the many possibilities and issues in perspective, the next section presents a framework for understanding and integrating HR research, measurement, and evaluation.

◆ ◆ ◆

INTEGRATING HR RESEARCH, MEASUREMENT, AND EVALUATION

This book has presented many possibilities for conducting research in human resources in terms of different designs, levels of measurement, and evaluation techniques. Trying to keep track of all the possibilities—not to mention trying to fit them together into a research study—can be difficult at best and overwhelming at worst. Therefore, this section attempts to give some perspective on the topic of human resource research.

Although each of the main research topics has been discussed separately, they are, of course, closely interconnected. Therefore, it helps to put them in a context in which they are integrated and understood together as part of a single study rather than as separate parts. For example, we can talk about the individual parts that make up an automobile, but ultimately what one is usually concerned with is the entire vehicle and issues pertaining to its appearance, durability, performance, and so on.

Let's review the three main components of HR research: design, measurement, and evaluation. Following the identification of a research question, concern, or problem situation, the researcher must choose a research design. This can involve conducting a survey or experiment, the use of qualitative designs, or a review of existing research and meta-analysis. Each of the research designs can serve particular purposes better than others.

Surveys are effective for tracking employee attitudes over time, investigating the effect of a program or intervention, or studying human resource practices within and across organizations. In addition to the traditional paper-and-pencil survey, alternative forms such as telephone and electronic surveys can be used.

In order to examine the effect of a human resource program or intervention, *experimental* designs are required. Research on training programs, job previews, incentive plans, and so on, usually involve nonexperimental, true experimental, or quasi-experimental research designs.

Qualitative research designs such as observation, interviews, and archival techniques are often used in human resource research, particularly when the researcher requires detailed and descriptive information. Many human resource practices, such as job analysis, employment interviews, and organizational diagnosis, involve qualitative research methods. Finally, if a particular HR area has been extensively studied, and if a meta-analysis has been performed, then a *review of existing research* may provide the information needed to make human resource decisions.

Determining the level and type of measurement should follow from the main objectives of the research and the study hypotheses. When the focus is on individuals' perceptions, attitudes, or behaviour, *individual-level* measures are required and can include objective output, ratings, or personnel comparison. If groups are the focus of a study, then the researcher will want to measure *group-level* variables, such as group inputs, processes, and/or outcomes. Research in human resources is increasingly focusing on the organization in terms of inputs and outputs. This type of research requires the measurement of independent variables at the *organizational level*, such as organization structures, HR systems, and/or organizational development/process variables. As well, dependent variables at the organizational level may include goal attainment measures, employee outcomes, HR outcomes, and/or open-systems variables.

Finally, once a research study has been conducted, the key variables measured, and the data collected, the focus turns to evaluation. This has most often involved some form of *statistical evaluation*, such as the analysis of descriptive data, tests of mean differences between groups, and/or measures of association. Experimental and survey research usually involves some statistical evaluation, and in some cases so does qualitative research. *Financial evaluation* has also been used to evaluate human resources. This has involved human resource accounting, return on investment, and utility analysis. However, financial evaluation is still relatively rare, and in the case of utility analysis, it has been used mostly to evaluate selection and training programs.

Human resource system evaluation involves the evaluation of human resource functions and systems. Human resource audits and benchmarking are increasingly being used for these types of evaluations. Thus, while statistical and financial evaluation are used to evaluate human resource practices or programs, HR audits and benchmarking are used to evaluate a functional area (e.g., compensation) or the entire human resource system.

Figure 14.1 presents an integrated framework of human resource research, measurement, and evaluation. To learn how this framework can be used to design and understand HR research, we will consider a study on work teams that was conducted by Banker, Field, Schroeder, and Sinha (1996). The authors were concerned that, although a great deal has been made about the success of work teams in the popular press, most of the evidence is anecdotal and in the form of descriptive case studies. Therefore, in an effort to learn more about team effectiveness, the authors conducted a study to examine the impact of work teams on manufacturing performance. This raises a number of key questions in terms of what design to use, what variables to measure, and how to evaluate the data.

The research site was a unionized assembly plant that manufactures small motors. The study was conducted over a 21-month period, and is described as a naturally occurring field experiment. The researchers investigated the conversion of the plant assembly lines to high-performance work teams (HPWTs) over the 21-month period of the study. They also collected qualitative information before and after the formation of the teams in order to study the evolution and functioning of work teams. The qualitative information included the teams' meeting logs, training documents, and interviews with the team facilitator, team leaders, production engineers, plant manager, and the divisional director of manufacturing operations.

In terms of measurement, the researchers noted that group effectiveness can be defined in a number of ways and that their focus was on the performance of the group rather than the group's ability to work as a group or individual members' satisfaction. In particular, they measured group quality and productivity. Quality was measured as the percentage of total units produced that were defective, and labour productivity was measured as a ratio of the number of units produced to total production. The independent variable was the formation of the HPWTs and the dependent variables were group quality and productivity. The researchers also measured a number of control variables that could influence manufacturing performance, such as managerial policies.

To evaluate the effect of the formation of the HPWTs, the researchers performed a number of statistical tests to examine the trends in the dependent variables before and after the formation of the HPWTs. Data were collected on a monthly basis for labour productivity and on a weekly basis for manufacturing defect rate.

The results indicated that there was no trend in the manufacturing defect rate prior to the formation of teams; however, in the weeks following team formation, there was a significant reduction in the defect rate. In total, there was a 38 percent reduction in the defect rate from the time of team formation, to the end of the study. Similar results were found for labour productivity. That is, there was no change in labour productivity prior to team formation, and a significant improvement in the weeks following the formation of teams. In total, there was a 20 percent improve-

FIGURE 14.1   Integrated Framework of Human Resource Research, Measurement, and Evaluation

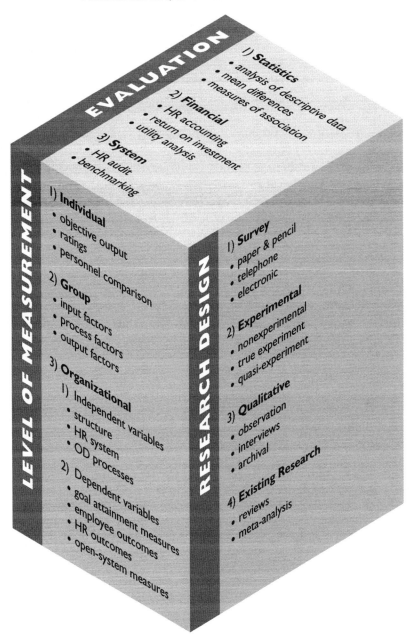

ment in labour productivity from the time of team formation to the end of the study. Finally, more than a year and a half after the study ended, the researchers met with plant personnel, who indicated that the teams continued to function effectively and to demonstrate performance improvements.

Referring to Figure 14.1, we can classify this study as both a *quasi-experiment* and a *qualitative study* that included archival information as well as interviews. The dependent variables were *group*-level variables. In particular, both measures are group output measures, and, based on the description of these measures in Chapter 10, they are measures of quality (total units produced that were defective) and efficiency (the number of units produced to total production hours). The evaluation consisted of *statistical* tests of the changes in the dependent variables over time.

Thus, as you can see, the framework can be used to classify and make sense of research. This not only makes it easier to understand the study, but it also makes it possible to critique and evaluate it. For example, do you think that the research design was appropriate, given the objectives of the study? Were the two dependent variables good measures? And was the type of evaluation sufficient to answer the research questions? With this framework one can also consider whether other designs, measures, or evaluation procedures should have been used.

Just as important, however, is that the integrative framework can be used to assist the researcher in the design of a study. It allows the researcher to consider various designs, levels and types of measurement, and evaluation procedures simultaneously. In effect, one can use the framework to develop a research plan or outline for a research study.

In summary, while a great deal of information has been presented about the many factors that must be considered in the research process, this framework can help one develop a clearer picture and understanding of how to research, measure, and evaluate human resources.

◆ ◆ ◆
THE RESEARCH REPORT

Throughout this book reference has been made to research articles and reports. Therefore, it should be clear that the results of research are usually written in the form of a research article or report. In this section, a brief overview of the nature of research reports is provided.

Although the nature and content of academic as opposed to practitioner reports will differ somewhat, they will contain information that reflects the research process that was first presented in Chapter 1. For example, after the Executive Summary or Abstract outlining the purpose and major findings of the study, a research report begins with an Introduction section. The Introduction presents the background information leading up to the research. This should include some discussion of the major research issue or question, or if the research was conducted to address a problem, then the problem should be clearly presented. The Introduction should also include information about the research topic, such as previous research, existing knowledge, as well as any relevant theories or frameworks.

Once the relevant background information has been discussed, the Introduction should clearly state the major purpose(s) and objective(s) of the study. This should then be followed by a series of research questions, propositions, or hypotheses that the research was designed to answer or test.

The second major section of a research report is the Method section. The Method section should include all of the relevant information concerning the research design and the measurement of the variables. The Method section usually begins with descriptive information about the research site and the study participants. Some of the most important issues that need to be described include how the participants were chosen and contacted, how many participated, the response rate, and any differences between respondents and nonrespondents.

The Method section should also include a description of the procedure used to conduct the study. For example, if the study was an experiment, it should be clear how participants were assigned to conditions, and what occurred before, during, and after the experiment. If the study was a survey, then the distribution and collection of the surveys must be described. If the study involved interviews or observations, sufficient information must be provided so that the reader knows how the researcher conducted the interviews or how observations were made.

Once the research sample, design, and procedure have been described, there should be a section on the measures used in the study. This section should describe what variables were measured and how they were measured. It is also expected that the reliability of the measures will be reported, and very often sample items or entire scales are provided. Usually the measurement section includes a description of independent, dependent, and control variables.

The third major section of the research report is the Results. The Results section should first describe how the data were analyzed, and then present descriptive data and correlations among the study variables. This is usually followed by more sophisticated analyses to test the study propositions or hypotheses. The Results section should include Tables showing the results, which should also be explained in the text of the paper. Most research reports contain at least some statistics, even if they are only means or percentages. In the case of financial evaluation, the approach used and a description of the variables and their values should be provided, as well as the formula or equations used to calculate the values.

The final section of the research report is the Discussion. In this section, the researcher will try to make sense of the results and interpret the research findings.

This usually involves explaining the results that support the study propositions or hypotheses, as well as those that do not. The researcher should also rule out alternative explanations for the study findings, and shed light on those that were contrary to expectations. The limitations of the study should also be noted, as well as the implications for practice and future research.

When the research report is being written primarily for a management audience, the Discussion section should focus more on action plans and recommendations. For example, audit and benchmarking reports focus on an organization's strengths and weaknesses, performance gaps, and, in the case of benchmarking, best practices. Action plans are also provided in order to deal with weaknesses and performance gaps. Thus, when the readers are primarily concerned with making improvements and solving problems, there should be a detailed discussion of the possible courses of action.

Finally, an exception to the research report just described is a case study. Sometimes the results of research are written up in the form of a case study. A case study involves a narrative description of the results of a study. Very often an investigator will use a case approach to communicate the results of a study because he or she is interested in descriptive information about the nature of some phenomenon. It should be noted that, although case studies are very often associated with qualitative research, the ways in which the investigator obtains information for a case study can be as varied as the methods covered in this book. It could be from an experiment, self-reports produced by a questionnaire, or the use of archival records, interviews, or observations. Whatever the method used to conduct the research, the goal of a case study is usually one of complete description. A case study can provide the groundwork required to orient a researcher to a new area of research or practice. Similarly, it can provide insight regarding the boundaries of a research domain, and it can be the source of ideas that may be more systematically examined or tested in future studies.

◆ ◆ ◆

INNOVATIONS IN HUMAN RESOURCE RESEARCH

The history of research in human resources is relatively short. Thus, it should not be surprising that new and innovative ways to study, measure, and evaluate human resources are an important part of the growth and development of the field. Several of these methods have been discussed throughout this book.

Consider the following innovations, presented in earlier chapters:

- The use of hindsight ratings in order to determine if differences between survey measures over time are due to alpha, beta, or gamma change (Fishel, 1998) (Chapter 2).

- The development, implementation, and validation of a strategically focused employee attitude survey (Schneider, Ashworth, Higgs, & Carr, 1996) (Chapter 3).

- The use of the Internet for conducting survey research and concerns that need to be considered when using the Internet for survey data collection (Stanton, 1998) (Chapter 3).

- The development of the "internal referencing" strategy as a way of dealing with some of the limitations of the pretest/post-test research design in training research (Haccoun & Hamtiaux, 1994) (Chapter 4).

- Audiotaping employment interviews to obtain an in-depth knowledge of interview interactions and processes (Stevens, 1998) (Chapter 5).

- The development of the Organizational Cultural Profile (OCP) for assessing work values and person–organization fit (O'Reilly, Chatman, & Caldwell, 1991) (Chapter 7).

- The development of a job analysis technique called the Personality-Related Position Requirements Form (PPRF) for identifying relevant personality variables (Raymark, Schmit, & Guion, 1997) (Chapter 7).

- The design of a survey (Staffing Service Delivery Satisfaction Survey) to assess managers' satisfaction with staffing services (Heneman, Huett, Lavigna, & Ogsten, 1995) (Chapter 13).

These studies demonstrate that an important component of the research process is the development of new and innovative approaches for studying, measuring, and evaluating human resources. The increasing need for research in human resources is likely to lead to more innovative approaches. In this vein, *Personnel Psychology*, a major research journal that publishes HR and applied research articles, now has a separate section in the journal, titled "Innovations in Research-Based Practice," that is devoted to new ideas and innovations in HR research.

Thus, research in human resources is still developing, and many areas require new approaches for conducting, measuring, and evaluating HR research. For example, procedures for conducting organizational analysis are required, as are selection methods for hiring people for organizational fit. In the training literature, new measures have been discussed for evaluating training programs (Kraiger, Ford, & Salas, 1993). As well, recall from Chapter 6 the importance of utility reaction measures in addition to more traditional affective reactions (Alliger, Tannenbaum, Bennett,

Traver, & Shotland, 1997). While research is important for HR practice, the research is only as good as the methods. Therefore, the future of human resource research must include the development of new and innovative approaches.

◆◆◆
CONCLUSION

The last decade has seen tremendous growth in the field of human resource management. There has been a substantial increase in the number of individuals entering the field and seeking certification to become human resource professionals. Many provinces in Canada have human resource professional associations, and the Human Resources Professional Association of Ontario (HRPAO) has established the Human Resources Research Institute to encourage and support HR research. In addition, more and more organizations today are realizing that the success of strategic initiatives requires the inclusion of the human resource function, and that the impact of HRM on organizational effectiveness can be substantial. In the research arena, there are more human resource research journals today than ever before.

The implications of these trends are clear: HR professionals must have the ability to understand, conduct, and interpret human resource research, and be capable of using research to improve human resources in their organizations. This is likely to be a key factor for making organizations more effective and competitive in an increasingly global and changing world in which people are the most important factor for an organization's competitive success (Pfeffer, 1994).

EXERCISES

1. Find an article on an HR topic of interest to you. Describe and classify the study using the Integrative Framework of HR Research, Measurement, and Evaluation in Figure 14.1. In other words, what research designs were used, what variables were measured and how were they measured, and how were the data evaluated? What are some other designs that could have been used to conduct this study? What other variables could have been measured? Could other forms of evaluation have been used?

2. Choose a human resource research topic that interests you, and develop several research questions. Using the Integrative Framework of HR Research, Measurement, and Evaluation in Figure 14.1, describe how you would conduct a study to answer your research questions in terms of design, measures, and evaluation. Be sure to explain your choices.

3. Review a research article on a human resource topic of your choice. In your review, make note of all sections and subsections in the article, and the content that is discussed in each section. Prepare a summary of the content of each section of the article.

4. Review the innovative approaches to HR research discussed in this text. For each of the eight studies highlighted in the section "Innovations in Human Resource Research," answer the following questions:

   a) What is the main topic or issue of concern?

   b) What is the contribution of the study to HRM research?

   c) What are the practical implications of the study?

   d) How will the study change HRM research and practice?

RUNNING CASE: THE VP OF HUMAN RESOURCES—PART 8

Use the Integrative Framework of HR Research, Measurement, and Evaluation in Figure 14.1 to develop a complete research program to demonstrate the value of human resource practices and the contribution of the department and programs to the organization. Describe in detail what design(s) you will use, the levels and types of measures, and how you will evaluate the data you collect in order to demonstrate the value-added of the HRM department and its programs to the organization. For each of the things you will do, describe the knowledge and skills that are required to perform them effectively. What are the advantages and disadvantages of your research program?

References

Alliger, G.M., Tannenbaum, S.I., Bennett, W. Jr., Traver, H., & Shotland, A. (1997). A meta-analysis of the relations among training criteria. *Personnel Psychology, 50*, 341–358.

Banker, R.D., Field, J.M., Schroeder, R.G., & Sinha, K.K. (1996). Impact of work teams on manufacturing performance: A longitudinal field study. *Academy of Management Journal, 39*, 867–890.

Becker, B., & Gerhart, B. (1996). The impact of human resource management on organizational performance: Progress and prospects. *Academy of Management Journal, 39*, 779–801.

Fishel, B. (1998). A new perspective: How to get the real story from attitude surveys. *Training, 35* (2), 91–94.

Haccoun, R.R., & Hamtiaux, T. (1994). Optimizing knowledge tests for inferring learning acquisition levels in single group training evaluation designs: The internal referencing strategy. *Personnel Psychology, 47*, 593–604.

Heneman, H.G., III, Huett, D.L., Lavigna, R.J., & Ogsten, D. (1995). Assessing managers' satisfaction with staffing services. *Personnel Psychology, 48*, 163–172.

Kraiger, K., Ford J.K, & Salas, E. (1993). Application of cognitive, skill-based, and affective theories of learning outcomes to new methods of training evaluation. *Journal of Applied Psychology, 78*, 311–328.

O'Reilly, C.A., III, Chatman, J., & Caldwell, D.F. (1991). People and organizational culture: A profile comparison approach to assessing person-organization fit. *Academy of Management Journal, 34*, 487–516.

Pfeffer, J. (1994). *Competitive advantage through people: Unleashing the power of the work force.* Boston, MA: Harvard Business School Press.

Raymark, P.H., Schmit, M.J., & Guion, R.M. (1997). Identifying potentially useful personality constructs for employee selection. *Personnel Psychology, 50*, 723–736.

Schneider, B., Ashworth, S.D., Higgs, A.C., & Carr, L. (1996). Design validity, and use of strategically focused employee attitude surveys. *Personnel Psychology, 49*, 695–705.

Stanton, J.M. (1998). An empirical assessment of data collection using the Internet. *Personnel Psychology, 51*, 709–725.

Stevens, C.K. (1998). Antecedents of interview interactions, interviewers' ratings, and applicants' reactions. *Personnel Psychology, 51*, 55–85.

Ulrich, D. (1997). *Human resource champions: The next agenda for adding value and delivering results.* Boston, MA: Harvard Business School Press.

Index